THE WAY TO THE SACRED

Rudolf Steiner's path to spirituality through meditation

DR. ADRIAN ANDERSON

2003 ©

THE WAY TO THE SACRED
Copyright © 2003 by Adrian Anderson

Threshold Publishing
www.rudolfsteinerstudies.com

Australia

Anderson, Adrian, 1950- .
    The way to the sacred : Rudolf Steiner's path to spirituality through meditation.

    Includes index.
    ISBN 9780958134101 (pbk).
    ISBN 9780958134163 (hbk)

    1. Meditation. 2. Spirituality. I. Title.

    291.435

All publishing and distribution enquiries to Threshold Publishing.
All rights reserved. No part of this book can be reproduced in any form without the written permission of the publisher, except for brief excerpts embodied in critical reviews and articles.
Lecture extracts, illustrations, verses from Rudolf Steiner are, in the main, copyright to Rudolf Steiner Verlag, Switzerland, these are noted in the text.

By the same author:

The Rudolf Steiner Handbook
The Foundation stone meditation - a new commentary
Living a Spiritual Year - seasonal festivals

Forthcoming:
The Grecian Mysteries & Christianity
Horoscope interpretation: a Rudolf Steiner approach

And see
Damien Pryor: The Origin & Nature of the tropical zodiac
        Lalibela
        Stonehenge
        Externsteine
        The Great Pyramd & the Sphinx

Third revised edition 2014

CONTENTS

Introduction   3

1 Esoteric meditation: the path to the divine   17

The purpose of esoteric meditation is to develop a consciousness capable of direct insights into the divine, both in creation and within the human being. There are three kinds of higher mental states which can be achieved through meditating. What are the higher spiritual 'realms' that the meditant may experience? What is experienced when consciousness rises from the physical plane to perception of one's soul and the soul world; and beyond that to the divine in the spiritual realms? One result of meditating is clairvoyance; what does it reveal and why does it happen? Some genuine non-visionary spiritual experiences. What is happening in the mind during meditation; entering the silence; when the silence speaks. The difference between prayer, contemplation and meditation, and between some classic Eastern meditation and this approach. How does one do this kind of meditating ?
Glossary of terms
Appendix: Concerning Esoteric Christianity

2 But I can't do it ! Learning to focus the mind   60
Overcoming the problems. Six vital exercises which result in a really 'centred' personality with the ability to concentrate one's thoughts on a theme, summon up the will to start self-transformation, remain calm in stress, and in charge of instinctive feelings, refrain from negative criticism, remove subtle prejudices, and become open to the full reality of life. Developing these qualities builds up the inner strength and mental integrity needed by the meditant. Reviewing the course of the day: "The Evening Review", an essential exercise for self-knowledge. How to do this, and important benefits.

3 Preparing the intellect and attuning the heart   77
Attunement and preparation. For meditation to succeed, the moods and attitudes must be attuned to the spiritual. Learning to think spiritually is also an essential step to the spiritual. Materialism sits in the intellect, not in the emotions. Rudolf Steiner's golden rule: "For every step you attempt towards knowledge of hidden truths, take three steps forward in ethical development". Unlearning adult insensitivity by re-enlivening the 'primal infant within', or finding the door to the enchanted world. Meditation links us to the spiritual only if the mental attitude and mood of heart are right. The divine spirituality which we each possess as infants. Practical exercises for re-enlivening the sense of awe, the

experience of wonder, the power of reverence, and the capacity for devotion to a task.
Appendix: Introductory books

4 First spiritual experiences   98
In esoteric meditation the connection between our soul, the body and our life-forces is loosened. Knowing this is the secret key to success: the ancient and the modern way to utilize this. Why does meditating cause visions or odd sensations, etc? What to do about them, why they are occurring – various experiences to expect, why they happen, and how to deal with them. First spiritual experiences: the author's experiences, and practical guidance regarding psychic experiences given to meditants by Rudolf Steiner. True results are at first very subtle. Other results are intrusive eg, blissfully expanding/cool-wind sensation, immediate visions, odd sounds and words, seeing clouds of colour, being lost in a void, etc. "Etheric vision": the student first encounters a realm of life-forces not a divine realm.

5 The dark night of the soul   117
A protector of the threshold, crossing the threshold into the spiritual world by meditating. Why we don't and shouldn't succeed at first. The existence of a "guardian of the threshold", and its role, encountering this being occurs on two levels, in daily life, and later, clairvoyantly. Encountering 'the double' or lower self, the necessity of conquering the hidden shadows in the soul. Our ethical motivation invokes a corresponding force that 'opens the door' for us and influences what we experience. The tempters, messengers of a false paradise, and the adversaries, beings who harden our will. The middle path from our "guiding angel". The three monsters, the shadow-side of the emotions, thinking and will.

6 Sleep, dreams, the guiding angel and the three auras   151
The "guiding angel" and the meditant, esoteric guidance about the approach of our angel to our consciousness in meditation. Going into sleep - preparing for the nightly immersion in realms of spirit. Sleep and the guiding angel, where are we when we dream? Awakening in the morning – how to live into the after-echoes of the night. What changes occur to the soul, as it becomes spiritualized? What 'colours' does the aura manifest? Illustrations of the colours in the soul-aura and in the spiritual-auras, how the aura changes through meditation. A pastel drawing by Rudolf Steiner showing the spiritual influences affecting the meditant. Experiencing the higher self through meditation, and the nature of the so-called Masters.

7 The chakras   175

What are the chakras esoterically; are all New Age ideas about the chakras accurate? Secrets of the heart chakra from modern initiation wisdom: the crucial role of the etheric-energy counterpart of the heart. Holiness and the spiritual-love energies offered to the heart chakra since the incarnation of the 'The cosmic Christ' (the Logos). The forehead chakra as the 'lamp of the pilgrim', and its connection to moon and sun. The throat chakra; the Holy Grail's connection to it, and to the esoteric meaning of the Beatitudes. Atavistic clairvoyance, what is this? Why astral projection is regarded as ill-advised to new students on this esoteric path. What is the kundalini force, should it be stimulated ? The new **etheric vision**: many people already have a glimmer of this but do not know it. Practical exercises for sensing ethereal forces; what one sees when ether vision develops.
Appendix 1 Archangel Michael
Appendix 2 Union with the archetypal higher-self

8 Higher consciousness: past-life recall   224
The modern meditative path brings about knowledge of the soul's inner being, as well as of cosmic forces, and of their interconnectedness. The reliable way to past life remembering (i.e., widening consciousness beyond the usual ego-sense) is via this kind of meditation. Breathing exercises: why they are not used here, except one which etherealizes the physical body.

9 Practical advice regarding meditation   241
Initial difficulties, perseverance; pictorial images of use in meditation; protection from negative influences; avoid falling asleep in meditation; whether to speak about your experiences? Steiner's view of the two kinds of group meditating. The higher-self, how does it respond to your meditating ? Reliability of a higher experience; positions to adopt, using mantra – how do they really work ? Clothing and a meditation robe.
Appendix: attending Liturgical religious services and meditation

10   Meditation texts   259

Meditations by Rudolf Steiner to develop 'Spiritual Enlightenment' and to develop the chakras: the Rose-Cross meditation and the great **Foundation Stone** meditation: a new translation with commentary. His "Prayer to God; ineffable, infinite Lord of all Creation". A contemplative text on the Vedantic 'aum'; on the primeval eternal Self; on the Buddhist concept of illusory ego (Anatta) and eternal self; and on the esoteric meaning of the Christian Beatitudes. Communing with the guiding angel, as the effect of meditating strengthens. Texts to assist in realizing the higher-self (or Manas), and for attunement to the cosmic

Christ or Brahma; for developing an enhanced sense of destiny (karma). The Noble Eight-fold Path of Buddha reformulated in a modern manner. Appendix: Illusory self in Buddhism and Steiner's concept of self.

11 Influence of nutrition and life-style   292
Vegetarianism, a brief outline of its advantages for the inner life, and which foods contain malignant elemental energies. The hidden effect of alcohol on the chakras, why it is not used in this path. The harmful effect of psychedelic drugs on the ether energies and on the aura, and for the self. Asceticism and sexuality.

Appendices 1 – 4

Index

Illustrations acknowledgements

Illustrations
1   Rudolf Steiner ca. 1912 (photo)
2   Twisted concrete chimney, Switzerland (photo)
3   Rose-Cross symbol (drawing)
4   The Red Window (enhanced coloured drawing)
5   The glass Red Window (modified photo)
6   Colour qualities in the unevolved astral aura (painting)
7   Spiritualized astral aura (painting)
8   Spiritualized lesser spiritual aura (painting)
9   Unevolved lesser and higher spiritual auras (painting)
10 Spiritualized higher spiritual aura (painting)
11 "The human being in the spirit", R. Steiner (pastel drawing).

Diagrams

1 Relative size of the soul aura to the physical person	**164**
2 Relative size of the evolved **second** spirit aura to the physical person	**166**
3 Seven planets co-forming the 7 chakras	**200**

Illustrations 5,7,8,9,10 and 11, Julie Harmsworth
Diagrams 1, 2 and 3, Joel Harmsworth.

Preface

The author is aware, in presenting this volume to interested readers, of the substantial responsibility involved in undertaking such a task. This volume is intended to help those who will to take up the earnest but joyous task of spiritual development, with the intention of eventually becoming a person whose heart and mind is spiritualized. This process gradually enables one to attain to high spiritual realities, as is reported of initiates in ancient and medieval esoteric-spiritual streams. Today this is a self-initiation process, as most of the impetus for this must now come from the individual who engages with daily life in such a manner as to make it a pathway to higher their higher-self. The goal is a state of spirituality that transforms the soul by suffusing it with sanctity of the spirit, and leads to higher faculties.

As a result of this process, selfless compassion, a deeper understanding of spiritual truths and an active will to be of help to others, become the central dynamics of one's being. This transformation process derives from the light of the sacred and mysterious object, the Holy Grail; a theme that shall be explained in this book. Especially insightful teachings on spiritual development in this sense are found in the works of Rudolf Steiner, a European initiate. His works, like any great spiritual teaching, have to some extent, been subject to dogmatism and sectarianism; in this book I have attempted, as an independent teacher in spirituality, to avoid these pitfalls. This is intended to be a complete and practical handbook based on his approach to enhanced spirituality, wisdom and higher faculties, through meditation. Since the first edition of this book appeared, the author has written many other books, see the website, www.rudolfsteinerstudies.com

In particular the **Rudolf Steiner Handbook** is recommended for those who are new to Steiner's works or who need more clarity about this.

Copyright note

The copyright for all the published German verses and lecture extracts of Rudolf Steiner's quoted here, is held by The Rudolf Steiner Verlag, Dornach, Switzerland, and are reproduced with their kind permission. The English translations are by this author. These texts are published in *Anweisungen für eine esoterische Schülung*, or in *Wahrspruchworte*.

Dedication

This book is dedicated to my dearest companion on the path, my wife Marguerite.

Editorial Note

I always endeavour to acknowledge when an idea was found in the work of Rudolf Steiner. This means that his name will be mentioned many times. To avoid a repetitious style, I shall at times simply refer to him as "Steiner"; but this is always to be understood as an abbreviation of something like, 'the initiate Rudolf Steiner".

Throughout this book I have altered Rudolf Steiner's text in one instance only; where the German says 'he' ('him'), I have changed this to 'he or she', or to 'him or her'. This gender inclusive style is actually more accurate to the meaning in German, and to the totally non-sexist attitude of Steiner himself. It is simply that in German as in other Romance languages, each noun (such as 'human being, 'Mensch' in German) has to have a gender; regardless as to whether one is referring to a man or a woman. Thus for example all archangels are masculine in the German language; but this does not mean that there can not be feminine as well as masculine archangels, in terms of the impression they give to the seer.

I realize that much of the material presented here is extraordinarily challenging in its implications, but the more earnest meditative path does have transformative implications of great significance. This book provides the only comprehensive guidance to the inner life from this great teacher (with an experiential basis, from the author's experience). In making this available I am following the attitude adopted by Rudolf Steiner with regard to his disclosures about the deeper meditative path, namely there are two reasons for doing this. Firstly, it provides an essential guidance for those who wish to take up the challenge of the pathway. Secondly, it is valuable for those who feel it is not yet possible to enter into such an inner journey, but nevertheless would like to know what the pathway might entail for them, at some time in the future.

Introduction

Within the heart of every seeker for the spirit lives the inspiring knowledge that the very advanced meditant achieves a Spiritual Enlightenment, unbroken by the journey beyond death – so childlike in its awe before the good and beautiful, saintly in its purity, familiar with both earnestness and joy, pulsing with selfless love – yet always seeking to help and refine our limited earthly reality. The question that arises for every person who glimpses the spirituality of a truly great person is; How can I so live that this kind of consciousness gradually blossoms within me, replacing my ordinary self ? How did the earlier students of the path to initiation transform this illusory, unfree, even potentially ignoble self into a spiritualized higher self ? This book provides the answer to this question as given by Rudolf Steiner, a great European sage.

Steiner was a teacher whose selfless love of the spiritual within humanity was the motivation behind his life-long teachings, tireless research and pragmatic humanitarian projects. The answer, in brief, is through esoteric meditation, assisted by spiritual study, and by nurturing a preparedness to act decisively for the common good. Meditation of this kind releases the meditant from egotistic illusions and from ethical imperfections; it is the way to transcending the limitations of one's understanding of the spiritual dimension of life. When earnestly followed with real enthusiasm and commitment, meditation can gradually enable the meditant to transcend the personal ego and achieve an eternal consciousness, the kind of consciousness that occurs in the higher spiritual realms.

This book is about the method of meditating designed to gradually achieve, over years of meditative activity, a state of enhanced integrity and wisdom, which eventually leads to experiences of the sacred realities of the human spirit and therefore of the spiritual realms. It is not a method which brings an encounter with the 'divine' that may leave one disinterested in the Earth and the future needs of humanity. It is designed for everyone interested in the question of attaining higher spirituality; and is not only for people with a prior acquaintance of Rudolf Steiner's research, although an inner resonance with the pathway he represents is assumed.

The author's experience of the path to self-initiation extends over 30 years of meditative experience, for a substantial part of this using approximately 220 lessons given in the Esoteric School of Rudolf Steiner (1904-1914), and the 19 esoteric lessons of 1924. In addition to my academic studies, I have undertaken twelve years full-time study of spiritual literature (not exclusively from Rudolf Steiner), seeking to achieve an esoteric understanding of the deeper questions of life, which is clear and rational, in so far as that is possible with matters transcendental.

A quarter century ago, I lived alone for many years in Queensland in a bush hut, on the side of a hill, accessible only on foot. While doing part-time work, I devoted my life to studying spiritual truths, and used Rudolf Steiner's teachings on meditation in a systematic way. This meditative life style brought about my first experiences of a higher realm when I was 21. These experiences clearly showed me the potential of this path to bring the seeker ever nearer to the lofty spirituality of the higher-self. The ethereal beauty and wondrous nature of those experiences, experienced whilst living in the majestic beauty landscape of the ranges and the distant sea-shore, spurred me on to go further.

Aware of the need to gain the discipline needed for concentrated meditation, and to gain a clearer knowledge of the spiritual realities that I would be encountering, I spent many years in comprehensive esoteric study, and striving to live these truths in my life. This book is not about my life, but to me it is experientially true that when some progress has been made on this path, then without losing touch with earthly reality, such as the obligations in our karma, it is possible to enter into an effective self-initiation process. In doing this, the meditant can by degrees begin to become aware of a sacred presence, a holiness, drawing nearer as the years pass. This book makes available the valuable advice to Steiner's personal students about meditation and the spiritual experiences which it causes, given in two hundred private lessons.

It is presented here in a clearly contextualized manner by one who has been his student for decades, and who has personal experience of much that will be discussed. A selection of meditation texts from Rudolf Steiner for deeper meditation are published here, including several for the first time. His teachings, which fill 360 volumes contain the most comprehensive system of spiritual knowledge ever developed within the uniquely rich heritage of central European cultures. Illustration One is a fine photograph of this initiate, taken just after his esoteric activity had imbued him with a remarkable majesty and integrity.

In addition to presenting the essence of his lessons on the inner life, I have also included a number of meditative verses of profound depth in order that this book could become a comprehensive manual for all those interested in following this pathway to spirituality. Its value then is that it is primarily a compilation from the teachings of Rudolf Steiner. This author has experienced the higher worlds to only a small extent, but offers his insights, derived from these experiences, in the hope that they may be also of some help to the reader.

Steiner's knowledge derives from research undertaken with his higher consciousness and this knowledge can be practically applied to life. For example, there are entire hospitals based on his medical system; hundreds of schools using his child psychology thrive around the world, providing really human-centred educational opportunities, and many acres of agricultural land are now farmed without chemicals, using his enhanced organic (bio-dynamic) technique of farming. Steiner was more than an intellectual genius, or a mystic or a psychic, for he developed higher faculties through meditation, and he used these higher consciousness states to research many aspects of human life, in a disciplined way. In keeping with modern consciousness dynamics, Steiner's spiritual research can be interpreted by clear, rational thinking, and then pragmatically applied to a large range of modern problems. The results of his research are increasingly confirmed with the advances of modern knowledge, and have brought a wholesome rationally-holistic renewal of life and work for many people.

Steiner was able to offer profoundly comprehensive insights and detailed knowledge for a modern path of initiation. He wanted to assist in the re-development of what was called in ancient times, The Mysteries; that is institutions in which ongoing, consistent wholesome forms of spiritual development were nurtured, and indeed seen as vital to the continued existence of humanity on the Earth. This modern path of spiritual development is in effect, a path of self-initiation; the seeker formulates a system of meditation, and a corresponding life-style, taking advantage of material given by Steiner. Rudolf Steiner was born in 1861 and died in 1925, so all this was begun during the 19th century, about 50 years before New Age spirituality developed in the west. Thus he may well be regarded as the foremost holistic researcher and seer in European or Western civilisations, and a master of meditation who attained an exceptional understanding of the mind and its higher potential. If you are not familiar with the basic texts of Rudolf Steiner, then you will need to acquire these **before attempting the meditative process explained here.**

From this process, the meditant can be enveloped in a peace-filled timeless serenity during deep meditation; and sense the nearness of a divine spirituality quality that is emerging into consciousness from within. The meditant also discovers that a higher integrity and an enhanced spiritually-attuned sense of 'purpose' has developed. So, after some time of consistent effort the meditation session becomes permeated by a wonderful mood of holiness. Gradually, as one learns to enter deeply into an inner stillness, yet retaining self-awareness, one's consciousness starts to function on another level, it could be termed an intuitive level. The kind of consciousness states that are achievable will be examined in detail later.

Esoteric meditation
Such meditation as is explained here is derived from what could be called 'esoteric' knowledge. That is, knowledge directly learnt from experiencing the higher realms and their symbiotic link to the physical world, through merging one's consciousness with the transcendent-eternal self. This is achieved through a systematic disciplined path of inner development, or self-initiation. One could also say esoteric knowledge is derived from attaining higher cosmic states of consciousness. In its fullest, highest form, such wisdom is only attainable by a true initiate, that is, someone who can in full consciousness raise their mind up to the divine realms beyond time and space, wherein the divine-spiritual beings exist, and through whom creation is sustained. It was precisely this ability which Rudolf Steiner had attained, and from which his teachings derive.

To pursue the meditative activity explained here, the student will however need to make a study of several of Rudolf Steiner's primary texts. This activity need not result in a sectarian path; his teachings are in themselves completely non-sectarian, they are not life-alienating. When read in translation, they may at times give that impression, because the translations date from early last century, so his texts may need to be updated in their style. In 1920 Steiner requested that his primary texts be revised so as to have a context suitable for the generation born a decade or so earlier. Before we consider how to meditate, what is the underlying motivation of this deeper esoteric meditating that Rudolf Steiner taught? It is similar to that of people in earlier civilisations who gained acceptance into the Mystery Temple or an esoteric order. I attempt to summarize below the several motivating factors involved.

Wisdom
This is the search for a gradual attainment of understanding of deep spiritual truths; a process that is not completed in one sudden moment of insight (although it may include such moments). It is rather an enlightenment that takes years to attain, and which results in one becoming more engaged in the needs of humanity, considered spiritually. It is the quest to so spiritualize the mind that deeper truths of a cosmic nature can be perceived and comprehended. To finally understand sublime truths that cannot at first be grasped intellectually, yet which answer the deepest questions of life. Behind this motivation there is an important ethical consideration; namely the perception that it is precisely because modern civilisation is devoid of a substantial spiritual wisdom, that we have the serious social problems of today.

Compassion
This is the deep urge to become a being of love and of purity; a person in whom personal desires are overcome and one in whom selfless

dedication to the greater purposes of life can be achieved. This motivation has far-reaching consequences, for love is fully present in us only when the will, as well as the feelings, is spiritualized. Then our volition becomes naturally inclined to do the good; humility and compassion become eternally present, unshakeably real.

Inner strength
The ability to be a person of courage, with iron will. The goal here is to be able to stand firm in life's challenges, and work to overcome evil tendencies in the world. The challenge is to be able to recognize the real tasks for our life and to face these with enthusiasm. To be able to take up a task of importance to the community, and to stay resolute and faithful to it. But especially to align one's will with the divine purposes of our Creator, and of those great divine-spiritual beings, such as the archangels, which seek to manifest His will. The motivation here is really to help build a new and better world in the future.

Higher consciousness
To expand one's perceptions beyond the physical material plane. The ultimate aim here is to seek to develop seer-ship with such accuracy that it is reliable and sure. In this way precise and clear research into spiritual realms can be undertaken.[1] On this basis, investigation into the interconnection of humanity with other realms could be made, some results of this could be for example, advanced holistic medical research, the creating of seasonal festivals, and developing new ways to help those souls who have entered the spiritual realms. The arts originally have their origin in such clairvoyance. These are vital tasks, now almost vanished, but needing to be reinstated on the Earth.

Very importantly, for our personal life, to have a higher consciousness whilst still in the body, means one is also able to commune with one's beloved partner, family and friends, when death robs us of their presence. The development of real higher consciousness enables us to assist the souls who are now already on the journey to the realms of spirit, the journey of the soul after death. This same capacity has enormous esoteric significance, connected to the theme known as **continuity of consciousness,** stretching across all realms and stages of the cosmic journey of the human being.

---

[1] This is the kind of clairvoyance research which Steiner developed to a unique degree; thus from his 'anthroposophy' or inner wisdom/higher consciousness, he conducted what he called 'spiritual-scientific research'. Its validity can be assessed by the success of Steiner's work in exacting specialist areas of work, e.g., its capacity to formulate precise medical therapies, and design very efficient, harmless 'herbal' horticultural sprays and a precise educational psychology which produces verified, excellent results in terms of psychological well-being and societal integration of Steiner school graduates.

Through a balanced path of spiritual development all of these goals can be effectively worked towards and – to some extent – achieved. In essence, all these various motivations could be summed up as: **seeking union with the higher-self, the spiritual potential of every person, the eternally self-conscious 'I am'. These goals are often understood in general spiritual literature as seeking fully conscious union with what is normally called God.** The term 'God' is however often used without clear understanding of what Being is involved (and of the ranks of divine-spiritual beings through whom the Creator manifests Its will). Later we shall examine what happens when the meditant raises his or her consciousness to the 'divine', as understood in the esoteric knowledge developed by Steiner.

I have journeyed along the path, and to a small extent, across the threshold, through developing methodically – to a limited degree – the higher faculties needed. This has enabled me to make this valuable material available in an experiential form, so that it can be practically used by any one who seeks to meditate in the way Steiner recommends. This involved the work over many years of sifting through thousands of pages of manuscripts from the students in Steiner's Esoteric School; there are up to six differing versions of any one lesson. These reports in the original language are of varying quality and length, hence close textual analysis is needed to determine his actual teachings.

A very little known aspect of Rudolf Steiner's work was his training of people in meditation over a ten year period, from 1904 to 1914. It was continued in a small way thereafter until his death in 1925. During his life he gave about 220 lessons to the various groups of students, who numbered approximately 1000 persons. The advice given was designed for the specific people in attendance, people personally invited by him, according to their inner development. It dealt with intimate spiritual matters, and hence notes of the lessons are not suitable for publication. Publishing such material is against his specific instructions, as it contravenes a fundamental principle of the spiritual life. It was understood in earlier cultures, and is still understood in certain ethnic groups today, like the Aboriginal people of Australia, that it is harmful in various way to make esoteric material prematurely available to someone who has not been prepared for such potent truths.

The higher spiritual truths if encountered too soon will appear odd or trite or perhaps grotesque. Rudolf Steiner told his Esoteric School pupils in 1907 that most of them would leave the room if he were to speak too directly on the sublime mysteries of the higher worlds. This perspective is still valid today. It is also to be found included amongst the New Testament teachings, e.g., in Revelation (10:4) where the seer was told to withhold certain experiences from dissemination.

When participants began to make their notes available to people who were not invited to join the classes, he announced in a lesson in 1914 that the school was to end. The first World War had also begun and this was a factor, too, but not the deciding one. Modern society has very little understanding of such matters, and hence in some circles these notes are today regarded as publishable, an attitude which is questionable, with regard to the more potent material of this nature. On the other hand, the fact is that copies of such material are anyway in circulation.

So, if one purchases a book of such lectures it is important to note that it may well be from such private lectures, some of which are now published. Hence some of the books in the Complete Edition are quite incorrectly integrated into the general category designated as 'lectures to members of the Anthroposophical Society', for in fact membership in that Society did not, and would not, qualify the persons to attend those lectures. Rather, one had to be a member of the particular, often strictly private esoteric meditation group; such persons were also, certainly members of the Society, but that was not the deciding factor.

So, it could be said, that to give oneself access to such material, which has been retained and subsequently published, is similar to travelling back in time to 1904 -14 perhaps by an out-of-body journey and then slipping into the lecture room and listening in. It is nevertheless true that quite a substantial portion of his advice is suitable for wider distribution, provided it is made available with a commentary, by an experienced esoteric meditator, so that the material is not too esoteric nor abstract nor 'intellectual'.

In view of the growing interest now for clear guidance in the matter of spiritual experiences, publishing of some of this confidential guidance on meditation, which is accompanied by a suitable commentary, is appropriate. In this book I am therefore presenting the essence of his guidance from the ca. 200 lessons, inter-woven with my commentary which derives from personal experience of much that is presented in this book. However, this book is intended to be read in conjunction with Rudolf Steiner's "Knowledge of the Higher Worlds; how is it attained?" The process of becoming spiritualized through earnest and regular meditative activity is in the modern worlds a path to what could be called 'self-initiation', a term that needs some clarification.

Initiation
Initiation refers to a systematic pathway of soul-exercises and meditation, and the adoption generally of a life-style that assists rather than hinders the spiritualization of the personality. The meditative activity undertaken in a genuine and wholesome path to initiation will derive from persons who have themselves already journeyed along the

path, because they have achieved substantially enhanced purity of heart, wisdom and selflessness of intention. Such higher initiates are rare, but they understand the higher realms and the pitfalls that may await the student.

The term 'Initiation' is again becoming a common term, but it has not yet attained the depth which it should have. In the European mystery tradition, there have always been at least a tiny handful of such meditants, in small and secret groups of esotericists. We shall begin the journey of discovery into Steiner's advice about taking the Path to self-initiation with a passage about initiation from his book, Theosophy, from the Chapter, 'The Path of Knowledge';

> "The person who is able to effect changes in the inner life in such a way, advances from stage to stage in spiritual knowledge. The fruit of such inner exercises will be that certain vistas into the higher world will unfold to his or her spiritual perception. The student learns what is actually meant by the truths communicated about this higher world; and these truths shall now be confirmed through personal experience. If this stage is attained, then something approaches which can only become experienced through treading this path. Namely, in a manner whose significance only now becomes clear to him or her for the first time, the student shall receive the so-called Consecration (Initiation), through the 'great spiritual guiding powers of the human race'. One becomes a 'student of wisdom'.
>
> The less one sees in such initiation something which consists in an external human relationship, the more correct the conception formed about it will be. What the seeker experiences after this can only be indicated here. She or he receives a new home, through which the student becomes a conscious dweller in the higher worlds. The source of spiritual discernment from now on streams to one out of a higher realm. The light of knowledge no longer illumines the seeker from without, for now she or he is placed within the fountain-head of the light. Thus within the seeker the deeper enigmas of the world are seen in a new light. The seeker no longer converses with the things which have been fashioned by the spirit, but directly with the forming, shaping spirit itself. The separate-life of the personality in such moments of spiritual-perception is only there in order to be a conscious image of the eternal.
>
> The characteristic of those who have attained to discipleship on the path of higher knowledge is **freedom**, freedom from the prejudices of the personality, from doubt and from superstition. However one should not confuse this 'becoming-one' of the

personality with the all-embracing life of the spirit, with an **absorption** of the personality into the 'all-pervading spirit' which annihilates the individual. No such disappearance of the self occurs with genuine {wholesome} inner development.[2]

Personality remains preserved within the relationship that one develops with the spiritual world. It is not subjugation of the personal self which occurs but rather a re-forming of it into something higher. If one wants an image for this coinciding of the individual with the 'all-spirit', then one can not choose that of various circles which merge together into one. Rather one needs to choose the image of many circles of which each has a distinct shade of colour; and do indeed coincide, but each and every nuance of colour preserves its being-ness within the totality. Not one of these circles loses the fullness of its own forces.

The **ethical background** to this system of spiritual development has been considered earlier, but there is a kind of Golden Rule underlying Steiner's approach. He formulated this axiom in his book, "Knowledge of Higher Worlds, How is it Attained?"; **"When you attempt to take one step forward in the knowledge of hidden truths, make three steps forwards in the ethical improvement of your character"**. This sentence and the over-all ethical basis behind this path will be examined in depth later. It is clear from the above that initiation today is really self-inaugurated, not carried out secretly in a remote secluded place.

---

[2] Note that any text placed in italicized brackets like these { } within a quote is a clarifying addition from the author.

CHAPTER ONE
Meditation: path to the divine

There are many different ways to meditate, depending on what one means by 'meditate'. Complex books exist on various meditative systems. The goal of the meditation method taught here is esoteric spiritual development. That is, it is designed to assist the meditant to achieve union with her or his own divine spiritual potential. The approach to meditation taught here is not complex, although some effort is required, but that is true of any worthwhile thing in life. Indeed it is emphasized here that the amount of real effort which a person makes is actually what counts, not the results. All that is brought about by making effort is of great value, because it is having a transformative effect on the soul, and shall bring results later in this life and in the next life. The purpose of this chapter is to explain **exactly how to meditate** in the esoteric deeper sense, and what kinds of higher consciousness states the meditant can develop. Chapter Nine gives further pragmatic advice about how to meditate.

This book is about how to systematically develop through meditation our **spiritual** potential, not our psychological potential. It is **not** a guide to meditation for relaxation, for personal growth, or as a method for attaining bliss. It is a comprehensive guide to the system of meditation, used by those seeking initiation under the light of the esoteric but cosmopolitan Christian stream of wisdom, associated with the mysterious Holy Grail, presented in a form suitable for modern times by Rudolf Steiner. It is a system which was devised to help people who seek union with their highest spiritual reality. Often when we say 'spiritual' we mean **psychological,** so here I need to make it clear that in this book, soul/personal growth is regarded as a psychological process, quite distinct from spiritual matters.

The human spirit is really a spark from Deity, and derives from sublime realms above the soul world, also known as 'the astral plane'. These realms of spirit are called in this book Devachan or the Kingdom of the Heavens. Devachan is a Sanskrit word used in Theosophical literature which means 'realm of the resplendent gods'.[3] An open secret of the human dilemma is that the human spirit exists in a germinal form and it seeks to become fully realized within each adult. The germinal spiritual entity itself inspires the incarnate personality to the right use of our soul-qualities, that is, our head and heart, for the active pursuit of spiritual development. However, psychological growth is certainly

---

[3] R. Steiner describes the nature of these realms of the soul and of the spirit in his 'Theosophy'.

important, it encourages a person to become more positive, life-affirming, sensitive, and more capable.

Books on personal psychological growth are valuable, for they serve as guides to integrating our personality. But I will assume that you have undergone, or are undergoing such personal growth activity. I will focus on working with the impulses from our higher self that seek to allow the potential for initiatory spiritual development within us to unfold. It may well be that you feel the need for further consolidation of your personality before entering seriously into the process of meditation. However, as I know from my work as an advisor in personal growth using Steiner's psychology, by taking up the soul exercises explained in detail here, much of the inner chaos and disempowerment can be effectively resolved. The study process, and the basic parallel exercises, explained in the next chapter, themselves gradually transform the soul – one becomes a different person, much more integrated and endowed with inner strength.

The term **'esoteric'** means here that this kind of meditation enables one, in the course of time, to directly experience the divine spirit which is part of our human nature. Drawing near to this spirituality starts to bring into being within the meditant spiritual wisdom, selfless love, and inner strength. It brings this about through a merging of the personality with the human spirit. As this occurs, higher faculties (so-called clairvoyance) also arise. Later chapters will discuss at length the experiences that this process causes. These chapters will explore various other aspects of meditating, including techniques to empower oneself so that the necessary faculty of concentration can be developed. We will also consider soul exercises to access the source of spirituality hidden within our being. Once this occurs, one begins to become aware of brief flashes of insight, concerning the theme of the meditative text on which one is meditating.

These brief moments become deeper and more prolonged, and one becomes aware, that from spiritual realms, from a source of holiness, **my 'I' is being 'enlightened'**. The 'I' is now becoming illumined, becoming transcendent. It is taking on layers of richness and depth that interface with a realm that transcends time, and space and the 'substance' of which is formed from God. This higher self is also permeated with the consciousness and creativity of a multitude of divine beings.

As this occurs, the 'I' is actually changing and deepening, one feels that it is expanding, in the sense of merging with a sacred all-encompassing reality; a reality that previously was only an exquisite, momentary sensing of a radiant point of consciousness, 'above' one. A point that in itself transcends time, and beckons to the personal self, as it lives with the flow of time, within the painfully empty widths of space all around one. One example, decades ago, prior to my developing at least some perception of higher realities, on this pathway of self-initiation, was that I could feel disturbingly small in the sensing of time's flow; and alien within the apparently empty and immeasurable expanse of space around me.

Another example, the space between the legs of a chair, or between several trees, would resonate with a disturbing barrenness, and the awareness of the flow of time in which I was carried along, without an overview of the beginning and intend goal of this flow, was constrictive. Meditation in the sense meant here, brings about within the kernel of one's consciousness, the gradual development of new qualities, and a sense of becoming gradually merged back into a welcoming nexus of being-ness. The meditant perceives that this new and sacred experience is itself an encounter with the divine, in ways that become transformative. These encounters or inner realisations do not remain fuzzy mystical feelings, they become ever more substantial, and show clearly and specifically the interrelatedness of the divine to human nature.

There are also psychic, visionary experiences that occur quite soon, but these normally fade out. This book explains practically, not theoretically, from experience, just why this happens, and how to deal with it. Furthermore, through such meditation in a slow, wholesome manner, higher faculties develop that also bring visionary experiences, but of a much more uplifting kind. This is not the goal of deep meditation, but it is an inevitable consequence of meditation. Consequently, you shall find that daily life brings direct awareness of the spiritual reality. For example, walks in nature become a door-way into an increasingly enchanted world. The various life-energies of the Earth's ether-aura become visible, constantly pulsing and moving against the background of the pale blue sky or the violet-blue night. From the leaves of trees, mauve coloured fingers of ether-energy stream out into the sky. At night the gentle auric glow which is to be seen around each star, or the complex coloured aureole around the moon bestow an enchanting beauty on the night sky, and affirms the aliveness of the cosmos.

The night-time also becomes a kind of portal into the spiritual realms, for the meditant begins to experience upon awakening in the morning, that one's dreams become ever less confused, and in their place, clear memories of profound spiritual 'messages' begin to occur. Furthermore, upon awakening, one can also have glimpses of the cosmos, imbued with a spiritual presence which speaks of some connection of the soul with the cosmos. This is because the meditant whose soul is being transformed by the inner discipline, can have a measure of awareness of the spiritual spheres through which we return as we journey back down to the body. **The hallmark of the path offered here is that one can quietly integrate this meditative path into a busy life.** This pathway can also help one to work in a new way in one's career or daily tasks. There is no need to retreat from life in order to pursue it.

In this esoteric path, the central spiritual being of our solar system, called here the cosmic Christ, is regarded as providing forces in the Earth's aura which assist the spiritual seeker to spiritualize the soul, so that the human spirit becomes "born" within. So, we could say that the purpose of esoteric meditation is to follow in the footsteps of the great initiates, to achieve Spiritual Enlightenment, which really means to achieve attunement of our consciousness to the divine-spiritual realms where the human spirit exists. **Hence to meditate successfully is to permeate our consciousness with spiritual truths, so that eventually these truths become one with us.** The transcendental truths will be presented in the form of a verse and/or a symbol, such as the Rose-Cross. A Rose-Cross symbol became famous through the interest shown in the medieval Rosicrucians; it is a simple wooden cross, which is of dead black wood, and has seven fresh, living roses around its centre. In later chapters this symbol will be explained, and meditative texts given that can be used whilst contemplating this symbol.

The verse or symbol must be something that proclaims actual 'spiritual' reality (i.e. a reality that transcends the sense world). The actual component ideas in the verse or symbol may be readily understood, eg, a wooden cross with some roses, or the words 'light', 'heart', wisdom, 'pure', etc; but the over-all 'statement' that the verse or symbol is conveying must transcend logic. It must be ineffable, that is inaccessible to the logical rational intellect. This is the essential point; our intellect's logical ability must **not** be able to completely comprehend and analyse the over-all meaning of the material used for meditation. Good examples of such texts that are easily available are two important meditative texts, used by thousands of meditants: the prologue of the Gospel of St. John (the first fourteen verses) and the eastern mantra, "Hail to the Jewel in the lotus".

It is immediately obvious that although logical thinking can analyse the component-ideas in these verses, the full significance of the statements is not comprehensible in its fullness to the logical mind. For the sublime truths that these words are proclaiming are 'transcendental', their meaning derives from higher realms and dynamics other than those of the mundane world.

Another example, from Rudolf Steiner, is the phrase; "**Wisdom lives in the light**". It is tempting to decide that these words are just too simple to be of any value for meditating. The reverse is true. They are of immense depth. Our intellectual mind quickly comprehends the elements of this phrase, but it gradually also realizes that it has failed to discover the supra-physical truths it is proclaiming. That is, the intellect just cannot understand how wisdom could be present within a ray of light. It takes perhaps many months before the meditant using this verse discovers the truths within it.

Likewise with the symbol of the Rose-Cross, and the prologue to St. John's Gospel; this symbol and text has an infinite meaning, which is obviously not logically accessible; only by intuitive consciousness is its meaning to be found. They will be considered in detail later; for now we need to simply note that they convey a spiritual truth beyond the power of analytical thinking to fully grasp. This is the essential quality of a true meditation text; therefore it needs to be formed by a highly evolved person who has experienced the higher worlds. A selection of meditative verses will be explored in a later chapter.

Now let us consider what **esoteric meditation** is. The meditant is to fill his or her consciousness with the verse (or symbol), to the exclusion of all other images, ideas, and worries, etc. No analytical logical efforts or striving for emotional experiences are to be allowed. You concentrate your attention on the text or symbol. **One simply permeates one's mind with the divine transcendental 'message' of the verse.** The mind is relaxed yet alert, it is 'tasting' the verse; its meaning is being sought through attunement with the words, or rather with the images that the words invoke. Subtle responses are occurring in your soul to the presence of the meditative verse. In other words, we totally suffuse our mind with the verse; which, as an esoteric 'message' of substantial depth and power, **will invoke into action a higher consciousness, a faculty for holistic insights.** This kind of consciousness is described by Steiner as a thinking that transcends the physical plane.

The human soul possesses an intuitive ability, but this is usually not required to become strenuously active for a prolonged period, nor to focus itself on a definite goal. It usually simply works for a split second when important moments or crises demand more than just logical deduction. In meditating, however, one is calling forth this ability and focussing it on the verse. Gradually one will experience as 'intuitions', certain insights into the sacred theme of the verse, insights that we can not at first explain or indeed even retain in our mind. But their presence is an exquisite and uplifting blessing, and **unknown to us, their presence is commencing the process of transforming our very being.** They are also beginning to attune our soul to the spiritual realms. The sacred reality that the verse proclaims is becoming one with us; making us into a vessel fit for its presence, permanently.

So one is not logically thinking, yet intense 'thinking' of a spiritual kind is occurring in such meditative activity. We could call this mental activity a perceiving by the mind itself, or apperception. Normally through our senses we perceive physical reality; now we perceive higher truths, not of course with the senses, but with the mind, or really, with the spiritualising soul itself. Such perception however is not occurring through the normal brain-bound intellect, and it thus results in holistic insights, these may manifest in the form of pictorial images. It is important at this point to understand that the process of consciousness, of registering reality is not derived from our brain! As Steiner explains, the brain simply registers (some of) our thoughts as prosaic logical concepts; both logical and intuitive thinking arise in the soul, not in the brain.

This point about thinking is extremely important; what one registers as thoughts in one's consciousness – as a person inside the body, using the brain – is only a pale silhouette of the real thought. Indeed many of the spiritual insights just don't become registered at all. An idea arises firstly in the soul, and is thus to be seen as thought-forms in the aura. It then is registered by the brain, so far as that is possible. Many people who are not interested in every day intellectual ideas say that in meditation one strives to get away from thinking, to something higher. That is reasonably accurate, but not if we understand thinking in its spiritual fullness; and therefore include in this term 'thinking', all holistic and intuitive insights. This is exactly what Rudolf Steiner does, because he experienced just how powerful and real is the spiritual activity responsible for holistic insights.

He also saw that most of our every-day thinking derives from this same power even if it focussed only on mundane themes.[4] So the process of meditating is quite simply to become absorbed in the meditative text, to let spiritual insights arise in the soul. The meditant then experiences these insights faintly on the periphery of consciousness. These are naturally transcendental, they speak of matters beyond the normal physical world which we know. Therefore they are not easily put into logical form, and also for this reason it is not easy to perceive them at first.

When this is achieved however, then we are consciously registering spiritual insights that are present in our soul, in our aura; **insights that are not registered by our brain** in the way that earthly ideas are registered by it. This is the most healthy out-of-body-experience of

---

[4] When you begin to read Steiner's works, you may at first think it is 'intellectual' and un-spiritual because he refers to thinking quite often, but actually he is referring to higher spiritual understanding, for example to a flash of insight. He is not referring to the normal logical thoughts or pale mental images of these which we normally have.

them all ! For one could describe this as body-free consciousness whilst still encased in the flesh; an experiencing of sense-free thought. It is important to note that these transcendental holistic ideas that are glimpsed as flashes of insight, without any tangible form or logical structure, are actually existing in one's life-force field, or so-called 'ether-body'.

This matter of the ether-body is extremely important; no understanding of higher experiences or indeed of spiritual psychology as such, is possible without knowledge of its functions. Although higher insights come from the astral/spiritual realms, and are perceived by the meditant's astral body or soul, the meditant will only be aware of them **after they are reflected** in the network of life-forces that link the soul-body to the physical. This life-force organism is called the **ether-body** by Steiner; it is made of life-energy, which is called 'prana' or 'Ch'i' in other languages.

So, actually, in meditation, one is in the first instance, striving to develop awareness of the holistic ideas that are living as images in one's own ether-body. Many of these can then become perceived, in a less living form, as 'thoughts'. These **images depict their meaning in a symbolic way** through their form and colour, etc. We need to just note that when this first stage of higher consciousness is highly developed, the meditant will directly perceive these holistic truths, that pervade the cosmos (in the astral level) as actual images within the astral world; these are then termed, 'visions'.

The term 'astral' is Latin and refers to the stars. Amongst the stars there are multi-coloured flowing fields of gas and dust, called 'nebula'. Therefore this term 'astral' was used as a name for the soul, (which appears as an aura around the physical body), because to clairvoyant gaze, there are similarities between the appearance of a starry nebula and the aura. So the term, 'soul-body' or 'astral body' came into being to refer to the soul, when seen as a separate organism around the physical body; it is a 'body' of astral nature. Those people in earlier times who had psychic perception were able to see the soul as coloured forms of various shapes, with a scintillating radiance.

One can readily understand that this must be so, since the sensing of insights is already a kind of inner seeing. This living in 'body-free thinking' is at first a kind of vague sensing of images that weave through the periphery of the aura. This sensing can become greatly enhanced and manifest as actual visions; then a fantastic display of shapes and colours, brilliantly hued, are inwardly 'seen'. It is possible at this point that the person learning to meditate may decide to stop, as such results are disconcerting. Yet all that is needed is to understand what has happened to your consciousness; this book has been written to provide help, in the absence of personal guidance from an advanced meditator, with these experiences.

This level of consciousness I call the **psychic-image consciousness** stage, because once it is fully developed, images of astral reality begin to be seen, and these can even become quite specific visions. In any event, a visionary mental ability develops, which places before the meditant the challenge of interpreting these experiences, which, like works of art, can convey multiple significance, beyond what can be conveyed in a text. A preliminary form of this first level is experiencing holistic insights weaving in the ether-body. The meditant is then becoming capable of consciously perceiving and processing insights that come from outside the normal limits determined by one's brain. In one report from a lesson by the initiate, Rudolf Steiner, on esoteric development the following was explained:

> By focussing our self in our ether-body through meditation, that is by seeking to sense the insights that exist there, we should be able to release ourself from the 'shadowy abstract every-day thoughts'. In this way one attains to the actual primal reality of the thoughts, which is present in the ether-body. As we train ourselves to recognize the mere shadowy nature of normal thinking, and the illusory nature of our external environment, then we gradually grow into the spiritual world. Then we will also recognize that all thoughts of the good, the beautiful, the noble, which we form here on Earth change into permanent factors of much value in the ongoing future of the world. We see these ahead of us, in the future, for there they live, bringing healing and happiness to humanity." (1914)[5]

The word 'illusory' as used by Steiner here means that the sense-perceptible world is much more than what our senses tell us it is; it is an illusion that creation consists only of self-sustaining molecular particles. There is a phenomenon that occurs as this state is being achieved; it is a sensation of getting wider, or expanding into a vast world around one. In Chapter Four this and other such side-effects of meditating are described.

In a more advanced stage of meditating it is as if one is 'spiritually breathing' higher truths into one's being, not just becoming aware of insights and the images they create. The process is like inhaling an inspired thought; yet what is perceived (mentally) lives in us just as

---

[5] Note that when a year appears in brackets like this anywhere in this book, it designates the year in which the statement was made in the private meditation lessons.

vividly as does the mental image of a rose which we see with our physical senses. Hence we are seeing, but not using the eyes; we are thinking, but not using the brain, i.e. not using the usual deductive-empirical logical faculty. This kind of higher consciousness I will call Spiritual Enlightenment. This term will be explained in detail later along with other aspects to meditating, which are more complex. See the Glossary of terms at the end of this chapter.

Firstly though, we need to understand more about the processes occurring psychologically during meditating. In particular the question, what kind of higher states can we expect to attain as a result of meditating? This needs to be outlined before detailed descriptions of the results of meditating are explored. Then the relationship of meditation to prayer, contemplation and other inner exercises of the soul will be considered.

There are three distinct kinds of higher consciousness-states that lie dormant in the soul and which are developed by meditating. The first higher state that we have discussed, enables one to sense the living essence of our thoughts, not just the mental images we make of these. As this sensitivity to the spiritual insights which live in the soul develops, it brings a form of clairvoyance. As I briefly indicated above, it causes images of considerable intensity to form in the aura; these are what people refer to as visions (or in New Age idiom, 'movies'.) I will use the term 'psychic-image consciousness' or 'astral vision' for this.[6] This faculty is well known, and is often called "astral clairvoyance". To understand what is happening, we need to consider briefly how a person attains to knowledge of this world.

Seeing visions through meditating

The meditant experiences colour-filled living images or forms, of any shape; an extraordinary world of forms that also possess a colour-quality. Yet physically, nothing is there. I say colour **quality**, because it is not so that one sees a colour-cloud made of rarefied or finer molecules. There is no matter in the soul world. When someone's aura is perceived, it is really that the soul-dynamics of a person are perceived. These are felt by us as if a colour is seen; actually, the soul quality is registered by the aura as a colour. Why is this? Because each physical colour derives from a corresponding astral energy, and thus has a soul quality or 'astral aspect' to it. If we contemplate colours

---

[6] Rudolf Steiner called this first of the three higher states of consciousness, 'Imagination' because root-words for this term mean to "form images"; which is what happens when one registers impressions from the astral plane. This term is fine for German readers, but confusing in English. The same word in common English usage often means of course, fantasy; which is also picture-forming, but undertaken by in normal consciousness.

carefully, we can sense that red has a different inner nature than blue, for example.

This is because in the astral world red is a specific mood or feeling, quite different to that of blue. So, each colour is an equivalent of a soul mood. Indeed when these colours occur in nature (e.g., the colour of a flower), they are the expression of a corresponding astral force in a particular nature-spirit. The astral plane does not consist of matter, not even refined matter. In practical life one would speak of seeing a red form or a bright green stripe, etc, in an aura. It is important to note that this is an abbreviated way of saying that the astral energy that in the physical world manifests in red, is now being perceived. This subject is explained further in the section about the illustrations of the auras of the human soul and spirit.

Such images seen by the meditant are really scenes of the astral world, perceived by our own astral aura. (The astral world is also known as the soul world.) The human soul registers glimpses of the soul world in this way; that is, the soul registers the soul world as images which have an inner colour-dynamic. As we shall learn in Chapter Four, there are many other kinds of astral visions that occur at the beginning, but the really important experiences in fact begin in a very subtle way. The soul which appears as an oval-shaped aura around the physical body, has organs for sensing/seeing in it; these are the so-called chakras. The term **'chakra'** is Sanskrit and means 'wheel'; it refers to circular vortex-like centres in the astral body, through which the soul can perceive in the spiritual realms. The term chakra in oriental literature can refer to many different octaves of energy vortices; I shall be using it to refer to energy vortices in the aura, especially the aura of the soul-body (also called the astral body).

All that which one normally yearns to experience through visions is to be found in this realm, and is accessed through the first of the three kinds of higher consciousness. The human aura, the unborn babes awaiting incarnation, the devas and the enchanting world of faery, angels radiant with holiness, and those souls whose body has died and who are now journeying up into spirit heights. Vision is also possible of the spiritual dynamics within the human being; for example, Steiner describes that every act of will lighting up in someone results in orange-red flames of lightning flashing through the life-energy body, which then ray on into the astral aura. All this is gradually able to be perceived by the faculty of astral clairvoyance, and in addition there are unpleasant and disturbing scenes at times, too. It is often the case that people want to meditate for the purpose of this elementary clairvoyance; but the goal of meditation is much deeper than this.

For the earnest meditant, the psychic-image consciousness level slowly brings about some perception of astral and ethereal realities; this bestows access to the fascinating and beautiful nexus that pulsates 'behind' the material world. The night sky becomes a pulsing interweaving of softly glowing auras enveloping each star, seen through a shimmering network of life-energies in the planet's prana or ether-energy fields. In the daytime, sun-beams when viewed carefully and indirectly, from under a tree for example, 'open up' to become a delicate tracery of vibrating light-rays. Fully developed **psychic-image** consciousness (astral vision) brings sights of magnificent beauty, of colours not seen on Earth, and a multitude of spiritual beings. In addition, as the seeker learns, the attaining of **psychic-image** consciousness also means that at times one has to endure glimpses of unpleasant but equally real aspects of life. Consistent meditating will indeed cause perception of this realm, but it may take some years.

This condition of seer-ship, which accompanies the development of a more spiritualized consciousness is achieved by simply continuing to meditate; that is, regularly faithfully meditating with real concentration. Naturally, this means after strengthening of one's consciousness through the soul-exercises given in the next chapter, and an appropriate study program. That is, firstly, you focus intensely on the special verse which you have chosen for the meditative session, that is on the various images which form in response to the transcendental nature of the verse.

One remains alert whilst living within these images to the insights that hover briefly before the consciousness; the insights form in response to these images. In fact delicate images are starting to take form in the aura, in response to the spiritual 'message' inherent in the verse. These are registered by the meditant as insights. This is meditating; at least in its first phase. Gradually this phase develops to the point where one becomes able to actually perceive various coloured images within the astral world. In a later chapter, various meditative texts will be offered for your use.

However, and this is really important, such visionary experiences as those mentioned above, do not reveal the real spiritual world; for it extends beyond the astral plane, which is the 'emotive stratum' of the cosmos. Access to higher sacred realms, or to divine consciousness-states is the real goal of the serious meditant. These higher spiritual 'realms' or states of being are accessed by the higher state of consciousness that I referred to as "**cosmic-spiritual**" consciousness, which will be considered soon.

Illusion or reality?

This first stage of astral-plane clairvoyance brings a substantial challenge. Namely, how does the meditant know that these images, which arise without any sense-object being involved, are 'really there'? For obviously the possibility of illusion, fantasy, even hallucination comes to mind. How does one differentiate between a hallucination and a real astral vision which is a perception of something quite real, but real in the astral world? Only by trial and error; in other words, **by experience**, for the meditant has in effect, lost the ground under his/her feet. Only through experience will it be possible to re-discover some substitute for the firm ground which we know when on the Earth. We no longer have actual physical reality as a test of the reality of something you see, so some other kind of 'test' has to be devised. This is done by learning to understand how an other-worldly 'object' develops its own inner genuine-ness to the eyes of the soul, just as a table is inherently genuine and real to our physical eyes. Rudolf Steiner gave many cautions to his students with regard to these initial experiences, as we noted in the text sample, earlier,

> But the most important thing which the student must know, when these images occur, is that what he or she sees before them does not always express what it appears to denote. Although they are realities which are revealed there, nevertheless these are too often only dissembling, tempting images which we have awakened and woven from out of our own souls...

One can begin to experiment to ensure that there is a reality to the vision, and not a self-deception. For example one experiences the **inner equivalent** of a colour, say orange, around a person when a particular mood prevails in that person. If this is repeated when you are in the presence of someone else and they are in this same mood, then gradually you can determine the inner truthfulness of your developing inner vision.

Remember, a characteristic of a hallucination, or even just a fanatical belief, is that the person is totally and unshakeably convinced of its absolute accuracy. Indeed in ill-advised occult activity the striving for visions to which one holds fast, with great intensity and faith is common. However, in great contrast to such soul dynamics, the meditant on this pathway is again and again reminded that **initial visions are not to be regarded as really objective**. On the contrary, they are to be taken as presenting inner desires, yearnings, and subtle egotistical hopes. So right from the start a main factor of hallucinatory experiences finds here no real breeding ground. In addition the meditant, in the self-training, is to work with the repeating images in the way described above, so that their objective nature becomes clear.

The term 'objective' here means that it is really existing in the astral plane independent of your own inner subjective desires, etc.

One could also say, just to be precise, that a false vision or hallucination is also objective in that it must exist as images in your aura and ether-body to be perceived. However, whilst this is true, it is an inferior form of objective reality, because you have unconsciously formed these images yourself, so we will refer to these as 'subjective', that is, not fully real. In this way, a hallucination is to be distinguished from a genuine astral scene; but the process is more substantial still. For example, one perceives in a vision, a cloud of colour; if it is genuine then gradually over time, this 'cloud' becomes a proclaimer of a substantial reality. You begin to sense that spiritual beings have a connection to this cloud of colour; the astral image becomes inwardly ever more real.

Just as you are certain that the table is really there, so too you become certain that the nature-spirit is really there. It is quite true that an unbalanced mind can be just as certain that its hallucinatory "angel" is really there too. However as we have seen, such a belief is total, unshakeable, whereas the path of meditation offered here encourages the very opposite attitude. Despite the fact that we yearn with quickened heart to accept that first fabulous image as real, that is, as genuinely coming towards one from the astral plane, and not conjured forth from one's own soul, this attitude of being dismissive towards these first visions is essential.[7]

These first visions are a transitional phenomenon, they are helping us to learn how to determine reality from deception in the higher worlds. Naturally this does not mean one should dismiss a special moment wherein a spiritual being, through an act of grace, was able to commune with you, or at least reveal itself as a comfort and support. Such experiences, not being invoked by an initial attempt at meditation, and simply happening suddenly, are indeed probably quite genuine. Certainly the more balanced and sound the soul-life is, the better will be the results of treading the inner path.

The avoidance of extremes in the spiritual path is vital, then, so that as a person of sound mental health, you do not become impelled towards disturbed mental attitudes, and hence prey to self-conjured visions, or to visions wafted towards you by spiritual powers that seek to give false impressions to the meditant. Likewise, as we have already seen, the constant striving for ethical development must become a self-

---

[7] This is further explained in the lecture of 21/Nov/'12 (G/A No. 62 p. 128) as well as in various of his basic books, where he speaks about the path. His esoteric students were further cautioned against this.

imposed 'compulsory' part of this path. This is essential to ensure that egotistic yearnings are rooted out of the soul, for example a subconscious desire for grandeur, to be Someone Important. Otherwise we may live this out by invoking subconsciously from its dwelling place in our aura, a vision of some impressive scenes of a magnificent past life. We shall be considering the avoidance of extremes in a later chapter about life-styles.

It can never be over-emphasized that one's inner world – the content of the soul, its yearnings, cravings, ambitions, etc – become one's outer world, as soon as the seeker crosses over the threshold into other worlds. In other words, one experiences as apparently quite separate from oneself, as an independent vision, the semi-conscious dynamics that prevail in the subconscious. The visions that appear can be naively taken by the beginner as independent reality in the soul world.\

All this may seem at first to be too cautious, as if the possibility of error is being exaggerated. However, this attitude derives from the student's assumption that, as a meditant, one is opening a window in the ceiling of a spiritual loft, and looking out into the empty blue sky above to see, perhaps, a spiritual being flying by. The initiate knows this is not the case, for the spiritual realms into which one enters are filled with spiritual beings. Indeed the very air and the clouds so to speak, of the higher worlds are themselves formed from a living spiritual-reality; "everywhere where something is, is being...what is there, is being." (1912) Hence there is much which interacts with our consciousness. The 'substance' of the spiritual realm only needs to find a compatible energy in your aura to form itself into part of the scenery which you then perceive as out there, external to your own being.

The path offered here provides much help in these matters; but it also **demands a real effort by the meditant**, to ensure that the seeker will not be caught off guard. A detailed description of the processes in the aura that actually cause clairvoyance is presented in Chapter Four. Here we are concerned with clarifying the kinds of higher states of consciousness which meditating causes, rather than the actual chakra-related dynamics behind them.

These themes bring us to an immensely important point: that **the meditant who perseveres with this pathway to the divine reality of the higher-self, is in fact treading the same path that the soul undergoes after death.** Once this life is over, the soul enters the other worlds, where it sees its past life before it, in a panorama of pictures, through which it undergoes a gradual process of attaining real self-knowledge.[8] Then it becomes involved in a process of 'divinization', as it ascends ever nearer to the sublime glory of the spiritual realms. Exactly the same processes are invoked into the life of the meditant.

A meditation for the first stage, psychic-image consciousness

"Wisdom lives in the light"

This can serve as an example of the sort of text used in this system of meditating. Various other examples are given in a later chapter. The intellect will, of course, try to analyse the meaning; so, let it try, but not when meditating on it! After a while, it gives up, for the meaning eludes it. One understands that wisdom is a state of holistic knowing, of thinking which is not matter-bound. It is a consciousness in which the empathy power of the heart is present in the thinking, giving an additional sensitivity to the intellect. One also understands that normally light refers to the sunlight.

But just how these two could be thought of as interrelated, this is where the intellect becomes puzzled; the phrase or verse seems to have no real meaning. The meditant then sternly decides that the intellect, having had its try, will not interfere with the meditating. So, one then focuses intensely on the meditative words, yet in a mood of tranquillity; and no further analysing nor a striving for an emotional state occurs.

Gradually, one becomes aware that there is a profound meaning in this simple phrase, and that the mind, that is, the holistic thinking ability, is starting to sense this. In your aura, thus in your soul, images are starting to fleetingly hover; images that contain a wealth of meaning about transcendental truths. These are at first perceived as flashes of insight, elusive but wonderfully uplifting moments of illumination. Much later, the meditant finds these insights, or spiritual thoughts, lasting longer and growing inwardly more substantial. Later still, the ability develops to express in logical concepts something of this insight. For example, an image of the Earth enveloped in sunlight can take shape in the mind; not visible sunlight, but the higher spiritual sunlight. (This exists in two forms, one composed of 'astral' radiance, the other of actual true spiritual radiance, referred to as 'Devachanic' in some esoteric literature.)

NB - much of the material from Rudolf Steiner which I present here is not translated into English, it is often published in German: the number of the volume amongst the ca. 350 volumes of his Collected Works in which it may be found, is shown, together with the letters G/A; these mean in German;" Complete Works".

[8] You can read further about this in Steiner's "Theosophy" and lectures on life after death.

Soon, the vastly complex, wisdom filled kingdoms of nature, of the earth's ecology is connected in your mind to the in-raying sunlight. For you begin to realize that the kingdoms of nature in remote ages have been conjured forth in effect by the sunlight. Then images of the inner light in the human soul draws your attention. They can be considered a potential wisdom which is seeking to unfold itself. Then a connection between this and the inner sunlight from the 'spiritual sun' becomes a theme of the insights that occur whilst meditating on this phrase. Profound understanding of the link between the cosmos and the dead and the human soul arises; eventually to be conceptually grasped. Meanwhile the effect of this meditating, this living in spiritual verities, has caused the aura to become ever more refined, and through this the chakras are becoming more developed.

The following is a specific example of **psychic-image** consciousness occurring with a quite experienced mediator, a student of Steiner's whose last years were lived out in New Zealand.

> "I was listening to a lady singing the Lord's Prayer, as someone played an accompaniment on a harmonium. The composition was agreeable, although not outstanding, the voice and singing were not especially technically skilled, but very pleasant and enjoyable. She had scarcely begun when something happened within me, my ether-body became (somewhat) freed from my physical body. I did not miss one single note of the external music {because on this pathway self-consciousness is enhanced, never reduced}. However a second inner process occurred at the same time. I saw the dark Earth in space. There sprang forth from it three thick rays of colour, purple, blue and violet. The inner nature of these colours was like that of a fountain welling forth, and of living, crystal-clear colours, now transparent and then opaque. They had precise contours like a tree trunk but with an inner flowing and moving.
>
> These thick trunks of colour grew and changed, branches sprang from them, which continuously divided up into more twisting spreading branches. All this rose ever higher, finally reaching the edge of the solar realm. There this mass of colour branches bent down around in a circle, thus gradually filling our entire world. At the same time, as an expression of these three intertwined (but never fused together) 'colour-trees' a glorious music resounded, harmoniously flowing on.
>
> It was a harmonious jubilation, completely in unison with what my physical ear heard, there was never any discordance or any overtones. One thing was clear to me; this colour-music was connected to the timbre of the singer's voice, not to the harmonium, and the colour music accompanied her, raising her

into the ethers, so to speak. For the singer was a lovely soul. Then as the song came to an end, everything sank back down into itself. With the last note the colour-tree-fountains sank into the dark Earth, and so the vision disappeared, together with its music. I can not say that at this point I awoke, because I had always been entirely awake; the experience is to be defined as supplementing my normal consciousness, not altering it (in the sense of weakening it).

As I soon thereafter told Dr. Steiner about this experience, he said, quickly and decisively, "That's good, now familiarise yourself more and more with the colours." He then gave me on the spot a special meditative text for this purpose. I had thought that the colours were of secondary significance, and that the ethereal music was the most important element of my experience, but from his response, it became clear to me that it was actually the other way around."[9]

Such experiences as this can occur in very many different colours and forms, but their wonderfully alive, radiant imagery can not be compared with the encounters obtained in the higher states of meditation into the holy spaces of the spirit. These encounters or rather, intuitive insights, bring the meditant into communion with spiritual realities. Insights occur, and these eventually become direct perception of the divine hierarchies and their interconnectedness with the core of our being, and of the potential for unconditional love pulsing within the fire-force of the human will. Such experiences which derive from developing **psychic-image** consciousness, is not the same as the perceptual distortion which has recently gained considerable medical and psychological attention, wherein a person sees colours or detects odours in direct response to sounds, or vice versa.

In the classical traditions of great religions and esoteric orders, people undertake meditation to attain to a higher state of mind that brings spirituality to the soul, and which gives access to divine realms. Hence many who meditate are interested in the 'sacred' aspects of meditating, rather than visual clairvoyance as such, that is, astral clairvoyance. Well, this higher kind of experience really belongs to the faculty or stage of **cosmic-spiritual** consciousness, which was briefly mentioned above. Although this is actually higher than psychic-image consciousness, it can start to develop at the same time as the lesser stage of the clairvoyant experiencing of images. The initial stages of **cosmic-spiritual** consciousness result in profoundly joyous, deeply satisfying

---

[9] From unpublished memoirs of Alfred Meebold, a student who succeeded in developing some clairvoyance, but still retained many imperfections.

feelings of being close to the divine and sacred realities of the spiritual world.

Stage 2: the stage of cosmic-spiritual consciousness

Beyond the bewildering and to some extent illusory astral world, there exists the actual spiritual realm, known as Devachan or Spiritland; this is the same as The Kingdom of the Heavens in Christian terms.[10] Spiritland is a term used in various esoteric systems of knowledge; as the name implies, it is the realm where beings more evolved than minor astral entities exist. A detailed insightful description of this divine realm comes from Rudolf Steiner, who had the faculty of **cosmic-spiritual** consciousness fully developed. He called this faculty, "inspirational clairvoyance", from the Latin 'inspirare' which means to absorb or inhale something, for the way in which the consciousness perceives the actual spiritual realm is akin to an infusion, absorption or inhaling process.

But the term inspirational clairvoyance (**cosmic-spiritual** consciousness) is confusing in English. In his words, it is a state "of being infused by or en-filled with spiritual reality". In this chapter I am drawing especially, unless otherwise stated, on Steiner's fundamental texts, Knowledge of the Higher Worlds; how is it attained?; The Stages of Higher Knowledge; A Way to Self-knowledge of the Human Being; The Threshold of the Spiritual World, and also his Outline of Esoteric Science. Steiner experienced that it is in this realm where our spirit, our divine essence has its existence. Hence when we can consciously experience elements of this realm, we are breathing in real living wisdom. To the meditant striving towards the spiritual world, it is as if one does not only see in this realm, but rather, that one also **breathes in** the spiritual wisdom, so to speak.

During perception of spiritual realities through this second faculty, musical notes are also inwardly heard, as if sounding forth from everything in spiritland. One can also refer to spiritland as realms, since it has, like the astral plane, seven distinct aspects to it. To become a meditant who experiences consciously this divine lofty realm, is a very substantial stage of inner development. It means in effect to become an initiate at least to a small degree. You may not be aiming as high as this, but awareness of the possibilities for higher consciousness is important.

---

[10] The original text is in the plural, but historically has been translated in the singular. The initiate experiences a multiplicity of realms in both the astral and the spiritual realms.

At this point, a brief archive note (date unknown) from Steiner about spirituality, as distinct from spiritual gifts, is helpful, I've added some clarifying words in brackets.

"**Constantly repeated practising of occult techniques makes a magician**": {that is, someone who can perform miraculous deeds. This is also the basis of the fakir, a performer who may impress friends, tourists or potential converts by doing things that defy physical laws of gravity, etc.}

A clairvoyant is someone who has perception of the higher worlds {but not necessarily through enhanced spirituality or esoteric meditation. It may be simply through a variety of occult techniques, or because they possess unusual ether energies that cause psychic abilities. Such a person need not have substantial spirituality or profound wisdom}. Thirdly, **an initiate is someone who knows and deeply understands the laws or dynamics of the higher worlds**.

In other words, an initiate, through meditation and contemplation, and in willing to manifest the spiritual laws of creation, acquires such inner purity and wisdom that he or she becomes enlightened. So, an initiate is a person with spiritual wisdom who may not always be manifesting **psychic-image** consciousness, but whose thinking is powerfully intuitive; it is attuned to the consciousness of the divine-spiritual beings who created and maintain the universe. So the initiate has attained to what I have called **cosmic-spiritual** consciousness, which brings attunement to the higher spiritual realms. This may not include direct perception of the spiritual world, but it will usually be present to some extent.

Earnestly persevering in meditating will bring one to the beginning of **cosmic-spiritual** consciousness; we do not have to wait until several lives have elapsed ! Within a few months of beginning this meditating, you will probably notice the wonderful sense of peace and inner harmony that this 'going within' causes. This is because we have the ability, slumbering within us to gain real spiritual insights. The ability to meditate is a gift, a capacity that is inherent in our soul; it simply needs to be allowed to flourish. It is an inherent potential in the human soul to breathe in or absorb insights about higher realities.

Why? Because inter-weaving within our normal ego is the higher-self, the eternal self. The higher-self yearns to unite with our personality; it could be thought of as actively wanting to inspire our personal self with intense interest in meditation. There are two starting points for every seeker on the journey to the spirit. One is from within our struggling, questing soul, and the other is above it, from the higher-self, whose rays of light (which are themselves interwoven into a divine nexus of spirit) have brought about our initial interest in the spiritual life. This is profoundly true: **one is never alone in spiritual development, in**

seeking to be one with the spiritual world. It is these factors that confer on us the ability to meditate.

Through **cosmic-spiritual** consciousness experiences, the higher truths of existence are perceived; at first however, only as fleeting impressions or moods. We have already briefly described this at the beginning of the chapter. It brings moments suffused with a holiness, in which the meditant feels as if permeated by a divine ray from the spiritual world, purifying and ennobling one's inner being.

What kind of realm is spiritland? To answer this question, even briefly, is important, for it provides much help with questions about what specific kind of experiences Inspiration opens to the meditant. Spiritland is a realm that consists, in regard to its 'substance' of the same 'substance' of which thoughts consist. The archetypal idea of every created object and being in the lower realms (in the astral, etheric, and material worlds) exists in the heavenly realms. These archetypal concepts emerge from the consciousness of the divine-spiritual beings who, in response to the impulses from the Trinity, have created the world.

In the spiritual worlds, one is in the realm of the gods, or what in Christianity is called the hierarchies; there are various ranks of divine beings therein; some of which are mentioned in the Bible. For example, the archangels, dominions, and powers. There, the human spirit finds its Creator and its true home. There our spirit exists in its own 'spirit-body'; its divine qualities perceived as colour-qualities, by the developed seer. In the case of a highly evolved soul, it appears as a rich golden glow, suffused with rose-pink and superimposed on a heavenly blue oval form. However, in contrast to the soul-body, the spirit-body has a greatly enhanced inner radiance. Yet its very existence is invisible to a seer whose vision is limited to the astral plane, and to whom therefore actual spiritual 'substance' is not perceptible. Moreover, our spiritual-beingness is there experienced as an integral part of the being of the hierarchies; truly, there, 'all is one'.

To the advanced meditant, or the human spirit after death, it is as if one experiences being immersed in a glorious ocean of spiritual light. It is like being immersed in waves of spiritual being-ness, a pulsing interweaving of radiance and warmth, not physical warmth, but a **warmth which derives from divine love**, not physical or even astral light, itself of extraordinary brilliance compared to physical light, but rather, **a light that is itself a manifestation of the wisdom**, the cosmic consciousness of the hierarchies.

Here then the meditant is experiencing or inwardly perceiving something, yet there is neither physical object, with its corresponding mental image, nor an image from the astral plane. What is perceived is arising into consciousness directly from the spiritual realms. One has to in effect, **learn to read the cosmic script**, a term that Steiner uses for this process.[11] One learns to understand, to interpret just what is presenting itself to one's consciousness. This is already needed to some extent with **psychic-image** consciousness, but the task is profoundly deepened with the higher faculty of **cosmic-spiritual** consciousness, for then divine-spiritual reality draws near to the meditator. The experience of this higher state of consciousness intensifies the process of transforming the personality so that the spirit becomes present in it.

This higher state also includes a form of clairvoyance, a seeing of forms and beings, although this does not occur in the early stages, which are characterized by insights into the truths of the spiritual realms not accompanied by images. In other words, at first the meditant is gaining wisdom, in the deeper sense. Later, when various images are perceived in this higher state, the images are of the 'substance' of the spiritual plane, not the astral plane. The forms of the soul-world (or astral plane) are experienced as if interpenetrating the higher spiritual reality.

To have the emotions and feelings permeated by such spiritual experiences confers a purity, a true inner beauty. To have one's intelligence spiritualized, that is, one's consciousness permeated by this light is to become enlightened, to have holistic understanding which grasps the ineffable. It is, Steiner taught, as if the supernal light begins to commune, to speak with you.... "In earlier esoteric streams, this stage of higher consciousness was described as 'hearing the inner word'. This expression was used because such an enlightened person is in the condition of perceiving profound truths through allowing the spiritual realms to infuse his/her mind with their 'speech'."[12]

Thus the mental images belonging to a word are transcended and the higher worlds themselves speak directly to the mind, so the spiritual realms themselves stream into the meditants thoughts. It is as if the conversation is with a being from the higher worlds; the meditant is tranquilly immersed in her or his self, holding away all images and visions, and inwardly perceiving. This faculty results in the person who enters higher realms not only seeing the objects around them, but also

---

[11] See his Outline of Esoteric Science, or his lectures, "The Theosophy of the Rosicrucians".

[12] This initiation secret was known to the great German genius Johannes W. von Goethe, who embodied it in his fairy tale of "The Green Snake And The Beautiful Lily", where the golden king receives the answer from the old man that "dialogue is more quickening than light" But this has been poorly translated as "speech" in the otherwise quite good version from Floris Press. In certain regions of the heavens, the radiance becomes an actual dialogue between the hierarchies.

in the phenomenon that everywhere objects are 'speaking' to one. Such a person listens intensely to what now in this new realm is busily whirring around about one." (1905)

Contemplation: a deeper form of meditation
To undertake the kind of meditation which goes beyond astral imagery to **cosmic-spiritual** consciousness (or 'Inspiration'), one needs to extend the meditation session by undertaking another kind of inner exercise. After meditating one dismisses the verse, that is, the content of our meditation. The symbol or verse on which our attention was intensely focussed, is to be removed from consciousness; the mind becoming apparently blank. Then instead of just stopping the meditation session, one attempts to remain highly attentive, inwardly alert.

The main purpose of this additional part of the session, is to 'enter into the silence', and at length, to hear 'the voice of the silence'. What does this mean? Firstly, the meditant has to create in this second part of the meditative session, a condition of inner peace, indeed of inner stillness. This is not simply a stillness caused by withdrawing from the noise of the external world, nor from one's own unsettled moods, which modern civilisation's hectic pace make worse. **The stillness must be an active stillness, so restful and devoid of movement, that it is a profound inner silence.** One needs to feel that the world itself has become a peaceful tranquillity. Nothing other than utter stillness is within you, **and the world itself has (seemingly) become this**, so all-pervading and powerful is this stillness. When this is attained, one is on the way to achieving the goal. However, by simply striving towards a deeper inner peace after dismissing the actual verse, one is at least progressing towards this second stage.

How does one create this inner peace ? Rudolf Steiner taught that it is attained by undertaking certain spiritual exercises. Six important exercises are presented in the Chapter Two, which assist the meditant to develop this tranquillity. These exercises have ensured that one is prepared for the next stage, namely Contemplation. Such inner work is vitally important, it forms the foundation for this second stage of meditating. For an earnest meditator who has acquired a natural inner peace within, it becomes possible to enter into this peace-filled space, and yet still retain a sense of self-hood (though this has modified a little). The main requirement of this activity is that the actual content of the meditative text is to be dismissed from the mind, and one is to remain intensely but peacefully alert.

The attention is simply to be focussed on that subtle spiritual presence which resonates as an after-effect of meditating; not on any images or thoughts, etc. The soul has been brought near to certain spiritual realities through the meditating. It now empties itself of these, to allow another, a higher faculty of consciousness to stir into life; this is **cosmic-spiritual** consciousness. This state of inner stillness, focussed on no definable specific content, is called **Contemplation** by Steiner. This is the technique needed to reach awareness, that is conscious functioning, in the actual spiritual world (or Devachan). When the meditant brings about this condition, after many months or years of effort, then out of the silence, the cosmos will begin to "speak'. That is, one begins to have intimations of the spiritual world, resounding within one, as if the cosmos is whispering intimately to our receptive, stilled mind.

This is in effect a condition in which the meditant begins to experience the reality of having consciousness entirely free of the body, that is, a form of 'thinking' which lives in the human spirit, and is attuned to spiritual truth, not just astral imagery. However, before this major attainment fully occurs, the meditant will have to be able to also suppress that is, remove from consciousness the panoramic astral imagery.[13] A major element of such astral visions is what Steiner calls a tableau of images in which one's life (up to that time) is seen. So this stage of **cosmic-spiritual** consciousness, once it is strongly developed, is indeed an advanced state of consciousness.

The results achieved through Contemplation are a major goal of meditating, since the eternal higher-self exists in this realm, and gradually merging into this being bestows the continuity of consciousness which is so central to higher spiritual attainment. However, at first the meditant does not experience the resonance of the actual true spiritual realms directly in the soul, but in his or her ether-body (or life-force organism). The soul becomes aware of this resonance in his or her life-forces. This circumstance is not really so strange an idea, for whenever we experience a memory or recall a sense-impression, we are indirectly accessing our ether-body. In 'Contemplation', we access directly in our ether-body the after-effect, echoing on, of approaching the spiritual realms. Only much later does the meditant access **directly** the true higher worlds; at first, "The most important moments for our higher development occur after meditating, when we let absolute calm enter our soul in order to allow the content of our meditation to work upon us... we may have remarkable experiences in our ether-body, in the quiet moments after meditating.."[14]

Eventually, the meditant becomes endowed with **cosmic-spiritual** consciousness in the special sense meant here – that is, **the condition of being conscious of the spiritual realms and of various astral**

---

[13] R. Steiner, Lect. 26.Nov.1921 (trans. as a separate lecture)
[14] R Steiner in personal advice to Martina Limburger, see Ref. 86.

realities interweaving through these. The first aspect of the spiritual which is experienced at the cosmic-spiritual consciousness is one's own existence prior to conception. This is truly the beginning of a momentous transformation of the normal ego; it widens out to encompass the fuller spiritual elements of the human being.

When this awesome moment arrives, in addition to already seeing various images from meditating, we now, in this higher state of meditating experience insights which are very difficult to verbalize. There are also inwardly **audible** spiritual sensations, not just **visual** sensations. Musical tones are heard that directly reveal to oneself secrets of the archetypal spiritual world. It is as if our consciousness becomes suffused through and through with inner music, which in its own way, unveils the nature of spiritual reality. In the words of Rudolf Steiner, "just as the air penetrates into the lungs once they have emptied themselves by exhaling, so the Inspiration(-al experience) penetrates into the soul which has consciously and deliberately emptied itself." It is for this reason that he chose the term, Inspiration for this stage, and you may prefer to use this word.

It is however also often at this time, when the meditant is successful in having the first occurrence of **Contemplation**, that the **full** visual experience of the astral plane also occurs. Instead of just the occasional vision, one sees a panorama of an extraordinary nature of beings and forces; but permeated by a symphonic sea of celestial sounds. They are inner sounds, these musical tones are a kind of speech, they confer on you insight into their own being...

> "...a moment arrives for each meditant who has brought her or his soul to real inner peace. This is the moment when within your inner being resounds, and the great eternal truths are perceived. Then suddenly the world around you is radiant with new colours, and new musical tones resound, tones which you have not heard before. The new splendour shines from the soul world, the new tones come to you from Spiritland."[15]

Naturally, one begins with this process, and lets it develop over the years, and it becomes ever more real. In this state, the mind has awareness of both the astral realms and the real spiritual realms. For this stage to be **fully** developed, the meditant must have developed to a very high state. For then one has crossed over the threshold between the physical world and the actual spiritual realms in such a way that the link between those realms and your normal in-the-body-state is always maintained.

---

[15] R. Steiner   G/A number 53   p. 197 15/Dec/'04 (untranslated)

This is only granted to those who have substantially developed their spirituality.... "When the meditant is in the condition of living the reality of love, so that love is at all times a divine service to Deity, then the spiritual world begins to speak"[16] This indication refers in fact to the throat chakra, and the moral condition necessary for its development (see Chapter Six). Furthermore, this faculty of having consciousness in the genuine spiritual realms that is, having **cosmic-spiritual** consciousness, is only fully attained when the life-force organism (or 'ether-body') is transformed; it needs to develop certain new dynamics and energy currents. In Steiner's essential handbook for spiritual development, 'Knowledge of Higher Worlds, How is it attained'?, the exercises to develop the special structures and currents of energy in the ether-body are given; they are to be undertaken in conjunction with the Six Parallel Exercises which are explained in Chapter Two.

How then does one actually begin to at least develop higher awareness of the spiritual world, as distinct from astral plane visions? By simply entering the silence after deeply meditating on the text chosen, and holding this soul-state for as long as one can; perhaps two minutes in the beginning stage. In addition, the various preliminary exercises given in Chapters Two and Three provide a basis for acquiring this faculty. The following soul exercise is also an important factor in helping the meditant reach the stage of **cosmic-spiritual** consciousness; that is, raising consciousness up to attunement with the divine spiritual realms.[17] One strives to become so filled with **reverence for truth** that a deep love of it arises in the soul; it becomes so strong that untruth in any form actually causes pain.

Hence the normal attitude of having a personal opinion and putting it forward as if it were the truth of the matter, rather than one's personal preference, stops. It becomes ethically unacceptable to continue this way of being. A kind of methodology for attaining an accurate perspective on a theme starts to be developed; this is the signature of a person who has achieved this stage (or is on the way to it). A life attuned to a sincere process of self-initiation results in the ability to sense when one's knowledge and way of researching a subject are sufficient to yield truth. One becomes aware that a disciplined approach to researching topics, especially deeper spiritual themes, has to be consciously created.

Formulating an opinion with only partial awareness of the fact that one has not actually undertaken the necessary research with the necessary clarity and care, ceases to be an acceptable way of being. **The student,**

---

[16] G/A 53, p. 203, Lect. 15.12.1904 (untranslated)
[17] see: "The Stages of Higher Knowledge" by Rudolf Steiner, pub. R Steiner Press London.

in contrast to the advanced esotericist, simply is usually not aware that she or he does not really have a clear grasp of deeper topics. For it takes time to develop such a devotion to the truth that one's current position concerning a topic can be clearly perceived as being inadequate to yield accurate truths.

Secondly, one needs to become **more 'sparing' with pointless emotions**; such as, anxiety, jealousy, irritation, resentment, etc. One strives to simply live from a perspective in which these are too inferior to find any real place in one's emotive life. As a result of striving for this inner tranquillity, considerable 'soul-force' is being gradually created; a source of inner strength arises when the soul does not exhaust itself in giving in to such feelings. And the equanimity that this creates provides further inner stability for the seeker who intends to set sail into the ultimate voyage of discovery. The stored up soul-energies are important, for it is this which gives to the soul a certain power, which enables the spiritual realms to be accessed. Restraint with the sexual function is also advantageous for this higher stage of being; and this will naturally begin to occur.

Another excellent way to develop the kind of sensitive, living contemplative mood that allows access to the actual spiritual realms, is to make it a way of life to contemplate nature, especially **to follow the seasonal cycle.** Train yourself to become sensitive to the inner reality in nature, especially to the rhythmical seasonal cycle of the year, in which a transforming, metamorphosing process is constantly occurring. Rudolf Steiner laboured strenuously to give to his listeners and readers some knowledge of the spiritual beings and energies that become activated in each season; he taught that the soul exercise of attuning oneself to the seasonal cycle was of immense importance in the life of a student on the spiritual path.

My first book; "Living a Spiritual Year", is written precisely for this purpose. It provides a comprehensive esoteric guide to the seasonal activity of these beings and their activity, from the research of Rudolf Steiner.[18] In addition, Steiner's "Soul Calendar" is an excellent text to develop this awareness, although its verses are quite enigmatic. This exercise involves learning just what kind of beings and forces emerge out of a static state, entering an active mode in your hemisphere at solstice and equinox, each season. Then one starts to try to develop a sensitivity to these spiritual realities.

---

[18] see "Living a Spiritual Year; seasonal festivals in northern & southern hemispheres"; by this author.

You can start to learn where in the zodiac the full moon is situated each month, and become sensitive to the subtle differences between the various zodiac qualities of the full moon, over the course of a year. In addition one can walk slowly through nature, or take a seat and gaze over the landscape, all the while striving to sense the archangel and the other beings active in that season. For example, in the autumn, of that hemisphere in which you are living, the archangel Michael, most revered of these great beings down through the millennia, is actively present. One can strive to sense his presence then.

Once you can begin to sense the enhanced solar ethers present in the mid-summer fire-flies, or the 'incarnating' of tree and bush sylphs into the blossoming of spring time flowers, then real progress is under-way. The exercise involved here, is in effect, a striving to sense the ever-changing rhythms of underlying creation, and which derive from the high spiritual powers (ultimately, the cosmic Christ and Logos). To do this is to work towards a form of inner hearing, it is learning to have empathy with these spiritual forces. It has to do with sensitising the emotions and the life-energies, so that they can become attuned to the cosmic rhythms and forces that maintain creation.

Whereas, in contrast, for the development of **psychic-image** consciousness, or attaining to astral awareness, the study of and meditating about spiritual truths provides the inner forces which lead to success. This is further explained in Chapter Three. Spiritual study could be called "practising beholding the spirit" (in the mind's eye) to eventually see astral imagery. But this seeing of images is to be understood in a mature sense; namely seeing in symbolic images the cosmic thoughts of the gods from whom creation is sustained. By contrast, this contemplative exercise of attuning oneself to the living energies ebbing and flowing in the flow of time, could be called "practising contemplating the spiritual nexus of existence" in order to become inwardly attuned to the spiritual realms.

The third stage: **high-initiation consciousness**
As noted at the beginning of this chapter, there is a third stage of higher consciousness. This stage concerns that sublime goal so well known in the religious life across the globe, of being 'at one with God'. Steiner explains that this term 'God' can be a term that is used too abstractly, since historically it covers a multitude of spiritual beings. The term 'God' may refer to an uncaused primal creator, but this leaves the problem (that soon becomes abstract or emotive) of Natural Theology, i.e., is this being inside or outside Its creation ? Others have used this term to refer to their tribal deity, others to beings that specifically guide this planet's evolutionary needs, and others even use it, unconsciously in a context where really their own guiding angel is meant.

Steiner explains that awareness of God is brought to us by the ranks of divine spiritual beings, and thus in gaining the exalted stage of **high-initiation** consciousness, one experiences the inner being as an intimate expression of the divine hierarchical beings. This third faculty is developed and described only with difficulty, and I am dependent upon the descriptions given by Rudolf Steiner with regard to this state of consciousness.[19] In this third stage one actually merges consciously into the inner being of the being that one is observing. It brings about a kind of spiritual union or intimate at-one-ment with the object of interest.

At the **psychic-image** consciousness stage, psychic images arise; with **cosmic-spiritual** consciousness, the nature of the spirit being (angel, 'deceased' person, nature-spirit, etc) we are perceiving begins to 'speak' to our inner ear, even if we do not see a corresponding spiritual form. But with this third faculty, one **enters** into the other being. One looks into the very core of what one observes, becoming one with it. And then, from within it the meditant gazes outwards into the world, almost as if one has become that being. It is through this deepest perceiving that the highest level of wisdom is attained; however the initiate does not become one with the being in the sense of losing one's own integrity or independence. To understand this spiritual stage of consciousness, which is the highest state possible, one could say it is a merging into a oneness or a unity of consciousness with whatever being we are observing.

Such a lofty stage takes effort, for as Steiner points out, in normal life we have but one such spiritual union experience, namely our own ego; we perceive it from within, that is, we intuit our own self. We are at one with it; impossible though it may sound, the initiate can become one with the inmost self of other beings. **The human self must become so powerfully developed that it can surrender itself and become one with another ego, without dissolving away and losing its own reality.** This stage should not be confused with an elementary stage of apparent unity with another being, such as that caused by a merging of the ether-bodies (life-energies); or caused by a merging of the emotions and intellectual processes.

For with this spiritual union state, the actual evolutionary history of an observed being itself, perhaps an angel, occurring throughout remote cosmic ages, becomes known to the high initiate. In terms of comprehension of the cosmos, **high initiation** consciousness enables

---

[19] He calls this faculty Intuition, the Latin root words of which ('in tueri') mean: 'to look into' His use of these terms in the German language in which these three Latin words are scarcely used was quite practical, but in English it causes confusion.

the person to have a connection with the spiritual reality beyond our solar system, therefore to that which underlies the galaxy itself.[20]

Another way Steiner explains this stage is to say that the will-forces become fully conscious; this is an extraordinary achievement because most of the will is deeply subconscious. Within this subconscious sector there is a part of our will that is at one with the will-force present in all other people. Hence to become conscious of this is to become inwardly united with the rest of creation; and gradually with its creator. Steiner taught that when the will does become fully empowered and 'realized' in us, then selfless, unconditional love becomes a reality in the soul. It becomes a force empowering the intellect, and an organ of direct perception into high spiritual realms. **High-initiation** consciousness has then been attained by the meditant.

Exercises for high-initiation consciousness
How does one develop to this final stage of meditative experience?
As Rudolf Steiner reveals in his book, Knowledge of Higher Worlds, how is it Attained? attainment of this spiritual oneness consciousness develops when the meditant can meditate on the apparent void that is present when even the subtle after-echo which you focus on in Contemplation is actively dismissed. If we can still have an inner focus when even this content has been dismissed, and then within this void find ourself seemingly within a nothingness, then we are on the way to finding our true self, as an aspect of God. The meditant becomes successful, when in still retaining consciousness at this deep level, the ego-sense is now experienced as somehow different to one's normal sense of ego-hood. Now it appears as part of the higher-self, which in turn is experienced as a part of the divine-spiritual beings who maintain the cosmos.

You experience your ego as also having a divine aspect, which strives to inspire your normal everyday ego. It is as if one's ego is two-fold; an earthly personal mind, and a higher spiritual reality. However, to really achieve this also involves crossing over the threshold between this world and the spiritual world; this subject is explored in detail in chapter five. Then deep insights into the relationship of the higher-self to the hierarchies begin. Should one not be successful in attempting this high stage of consciousness, then one normally simply falls asleep or ceases to concentrate any longer on this subtle focus. On this point, it is important to note that to fall asleep in the first stage of meditating is in contrast, very bad; it is harmful to the meditant, see the beginning of Chapter Eight for more about this. Help with this very high stage of meditating is available from the many lectures on precisely this inter-

---

[20] R. Steiner "Theosophy of the Rosicrucian" lect. 8 & "Universe, Earth and Humanity" lect 8

connection of the human self with the hierarchies as an expression of God. (But one needs to start with the introductory literature.)

The following two short paragraphs are examples of the kind of experiences and specific knowledge of the divine worlds which this highest state of consciousness make possible.

The divine spiritual realms:
"The Universal life-force, which in physical life is bound up with the forms of human, animal and plant kingdoms, and is limited to the bodily forms thereof, is to be experienced in the second realm of the archetypal spiritual realms. There it flows freely like the waters of the sea, like a living ocean of life-essence, it has a delicate reddish-lilac colour and permeates all living beings equally. It constitutes the living fountain for all the multitude of forms which are to arise on Earth in the kingdoms of nature. In the fourth realm of these sublime realms, the {meditant who has become} a seer may observe the archetypes of the thoughts {not just the astral form} produced by the human mind.

Each time you grasp a thought, you bring about a change in the spiritual realms. First, the thought rays out, like a wave of light from a light-fountain. Then one can see how noble thoughts living amongst people are received by certain things in the spiritual realm where they form themselves into the shape of certain flowers, flowers not found here on the Earth. These flower-like thought-beings have the most beautiful geometric forms, they then move towards the person about whom the thinker was thinking. The advanced student of the spirit learns to work with this dynamic and strives to produce only thoughts which bring forth beneficial consequences in the divine realms."[21]

Life after death
"After death, and after the journey through the soul worlds, the human spirit, incorporating within itself the highest qualities of its soul-nature, at last enters the fifth realm of the Kingdom of the Heavens, or the spiritual world, and there it unfolds its wings so to speak, and arises in blissful freedom into the sublime heights. Radiant with a light not describable in earthly words, the purified human spirit sheds the last limitations, and moves in complete freedom onwards. It experiences its inner qualities becoming empowered, enabling it to prepare a new life on earth with the greatest potential for further self development. Here too one experiences that sublime beings exist within the streams of light,

---

[21] From unpublished archive material, notes taken during a lecture given in 1904.

and one experiences how these beings speak to one from within the light, and how the world had its origin through this cosmic dialogue, the cosmic word. " [22]

Obviously these experiences are for the advanced meditant. One way to work towards developing this faculty is to put considerable effort into a spiritual exercise taught by Steiner, known as the Evening Review, in which in the evening, the day's events are reviewed objectively, prior to sleep. This soul exercise is described fully in Chapter Two. It is an exercise that involves attunement to our real will, that is, to becoming aware of one's underlying volitional forces. Not only in terms of psychological qualities, but also of the spiritual forces that have created and now maintain the mysterious energy we call will. In addition, Rudolf Steiner taught that one strives towards a way of life that seeks to attune one's own will-impulses with the will of God; **thus the purpose of one's own life becomes ever more in harmony with the purpose of life of all other living beings.**

In effect, the effort is constantly made to intuitively harmonize one's own karma with world karma, and indeed in such a way as to bring karma to an end, in the sense of negative factors that subjugates creation to evil influences. The meditant, when this advanced stage is achieved, has a fully conscious existential insight into the nexus interconnecting all life, and which is formed by the higher gods in archetypal divine realms.

A preliminary beginning of this faculty is for example, the realization that one's own human consciousness state is interlinked in that archetypal realm with the existence of plants and animals on the Earth. Further, one realizes that God (or the divine-spiritual hierarchies that serve this uncaused being) is experiencing our own innermost being, and guiding our own karma and that of the Earth, through the interaction created by the co-existence of the plant and animal kingdoms. This insight then not only flows into the emotions, bringing a compassionate attitude, it also can be realized by our intelligence as a coherent philosophy of life, with many profound implications. Since **high-initiation** consciousness is achieved by accessing the deepest level of the will-life, as one gradually moves towards this goal, it naturally affects our volitional impulses, causing the meditant to formulate appropriate life values and goals.

Another indication from Rudolf Steiner of how to develop towards this high state of **high-initiation** consciousness involves understanding more deeply one's experience of life, its events and challenges. It is a question of viewing life's events in an especially insightful manner.

---

[22] From the same lecture of 1904.

Through normal psychological insight we are aware that a repeated illness or repeated relationship problem may be an indicator of a deep seated unfree dynamic in the soul. However, for the development of **high-initiation** consciousness, the meditant strives to sense how the soul itself undergoes a developmental process, that actually involves more than one life, through these life experiences. So, one begins to comprehend that **these life situations are linked to influences from the spiritual world**.

That is, via the spirit working through specific outer circumstances. An elementary example of this would be when a friend says something, quite unprompted, and startled, one realizes just how relevant their words are to one's own inner struggles with spiritual goals. A psychic would perceive that in just those moments the guiding angel is active, prompting the friend to 'deliver a message' to you. With the faculty of **high-initiation** consciousness the meditant would experience the complex web of karma (or destiny-forces) deriving from the past life which has enabled that moment of help to occur, and the implications of responding or ignoring this.

Steiner also refers, in this connection to "the drama of knowledge", by which he means the entire remarkable process of a human's being incarnating and learning through life experiences, becoming sensed on a deep level 'within' and one begins to see its connection to the 'without'. Normally one only comprehends this after death, during the journey through the spiritual realms. One's unfolding life, through which "the drama of knowledge" occurs, becomes experienced as a decree of destiny (karma) aimed at developing the inner-life of the soul.[23]

In other words, the subtle soul-drama whereby an understanding of life develops in us, through living on Earth, is now to be encountered on a deeper level. The advanced meditant is now gaining the ability, at least in a preliminary sense, to experience the unfolding destiny of a human being as an expression of the will that the creator and the hierarchical beings have poured forth into creation.

The soul's own internal development is seen as connected with a spiritual reality that manifests via the physical environment. Insights can occur which reveal, for example, that an aspect of oneself – of our will forces actually – is present within other people, and especially people with whom we have a karmic connection. The beautiful old saying; **'We are one another'**, becomes an increasing potent proverb for the meditant who has growing awareness of the extent of her/his connection with humanity. Steiner taught that persons who fully attain

---

[23] Rudolf Steiner: Lecture 5/Nov/'17 in G/A 73, (untranslated).

to this third stage "are able to give names to all things; such a person has merged with the cosmic-self, he speaks from out of this cosmic-self." [24]

Obviously we are dealing here with a very advanced state of human spirituality, it is important that people actually know about the possibilities inherent in humanity, even if one feels that one can not attain this, in this lifetime. As a help towards understanding **high-initiation** consciousness, it appears to me from the various indications of Rudolf Steiner, that one can make an experiment to sense the connection between the kind of nature environment in which one 'happens' to be living during a time when a particular inner exercise or life-challenge was being experienced. For example when the theme of sacrificial selflessness existentially entered one's life and the need to discern the difference between selflessness and having insufficient will to protect oneself from being dominated, was one then living by the sea-shore, or a crowded terrace housing estate?

When the death of a significant friend or the opportunity for a new career occurred, in what kind of environment were you then living, and at what age did it occur, and what astrological dynamic was at work then ? Was one living amidst rows of old pine trees, and in contact with friends who all had a common connecting link to us? As we walk along the lonely beach, what animals or birds were seen: sea-gulls often wheeling overhead and an occasional shark appear in the waters? If we lived then in the city, what was the main element in the environment of inner-city streets, and did we often encounter a friend who is afflicted by a certain illness, and were there young children, always intent on a specific kind of game?

Could there be a specific connection between these external environments and our inner task and struggle? The external environment could also include the current social themes and issues of the day, or even of the generation. All the elemental powers and differentiated will-forces 'out there' striving to exist, is there not a link to our own will at that important time? The meditant begins to glimpse a connection between that environment, mineral, plant, animal and human, with his or her soul's own inner growth. Awareness of such subtle mysteries as these gradually causes the ability for **high-initiation** consciousness to develop. Whereas normally we may note how a particular opportunity or unpleasant destiny-event was coloured by the local situation we were in, this exercise is much deeper.

In addition to such subtle exercises, this faculty also develops through exploring in other ways the interconnectedness of all life. The following

---

[24] R. Steiner, Lecture, 16/March/1905, in G/A 53, p. 272 (untranslated).

words from Rudolf Steiner provides a profound meditation on this theme:

> "If my mind absorbs a spiritual teaching I do thereby bring myself higher {spiritually}, but not entirely effectively. If however, I also **incorporate** this teaching in (for example) the building of a Gothic cathedral, or let my understanding of this wisdom flow into the soul of other persons, or even just into my contact with other people; then this which I have spread **outside me** {in the will-forces of the living beings around me} becomes a part of my eternal spiritual-being (1906)." [25]

In these profound words a valuable perspective can also be found on that central Christian dilemma of salvation — is it through good deeds or through 'faith'; that is, developing spiritualized consciousness? In the above words, one learns that actively 'doing the good' also develops the higher eternal spiritual-self. A life of meditation, although immensely valuable to the world, does not allow one to fully develop one's potential. There needs to be some expression through the will into the community, even if that will-deed is occurring directly in the spiritual realms, a capacity open only to advanced meditants.

Finally, the more one develops the quality of selflessness and humanitarian interests, but as an expression of a consolidated ego, not by losing the centre of one's being, the greater is the ability to achieve **high-initiation** consciousness..... "Love is the relinquishing of one's own being into the other. This needs to be so strong that one is no longer focussed on one's own ego, as it manifests in the earthly body. Then comes the paradox, that precisely through selflessness, through the ability of this highest aspect of love, that one draws near to one's own true ego, which shines towards us then from the distant future. One has to lose one's {illusory} earthly-ego in order to behold one's true ego..." [26]

Prayer

We have considered the nature of meditation and contemplation, as these terms are understood in esoteric language. What then is the difference between prayer and meditating in the esoteric way? Prayer is another very valid form of interaction of the human being with the divine, and is also, in a different way, part of daily life for the esoteric

---

[25] That is it grows into a part of me: into the essence of my spirit-nature, known as "atma" in esotericism.

[26] Rudolf Steiner: Lecture of 22/April/'23, G/A 84 untranslated: other refs. to Intuition & Inspiration used in this chapter include; and G/A 73 5/Nov/'17 Anthroposophy & psychology (untranslated); G/A 60 lect 15/Dec/'11 (Untranslated) and "An outline of Esoteric Science"; Chapter 5. See the Appendix at the end of Chapter Three about what books of R. Steiner's to read first.

meditant. The practise of meditating is derived from a conscious intention to transform specifically the actual substance of the astral body so that the chakras develop, and hence giving the ability to direct awareness in a controlled manner into spirit-land. But prayer is not derived from such an intention, it has different origins which are not so specifically esoteric, although there are of course many kinds of prayer.

For example, one prays that a loved one may be protected from danger when travelling, or that a friend may recover from a serious illness. (Naturally, some prayers can be subjective and self-centred.) Another kind of prayer is that kind in which one dwells on the attributes of Deity, or of a great saint, and one becomes nearer inwardly, to that sacred person or being. This kind of prayer is similar in some respects to esoteric meditating, as indeed is deep 'wordless prayer'. Hence meditants also pray in this special sense. This more mystical praying is similar to the esoteric meditation, wherein the specific focus is on gaining direct awareness of higher spiritual realty, by forming the chakras in both the soul and life-force body.

Thus, **the cultivation of a prayerful attitude is an essential element of the meditant's life**; after each meditation session this mood needs to be present, to close the session. Rudolf Steiner recommended that prayer, in its aspect of gratitude, becomes a constant element in the meditant's soul-life. For example, when one has the opportunity to delight in the odour and sight of flowers, or beautiful artistic experiences, this mood should naturally arise. This approach to prayer is akin to the words in the Scriptures, "Pray without ceasing" (1 Thessalonians 5:17)

Yoga

The term, 'yoga' as a practise associated with the traditional approach to meditating in the orient has many meanings, and modalities. There are a number of differences in the ancient venerated oriental systems and the path presented here; in particular, the question of the individual's self. I will only briefly indicate that in the path given here, adopting specific body positions (yogic positions,) are not used. For as Steiner explains, yogic positions alter the flow of life-forces through the limbs of the body, in a way calculated to assist the astral body to become freed of the body's effects, and enter into the other worlds. However in the path presented here, **the individual ego** has to find the inner strength to transcend the various obstacles to higher consciousness **whilst within the body**.

For in this path **the individual ego is to be upheld**, not dissolved away; it must become strengthened yet also selfless. So that in the current personality a divine presence from the higher-self can come into being. For the same reason, in this path, a very advanced person may indeed become an adviser to the meditant, but not a 'guru'; that is, not an authority to whom one must give obedience. Another difference of the path offered by Steiner, is that depression, which is often reported amongst students of various other meditation systems, is not normally caused by the meditating advised here. This has to do with the fact that the student's life-forces are not specifically separated from the body, to induce a feeling of ecstasy. Hence they are also not later impelled into the reversal of this, namely a too constricted in-drawing into the body, which causes depression.

It is axiomatic in this pathway, that humanity can acquire the ego-strength needed for spiritual development, ever since the resurrection of Christ, because as Rudolf Steiner explains, this is the event in which the cosmic Christ 'incarnated' into the Earth's aura. That is, each human being can draw on a source of divine light, now permeating the earth, to attain a consolidation of ego-hood, as well as to begin the process of transforming it into a selfless higher ego. The sublime truths learnt by initiates about the incarnating of the cosmic Christ are not the theme of this book, but the scene observed by Rudolf Steiner during his research (into the spiritual history of the planet) is significant for this subject.

He reported that when the Incarnation event occurred, the oval-shaped aura of the Earth, observed from a point in the solar system, took on a radiant form, that will become ever more star-shaped.[27] So the cosmic Christ has become the central spiritual being within all of the beings that together comprise the consciousness of the Earth. This collective consciousness – all nature-spirits, higher divine spirits active with our planet, human souls, etc, is called by Steiner, the "Earth-soul".

Nature mystics who gain attunement to higher elemental beings become aware through them that indeed the Earth-soul has this sublime light-being within it; a being that is connected to and strengthens, the self of individual human beings. Hence in this path, it is taught that you must make your own decisions yourself. Naturally the advice of someone whom you recognize as more experienced than yourself is of value, but their advice and wishes are not binding on you. The kind of meditating presented here also does not require a person to leave their suburban life situation and karma; it can be integrated well into a busy modern life.

---

[27] Steiner refers to the alteration in the planet's aura in most of his lecture cycles on Christology, but only rarely to the star-shape, this is done e.g., in a lecture (untranslated) on 1.April.1918.

Glossary

Rudolf Steiner's terms:	Terms used in this book:
Imagination	**psychic-image** consciousness
Inspiration	**cosmic-spiritual** consciousness
Intuition	**high-initiation** consciousness
Astral body	Soul soul-body astral body
Etheric body	ether body ethereal body life-force organism

The term "thinking" can be used by Steiner to refer to four kinds of intelligent consciousness processes.
1 Logical thought
2 Holistic ideas, which may have a psychic element to them (this occurs as psychic-image consciousness is being reached)
3 The flashes of wisdom that happen when cosmic-spiritual consciousness is being reached
4 The inexpressibly profound consciousness dynamics of **high-initiation** consciousness, which is the highest level possible.

Appendix 1

Esoteric Christianity – a brief explanation of this concept

The sun as the central organism in the solar system is the manifestation of the highest creative divine beings, hence the most revered mysteries in antiquity were those of the sun. There is a spiritual aspect to the sun, it is an immense centre of sublime spiritual forces emanating from the divine-spiritual hierarchical beings who manifest into the physical world via the sun. (These were called in ancient times, the 'sun gods'.) This understanding that there is indeed a spiritual (and astral) level to creation, hence to the planets and the sun, was widely held in the Hermetic-Grecian Mysteries.[28]

The initiate of the Sun-Mysteries would ascend into the spiritual heights to seek union with the same divine being who is called here, 'the cosmic Christ', for, until the events on Golgotha hill in Palestine (the crucifixion and resurrection of Christ) occurred, this being had not yet united within the Earth's soul. Rudolf Steiner taught that initiation (within non-decadent streams) has for millennia involved seeking attunement with the sublime divinity now known as "Christ", (as distinct from the man, Jesus). So even in past ages when the descent of that deity from the sun-sphere into the Earth through over-shadowing Jesus had not yet occurred, the acolyte was brought into a nearness to the 'cosmic Christ'.

The ancient initiates knew of this being, who was revered as the source of the human spirit itself, although naturally in ancient times different names were used in different civilisations for this same being. The sun initiation occupied a central place in the ancient Egyptian culture, Osiris and Horus are deities who represented aspects of the cosmic Christ, the sun-god. An especially deep truth is indicated when the cosmic Christ, and therefore our higher-self, is referred to as linked with the sun. Secondary spiritual influences derive from planetary spiritual streams; hence the Moon Mysteries, the Venus Mysteries, etc were less elevated than those of the Sun Mysteries. Although various stars, such as Sirius and the Pleiades, provide influences that are also fundamental to the spiritual dynamics of the Earth, these are a theme only in more confidential, higher esoteric strivings. The quest for the spiritual in the cosmos should begin by focussing on the moon and the sun, and the planets in our own solar system.

---

[28] The emperor of the Christian-Roman world in the fourth century, Julian the Apostate, attempted to explain this mystery in a treatise dedicated to the spiritual Sun; he made it clear that his esoteric insights were the result of being initiated in the Mithraic cult.

The mystery of the origin of the higher-self or the human spirit, was profoundly researched and taught in ancient Egypt. It was in that country that the seventh degree of initiation, which leads to inner union with the Father-God, was made possible.(1910) The initiation processes were carried out in the awesome underground temple complex beneath the sphinx and the great pyramid. Meditants from many lands journeyed there to further their initiation. Steiner concludes, from his research, that a number of saints or prophets of both Old and New Testament times were involved, such as Joseph, Moses and St. Mark.

Because the 'pre-Golgotha Christ Sun-Mysteries' were so powerfully active there, the ancient Egyptian spirituality has an extraordinary attraction for many people in today's time-cycle. Moreover because that civilisation was for many souls the last incarnation in a culture which had the initiatory Mysteries as a prominent part of its life, the old Egyptian spirituality has a special attraction. The ancient Egyptian initiate pharaohs revered this cosmic Christ who manifests through the Sun whom they called Osiris, and Zarathustra the ancient Persian sage too, spoke of this being, of its immense aura which he called Ahura Mazdao. So the cosmic Christ is a central cosmic deity, the highest divinity of the solar system.

In short, the most sublime of the lofty spiritual beings of the sun-sphere, that is the hierarchical beings who manifest indirectly in the physical plane through the sun's life-forces. For perhaps 300 years after the events in Palestine such truths were known, but it was then eradicated by church authorities who no longer understood these esoteric truths. One of the few references to this long suppressed truth which escaped the fires and censors is that of the great saint Origenes, who taught that "Christ is the highest and foremost of the 'powers'."[29] The term 'powers' was the established name for the beings who manifest in the sun sphere; there are other beings in the other planetary spheres. So the cosmic Christ means firstly a deity, not a human being, and a deity which is the highest of those spiritual beings who are associated with the Sun-sphere, in traditional wisdom.

There is only one real difference between the wisdom from which this book derives and that of the various other more ancient spiritual traditions that revere the same being. Namely that it is understood that the cosmic Christ descended to this planet by over-shadowing Jesus the Nazoraean, in Palestine, and became united to the Earth-soul.

I refer to Jesus as the Nazoraean, not Nazarene, because significantly, this is His description of Himself, especially in the gospel of St. John,

---

[29] In his commentary on the Gospel of St. John; Book 1 (end); see Commentaire sur S. Jean, Sources Chretiennes, Paris, 1996.

although this term is unjustly altered in most translations of the New Testament, because of uncertainty about this term. The term derives from 'Nazarite'. This word, and hence Nazoraean, refers to an esoteric stream within the ancient Hebrew religious life, that is, people who strove towards initiation. The term 'the Nazarene' is also used, but in several instances it is incorrect to the Greek not to have the term 'the Nazoraean'.

As we noted earlier, the spiritual stream from which this book derives, reveres a three-fold primal God, that has created and now sustains creation (both physical and spiritual realms). It also acknowledges the sanctity of the ranks of divine-spiritual beings through whom the intentions of the primal trinity are manifested. The three-fold primal Deity consists of the First Cause, the unknowable foundation of all creation, (called the Father-God in Christianity). Then as the second member of the trinity, a being who makes manifest the un-manifest hidden intentions of God. This being is known as the Logos in ancient Grecian initiation wisdom.

It is this being that is central to esoteric Christian wisdom, such as the Holy Grail movement, and the medieval Rosicrucians, in these streams this being is known as the "cosmic Christ". It is important not to confuse this name with any form of exoteric Christianity that has been involved in repressive actions, political machinations, repression of women, antagonism to other religions, etc. The being designated as the cosmic Christ was equally revered by noble religious-esoteric movements throughout history. It has been known by other names in various spiritual streams, and is not really known in its full nature in exoteric Christianity. The ancient Egyptian mystery wisdom of Aton, the Zarathustrian teachings of Ahura Mazdao, the inspiring spiritual wisdom of some major Buddhist-Hindu avatars, and the central deity of the religion of Mithra is regarded as a worship of this same being, or aspects of it.

The third being in this primal trinity is the being traditionally called the Holy Spirit, which is associated with the goddess Sophia. It is the task of this goddess, who is a vessel of the "Holy Spirit" to assist humanity in the striving towards self-initiation.

However, as indicated above, there are also a vast number of divine-spiritual beings who carry out the intentions of this trinity. In the Bible (Romans 8:38) these beings are known as 'the hierarchies'. There are some nine different ranks of them, from angels to seraphim, in the works of Dionysus the Areopagite. It is these beings which have been experienced by advanced meditants since time immemorial, and whom were called 'gods' by most cultures. We shall briefly note the relationship of the Christ to the Earth, and return again to further clarify the three primal beings underlying the vast numbers of divine beings.

Nature and mystical Christianity
A brief note now follows about the perspective underlying the approach in this book to nature or spiritual ecology, and to Christianity, indicating a pathway to resolving the perceived conflict between a nature-based spirituality and Christian spirituality. The following text is from a lecture by Rudolf Steiner, given late in his life, (1924) on historical karmic relationships;

> As late as the eighth century of our era, through the ongoing influence of pre-Christian initiation experience, an esoteric Christianity was taught in centres which had remained {in Europe} as ancient high places of knowledge, as relics of the pre-Christian Mysteries. In such places people were taught through a non-intellectual method of education about the physical-bodily and spiritual realities. They were in fact prepared for the moment when they might have at least a delicate glimpse of the spirituality that can manifest itself in our environment here on Earth. Their gaze was directed to the minerals and crystals, to the plant kingdom and to the animal and human reality.
>
> Then they saw, welling forth like an auric field, the spiritual-elemental beings which live in all nature, and which are themselves nurtured by forces from the cosmos. Above all, there appeared to these students of the spiritual, the goddess 'Natura', they could speak and commune with her as one would to another human being, except that she was a higher kind of being. They saw her in her full radiance before their soul. Such people did not speak of the abstract 'laws of nature', rather they discussed the creative power of Natura, working creatively everywhere in nature.
>
> She was herself a metamorphosis of Proserpina, who was known to people in antiquity. She was that creative goddess with whom in a certain sense every person united who sought for spiritual knowledge. She appeared to the seeker as existing within every mineral, in every plant, in every animal; from the clouds, the mountains, the river-springs. Of this goddess who alternately in winter and summer is active creatively above the earth and below, they felt; she is the helper of that God of whom the Gospels tell. She is the divine power who actually implements it all.

> The students experienced their connection to the four elements...the teachers saw to it that their students attained an intuitive feeling for the interconnectedness of the human being with the living, weaving forces of the elements; they attained a feeling for nature as en-filled with a divine being-ness, with the substantiality of God. Once they had attained to this stage, they were introduced to the planetary system, they learnt how, with knowledge of the solar system, knowledge of the human soul arises...and then they learnt of the stars, and of how knowledge of the inner nature of the human self, the ego arises from this...[30]

In short, as the above quotation indicates, **Steiner was able through initiatory wisdom and perception, to unite the spheres of Christian mysticism with the old 'pagan', nature-based spirituality**. As the initiatory stream underlying the pathway described here is an esoteric Christian one, there will be references to 'Christ'. But as noted earlier, it is understood here that Jesus is a person, who became the vessel for a spiritual being, called 'The Christ'. This latter is the most evolved of the divine-spiritual beings that have brought our solar system into manifestation through the sun. Hence these spiritual beings are also known as sun-spirits. Because of this cosmic aspect, the term, 'the Christ', is understood to refer to the 'cosmic Christ'.

Furthermore, Steiner taught that within this highest of the sun-gods was a ray of the much higher being, 'the Logos', or 'the Son'. That is, the second person of the primal triune Godhead. Now the second Logos is regarded by Rudolf Steiner as the same being as that primal cosmic deity of the Vedanta wisdom, Brahma. So there is no narrow, credal Christianity here. The initiation wisdom underlying this book understands the second Logos to be the regent of the cosmos, that is, that part of it which we experience – the Earth, the planets, the sun, and its zodiac system. In ancient Greece, some 500 years before the Christian era began, there are references to this being. About 500 BC a Grecian initiate, Heraclitus, wrote of "The Logos who is the divine soul of the cosmos, and although this Logos has existed since the beginning of the cosmos, yet humanity is unaware of it."

Rudolf Steiner called this being the "Welten-Seele" that is, "the Cosmos-Soul" (or the 'Soul of the Cosmos'), a name which reflects the fact that this being is so centrally active in creation, and that it is the macrocosmic archetype of our own soul and spiritual dynamics. The actual origin of the human spirit is from the primal Father-God, the first of the primal trinity, or in Rudolf Steiner's terms, the Cosmos-Spirit (or 'the Spirit of the Cosmos'). The second Logos, the supernal

---

[30] R.Steiner Lect. 13/7/'24 : in Karmic Relationships, Vol 3.

intelligence manifesting as the Cosmos-Soul, invoked our cosmos (our solar/zodiac system) into being, as a vast system of archetypal ideas. In doing this, it was expressing the will of the uncaused, primal Father God.

This second Logos radiates some of its light into the cosmic Christ. So the term, the cosmic Christ used here, refers to a transcendent divinity, from the sun-sphere, in whom is also present a ray from the sublime second Logos. It is important to understand this, because at the crucifixion and resurrection, the Logos (Cosmos-Soul) and the cosmic Christ united with the soul of the Earth. **This immensely significant event took place in Palestine, where the Earth's aura actually has its heart-chakra.** The third aspect of the primal trinity, the Holy Spirit, is here regarded as closely associated with the Sophia, which is a Mystery name for the Spiritual-Self, which arises as the Holy Spirit effects a real spiritualization in the human being.

CHAPTER TWO

But I can't do it! Learning how to focus the mind.

"From the power which holds all beings in its grip, that person frees themself, whom self-mastery does attain." Johann W. von Goethe in the epic poem, Die Geheimnisse ('the Secrets', or 'the Mysteries').[31]

Everyone who tries to meditate discovers that after a while, one's thoughts start to wander, so one finds oneself thinking about an entirely different subject, usually a major task or worry of the day. This is however only the most obvious aspect of a problem that can prevent the beginner from achieving success in meditation. The full extent of the problem involves the connection of the ego to the soul and its dynamics. Just what is the connection of your self to the soul's emotions, thoughts and volition? We will explore this question in the course of this chapter.

What is required is that the ego or self must be master of the three elements of the mind; emotions, thinking and volition, because successful meditation demands that the self is in charge of the mind. Consider now thinking; as we have noted, it is common knowledge that when the meditant seeks to focus on a more demanding matter, thoughts can start arising about a dominant concern and then associated thought pictures start to chase each other around.

The first exercise: controlling thoughts
These simply run on and on in circles if the ego does not step in and give direction. The relation of our self to our thinking capacity is rather like that of a star-gazer looking through a telescope on a motorized stand, which is however, malfunctioning. The instrument gyrates giddily all over the place, bringing a bewildering array of stars and objects to the eye of the viewer. The problem is that whereas you can give direction to thinking quite easily if you start to think about a daily matter, it is very difficult to be in charge like this, if you try to focus on a meditation. So actually we don't have the ability to master those whirling thoughts except by immersing our attention in a mundane subject; which is really only a way out of the difficulty, not a real solution. Consider the example of a person and a dog; real mastery is when the dog ceases to chase a cat and stands still at your command, rather than gives up chasing the cat and chases a ball that you throw to divert it.

---

[31] This highly esoteric poem is also translated under the title, 'The Mysteries'.

What advice did the initiate Steiner give to his students in this matter? There are six exercises and they take six months to complete, they concern control of the thinking, will and feelings, and also the development of a positive attitude and open-mindedness. In the first exercise, one is to take a simple object, say a pencil, and place it before oneself, then one resolves to think about this object and nothing else. This is done at a time of day when one is most mentally alert, it does not have to be at the same time each day. For just five minutes each day for the next month one vows to carry out this seemingly simple exercise. That is, one consciously formulates thoughts about it; especially what one's senses reveal about it.

What colours does it have, what are its (approx.) dimensions, what shape is it, if one were to try to bend it would it flex? If one were to touch it what kind of surfaces does it have? Then one briefly considers its purpose – here caution is needed! One must not start to think about actual letters that are to be written etc, simply note that it is to mark a writing surface; otherwise one's thoughts can go off on a wild tangent. Perhaps lastly one thinks of what **idea** is 'behind' such a simple object.

Perhaps it is derived from the wish to put burnt carbon sticks in a more useable form, that is, with a sheath around. Or does it derive from the idea that the old ink and quill writing method was too clumsy and so the ink was solidified into a carbon, and the quill instead of being dipped in to a dye substance was wrapped around it. So the applicator and dye substance were united as one. Again, it is important at this point not get into thoughts about a carriage travelling through medieval Europe and a writer at a Renaissance court, etc. Just simple thoughts are needed, which you can think without having to study the subject at university first.

This should take about five minutes, however the time should be estimated, not precisely set by having a watch next to you. Now, after a few tries it may be possible to do this, but then after a further while the entire exercise, having lost its novelty, becomes boring. At this point you need to summon up more will power to keep on doing it, reminding yourself of the goal towards which you are striving. Should after some weeks this become just too boring then of course another simple object can be chosen. These must not be manufactured objects with many moving parts and complexity; like a TV set, a camera, etc. So a hair-pin, a stick or piece of paper, a match, a tea cup, a rubber band etc are all fine. Further, if you are starting to do the task of producing the thoughts as if half-asleep, by habit, then that is not of any use. The thinking must be actively and freshly produced by you. So resisting a certain amount of boredom is a good way to 'flex your (ego's) muscles'!

Once you have gained some success with this first exercise of **controlling thoughts**, you will have an enhanced degree of inner stability and self-confidence. This wonderful new sense of empowerment is the result of the ego becoming ever more master of the thinking process; which is how the human being should be. Lack of this mastery is a cause subconsciously of nervousness and a certain subtle dissatisfaction with oneself. Practically, if you find that the object is becoming too boring, or the thoughts are being produced in an habitual manner, or in a mentally numbed state, then you can either attempt to be more active in the process, or change to a different object. Over a six month period, I would suggest that no more than a few objects should be needed.

The second exercise: control of the will
Now after about a month, **assuming you have gained some success with the above exercise,** then you keep on doing the exercise, and you add a second exercise in this second month. **The second exercise is designed to enable the meditant to gain mastery of the will.** One is then no longer to be driven by outer circumstances, but can determine one's own fate oneself. It can be difficult to meditate because the will to do this often seems to slacken off. This is a sign of a most important inner reality; if the motivation to meditate is there, then it has to actually come from your will - without any compelling influences. The motivation for this intention does not derive from instinctive will impulses, like self-preservation; nor from intense desires or thought-out ambitions.

Have you ever really summoned up your own will like this before - to do something which does not relate to personal needs, wishes, obligations or enjoyable moments ? The will for this would have to be **free**; that is, not impelled into action by what normally causes us to act. Behind every deed there is will of course, but how much of this will activity is really "free"; that is, how much of it was your will? If one really works hard to get enough money to purchase a prized object, is this will, pure and simple? No, for mixed in this is strong desire, which stirs the will on. Much activity is done because a desire compels us, or sheer necessity and pragmatic laws of life impel us. Will power is active when potent self-centred desires are lacking as a motivation, yet still one carries out the activity. Since the motivation for meditation is so closely linked with the urge towards spiritual development, it often lacks empowerment from the normal ego-centred urges.

When does one undertake an act of will without being 'forced' by any such consideration? When the motivation is from the influence of the higher-self within the normal ego. That is when personal desires, thoughts and intentions are not entirely the motivating factor. So in meditating one is dependent upon a will-force that is not normally invoked in life. Because the intention behind meditating, especially when one perseveres earnestly with it, is free of personal egotism and is influenced from the higher-self. The ego has to be able to manifest a power of will that is normally only possible if there is some more earthly motivating factor. The purpose of this second exercise is to develop the ability to access your will in a free sense.

As Steiner explains in his invaluable study of consciousness processes in his 'The Philosophy of Freedom', real inner freedom is actually possible, and it manifests in the volitional forces, the will. The exercise to develop this consists of this: one resolves each day to undertake a simple action for no other motivation than to begin to learn to empower one's will. There must also be a time gap involved; so in the morning you resolve that later on, say 11 am, you are going to do a simple deed. Perhaps pick up the clock on the mantelpiece and turn it around three times. However, note you must think up your own deed, you can not use the one I have just given. There should be some hours between the resolution and the time for doing the simple act of will.

The reason for the time delay is connected to a key element in anthroposophical psychology, namely that there is a deep link between the ego, the will and memory. For example, suppose you came home one night with $10,000 cash in one hand and your car-keys in the other. Next morning, you will surely know where you put that money, but perhaps not so sure where your car-keys are! The reason is that your ego was fully involved in the will process of placing the money in a safe place, but it left the deed of putting down the keys to habit, to your habitual being-ness. So, as the ego was not really present in the act of placing the keys somewhere, it can not remember its action. Because it did not really do the action, it did not summon up the will for the task.

Hence you may find that upon doing this exercise, you simply forget to carry it out; because it requires an alert will to remember such a planned action. Then perhaps in mid afternoon you suddenly remember that you were meant to turn that clock around three times. This 'forgetting' may go on for weeks; this is itself a sign that the ego can not yet access its own will forces to the extent that is necessary to carry out even this small resolve. The only way to overcome this is to keep on trying! However, once you remember your resolve, even if some hours late, just go ahead and carry out the deed anyway. Gradually, as the weeks go by you will actually start to remember to carry out the will-deed in good time.

That is an exhilarating moment! One discovers that shortly before the time when you resolved to act, a mental bell rings inside the soul, reminding you of your decision. Once you have this happening, you will feel inwardly changed, a sense of empowerment grows; "I feel more capable than ever before, I can really achieve something" is the kind of feeling one gets. As with the first exercise once you find that you are not really carrying it out, but simply acting from habit, then it is time to change both the actual deeds you are resolving to carry out and the time of day.

It may well happen that one decides not to do the will-exercise because "I don't know where I will be at 11 o' clock today". This is only a subtle indicator of the forces that oppose our journey into inner freedom; for it is easy to decide upon a simple little action no matter where you may be. For example, let's say you wear glasses, all you need to do is some normal little touching or altering of them which other people won't find odd at all. Finally, should it be very difficult precisely at the right time to do your will-exercise, then note to yourself that in five minutes you will do it. After developing the ability to empower yourself in the deepest sense of the word, you will start to notice the benefits of persevering with the exercises. A wonderful sense of inner peace is felt, this is however only the beginning of the process. Once all six exercises have been carried out for a year or so, then indeed a profound new inner peace develops. **For this is deeply true: the way to inner peace is by developing inner strength.** I mean an inner tranquillity that becomes part of your reality, not one which lasts for a month (or a weekend) and then gets thirsty for another 'happiness seminar'. During training for the development of higher faculties, I found it was eventually possible to multiply the demand by carrying out several such deeds per day for many months.

Practically, should one keep forgetting to do the exercise, then reduce the amount of time between making the resolution and the appointed time to carry out the action; e.g., to only 30 mins. Try to gradually increase the time lag. Then over time, perhaps in the second six month period, the time has increased to 2 hours or so. If the action has become habit, then indeed one should replace it with another action, at the same time (to make it easier for you at first) but then after a while set a different time, perhaps 2.30 pm, instead of 12 noon.

The third exercise: establish a tranquil emotional life
Now we enter the third month, and so a third exercise is added; this is designed to develop **equilibrium in the emotional life**; it also confers a certain capacity for **perseverance**. We have found that our thinking life is not under our control, and that the will needs to be accessed. So too, do we discover that the emotions are not answerable to the ego, a condition which is of course well known to all of us, and which can cause much embarrassment, discomfort even unethical behaviour. It is as if the emotions surge back and forwards, running over the ego in the process, and disturbing our equilibrium as well.

If however, one is seeking to find the lofty heights of spirit reflected in the mind as it opens itself in meditation, then the surface of the soul must be as clear and calm. To borrow an widespread metaphor from ancient Indian spirituality, towering snow-clad mountain peaks, burnished into a shimmering gold and pink by the setting sun can not be reflected in the lakes below if these are restless and ruffled by incessant breezes. So too our soul must be tranquil and calm to sense the ethereal revelations received from the higher-self in which the light of the spiritual sun is living.

The previous exercises certainly help one to develop this inner quality, but further exercises are also needed. In the third month, the task is to respond to the emotional surges in a more controlled manner. It is certainly not the point that one should stunt one's emotional life, not at all. One is still to feel the inner life **just as strongly**, but not to allow the surges of emotion to **dictate** one's response. A temptation or annoyance is still experienced, but now one must strive to carefully weigh up the reality of responding directly to it. A feeling of caution when confronted with a dangerous situation is fully justified, but it need not lead to panic or hysteria. So too a feeling of anger for a bad deed is still experienced, but it may not lead the meditant into a violent response. Consider the relationship of the ego to the 'astrality' (the emotional forces): is our ego master of them at least as regards outer expression, or is it an unwilling servant?

Any dog seeing a raw steak on a low table will feel the urge to simply gulp it down, there is no ego to analyse whether it belongs to it or not, etc. In the animal kingdom pleasure is involuntarily 'grovelled towards' and pain is avoided. The emotional forces have this simple pendulum swing towards self-indulgent pleasure and away from pain. If this dynamic is predominant in the meditant then the 'surface of the lake' will always be ruffled, and the ego will be subject to the emotions and instinctive drives. An ancient metaphor used for this need of the self to master the astral forces is that of the charioteer; he must be able to ensure the horses move in the direction that he wills, not wheresoever they are impelled to roam.

So the exercise involves trying to be not so oppressed by pain, not pushed into unwise reactions by irritating, annoying events; rather to ensure that your ego is not submerged by such things. Likewise with pleasure, the urge for gratification must be ultimately under the control of the self. It may well decide, as it seeks through meditation to develop an inherent longing for higher realities, to be more objective about pleasure, not to simply allow the emotive life to rush into it. Gradually the soul learns to seek for a wondrous new world, the world of spiritual joys, rather than pleasure; it is exhilarating to experience one's inner being as free from egoistic pleasures. That is, pleasures which one prior to inner illumination is naively impelled to regard as the most enjoyable thing in human life, yet which actually weaken the ego's control over the soul.

One also becomes less anxious and resentful of painful and challenging experiences. This exercise is not as such a pain-control exercise, but it has that effect, as a result. I found that using the time at the dentist was an excellent way to test myself. Indications of success were appeared when the dentist after an hour (without anaesthetic) of substantial drilling, scraping, etc asked whether I was practising self-hypnosis, as I was so relaxed. Well, self-hypnosis is not involved, but the conscious ego striving to find a centre within the experience of pain certainly is. The first effect one notices is that anxiety about pain is reduced, this itself reduces the actual inner intensity of pain. Later, as my inner tranquillity and preparedness to listen to the lesson of pain increased, it became possible for even the implanting of metal pins from a kind of staple machine into the ground-down tooth to be done without anaesthetic.

So in this exercise one is learning to be in charge of the basic drive in the astral nature, which we share with the animal kingdom, rather than simply being driven by an instinctive response to pleasure and pain. The meditant is still experiencing these responses but they are not to impel the ego into action and reaction. During this third month whenever the opportunity arises the goal is to strive to respond in a more centred manner to life.

Further, this exercise also can yield insight into the profound question of what is the 'purpose' of pleasure and pain in human life? The esoteric psychology behind it is that one can learn much wisdom from being objective about irritation, anger, pain and on the other hand, desires and pleasure, "the less pleasure and pain exhaust themselves in the waves of emotion that they hurl up in the soul's inner-life, the more they can form themselves into 'eyes of the soul' (for perception of higher truths.)"[32] That is, through an objective 'listening' to the inner nature of pleasure and pain the meditant begins to gain insight into what the effect of these two experiences have on the human soul. This kind of sensitising to the inner-world also strongly helps the chakras to form. To really succeed in the exercise one needs to also carry out the Evening Review; see later.

So, the third exercise is to strive not to be driven into reaction by either painful or pleasurable experiences, as if one had no self. Rather, one is to attempt to respond in a manner which affirms the power of the self over the craving for pleasures and the withdrawing before pain or the

---

[32] "Theosophy" see the chapter; "The path of knowledge". R Steiner Press 1994

giving into fury, etc. A small part, at least, of one's inner being should be able to remain free to determine an appropriate response to such situations. For those with some background in esoteric studies, it is not irrelevant to point out here that there are many elemental beings that have an influence within our feelings and temperament.

By undertaking this exercise the meditant is developing the power to be master of his or her 'own' energies, that is, the influences from elemental beings which form a vital part of the 'temperament' or predispositional tendencies.[33] In addition, this third exercise creates a certain objectivity and insight about pleasure and pain that leads to an enhanced capacity for joy. Hence there is less need for diversions and pleasures which may hinder the development of inner depth. Spiritual joy is the result of experiencing something which one recognizes as an aspect of the spiritual reality of life.

It may be one's own higher potential or an intimation of the exquisite nature of the spiritual realms. For example before sunrise the hemisphere's ether forces are less drowned-out by the full light of the new day, bestowing a glorious freshness and enchanting ambience on the world around one. To wander through in nature in that enchanted hour can be a joyous experience, because at that time, it is easier to sense the qualities of the elemental energies, and even the efficacy in these of the higher energies, deriving from divine creative beings.

Also the successful carrying out of this exercise gradually enables one's soul to truly revere the spirit within other human beings, despite their surface qualities; this can be a source of real joy. This exercise also bestows an enhanced sense for artistic appreciation, the sublime beauty in the deepest of classical music that previously was hidden from one, can now become gradually perceived. As this sensitivity to musical truths develops, then a glorious world of inner nurture is opened. With such highly developed musical sensitivity, one can discern the revelations present in great works of music, for example, the last composition by Ludwig van Beethoven – a string quartet in *f*, opus 135. It is Beethoven's last work, and the culmination of the preceding group of quartet's, it is my conclusion that this composition (and to a lesser extent the three earlier compositions) portrays in musical tones the dynamics experienced by the consciousness of an advanced meditant entering into the divine spiritual worlds (the realm of Ideas of Plato, called the "higher Devachanic spheres" by Rudolf Steiner).

---

[33] As a psychic student of mine colourfully expressed her perception of a field pulsing with many different energies in or around her when anger rises, "Whoa – it's a **party**!"

Although this exercise is primarily directed to the astral body, the soul, it also involves the temperament or the habitual predisposition tendencies; this manifests in moods, and background attitudinal qualities, not emotions as such, although moods are similar in some respects to emotions. This exercise has another especial element for women, who are often more connected to these elemental energies than men. These energies are responsible for the background moods, they are not in the soul, but in the life-forces which maintain our body; these energies are elemental forces of fire, air, water and earth. They are affected by the moon's phases and also by what astrologers call lunar transits in the personal horoscope, that is the movement of the moon through the heavens which corresponds to a section of one's birth chart.

The fourth exercise: developing a positive attitude towards the world
So far, the first exercises have been to do with developing the ego's capacity to master thinking, willing and the emotions. They enable the self to really become empowered concerning one's own inner life. Their value becomes ever more confirmed as one works with them; after all, success in meditation is absolutely based on ability to control soul dynamics by the ego. However, there are two soul dynamics which if conquered by the self, will put the soul very substantially under its influence; for these are really powerful forces. They are the tendency in the heart to negative criticism through envy or jealousy; and the tendency of the intellect towards prejudice and a closed mind generally especially regarding new or unfamiliar realities.

The fourth exercise, to be undertaken in the fourth month, is to **combat negativity by striving to manifest a positive attitude**. That means, whenever one is aware of a negative feeling, which is about to be expressed in a sarcastic or cutting remark, one resolves not to say it. Instead, one replaces it with a positive feeling – even a positive remark. This can be done relatively easily when you are confronted by an impersonal situation. Perhaps seeing a stranger with a peculiar hat or irritating mannerism, you can easily then stop the negative thought or remark and find something positive about the person. There is nothing false or sentimental about doing this, it is not done to impress other people, indeed others need not know that this is going on. It concerns the problem of a negative attitude, brought about by subjective factors in oneself. These factors are actually elemental powers that dwell in one's aura, and intensify egotism, by invoking an unloving attitude to that which is different from oneself.

These same forces also cause antipathy to people where astral influences are present deriving from a past life, and if they dominate, then the reconciling with the other person is thwarted, so as with all these exercises there are profound reasons for them being recommended. This exercise becomes more difficult when the situation involves a work project where another person is a potential competitor to you or your project. This is the exercise; to become a person who does not let negative condemnation of others live in one's soul. **It is in particular also about developing the social interaction skill of tolerance**. The other result is that we develop a social interaction skill of great value through striving to be a positive person in this sense. It may well be that you find such an exercise is at first 'artificial', something that you have just 'put on' - but that does not matter. Because as the weeks and months go by it loses this artificial quality and the positive outlook really becomes your inner truth.

The modern personal growth technique of considering why you feel deep within such an antipathy etc, is another matter, it focuses on a different dynamic. This technique, often undertaken in a group, provides the valuable opportunity to identify the personal reason for a particular attitude. It complements the technique offered here in this fourth exercise, which seeks to transform the soul, to actually change the astral substance of your aura, thereby greatly reducing such antipathy and prejudice as a force in the soul. **There is a hidden cause to the general phenomenon of unjustified antipathy, and this fourth exercise counteracts the hidden forces behind it.** By now you may be wondering just why did the initiate choose these various dynamics.

Well, contemplate what happens when the person's karma brings them into a spiritual path that can be applied to professional areas of work, teaching, agriculture, medicine, the arts. One starts to work together with other people, probably on the basis of a spiritual ideal. This is true to an extraordinary degree with the teachings of Rudolf Steiner, for these can renew a variety of skilled professions in a healing and fulfilling way.

The meditant seeking an inner development will probably acquire a new group of acquaintances and colleagues; and here is where the dragon of criticism and personal antipathy could find potent breeding grounds. Many an initiative that starts with an idealistic basis, experiences bitter disputes shortly afterwards; often this is due to the inability to remove the urge towards critical attitudes.

So to become a person whose soul life breathes a fresh invigorating positive quality and enthusiasm has two important results. One is that the soul ceases to be a closed-off thing which relates to the world in terms of its own inner agendum. It therefore becomes ever more open to the environment in the best sense of the word. For our inner reality determines our aura and chakra dynamics, this point cannot be over-emphasized. I refer the reader to the book "Knowledge of the Higher Worlds, How is it Attained?" where an additional 'sensitivity exercise' is given for each of these exercises. These important exercises teach one how to re-shape the ether energies, in order to develop perception of the ether forces in the environment, and in order to consolidate the development of higher consciousness in general.

The fifth exercise: open-mindedness
The fifth exercise to be taken up in the fifth month combats the remarkably powerful and pervasive quality of the intellect of prejudice regarding new or unfamiliar realities. **It is designed to bring about an open-mindedness, an impartial attitude to the world.** It is important to realize that, as explained in Chapter Four, first spiritual experiences will be far more subtle and are going to occur in a manner quite different to what one has assumed. Hence it is vital that an open-mindedness is developed; **but this does not mean a gullibility.** An example of the kind of prejudice that must be overcome by those who seek success in meditation can be found in the story behind the discovery of the Dead Sea Scrolls. The elderly cleric who bought these scrolls from some Bedouin Arab people, was told over a period of perhaps 18 months that there was no such thing as really ancient original Jewish texts. About five or six experts in the subject simply refused outright to even seriously look at the scrolls! The possibility that they could be the greatest discovery of Old Testament related material ever was sufficient to prevent a serious examination.

Another example from Rudolf Steiner of the flexibility needed is that of the bent chimney. Imagine a friend rushing into your house to tell you that a brick chimney on a house opposite has been twisted around like a liquorice stick. In such a situation you must be able to refrain from rejecting the idea until you have gone and looked for yourself. He taught that the seeker never says about some new idea or research; "I just don't believe that !" This is not to say either that one should immediately believe the truth of the news before investigating; it is a question of refraining from the prejudiced attitude that simply dismisses **this sort of phenomenon out of hand.** He chose this example for deep reasons; for just consider what kind of phenomenon would cause a chimney to become twisted? That is, to be twisted around without cracking, as if temporarily made of rubber.

Before we go on to answer this question, the reader should know of the following incident, which actually took place in the town of Murten, Switzerland. In 1980 a cleric returned home after a brief absence, and cast an eye upwards to the roof. He stood there stupefied as he saw to his utter astonishment, that one of the three concrete chimneys on the roof was twisted around exactly as if made of liquorice. Just as in the example from Rudolf Steiner. It had been turned a full 180 degrees on its own axis! He checked with the weather office in case there had been a small local tornado or whirlwind; the answer was negative.

Since a whirlwind or any other physical force could only have produced physical damage, the twisting of concrete into a spiral shape, without cracking it, means that the rock-hard, non-elastic matter of the concrete had been placed for a moment into a different, and remarkable state of being. It had become elastic for a while, was then twisted around, and then returned to its normal rigid state. It is precisely the meaning of Steiner's example, that when an etheric energy is active, we need to be able to acknowledge that's see **Illustration Two**. Such an incident is similar to that of solid ceramic statues weeping tears, or miraculous healings, and the appearance of apports in mediumistic séances. These events, like all miracles, are **due to the manipulation of material substance from within the ether world**. A convoluted chimney is an example of an ethereal energy at work in the physical world, suspending physical laws. Ethereal energies usually work in a more normal fashion, but they can at times behave in this odd way. Now, all this is important, because it is precisely the case that the earnest meditant will start to acquire a sensitivity to the ethers, for example those which surge through the air around one.

Further, as explained in later chapters, when meditating causes a visionary experience, this is due to the ether-body imaging in itself what the astral chakras are perceiving. All higher experiences are mediated to one's consciousness via the ether-body; it mediates to consciousness what our physical or soul-body senses perceive. So, if the intellect is closed off and prejudiced, then the consciousness will likewise be numb to the holistic reality of life and hence closed to the first delicate glimpses of higher realities.

Those first experiences of external ethereal forces, (or astral images coming to you via your ether-body) will be as alien and hard to register as a very obvious 'miracle' is for the normal materialistic mind. Unless the student makes effort to develop real "open mindedness". (This seemingly complex matter of the ether-energies transmitting astral images will be clearer to you after reading Chapter Four.) It is not a question of being sensational, of looking for sensational things, it is a question of being open to the fuller reality of life. This in turn allows one to recognize that realm which is next to the mineral or physical plane. It is to this nearest realm that our faculties obviously become sensitive through meditation.

The kind of open-mindedness implied here results in the ability when perceiving an object, to sense something of the ether or astral energy from which it has been made. For example, a sea-shell becomes a remarkable testimonial to the existence of a living inter-weaving of ether forces in calcium and yet formed in connection with a spiral pattern that has a cosmic origin. In Rudolf Steiner's words; once this exercise has brought results, "...many common objects become a point of entry into an infinite or higher reality." Now, in addition he gave a special gem of wisdom about this exercise, of great value to the student interested in the mysterious term; 'faith'. **This fifth exercise is also designated an exercise to restore the ability to have faith in the spiritual reality of life.** One of the most common exhortations of the priesthood in earlier times, was "to have faith". If someone ceased to be involved in the church, it was said that they had 'lost their faith'. Well, this term, faith, like many others from the New Testament (and other old texts) have really lost its voice; the actual meaning of the term is today lost, and been replaced with an intellectual substitute.

This conclusion arises from the following teaching of Rudolf Steiner......"Faith as it originally was understood, referred to the quality of **not weakening the inherent spiritual reality of something that we come across, {especially for the first time}, by that which we are.**."[34] That is, what our inner being (eg prejudiced mind) brings towards the perceived object should not weaken our sensing of what that thing really is. Therefore, we were able to say above, of this fifth exercise ... "the kind of open-mindedness implied here results in the ability, when perceiving an object, to sense something of the ether or astral energy within it". It has a similarity to the exercises given in Chapter Three. It opens a path for modern humanity to that which is essential for spirituality, and which was once urged upon the laity by formalized religion.

The sixth exercise, undertaken in the sixth month is to combine all five of these activities into a unity, that is, **to integrate them into one's daily life for that month**. The result of such inner work is a tangible soul-harmony and also the acquiring of a strong will for inner freedom. Then it is worthwhile starting again from the beginning, if you feel you have achieved tangible success, then you can make the exercises harder. For example, in the second time around, the will-exercise can be done twice a day, and generally do the exercises more vigorously. The time to stop doing them is up to you, once you feel sure that you have achieved the desired results, then there is no need to continue.

The aim of these six 'parallel exercises' [35] is to enable the ego to step into centre stage, i.e. to be in charge of your soul-life. This enables you to focus on a subtle meditation theme for as long as you wish. Also, they work very effectively **as a way to integration of the personality**; for example, one result is a more tranquil encountering of life's shocks

---

[34] R Steiner Lect 7/Dec/'05 In G/A 54 untranslated.
[35] They are called 'parallel' because they proceed in tandem with meditating, until you have achieved the desired results. They train the ego to master the soul, they are not suitable for meditating upon.

and challenges. People who carry them out act from an inner certainty; a self-assuredness arises. It can even happen that one's hand-writing undergoes a change; this is a sign of deep seated inner integration.

I once had a dangerous life-threatening experience which certainly tested this ability to be master of one's soul, and so I can speak from personal experience of the advantages of the path to self-mastery. It happened 30 years ago, when I was living in a small bush hut. I was retiring for the night, getting into bed, when as my head rested upon the pillow my feet came to rest on a snake coiled up in the bed. As I later saw, it was a deadly full-grown brown snake. Since the old grey blanket was tucked in tightly right around the little bed, I simply could not pull it up quickly and jump out. This would have been a difficult process involving me pushing down with the feet, then the alarmed reptile would have then bitten in a flash. I realized immediately that only total calmness, which would not give any hostile signals, was the sole way to get out of this alive.

So I willed to enter the meditative calm state, and let the snake feel it could unhurriedly explore the way out. To do this, knowing that snakes have a keen sense of warmth, I slowed my heart-beat, and let the body become marginally cooler. This was vital because the snake soon realized it too was trapped, it could only get away by exiting up near the pillow. It had to feel free to do that, and it did; it slowly crawled up my body to my chest, and then poked its head out near my face, gazing at me with its dark eyes, for a few dangerous seconds, from about six inches away. But since I gave no signs of life or increasing warmth or increasing heart beat, it gradually slithered off calmly onto the floor.

The Evening Review
It was mentioned in conjunction with the third exercise that the "Evening Review" exercise is necessary. This exercise involves looking back over your day to gain an objective perspective on your personality, in the evening. In contrast to the exoteric approach to this, the esoteric meditant is advised to do this review **chronologically in reverse**. That is to start with the events that occurred in the evening and then go through until the events of the morning. Before we consider why this time reversal is advised, lets see exactly what is to be done. The meditant each evening, just for five minutes, is to note **what were the main events of that day**, and then to see them happen again **in your mind's eye,** starting with the **last** one.

Now, when doing this, there is a very important perspective one must have. Namely that in doing this review, **one is to consider oneself as one's higher-self**. If that is difficult, then think of yourself as some kind of celestial judge. In this way our attitude strives to be entirely objective. An openness to acknowledging one's faults, no matter how much one resents having them, is essential. Naturally, this 'judge' also has a preparedness to acknowledge evidence of all spiritual impulses one has manifested, too. Then, as you review the day, keep these two crucial questions in mind. Regarding any experience that occurred: has this personality (yourself) learnt enough from it?

Regarding any deed you carried out, could not this personality have done it better? It is important to note that this exercise has nothing to do with personal regret for bad deeds or failings of the inner life or clumsy deeds. Self-centred regret at having not done something as capably as someone else for example, is not to be allowed in this exercise. Regret for immoral deeds, on the other hand, is very valid, but does not belong in this exercise either.

This exercise is in essence very old; for example Sextius Empiricus, a teacher of the ancient Greek Stoic philosophy, recorded (early in 3rd century BCE) his practise of this.... "Every day I plead my case before myself. When the light is extinguished, and whilst my wife, who knows my habit, remains silent, I examine the past day. I go over everything and weigh all my deeds and words. I hide nothing, I omit nothing; why should I hesitate to face my shortcomings, when I can say (to myself) 'take care not to repeat them, and thus I forgive you today'."[36] It seems that the esoteric order of the Pythagoreans also carried this kind of daily review.

However in the pathway described in this book, one is to go in reverse order, as noted above. There are various reasons for this, one is connected with the deep mystery of our life after death. Namely, that during the first stages of the journey after death, the soul must then gain self-knowledge and come to terms with its personality qualities. However, this occurs for the soul in that the cosmos is so ordered that we see our life appearing as images in reverse order, that is, one sees the events of that life starting with old age and going slowly back to birth. Our task is then to contemplate our life with as much objectivity as possible. The meditant who regularly does the evening review exercise will greatly shorten the amount of time needed for the process of self-knowledge on the journey to the spiritual world.

Further, undertaking this exercise assists one in the task of gaining access to one's previous earthly life; as explained elsewhere, this is a gradual process through which images start to be seen from the past. These images as well as other images - for example, of the future - are present in the aura, but they are not normally seen. By practising this exercise until the day's events can roll along quite livingly before your

---

[36] His comments are recorded by Seneca, quoted by S. Angus in "The Mystery Religions" Dover Press.

'mind's eye' you assist the associated process of recalling memory of the pre-conception time; that is of one's existence prior to birth. Steiner explains that one aspect of this review exercise is that **one gradually can attain to perception of the phase of one's existence in the spiritual realms**, preparing for the next life. For this reason, he recommends that you try to see each event as visually as possible, as if looking at a video recording of the event.

But, he also advises that one can try to 'roll the film backwards' past the other lesser events until the next (earlier) main event occurred. Try to stay in the living backwards-moving flow, rather just like seeing a video film of your day. He taught that if one also attempts to do this vivid, but chronologically reversed exercise, then other valuable benefits are to be gained. One benefit is that one is learning to develop a new faculty of memory; a kind of memory which future humanity will develop. With this new memory, we will **see** a past event by accessing it in the ether-body, where it is stored as an image, no longer just vaguely recalling in outline the event. Further, if one goes in a chronologically backwards manner, then one is learning to function in higher realms; to orient oneself in a different continuum. Namely in realms where time as such ceases; where time flows backwards as well as forwards. It is precisely to such a realm that your meditation takes you! How often does one read that it 'seemed as if time had ceased' when a higher consciousness state is experienced. The importance of this process is high-lighted by Steiner in these words,

> When we thus control our memory in this way, so that the past becomes a school of learning, then astral vision forms itself. This activity makes the soul-body into an organ of our will which we can use to form images of the external (astral) world. This learning to be objective about the mental images recalled by memory metamorphoses the cloud shaped forms in the aura into radiant coherent forms. The radiance proceeds from the head and heart areas, showing the seer that this person's life has an inner centre from which their outer life is directed. [37]

For those who wish to proceed to more advanced esoteric development, such as becoming ever more conscious of one's night-time experiences in the spiritual realms, it is important to undertake the special additional part of this exercise. Namely, that upon recalling the day right back to that morning, you do not stop there! Instead, you continue on, trying to recall your entire night-time; i.e., all the dreams or other events that occurred during the night. This has some wonderful results;

---

[37] Archive lecture from 1904 Feb 2nd - "Knowledge of the Higher Worlds, how is it attained?"

for example, the dreams become not only recalled but more coherent and even more conscious. [38]

Finally, to really make full use of the power of this exercise to adapt the mind to the 'timeless' nature of the astral realm, more can be done regarding the reversal of the time sequence. You can select an event, such as yourself walking downstairs at lunch-time, and then strive to see this event in reverse order. That is, try to visualize your feet moving from the ground back up onto the last step, and then backwards up to the second last step. And so on until you are on the top of the stairway, just about to step down.

---

[38] Those with interest to do this will also find the way to take this matter further by exploring anthroposophical literature; this deeper aspect of esoteric development is not the theme of the book.

CHAPTER THREE

Preparing the intellect and attuning the heart

"The seeds of wisdom cannot sprout and grow in airless space. To live and reap experience the mind needs breadth and depth, and points by which to draw it towards the Diamond Soul (the supreme Buddha)."
   from "The Voice of the Silence", by Helena P. Blavatsky

The kind of spiritualization process we are considering, gradually develops over several lifetimes on Earth. It involves transforming and uplifting one's soul, so that the higher-self may become one with it. Through this deeper kind of meditating, one is in effect speeding up the evolutionary process. What would normally be achieved only after several more lifetimes could be attained in one life. That is a useful definition of a true Initiate; she or he has attained to that glorious state which humanity in general will attain only in future time cycles.

It could be said that it is precisely such 'future-people' who provide the present with the vitally needed spiritual guidance; without which the future may not be fully realized by the human life-wave. There is, according to Rudolf Steiner, in preparation in the spiritual realms, a future epoch on the Earth wherein a kind of golden age of moral integrity and spiritual-esoteric development will be the normal cultural goal, and for this epoch people need to work towards self-initiation, already now in this life.[39]

A deep tranquillity and joy results as the spiritual potential becomes ever more part of one's personality. One attains to deep tranquillity and joy through a higher state of consciousness. But also this new state of being, of enhanced spirituality, actually helps all humanity in general, around the world. Through the kind of esoteric meditation which Rudolf Steiner taught, the soul gradually develops spiritual 'substance' or energies within itself, as a pearl forms inside an oyster. Rudolf Steiner pointed out that such 'inner work' has the effect of ennobling world-karma; and thereby removing the underlying causes of much of the suffering to which people are exposed.[40] A successful meditant is in effect invoking the future spirituality into the present; as Steiner once commented to his pupils, a person involved in earnest study of the

---

[39] The time cycle occurs in ca. AD 4,400 - 4,700, but just to what extent the spiritual renewal will blossom depends on spiritual seekers of today and from now on.

[40] In a lect. 1. Jan.07, "Mephistopheles and Earthquakes".

results of his spiritual research, wherein there is a tendency to become contemplative with the material, can directly help their community.

He explained that another person, elsewhere in the town can be struggling to find the right ethical decision or insight, perhaps regarding parenting for example, and – because of the spiritual energies invoked by the meditant – this other person finds the illumination they need. Among the many oral traditions handed down from Steiner's lifetime, is the account of this initiate commenting, during a train journey in Germany that, if only a small but tangible number of people in each city would take up this kind of inner transformation, there would be less crime and misery in the world. This is possible because through the presence of actual spiritual qualities being drawn into incarnate meditants, lower forces seeking to exert their desires in people, are neutralized.

The soul substance (or aura) of the planet is tangibly more light-enfilled through our new being. That is, **our new being is not only consciously more wise, but also emanates goodness, thus reducing the hidden inner causes of hate and evil in the world**. The great initiates or saints are people who have developed this potential more fully than most people. Such great people would have worked with immense dedication towards their spirituality already in their past lives.

Our spirit derives from a far higher spiritual realm than our soul. Gradually, through meditation, the soul becomes transformed into this purified, divine reality; see the illustrations of the three auras in Chapter Six for more about this. Our spirit exists as a germinal essence in the spiritual world, whereas our soul derives from the soul world. In our spirit a divine state of being prevails; unconditional (not sentimental) love is natural to it. Further, awareness of all of one's past lives is contained within its consciousness, as well as the essence of our present destiny-purposes, (karmic requirements). But, before meditating can be successfully carried out, some preparation has to be done, and this involves study and attuning the feelings to the sacred.

Spiritual study: the essential basis for meditating

"Higher consciousness with its 'clairvoyant' perception begins with a thinking in which the soul has been inwardly illumined and has been mastered by its own will. From this kind of self-disciplined thinking the soul develops the clairvoyant perceiving referred to here. Such thinking is a prototype for higher vision. Naturally what one experiences {with **psychic-image** consciousness and **cosmic-spiritual** consciousness} is essentially quite different to normal thinking. It leads into the higher realms, where such normal thinking can not enter."

This quote from the 1918 foreword to Steiner's "A Way to Self-Knowledge" confirms what we discovered in Chapter One, that the term 'thinking' is also applied in this path to consciousness processes of high spiritual kinds. Well, how does one work towards achieving these goals? To effectively carry out the deeper kind of meditation, presented in Chapter One, a number of processes are necessary. **The first one is concerned with thinking, and requires a study regime**. However, the truths must be presented in **conceptual form**: and such material is not as common as one might think. The primary source of modern material of this kind is the works of Rudolf Steiner. **It is not a question of stimulating a mood of excitement or even belief in higher matters. It has to do with the need to develop the ability to conceptually grasp spiritual truths.** This is to so understand them that you can re-state them in your own words, or at least know clearly that one has grasped them.

The higher realms are by nature not of the Earth; the dynamics holding sway in such realities are transcendental. Steiner recommended that 20 minutes a day are spent in the study of spiritual truths. The student is cautioned that any attempt to commence the deeper kind of meditation presented here, without first having studied Steiner's basic works, and having strengthened the personality through the Six Basic Exercises, could lead to annoying, but not damaging disruptive psychological results. His 'basic works' means here; The Philosophy of Freedom / An Outline of 'Esoteric Science'/ 'Theosophy'/ Knowledge of Higher Worlds.

Most of our thinking, that is **the way** we think and analyse, is earth-bound, because it is connected to the material physical world, because we naturally think about and continually analyse what our senses tell us. We have to do this, or we could not do any daily action at all, such as crossing a road. So normally our thinking is not attuned to spiritual realities, rather it receives sense impressions of the physical plane, and analyses them. We may entertain **images** in our mind of higher things, without really thinking about them in a thorough way.

That is, our normal thinking life can not, at first, come to terms with spiritual matters. We are not used to functioning for example in a continuum where time does not exist or where space is four dimensional, or indeed even ceases. Or where separate beings can also be aspects of the one being! What is meant here is quite easy to grasp. Consider for example, the creator. It way well be that we have an image, an idea of this creator, but we have little capacity in our normal thinking life to conceptualize about It; to think through just what is the nature of the creator.

Once higher development occurs, we don't want to be like the proverbial moo cow gazing in non-comprehension at the passing traffic!

For such a bemused state in fact would be the beginning of a new unfreedom, not the wonderful herald of attaining to real truth and genuine enlightenment. This bemused state occurs when drugs or magical techniques are used to force higher consciousness states. So, a study of the 'laws' and dynamics of the spiritual realm is vital, for in doing this we are not just intellectually learning about higher realms, we are also acquiring the ability to attune our thinking to the spiritual reality.

Hence it is essential that the student strives by such study to gradually develop the ability to understand higher spiritual realities intellectually. That is, to approach the spirit first in the form of concepts, ideas that can be grasped by the mind.[41] For example, descriptive accounts of metaphysical experiences or theoretical conclusions are not of much use for this purpose. The texts need to be derived from an initiate's direct conscious experiencing of higher truths, not based on what someone believes to be correct. Then those contemporary spiritual experiences, having been understood, need to be grasped by that person's logical consciousness and presented in conceptual form.

It is widely accepted that Rudolf Steiner is a leading teacher of a path which presents spiritual truths in a logical, conceptual form. Yet some people may find his approach 'intellectual', and by implication, not spiritual. What they are discovering is that the student has firstly to grasp intellectually the underlying realities, for to just enjoy descriptive accounts is of no value for developing the ability to meditate. Steiner wanted people to be able to comprehend clearly in freedom the dynamics of the higher realities, and only after having attained some comprehension, to feel how inspiring and significant these spiritual truths are.

He strove to avoid any directly sensational accounts of the spirit; he worked to give a rational conceptual presentation of higher truths. Why? Because once a person gains understanding of a higher eternal truth through grasping it with the intellect, that truth then enters deeply into their being. It remains in the mind of the student, even if only a shadow of its real self. It does not disappear into thin air after the excitement dies away. It does not become yet another wonderful but soon to vanish 'high'. Naturally there is nothing wrong with a person having such experiences, the right way, and not being able to conceptualize it for others. But those who wish to become united in

---

[41] It is for this reason that R. Steiner's lectures and written books, are conceptual logical presentations of transcendental truths (so far as that is possible).

their innermost core with the spirit, need to develop the ability to think spiritually.[42]

Further, when making a decision based on a spiritual teaching, one needs to have intellectually grasped the ideas. This requires conscious effort by the person. Once the idea is grasped you will be able to determine quite freely how to relate to it. The emotions then become involved, becoming uplifted and inspired; but if so, this is because you have responded in freedom, after objectively understanding the teaching. You have not become **directly** stimulated to excitement and thence to commitment (perhaps financial) by an emotive reaction. Otherwise, the freedom of the student is at risk; decisions made emotionally, in the mood of excitement, are not free decisions. Apart from the above considerations, there are other reasons for emphasis on thinking, even though our usual rational thinking can not directly grasp the higher realities.

There are several very important reasons for this stipulation. Consider what you say when a friend shows you a new gadget: "Oh, I like that idea!" Or, if someone is discussing a matter, we might respond; 'I see what you mean'. These are very significant expressions, for they indicate that our intellect has the ability **to perceive ideas,** which are as real for it as a physical object is to the eyes. We can find, intuitively, the concept which belongs to what we perceive; the Idea from which the object was created. We sense that the concept is somehow real, even if it is invisible. Once we have found the idea belonging to something, then we are much nearer to it, we have formed a close association with it.

For example, an adult is much more attuned to the essential reality of, say, a fox quietly nearing a chicken house than a young child. For a child looking at the scene can not yet realize that the fox is drawn to the fowl for predatory reasons. A connection is formed between the observer and the observed once you have found the concept belonging to it; in other words, the idea behind it. For example, when studying a spiritual text about another planet or a nature spirit, you begin to feel

---

[42] Note that a book by Rudolf Steiner on Philosophy, "The Philosophy of Spiritual Activity" (also transl. as Philosophy of Freedom) is important in this context. It is a training manual for the meditant to acquire the kind of attitudes that enable the consciousness to grasp the transcendental nature of spiritland. The inner work that the ego undertakes in studying this book gives it the strength needed for assimilation of the transcendental experiences. In itself it is apparently not a 'spiritual' book; for its theme is the nature of the mind (epistemology); but behind its words is a potent description of the human spirit's connection with the mind.

as if you are almost seeing the matter being presented, not just inwardly seeing it in the mind's eye.

This inner comprehension forms a subtle union between observer and observed. Hence Rudolf Steiner speaks of a (holistic) philosopher as "an unconscious clairvoyant". Such mental focussing on divine realities has a power to prepare the student for the faculty of **cosmic-spiritual** consciousness, through which the mind functions consciously on the spiritual plane.

> When the person raises him/herself from the external thoughts that storm in upon the soul, to those that have an eternal significance, then that person lights up a flame within their being, which illumines for them the way beyond the soul world (to the spirit world). [43]

When we consider the chakras more will be said about this. For now, it is important to note that soul qualities, and an enlivened consciousness is what really counts, not occult techniques. In the same lecture, he gives a few examples.... "to become enlightened, one has to develop **self-confidence** but his must go hand in hand with **humility**. **Self-control** has to be developed but together with **mildness of character**. Lastly **presence of mind** and flexibility will be needed, but together with **steadfastness**."

So, if your meditative work succeeds, and you are in a spiritual realm, perceiving (with one's consciousness, not sense-organs), what is around you, what will you 'make of it'? If you have been developing the intuitive ability of the intelligence to find the concept of spiritual realities – by study of the spiritual in a rational format – then you will be more able to comprehend the profound transcendental verities around you. The eye of the mind replaces physical eyes, so to speak; one does not want to be simply registering the transcendental in bewilderment. The ability to perceive the reality (or 'idea') of the intangible higher reality is vital. This offers crucial protection against misunderstanding deeper meditative experiences; indeed the very first initial non-comprehending, occurring within the experience itself, becomes an open door to lower entities, who then insinuate a false perspective on life and on spiritual realities to the unprepared meditant.

This point can be illustrated by a mundane example. Consider a person gazing up at the stars, how often such a person then thinks about the infinite number of galaxies and the vastness of space, and then becoming aware of feeling ill at ease, has to stop. Whereas if one can intuitively sense the concept of what one is seeing (the idea behind it

---

[43] In a lecture, untranslated, of 15.Dec 1904, in GA No. 53, page 202-3.

all), this enables that person to enjoy such star gazing. For one then understands that our spirit-self transcends space, then the physical universe is not large, it is not even perceived as spatial from within the spiritual realms. One's inner being can be experienced as spread out across it; one feels that one's true being is derived from the All. Likewise, the unprepared meditant in encountering some spiritual reality, can be given a false attitude, but in this situation, the meditant will not be aware of the falseness of the attitude; but will live it out.

There is still more to recommend this study discipline, and we find this additional very important reason when answering the question, **where does materialism exist**? Well it exists in the intellect! The least spiritual aspect of our being today is the materialistic or abstract thinking. It is here that the opposition to our spiritual aspirations are found. It is easy to give oneself a spiritual feeling or emotion; for emotions are by nature in empathy to the environs.

They respond quite naturally to a spiritual experience; not so the mind; it doubts, it resists in very tenacious, subtle ways. The more subtle materialism is revealed in the mind - not in the heart - of seekers of the spirit. For example, someone declares their belief in the other worlds, then declares that these are composed of simply very refined matter! However, matter is unique to the material plane for material substance namely molecules, **simply vanish, as from the ether energies upwards**.

So, the being-ness of a spiritual being, of an archangel for example, is **not** composed of very tenuous, refined molecules; nor, of course, is the mind of God. It is composed of spirit. Non-material energies constitute the ether realm, and then soul-consciousness (also known as astral 'substance') is encountered in the soul world; whereas spirit-'substance' is what the spiritual world is composed of. All the beings or thought-forms in the soul-world may be referred to as consisting of soul (astral) 'substance', but this is due to the limitations of language.

For example, the English language has few options to describe the composition of spiritual being-ness without implying the innate presence of material substance in this being-ness. Hence, one says, an angel consists of soul substance; or a thought-form is composed of astral matter: both these expressions are materialistic, for such is earthly language.

The terms substance or matter in such usage as 'astral matter', or 'the substance of the spirit-aura' are 'emergency stand-ins', being totally incorrect. For there is no substance or matter in such realms. However, such understanding is not always there, as indicated above. They are material expressions that can imbue the meditant's mind with a subtly false concept of higher worlds. If subtle materialistic tendencies still exist, and the person is plunged into another realm, then a variety of unfortunate results occur, for the mental attitude will be incompatible with the experience. This theme that involves the fact of opposing spiritual powers, will be dealt with in a later chapter.

There are a thousand other examples of such subtle materialistic ideas that have their roots in the materialistic intellectualism of today. Hence the practise of 20 minutes a day of such study will help to remove this serious obstacle to successful meditation. In addition, when we practise this study program, another vital benefit is gained: the inner strength to defend oneself from deception and illusions as well as general disorientation in spiritual experiences. Why is this a result ? Because thinking is that mental activity in which the personal ego, our actual self-consciousness, is most awake. The ego is most intensely present in the activity of thinking; if we cease to focus on it then the thoughts stop, as if a light was switched off.

Where is our ego most conscious? In its thinking activity, rather than the emotions for example, for emotions come and go without our conscious self really being aware or in control of them. To Rudolf Steiner, this capability of directing of thoughts shows the 'awake state' of the ego in thinking – actively produced thoughts – is stronger than that of feelings, wherein so often no such control or directing is possible. The power of the emotion may well be greater than that of thoughts, but that is not the point here.

So self-consciousness has to undergo training to maintain itself in spiritual matters by striving to grasp transcendental ideas. Then in the actual moment of being 'body-free' or arising to higher states of being, the ego will be much more able to discriminate, in the most positive sense of this word; that is one shall have a capacity to **discern**, one becomes a person who can discern clearly the nature of whatever one is encountering. Discrimination in this sense is very ethical and important; it is the ability to objectively assess something, instead of being confused and overwhelmed, which may then lead to misinterpreting everything.

The self will be able to maintain itself, to retain its inner integrity. In addition, if we have learnt to maintain our alertness in the process of conceptually grasping spiritual truth, we will be able to maintain our ego-hood, our sense of self-hood when actually experiencing higher realities. **If you nearly fall asleep when trying to study the teachings about higher worlds, then how will you have the inner power to assimilate and assess higher experiences?** Through the study program discussed earlier, self-consciousness will be maintained and afterwards, the ability to assess the subtle implications of the experience will be there.

Since there are also forces that attempt to distort the meditant's impression of the experience, this ability to maintain one's inner alertness is essential. In Appendix 1 at the end of this chapter, there is a list of texts from Steiner that train the mind to think in spiritual ideas, as distinct from feeling or resonating with them.

Once the ability to think, to conceptualize spiritual truths is achieved, then from this activity, profound and profoundly transformative feelings can arise; and that is immensely important ! But the point of the study program is to develop the capacity to think spiritually, and this is a prelude to conscious functioning on lofty spiritual realms.

The Four Moods
The ancient Chinese sage, Mencius, said, "The great person is he who does not lose his child's heart...the moral problem is, how to maintain 'the air of the early dawn' in the heart of the adult."[44]

The second aspect to the preparatory stages involves something quite different: namely our emotions, moods and attitudes. I call it the path of the Four Moods. It is essential to realize that one reason for meditation not being successful is that the underlying attitude which one brings to this activity may not be appropriate. In other words, the attitude or mood prevailing in the soul of the meditant needs to be attuned to the spiritual realms. After all, a spiritual experience is the result of some aspect of the spiritual realms becoming perceptible to the soul. However it won't be perceived if the person's background mood is not attuned to the divine qualities of such realms, **where love, beauty and goodness are interweaving continually like three 'substances'.**

They are a tangible reality in the spiritual realms, they are the 'background' of those realms, just as mountains and clouds form the physical background to our world. The idea of 'holy' came from the experience of this triune reality in which these three fundamental 'elements' are fully present. This word originally signified that a 'wholeness' prevailed, a wholeness deriving from Deity, from the primal trinity of spiritual creativity. This is an extremely important point; the esoteric wisdom given by this initiate, such as that given in 1924, if purchased as a book and simply 'studied', that is, read as a body of

---

[44] Mencius lived 372-289 BCE, in that earlier Age of the archangel Michael, when so many great sages became inspirers to humanity, in both the Orient and Greece. Quoted by Lin Yutang, in "The Wisdom of China", 1963, 200-226.

knowledge, will have almost no value for the soul. It is better to contemplatively read such material, only after a few minutes of attunement, and after the meditant has really developed the capacity for reverence. Then it will be a powerful transformative experience.

The following exercises are necessary to acquire the soul-moods that confer attunement to the spirit. They need not be followed in any particular order; these are to be found in various works of Rudolf Steiner.

Exercise 1: Wonder
This exercise involves taking the time when perceiving a particular object or process, to try to be open to gaining insight into an additional quality within the properties of the perceived object. One needs to develop the capacity for experiencing wonder, to learn to wonder at the world. Every day some effort is to be made to pause a little in the midst of perceiving the world. To pause and take a moment to realize that although our logical mind has indeed 'sorted out' what the object is, yet it has totally failed to consider the deeper significance of the object, and the extraordinary context in which it exists.

For example this includes the **deeper meaning** of that object for the world. Consider a comet streaming across the night sky; its physical nature is known and registered by the intellect. Still, just why it exists, what significance it has for the cosmos has not been perceived. To develop the capacity for wonder, one looks at the comet and then gazes in a quiet manner, giving time to sense the especial ambience which resonates from a comet. Of course in the view of materialism, wherein non-causation prevails, everything is the result of chance; so there can be no deeper significance to a comet. Assumptions of this kind tend to linger in the meditator. This exercise of allowing oneself time to feel what is the larger, deeper reality of a perceived object, is a wonderful antidote.

When a rain-drop falls, or some water falls onto a bench, it forms, where the surface is smooth, into little round droplets, not irregularly formed blobs. When water freezes and forms into snow crystals, all these, in their billions, always have the form of a six pointed star. The deeper significance of such extraordinary facts is unknown, and indeed disregarded in the analytical process. It is precisely the point of this exercise to wonder about such things, to be syncretistic in one's thinking. One is not to become more analytical, but to ponder that **there is a hidden aspect to the sense world which the logical mind can not perceive**. This exercise also involves refraining from making abstract theories about things in the world, and to let these various things convey to us what their reality is. It is a question of trying to become aware of just what the reality is, not intellectually deciding.

One soon realizes that purely logical thought cannot actually discover the deeper truths of life. One tries to place oneself wisely in the living nexus of the world, so that it speaks its reality to one. This attitude is an integral part of experiencing wonder at the world. An easy way to learn to experience wonder is of course, to contemplate the stars. When the stars come out at night, they are cognized, but this does not mean that their deeper meaning is grasped. To wonder about their meaning is not difficult, the challenge is to do this for many common things! When we take time out to gently ponder these phenomena, to wonder at these beautiful mysteries, then we are doing something much more important for successful meditation than we may at first realize. Before considering what that is, the rest of the exercises will be described.

Exercise 2: Awe
This second exercise involves taking the time when perceiving a particular object or process, to try to feel an additional quality within the properties of the perceived object. One is not to invest the world with artificial grandeur, but to learn **to become sensitive to the dynamic living nexus of life that can be glimpsed behind what the senses perceive**. For example, what before was simply a walk along a suburban tree-lined street becomes an experience of a remarkable environment filled with an interweaving of specific colours and of symmetrical forms, each of which is significant. The basic shape of the leaves of trees and bushes and the pattern of their branches show a characteristic quality that now hints at the presence of a specific planetary ether energy. Hence a pine-tree, with its somewhat severe, Saturnine quality, becomes a conical shaped tree with branches spiralling out in a sophisticated spiral formation, but almost on a horizontal plane, not pointing steeply upwards, which is the case with trees whose ether-energies bear the imprint of different planetary influences.

The pine leaves are solid rectangular needle-like formations, and within these 'leaves' there exists an oil possessing germicidal qualities stronger than many chemical germicides. Gradually these facts can become awe-inspiring. Next to it may be a fruit-bearing tree, and again the awesome quality of a plant that condenses into material substance a fine nutrition for us humans from the ether, becomes a living, experiential fact. The complex panorama we have been describing are qualities that we naturally see at a glance, but often fail to livingly register.

Importantly, this exercise is also about becoming quite simply filled with a sense of awe just at the fact of quite rudimentary sense reality. For example; consider the grass and trees that cover the earth's landmasses; why are they green? This fact, if living fresh and clearly in the soul **is awesome**. How irritating it would be if red was the colour of the world's flora, and how uncomfortably 'closing-in' upon us and dampening if the grasses were blue. Yet it **is** green; the most relaxing, neutral colour for humanity. Consider too the form of clouds and indeed of all things, they are all non-lineal except crystals, which are usually not seen, as they exist beneath the soil. That is, they are rounded; they have a wave-form, flowing and curving, or perhaps have forms of a symmetrical type, like the fir tree, a cactus, an oak. The presence of other pedestrians, each moving along, impelled by their will, yet together forming a cloud of human volition, imbued with karmic forces, is again a remarkable fact.

In nature, except where decay occurs, and with regard to malignant beings or plants, beauty exists everywhere; yet one could say, that it need not be beautiful. Clouds could be grey squares, trees look like boxes, butterflies like flying hinges. One must learn to experience this as an awesome reality as an obvious, yet overlooked fact, that beauty is given to us everywhere in the environment. Of course, a rainbow or the sunset are more easily experienced as awe inspiring, but virtually all that we find in nature, is awesome. For instance, consider a sea-shell; it is not just a calcium sheath. It is formed on a sophisticated spiralling pattern and grows quite pliably as the marine animal grows, yet the calcium then forms into a rigid hard bony shell. This is intelligent living engineering, yet the marine creature inside has virtually no brain. One just needs to make the effort to develop the awareness of this. This is vital for success in meditation.

Exercise 3: Reverence
The third exercise involves developing the capacity for reverence. **The higher-self can not manifest in us if there is no capacity for revering that which is from the spiritual realms**; this is the meaning of reverence. It is the power within the soul to respect that which manifests the qualities of the spiritual realms. This is in fact a useful definition of what is sacred. In this context, it is especially to respect deeply and joyously acknowledge a spiritual reality greater than what is normally manifested by oneself. The people of the European spiritual life, such as the medieval Knights Templars, and the medieval Rosicrucians, revered the cosmic Christ and the sacrifice this divine being made 2000 years ago, which occurred geographically at the Earth's own planetary heart chakra.

It is also necessary to be able to revere any good, true or beautiful deed (or quality) which comes to our attention. When someone manifests outstanding honesty, goodness or wisdom for example, then the soul must be able to experience deep reverence for those qualities. For such qualities are inherent in the spiritual realms. Not to have reverence for these is not to be attuned to those realms which one is trying to reach through meditation.

The importance of reverence can be further understood when its role in the aura is known. Reverence is in many ways the opposite of jealousy and envy; hence striving to develop this inner mood helps in the struggle against these twin evils. **When a person emanates reverence, they are sending out the kind of astral thought form (or emotive form) that impinges upon the astral substance of other people, who strongly absorb it**. One virtually transfers this astral 'substance' of reverence to others; it has the quality of warmth, warmth streams from it. The appearance of this in the spiritual world is a bluish coloured astral form. The warm, reverential attitude creates a thought-form of bluish colour. (1904)

One sends this towards the other person opening the possibility for this warmth to ray into their own soul. However, if one's attitude regarding another person is filled with the mood of jealousy, then this produces a red coloured thought-form permeated by self-love. This red form encloses around a thought-form which is full of mental pictures of oneself. This situation may have its origin in our personal ambitions. Such a soul-state comes to expression in one's aura as a substantial thought-form that is particularly 'full.' It has no room for other astral energies or dynamics. The resulting effect is one of coldness; an inner coldness that repels everything. The red astral form closes itself off, hindering the absorption into the aura of other dynamics and forms. (1904)

Exercise 4: Devotion
Fourthly, the mood or attitude of **devotion** is required; like the other moods, this must become a naturally present quality of one's soul. By devotion is meant **the capacity to apply oneself to a task that is of service to others**. If one has devotion, one is able to keep on applying oneself to a task that is not gratifying to any personal desires. For example, devotion to a soul exercise, or to helping an elderly relative, and doing this for years – within the possibility of one's own time-schedule. Devotion to such a resolution, or to some inner exercise is the kind of mood that is meant here. In particular, it is the ability to carry out such an activity, over a long time, and not fade away after a few months.

It is obvious that these four qualities are wholesome classical virtues, but the profound reason for their selection by Rudolf Steiner may not be so obvious. These four moods have a common quality, namely to be carried out, one must reduce the natural egotism in oneself. Consider wonder: this challenges the intellect, for **the thinking-life** is required to step back a little, so to speak. Instead of presuming confidently that it has the matter clearly labelled, one has to yield on that point and make the space to query and ponder the subject. It is a question of letting the greater, transcendental picture arise, to envelop the analytical conclusion with many open-ended possibilities. It's an exercise in gradually yielding the normal every-day way of being which the personal ego has formed, in its intellectual life. It opens itself to a greater reality; it is learning to become more intuitive.

Our intellect already functions by an intuitive process, for this is how it finds the concept or grasps the idea behind a perceived object. In this exercise the intuitive sensing is to greatly increase, so that we can perceive the concept (the idea) of something in a much more important way. Namely, to sense its significance for the world, not just register whether it is an animal or plant. We see a sea-shell or a butterfly, and as adults we inwardly know what the creature is; its idea is clear to us. Yet only in a basic way, we don't really know just why it exists, what role it plays in nature. Not only in a physical sense, but also in regard to the ethereal life-energies in the planet. Precisely this ability is what the advanced seeker has to develop; to be able when thinking about a being or dynamic, to inwardly grasp the intention of the spirit living within that being or dynamic.

This ability to really sense just what kind of object it is which one is seeing, must extend to spiritual things too, such as a being or coloured form that appears to you in meditation. So long as the natural analytical function is allowed to prevent this more holistic thinking, then the ability to dialogue with the newly developing spiritual experiences will remain poor. To such developed "body-free" thinking, objects that manifest physically will also be seen in their full reality. For example, in mid-summer the wondrous phenomenon of luminous fire-flies occur. To the logical mind, despite the fact that this is a courtship process, it is an eerie exhibition. However, to the holistic thinking faculty they confirm that the solar ether-energies from which light derives are especially dominant on a subtle elemental level in summer, causing the phosphorous substances in some insects to light up in response. They confirm that the living interweaving of Earth energies with solar forces, is now at a maximum. We can take another example, this one from the cosmos.

A comet, with its little head and long tail streaming through space, with millions of others, comes towards the vast oval sphere of a solar system. This brings forth an inner picture that is all about the 'fertilization' of a solar system; on the level of elemental life energies. In this connection, it is interesting, according to the experience of earlier European vintners, that the wine harvest is different when a large comet comes close to the Earth. Humanity's consciousness is also subject to subtle influences from comets.

Similarly with the exercise in Awe; here the **sense-perceptions** are required to be much more open to what they are really perceiving. The normal everyday way of sensing the physical world is required to be more open, less assumptive. The interface between us and the world must be enlivened, sensitized! Just consider that some reality in the ethers or astral plane has condensed a material object (or sound/colour) into existence. Hence 'behind' the object, so to speak, there is an ethereal energy, vibrant with its own colour and other qualities. This subtle counterpart is actually 'seen' by one, but it is at the same time blocked out of awareness by the matter that constitutes its material existence. It is in this sense that the physical world which we see is 'Maya'; it is an incomplete seeing, and it is subtly accompanied by a false idea; namely, there is only matter.

Only when the soul strives to develop a sensitivity to the more subtle elemental energies behind the physical world, can the inner reality be seen in the act of perceiving a physical object. Learning to wonder at the world is to train oneself, in a wholesome way, to be open to that which lies behind the physical sense impression, and which one's life-force organism and aura is perceiving. The forces that sustain our everyday normal ego in its registering of the perceived world have to retreat, and allow a greater openness, a finer sensitivity, a less self-enclosed attitude to emerge. Like the preceding exercise, it involves a **lessening of the normal ego-centred attitudes and opening to a fuller reality**.

Regarding the third exercise; reverence, this same requirement is obviously also involved. If one can not bend the knee, sensing that the ego needs to acknowledge humbly that it is in the presence of something of exceptional goodness, then reverence is impossible. The point of this third exercise is to develop a selflessness in the emotional life; this is of enormous importance for the path. No progress of a wholesome kind can be made if this is not present. Indeed danger lurks ahead if we carry any arrogance or selfish goals – and this includes the unsuspected subconscious type – into esoteric matters. So long as a continual earnest effort is made towards the removing of arrogance from the soul-life, then there is no danger. This third exercise, which like the others is designed to develop permanently a new quality in one's personality, is especially effective. It works strongly against normal subtle egotism in the emotive-desire life.

The fourth exercise, of devotion, is very clearly connected to learning how to reduce the personal egotistical qualities, this time in the will itself. The will is a powerful part of the soul-life; it is here that self-centredness has its real empowerment. One wills to get to the top, to have the best for oneself, for example. To be determined is basically a matter of will, if there is a tempting reward for us, then our will is enthused. If there is no personally pleasurable reward, the will is curiously weaker. This is personal ambition, it is not connected to devotion, which is selfless willing. By practising this fourth exercise, one is gradually working at reducing the self-centredness or personal ambition in the will, and replacing it with a selfless will. It is a vital process to so spiritualize the will forces; otherwise hardened power-seeking develops as esoteric knowledge grows, and one then seeks to dominate others through occult abilities.

Seeking power over others is the nature of the 'shadow of the will'; its darker side. For example, this exercise can be done as part of the task of living in attunement with your the higher-self in daily life. For example, when selecting your organic fruit at a shop. Such produce will have various external flaws on them, and some will have the occasional inedible bit showing up as a patch on the skin. Why should one actually select from the bin only the most perfect items, leaving the less perfect for 'the other people'? Is not the will revealing even in such little matters, its self-centredness? Naturally, I'm not suggesting we take entirely only the least attractive items, but rather a mixture of good and imperfect produce.

In this way others also may share the good items, and the grower/seller will not have the expensive problem of rejected produce. Here we see in contemporary form, the concept of surrendering one's personal self-centred existence, and opening up to a selfless condition. But its primary application is in staying with a task that does not benefit oneself personally, rather it benefits the rest of humanity. This was expressed in the Scriptural words... "Whoever loses his soul for my sake will find it..." (Gospel of St. Matthew 10:39) The great esoteric dramatist, poet and scientist Johann Wolfgang von Goethe expressed this idea in these words: "So long as you have it not, this dying and becoming, you are but a dreary guest upon this dark Earth".[45]

Now, it is clear that these Four Mood exercises are very important not only from their ethical aspect, but from their ability to greatly promote success in meditation. However, there is yet another extraordinary importance to these exercises; it is connected with the mystery of the 'primal infant'; this is not be confused with the more exoteric 'child within' concept.

Becoming one with the primal young child within
Consider again, that there is another common link among these four exercises, something that connects them. To find out what this is, we need to ask: is there anyone of whom it may be said that they have all

---

[45] Goethe: The West-East Divan, in the book of The Singer.

these qualities? To have a natural sense of how awesome the world is, to be spontaneously wonder-filled; to revere beauty and abhor lies and evil; to be socially loving, devoted to others or the common good.

The answer is; yes! In fact millions of such people exist, or rather, millions of such **young children** exist! For these divine qualities are precisely what each infant has within its innocent little being. Every sensitive parent knows just how awe-struck, how wonder-filled, a tiny child is at the moon, or a sun-set, a musical note, blossoming flowers, and so on. One knows too, that they have an exceptional ability to revere that which is holy and good; this is already evident in infants, although they may not be able to express it so well, but it is there. Another way to see this ability is to recall how they inherently experience indignation and repulsion when someone lies.

The quality of being devoted, of being selfless in the will is also present in the young child but not so easy to perceive perhaps. There are however, times when the young child will spontaneously yield up something, or offer comfort when it perceives someone in distress. These moments speak of a powerful social sense and this is due to a selflessness in the will, the volitional life. What is actually offered to us through these four moods? That method whereby we can access the source of true spirituality; and the qualities present in the human spirit, qualities which illumine the being of every infant. That method whereby we can restore to our adult personality the divine spirit-attunement inherent in our being, but which is normally only present during our infancy.

A wholesome yet profoundly esoteric path through which those divine qualities that waft through the aura of an infant can become once again present in the adult personality. The divine reality in which the infant was living until its descent to the Earth is the origin of this spirituality. Because it has only recently descended from the spiritual world, this nearness to the spirit is possible. One could also say, the infant is enveloped in its higher-self. Furthermore, not only is it recently descended from the spirit realms, but another significant factor is the absence of any real ego, and hence egotism. As the child grows, usually a little after its second birthday, it begins to say "I". As this occurs, and earthly ego sense develops, the primal spirituality fades away.

Relevant here are the words of the cosmic Christ concerning gaining attunement with the spiritual realms. "Unless you change, and become like little children, you shall not enter into the Kingdom of the Heavens." (Gospel of St. Matthew 18:3) In other words, unless an adult undergoes an inner change, becoming childlike, she or he can not merge their consciousness with the spiritual realms. On the basis of the above, inner study of spiritual ideas, and developing the appropriate moods of life, one can approach the deep mystery indicated in these words. Success in meditation is not likely if the process of self-transformation, in the sense of the above exercises, is not being actively lived.

The golden rule

In "Knowledge of the Higher Worlds" a golden rule is given, the very kernel of this path. **"When you attempt to take one step forward in the knowledge of hidden truths, make three steps forwards in the ethical improvement of your character"**. This statement is often referred to in a brief form, as "for every step forwards in esoteric development, take three steps forward in ethical development." This, like the above exercises has more to it than what we at first realize. In his psychological teachings, Steiner defines the mind as having three distinct qualities or powers. Namely, thinking (logical faculties), emotions (desires and yearnings etc) and volition or will, this latter being the capacity to make a resolution. It is axiomatic in his approach that we are to transform our soul (or mind) to allow its spiritual potential to emerge.

Hence it is clear that this golden rule is in effect saying that only upon the basis of personal moral betterment can esoteric development be properly achieved. In this process, the emotions and desires lose their earthly sensuality and innate self-seeking quality; a wonderful beauty or purity of soul emerges. Further, the thinking life loses its abstract deadness and hence materialism recedes. The thoughts thus become more alert, sensitive, and holistic. And the will or volition loses inherent aggressive, competitive tendencies. This is replaced by a sense for community, of working for the common good.

The reader will know that there are a variety of organizations that offer techniques for the developing of occult powers and clairvoyance, or 'clear-seeing'. However, any such techniques which do not have the intensive moral renewal process as their basis, as elucidated above, but rather just utilize occult techniques, are not recommended by the teachers of the path presented in this book. The purpose of spiritual development is often associated with "self-knowledge", but there are two sides to this idea. Firstly, there is the process of becoming more informed and insightful about one's personality.

Both negative and positive tendencies may not be clearly perceived, so making the effort to integrate the personality and learning about the various less obvious aspects of our personality is most valuable. This is indeed gaining knowledge of the self, the personality. However, the second aspect to this expression 'self-knowledge' is about the great task of merging the current personality with the higher divine qualities of our spirit. This is seeking "Self Knowledge"; self with capital 'S'. To gain knowledge of this self, is to set one's foot upon the path to the divine spirit within our inner being. Naturally, before an acolyte attains to union with the real **Self**, there must be **self**-knowledge.

A dialogue about this by Rudolf Steiner expresses the essential truth of real spiritual development, namely that one's personality transforms, and upon the basis of that the journey to the spirit is possible:
The Master questions: "You are seeking self-knowledge? Will your so-called self have more significance for the world tomorrow, once you have found this self?" (The master then gives two possible answers.)
First answer: No, if tomorrow you have not changed, and the knowledge of tomorrow which you gain is only a restatement of your being of today.

Second answer: Yes, if tomorrow **you are different** from what you are today, and in fact, your new being of tomorrow is the result of the self knowledge you are gaining today".

The initiate perceives this 'becoming different' as a result of seeking spirituality through the exercises of this path. It is as if egotistical soul-substance dissipates from the aura of the meditant, and in its place, new light-enfilled substance comes into being. This 'dying and becoming' occurs both through the study and Four Moods exercises and is the elusive vital factor upon which success in meditation depends.

We must permeate our adult personality with the spirituality of our infancy, then the light of the spirit may arise within us. Then our divine higher-self may find something in us with which it may unite. Having united, it may then begin to transform our soul.

Appendix 1

Rudolf Steiner's works are not as easy to read as New Age writings. This is because he does not intend giving fascinating and thrilling descriptions of higher realities; he has a different purpose. Namely to provide material that conveys in concepts, in ideas, the actual nature of the spiritual reality, and to demand some effort to rise above everyday thinking. . If one perseveres in the study then one learns to **think spiritually**, not only to feel higher feelings; when this happens then those truths have become integrated into the self. There are however some problems for the new-comer to his writings. As there are about 150 books/booklets in English, where does one start?

The author's new book **This is Anthroposophy: a Rudolf Steiner Compendium** provides a clear and insightful introduction to his teachings for the modern reader.
And also written by Rudolf Steiner himself is his introductory book entitled; "Theosophy". The new edition of this book has been very well up-dated in its language, but it retains the rather misleading title, "Theosophy". Theosophy, as you will know and expect, is primarily a body of oriental wisdom, not connected with Rudolf Steiner, but connected to ancient Indian wisdom.

However this book is challenging, it is not designed to be easily read. Its remarkable style demands totally conscious involvement with the text. There is another Steiner text which offers an overview of Anthroposophy, and includes a chapter on the above themes. it is titled, "An Outline of Esoteric Science." It is not written as a challenging test, but its main chapter, on cosmology, is at first difficult to grasp. However even if you at first just absorb some of its powerful and awesome images, and then proceed on to the rest of the book, that is of real benefit. You can return to the main chapter later, in a more analytical way.

However, once you have read these texts you will then be able to read other titles, which are mainly the lecture cycles, for these use specific terms which are explained in the above book. It is the study of this material which is so valuable for inner development. It has the conceptually based presentations of spiritual truths that assist the soul to develop the chakras and to thereby remain an integrated person, whose ego-sense is retained in spiritual experiences. There are also introductory lecture cycles such as "The Theosophy of the Rosicrucians" or "At the gates of Spiritual Science", but again they are archaic and awkward in translation. However, you will probably find his smallish book, "Cosmic Memory: Atlantis and Lemuria" fairly easy to read and very enjoyable.

There is also a large and growing body of secondary literature, which often expresses in clear contemporary language a specific aspect of Rudolf Steiner's teachings, such as family dynamics and parenting, personal growth, the education system and bio-dynamic agriculture, etc. These are available in Steiner book stores.

CHAPTER FOUR

Clairvoyance and threshold experiences
Exploring the various phenomena which occur when meditating.

As I commented in the preface, the purpose of such chapters as this, is to provide the reader with the knowledge of the processes and demands placed upon a meditant who is seriously seeking to enter into the initiatory pathway. One does not have to feel daunted by the rigours of the journey, it is enough perhaps to know the challenges encountered by a person crossing the threshold.

In Chapter One we saw that visionary experiences are quite naturally connected to developing higher consciousness. This means that even if your interest in meditating is expressed in terms of enhanced spirituality or nearness to God, one should anticipate visions and even clairvoyance as a result of meditating. This chapter will explain why this is so, and consider some of the deeper aspects of clairvoyance, **even though psychic faculties are not a goal in themselves.** The idea is often expressed that a technique is needed to directly stimulate the chakras, in order to acquire clairvoyant experiences; this is not the viewpoint of Rudolf Steiner. The chakras are vortices in the aura, by which higher vision is possible; their nature will be explained in detail, later. How does true initiation knowledge strive to develop higher vision actually? Although clairvoyance (**psychic-image** consciousness) is neither the sole goal of meditating, nor is it the only theme of this book, it is nevertheless important that we spend some time considering this aspect of the path.

Rudolf Steiner, who developed and trained his higher faculties to a degree seldom attained, was able to study with great precision, the intricate changes occurring in both ether-body and soul-body. He found that in meditating, both of these 'subtle bodies' are lifted partially out of their normal connection to the physical body. It is one of the aims of esoteric meditating to create a slight 'inner' tendency for this to happen. This process however is entirely unable to induce out-of-body experiences or any other strange change of consciousness in a person with a healthy soul-life. That is not its purpose.

Before we explore what the body of initiation knowledge provided by Steiner has to say about the chakras, it is necessary to consider further the theme of loosening the connection between the soul and body. We noted above that, in a certain sense this is the aim of deeper meditation; now a brief historical survey of the path to Initiation is needed. Historical research into the ancient forms of spirituality confirms the teaching here, that in order for a person to really gain a permanent **cosmic-spiritual** consciousness in ancient times, it was necessary for them to be taken out of the body for three days. Such a process was given to a prepared acolyte as the climax of their inner development, and consolidated their higher consciousness. The acolyte was placed in a sarcophagus, like the one in the great pyramid of Egypt, and then carefully guided out of the body.

To understand what this mysterious process was, we need to briefly consider some aspects of our higher being. The human soul appears to the seer as an auric cloud; in this our consciousness dynamics manifest, forming a variety of forms and swirls of colour (or rather 'colour-impressions'). In addition to this well-known 'aura'; we also have a body or coherent organism formed of life-energies; called ether-forces in this book. This life-force organism or ether-body is the actual vivifying energy behind our sense impressions; it is also the energy utilised in healing and involved in sexual activity.

Without this ether-organism our sense impressions would be simply of a 'flat' lifeless physical nature; the vivid livingness of a musical note, or a colour, which we constantly perceive (although semi-consciously), would not be registered. This ether-body is the intermediary between soul-body and flesh body; it mediates that which occurs in the soul – thoughts, emotions, intuitions, and spiritual insights through to our physical consciousness. Whatever our soul perceives is imprinted into the life-force body as images or moods, and in this way we become aware of these experiences.

Therefore throughout several millennia, the ancient Mystery Centres carried out the above procedure. The acolyte was taken out of the flesh body, which lay in a hidden crypt, and directly experienced the spiritual realms. After three days he or she was brought back carefully into their body. However, before returning the person to the body, this vital task of imprinting into the ether forces the vortex-pattern of chakras that had developed in the soul was carried out. In fact, by having the ether-body likewise a little detached, it in turn is especially exposed to that which exists in the soul. Furthermore, as the meditant lives faithfully and regularly into the daily meditating, a new and potent spiritual reality develops in the soul. During the night-time this reality gradually permeates the ether forces, slowly attuning them to the soul's chakra system.

Inside the great pyramid of Egypt is the famous empty sarcophagus; likewise at the once sacred ancient Mystery Centre 'The Externsteine' in northern Germany one may see a stone sarcophagus. These sarcophagi were not built to house a preserved mummy, but were used by acolytes at the time of their extraordinary three-day out-of-body process, which was the age-old classical method of initiation. However, the skilled assistance of various helpers was needed, for example in medical procedures, as only with this help could such a process occur.

As Rudolf Steiner explains, this same process is referred to in a veiled way in the Bible; namely in the story of Jonah being swallowed by a whale, an event that lasted for three days (Jonah 1:17). It is significant that the cosmic Christ, in His 'over-shadowing' of Jesus (and becoming one with him gradually in many respects), declared that He would give the sign of Jonah to His contemporary world. This is a reference to His sacrifice involving a sojourn of three days in the spiritual world (whilst the body was on the cross). Modern theology does not consider these esoteric matters, as mainstream Christianity, in the main, does not give credence to the esoteric depth that once lived in its own tradition. It is a matter of initiation, presented in imaginative form, obviously in accordance with ancient classical guidelines for presenting spiritual verities to the wider community. The enormous fish refers to the soul world, into which Jonah was cast.

So, summarising the invaluable teachings of Steiner on this subject, in the ancient process of initiation the high initiate guiding the process would **impress the pattern of developed chakras existing in the astral body into the acolyte's ether-body.** Once this was done, then the person could remain clairvoyant, whilst living within their physical body, and could remain in communion with the higher worlds. For clairvoyance (or the higher experiences of **cosmic-spiritual** consciousness) to be present, the ether-body must have received a copy of the chakra-pattern that has by now developed in the soul. That is, the life-forces of the meditant have to receive this pattern into themselves, like the image on a metal stamp impressed into a warm wax. This is the secret of attaining to actual reliable, accurate clairvoyance.

If the ether-body lacks this replicated pattern, then the acolyte can have awareness of the spiritual realms only in exceptional circumstances, or during the night-time. What is being experienced by the soul (or astral body) would not become registered in the consciousness of the person. Because, as we saw earlier, all impressions from the senses or from the soul have to be conveyed to us by the ether-body. Whether the impressions are from the sense-organs, or from the soul, with its 'eyes'.

Rudolf Steiner's lectures and writings reveal this secret of the process and also explain that this is the key to developing higher consciousness, although in modern times it must be carried out in a different way. Concerning the matter of chakras, it is the primary intention of this path to ensure that meditating on transcendental verities will direct the soul's attention up to the spiritual. As a result of this concentrating on such 'higher' matters, the ether and astral bodies slightly rise out of their normal dense connection with the physical body. Then, to the extent that the meditant has developed the astral chakras, these will imprint their pattern into the ether-body. When the soul is a little lifted up from the body, as it is in esoteric meditating, it is much easier for the chakras to form.

Meditating in this sense is the method that replaces the now obsolete 'sign of Jonah', the difficult and odd state of being taken out of the body for three days by other persons. It has the equivalent impact on the 'finer bodies' of the meditant. Having this imprinting process undertaken with the help of a hierophant (that is, the leading initiate) is no longer possible or advisable. For today the ability exists to inwardly lift one's consciousness up to the spiritual by the will of the individual, who seeks spirituality. Naturally, this process also needs **the grace of the spiritual powers to be fully achieved**.

The development of spirituality (overcoming the lower self) is now achieved by **the power of our own ego,** through the effort made by the self, the ego; indeed this is the gift to humanity of the Cosmos Spirit, and the purpose of the crucifixion. It is vital that the conscious ego decides to undertake through its own effort, a path of refining its current personal reality. For what was once done in total secrecy, the three day initiation rite of entering in a death-like state, can now be done in the context of daily life, through the way we encounter our own inner reality and outer destiny. This ability is relatively new, and became possible because the ego can now attain the inner strength through connection to its higher aspect. In other words, there is a viewpoint here, expounded by Rudolf Steiner in many lectures, that human consciousness actually changes and evolves over the centuries.[46]

However, in the process of meditating in this deeper esoteric manner, a variety of unusual experiences can occur. This is particularly so in the beginning stages, as the subtle 'lifting up' of the higher bodies from the physical body begins. The next section explores what kind of experience ensues once this state is attained, and what causes them.

Threshold experiences
The following advice about the nature of first spiritual experiences on this path derives from the esoteric guidance lessons given by Rudolf Steiner, to which I have added the fruits of my own experiences. The reader is reminded of the motivations mentioned in Chapter One that lead people to take up this form of meditating. It is not to have bliss, it is not simply for relaxation, nor is it to have visions that are thrilling and powerful. Rather, the aim is to become so spiritualized through consistent meditating on a sacred text that the personality is merged

---
[46] See Appendix at back of book

with the higher-self. This in turn brings communion with the divine-spiritual beings through whom the will of God is manifest.

This in turn brings deep joy and also the ability to become conscious in, or to 'see' in higher realms. As we saw in Chapter One, the goal of esoteric meditation is to become attuned to the transcendental spiritual realms; where the human spirit has its origin. In human terms, the meditant is becoming ever more an aspect of their own higher divine self. On the way to this goal, perception into either the ethereal realms or the soul world may occur, but that is a lesser form of 'divinization' of consciousness.

What happens when higher faculties unfold? **The experiences will be entirely different to what the meditant is expecting** ! This point can not be over-emphasized. The meditant will at first have expectations that don't harmonize with the reality of higher experiences. Because, until one has actually 'been there', one is an armchair traveller with abstract ideas. Further, the real results take time, unsuspected flaws still lurk in the depths of the soul, and there are also opposing powers in the spiritual cosmos. Hence a number of complex results can occur, and without guidance from real esoteric knowledge, much can at first occur which is bewildering. In my seminars people often speak of these experiences and the confusion they cause, and so it is my aim in this section to explain what happens in these initial experiences.

In Chapter Two we discussed the Six Basic Exercises, including the preparatory exercise of flexibility and lack of prejudice in how one thinks. Now the results of that inner work show their value, for without an unprejudiced attitude, one can be quite baffled by the first results of esoteric meditating. The following statements may appear to be absurd. For example; those powerful, clear visions arising almost immediately when a person is learning to meditate are not the best results. Further, one may manifest in the early stages, **intensified egotism**, including the lower desires, to a degree that is really disquieting. The purpose of the following pages is to reveal the causes of various results of meditating, especially the unusual beginning experiences. In Chapter One the genuine results of meditating were described, in outline, these will also be further described here, and again in Chapter Six.

Blissfully expanding
An intensely blissful mood arises, accompanied by the feeling of spreading out over the entire world, a feeling of expanding endlessly. Contrary to popular attitudes this phenomenon is regarded in this esoteric path as something to be discouraged, not encouraged. From Steiner's advice it is clear that bliss is certainly not the goal of meditating; although it does bring a blissful sensation, this is secondary to the real goal of the path. What causes this feeling of bliss ? The

phenomenon itself is due to the fact that as our ether forces emerge out of the physical body, **they interweave with the Earth's own ether-field.**

The ether-body becomes one with the ether energies in the Earth and its atmosphere; these envelop the Earth in four layers reaching up to about 150 kilometres, and then they merge into a vast interplanetary ether field.[47] This merging of your own ethers with the planetary ethers greatly extends your field of perception, because the world-ether boundaries extend across the solar system. A sensation of expanding lightly into a vast ethereal realm is the result. (1911) Whilst this is quite naturally enjoyable, if kept in check, it is not the real goal. It is certainly not yet due to 'becoming one with God', to attaining to the lofty state of 'union with the All' referred to in ancient mystical texts. Nevertheless that is how the inexperienced meditant is tempted to think of it; and there exist various 'fallen' spiritual beings who seek to draw one up into that dynamic, and induce a yearning to prematurely escape from one's karma, and from earthly life.

Only when one's ego so spiritually empowers its own nature through merging with the higher-self, does it connect to the true divine spiritual realms. This is the result of real inner work, of expanding the actual consciousness of the ego; this brings deep joy of a wholesome type. The other 'expanding into the infinite' is an artificial or **de-facto** form of this; it is caused not by one's inner development, but simply by the dynamics inherent in the ethers. We will return to this matter when considering the nature of the tempting beings (Chapter Six).

Immediate powerful visions
Another experience the meditant may have at the beginning is startling clear visions, perhaps of a face; these visions are very hard to forget, or to get out of one's mind. Their effect is powerful and can be quite overwhelming. It suddenly happens when you are a novice, only just beginning to really meditate. Generally this phenomenon is not a sign of progress towards higher faculties. A little reflection will show that such occurrences are **not** the kind of higher vision you are seeking, for they are not controllable by you. Nor did they really arise through your efforts, except in so far as you 'opened up a window', or rather, turned towards the window.

That is, such a vision is not the result of your developing ability to **gaze into** the spiritual realms, by **the light of your purifying soul.** Rather the vision **was imposed upon you**, it suddenly appeared as you set out to find how to open the window to higher realms. There is a mighty difference here, for how does a soul see into the higher realms? By the

---

[47] See "Living a Spiritual Year" (ref.8 in Chapter One) by this author.

light developed in the purified and therefore **radiant** aura! This mystery will be discussed when the chakras are considered. For the moment just consider that **the 'power' to gaze into the spiritual is actually a power**. The more radiant the aura, the more one can behold. A powerful vision occurring almost immediately that one starts to meditate is obviously not the result of the empowerment of the inner being, for we have not yet acquired the inner radiance nor have the chakras been developed sufficiently. As we saw in Chapter Three, **meditation is designed to bestow on us properly functioning chakras, and this takes time**.

Most students who experience such a thing, have been involved in esoteric activity or in religious experiences involving potent rituals and sacramental ceremony in their previous life. (1912) In meditating one makes initial contact with one's own inner soul-life. In the case of the people mentioned, some powerful transcendental images or dynamics have been absorbed, and are present deep in the soul in this life as memories. These, being the most potent of the memories or dynamics from the past life, are the most likely to now surge up spontaneously as meditating begins.

The same phenomenon can also be caused by atavistic clairvoyance. This is an unusual condition of the soul or ether-body, derived from the widespread psychic capacities of an earlier epoch in evolution, which induces such visions. This state of consciousness will be discussed later. For both groups of people, visions of this kind can happen; it is generally better if they don't, because forces are involved which are not controllable by the student. Steiner's advice is to focus on results that are normally experienced, and not seek to have further involvement with those first images. Then they should not be able to exercise an unwelcome influence on the mind.

Another cause of strong visions which are rather peculiar and which occur soon after beginning meditating is connected with the physical body. The initial effect of meditation on one's astral body can cause a variety of short term results. For example, one unusual process that can arise is that it transmits to you, in imagery, its involvement with internal body processes. Physical-ethereal processes maintain the internal organs and general life of our body, but these are interconnected with our astral forces, there is an intimate interweaving taking place between them. For example, the health of the lungs is connected with the emotional life, for instance, and thus breathing and feelings are interwoven. The reciprocal interaction of body, life-forces and soul which is normally hidden, can be temporarily experienced in startling images by the meditant, until the soul 'settles down' into its new dynamics, and begins to form the chakras. There are other bodily experiences which meditating can cause, these will be dealt with in

Chapter Seven when the actual practical realities of meditation and life style are explored.

Experiences caused by real inner development
Here we touch upon an important point, that real esoteric spiritual development brings at first, only very subtle changes in our inner feelings, they are not powerful and dramatic. By 'esoteric' I mean experiences that derive from the effect of esoteric meditating. We now come to a vital fact of the inner life: **the most wholesome, positive spiritual experiences at the beginning stage of meditating are those which are especially subtle and unobtrusive.** For example, gradually you become aware that your consciousness is now "**body-free**" in the deeper sense of this term, (astral projection is something different; see next chapter).

You become aware that the thinking life has inwardly deepened and vivified; abstract thinking gives way to holistic insight. It is as if your consciousness is no longer body-bound regarding ideas and thoughts. Instead, intuitive insights flash across the mind's horizon; these are experienced as having a more living quality than the normal intellectual type. When this stage is reached, it is an excellent sign, because it signifies that the ether-body, the life-energy organism is now able to vivify our incarnate consciousness. Putting it the other way around, it signifies that the meditant can access spiritual, holistic insights living in the ether-body, before they reach the brain. Our thoughts are registered in the ether-energies before impinging on the brain. Consciousness is no longer so 'body-bound or 'earth-bound', it is no longer dependent upon the brain's functions for the experiencing of ideas, insights, thoughts.

Most people aren't aware of just how much our consciousness – especially higher ideas – is dominated by the body, which dims our 'inner seeing'. We often simply don't register a majority of the more subtle insights; and what we do register tends to become somewhat flat and abstract. In other words, by now the meditant can begin to contact the kind of holistic and vividly pictorial thinking that we experience as souls outside our body during sleep – and after death. One starts to sense a kind of special 'atmosphere' in your mental processes, an atmosphere or mood that is hard to describe.

Such subtle enchanted atmospheres also occur in other ways, during the beginning phase. They are hard to perceive, until you develop sensitivity to such things. For example, suddenly in the midst of doing one's daily work, some hours after meditating, the following may occur. For just a few seconds you become a little withdrawn, focussing on your inner being, enveloped in a special, inviting, enchanted mood or subtle ambience. Just what mood or thought caused this, is most difficult to describe, because as you become aware of the situation, suddenly it's gone.

Just in this subtle way, higher consciousness gradually unfolds itself. We have to form the inner eyes of the soul to behold spiritually; and this after all, takes time. It is naive to expect immediately an intense, fully formed result. These beautiful, brief moments are the result of the inner eyes starting to open. It is precisely the value of the awe and wonder exercises (described in Chapter Three) that make the student sensitive to these subtle experiences ! Insensitivity to the presence of subtle atmospheres in our soul-life will delay spiritual progress.

The student learns to be alert to these tenuous zephyrs, these spiritual breezes that shyly arrive and so quickly fade. In that way the technique is acquired of working with them; the conscious personality learns by this to become ever more sensitive to these. Gradually this ability deepens, and what was at first subtle, ethereal moods or memories become more substantial experiences. The exquisite atmosphere of these moments wherein one is at the portal of a divine reality becomes more tangible, and one can retain it for a while. These ethereal moments are of two kinds: one involves vivid memories, suffused with an exquisite magic, of your childhood; the other is of your thoughts, as if they are independently thinking in you.

There is another very important way in which real spiritual development of our soul manifests, namely in our dreams. Apart from the above subtle indicators of sanctification of one' s being, it is whilst one is asleep that the first signs emerge of an inner harmony with the spirit. Namely that dreams become clearer, much more coherent, instead of a jumble of confused pictures. And the dreams slowly become more **conscious,** which really means more self-conscious, as if you are almost aware of your day-time self in the dreaming process. This is a phenomenon of immense significance; but we will here only note these points, in Chapter Eight dreams and 'dreaming true' will be discussed in detail. In other chapters the nature of the other genuine experiences will be explored fully.

It is now necessary to clarify what is meant here by the difference between real yet subtle results of spiritualization and the temporary, less important but more obvious results. So, I will now discuss a variety of fairly common experiences of the second type – those which are quite strong but really of less long-term worth.

Nebulous colours
Quite suddenly during meditating, with your inner eye, you can see a cloud of colour, an impression of colour. Such a colour cloud could well

be an indicator of your own auric quality. Nevertheless it is advisable to consider whether it is not quite a different 'message'. Let's say that the colour is a delightful gentle rose-pink, which is the astral 'colour' of truly caring love. Instead of concluding that now one's intuition is enhanced by meditating, and is now revealing that one has much real love in one's soul, there is another very real possibility. Whereas for an advanced soul, this first interpretation may be true, Rudolf Steiner suggests that the beginner is well advised to consider whether the **opposite** is true.

Namely, that the appearance in our consciousness of such an inner colour sensing is the way our higher-self tells us **that we need the quality which that colour represents.** Often the correct interpretation of such a phenomenon, especially for the beginner is; "I am being told that I don't have enough genuine selfless compassion, I must work harder to acquire this quality within me". If one then works with this, then in the course of time, this pink colour impression changes to its counterpart, green. (1904) Then the process has been successfully completed. Then the counterpart colour is saying that the aura now has a strong presence of love within it. In this gentle wholesome way the higher-self begins a process of communing and instructing you. Likewise if one often senses a purple cloud nearby, this may be the sign of a lack of selfless, devout piety, the quality of being reverential in a devout manner. Our guiding angel is whispering that we need to strive more strongly towards this.(1904)

Cool wind
The meditant experiences the sensation of a cool wind blowing over the forehead, between the eyes. This is so perceptible that you stop whatever you are doing, and put a finger to the area, to see if perhaps some moisture is there. Yet there is nothing at all, no physical reason can be found for the cool sensation at all. The cause is that a centre in the aura, inside the forehead, known as the two-petalled chakra is starting to develop.(1913) It is most important to strive **to ignore** this cool feeling !

Rudolf Steiner advised that one just let it be, and keep on meditating; any focussing on it will cause a disturbingly irritating feeling. As the chakra develops further, the cool wind sensation is not so constantly present. However, it is also possible that severe head-ache can occur during the development of the forehead chakra, but the pain is localized in the area of the third eye. The pain can in some cases become really intense, but then it ebbs away.(1913)

Being lost in a vast void
This phenomenon can be a result of meditating, but it occurs only slightly and usually only if one's preparation is not properly done. It is

an unpleasant feeling of being spread over the cosmos, but it creates a feeling of not belonging 'out there'. This is another result of the ether forces spreading out and merging into the world ether; they have been too loosened from the body. This is not a major problem, if one has undertaken an intensive study of fundamentals of the spirit – as described in Chapter One – then it should not be other than a mild problem. The advice regarding this experience is that the study must be considered so important, and done so earnestly that the emotions and mood are stimulated and uplifted by it. It is this permeation of the heart (not just the head) with understanding of the structure of the cosmos, which protects one from this problem.(1910)

Croaking of the ravens
Here we come to an important secret of this esoteric wisdom, namely that as the soul arises slightly from the body, we become aware of the **astral world within us!** It is not only that one becomes psychic, and acquires awareness of things 'out there' in the astral world. It is also the case that desires, yearnings, fears and thoughts living in our own astral body (soul) are perceived. These are part of the content of our so-called subconscious. It is inevitable that the meditant takes the way to the underworld, and enters into a more conscious connection with a variety of urges deeper in the soul. However, amongst these urges there are also certain 'elemental' forces in our ether-body and in the physical body.

These resist the process of spiritualization. These urges do not manifest in an intellectual, theoretical way; they manifest as psychic visions, but especially as strange sounds. They are present in our soul subconsciously; through meditating they 'find a voice'; they become perceptible, or rather, audible, for they also produce sounds like musical notes or more often like words. For example if one has recently become vegetarian, the yearning for meat may still there but is now suppressed. Then this frustrated desire, or any other such desire, can arise as vision of an astral form, hearing of a tone or even a word.

Certain forces inherent in our physical and ethereal bodies resist the process of spiritualization; this causes the phenomenon of the 'croaking of the ravens'. People who eat meat will have this experience much more than vegetarians. (1910) If you have ever heard a raven croaking, then this term becomes quite a meaningful description of the strange sounds (or perhaps odd visions) that occur. As the preliminary resistance to spiritualization is overcome, and the subjective attitudes cast off, these cease. Real spiritual experiences do not have the quality of being uttered from a physical larynx, with few exceptions. Hence most of these tones, words, and noises are to be ignored. One must not focus on them, nor take them as signs of deep spiritual significance.

Regularly recurring theme-vision
Symbols or scenes from what are apparently past lives can appear already in the initial stages of meditating. A potent cause of these experiences is the yearning for fascinating spiritual experiences. This hankering after visions can **actually cause** images to appear to our mind as visionary forms and scenes. For example, there may be a powerful wish for success in meditating to impress our friends, or to confirm a delusion about a past life (**I'm** the **real** Mary Magdalene, or I was Gawain), or to view colourful scenes as replacement for boredom. Also a variety of convictions and prejudices can cause these; for example one sees a friend or colleague as if in another earlier life. This is often an expression of one's own wishes or convictions.

Any such predominating themes about spiritual issues that exist in the subconscious can repeatedly be seen as a vision once meditating starts. It is the meditant's task to attempt to identify the cause of such experiences. It is important to note that when such a vision occurs, if it is a false preliminary type, **it will dissipate when one objectively focuses on it.** (1910) When the meditant really thinks about the image with humility and clarity of mind the vision fades away. To be objective is not easy, if the vision is in fact the expression of some subjective attitude. It could be a valid portrayal of a crucial experience from a past life or a vital dynamic living in our soul now. However it is usually a subjective image manifesting some dominant motif in one's ego-centric yearnings.

The best advice here is to not become flattered or fascinated by such initial visions, as most of one's initial experiences are not objective. There is another aspect to this matter; some objective image is granted to you, but unresolved desires colour the vision so that although it is genuine, it becomes distorted. As one cleans out these little dusty corners of the soul, the visions become perceived correctly. Hence to place trust in those first experiences is rarely wise. As an ego-centric impulse about your past life, dies away, then a deceptive vision of you as Master of the Knights Templars will also die away. Then a true vision can gradually be experienced at a later stage.

We can also enter our own inner world of lower desires and impulses insofar as these have not been overcome; sometimes moral codes in society do not allow these to be expressed. So a variety of tempting visions or subtle desires can be experienced. It is very sound advice to distrust all such initial visions, but in humility to contemplate what may be the cause of them. If they are valid, then in time they will metamorphose into a truer form. If they are false, they will disappear, as noted above. Later we will see just what kind of beings attempt to distort one's inner life; in any event, caution is advisable.

Discomfort and ill-health
The meditant on the path of an ongoing study program and exercises of the Four Moods, will become a more sensitive person. She or he will become less 'at home' in the physical body and more aware of the quality of its different parts and processes. Subtle changes in the dynamics of an internal organ are now sensed, whereas in the past, it would not have been noticed until definite pain began to appear. Furthermore, it is usually the case that our physical body and life-force organism usually do not perfectly match and harmonize; Rudolf Steiner reports that small areas of friction exist but are not very perceptible.

They are not perceived that is, until meditation brings one to a greater sensitivity to life and to one's own ether-organism. Such increased sensitivity often results in one becoming aware of these friction areas, and hence it may seem as if since starting to meditate you have become unwell. This is not really the case, and with increasing sensitivity comes increasing inner strength with which to cope with these minor irritations.(1911 & 1913)

Furthermore, **temporary ill-health** can arise as a direct consequence of meditating, because it slightly releases the ether forces from the physical body, as a new general condition. This has the effect of reducing very slightly the flow of rejuvenating life-energies through the physical body; hence wheresoever your body has a weakness, an illness tendency, this may manifest. One becomes a somewhat more fragile person for a while; the usual remedies may not work as effectively as before.

However, as the inner work continues then the ether-body starts to compensate for this by mediating forces into the physical body from the world ethers. **Then, the process reverses**, and one's health improves; wounds may even start to heal more rapidly. (1913)

A further point concerns a feeling of dizziness. If this happens then you need to shorten the time you meditate; and one also needs to earnestly ask oneself just what is causing the problem. There may be some other cause for this apart from making yourself meditate too long; your intuition will gradually reveal what is the underlying cause. (1911)

The parting of the ways
A major change of considerable importance will be an inner uncertainty that effects your self-expression. It is not permanent, but it lasts for a while. That is, you find that your thoughts express themselves without you really sanctioning it. Another expression of this is that you have to

consciously determine what you think about something, whereas previously you quite naturally formed your conclusions. Amongst the immense contributions made by Steiner to psychology is an insightful modern re-statement of ancient knowledge about the mind's structure; that it has a three-fold dynamic. We have thinking - logic, rational deductions, and emotions - desires, wishes and 'feelings'; and we have our will -a volitional capacity through which we make decisions. One discovers after meditating for some years that the emotions, desires and the will also take on a life of their own.

Your ego must determine by inner effort just how your mind will function; it no longer simply goes on as it used to, gliding along in the natural way that the mind usually functions. What is happening? These faculties that constitute the threefold mental power, no longer simply 'automatically' interrelate their functions to each other; you have to consciously interrelate them to each other. This is the result of an inner awakening tendency, through which the thinking, emotional life and volition separate into independent faculties. The uncertainty that manifests in one's way of being because of this new development, in self-expression for example, settles down as you take up the challenge. Later this 'splitting up' becomes a very substantial new dynamic. It is actually of great importance.

These three aspects of our consciousness are kept in a healthy inter-relatedness by our ego or self. However, upon crossing over the threshold, we discover that these three elements separate, so to speak. The esoteric path brings true self-knowledge; for example, the meditant discovers what the contents of her/his subconscious really are, for this becomes perceived as astral forms. Likewise the higher-self becomes an experiential reality. With regard to the normal soul-life, this becomes experienced as three distinct strands each with their own inner spiritual reality, and with an inner life of their own. This phenomenon is described in detail in "Knowledge of the Higher worlds; How is it Attained?". Here we need to note that in normal life our thinking, emotions and will are interwoven into a seeming unity. However, as the meditant's consciousness attains a higher state through meditation, these three faculties tend to become independent.

Our guiding angel no longer gives a sustaining underlying support to the mental processes; **one is now to more consciously experience thinking, emotions and volition**. The ego has to exert itself more to ensure a normal healthy functioning of the mind. Eventually, in a striking confirmation of anthroposophical psychology, a meditant begins to livingly experience herself or himself as having a threefold or triune being, not just a generalized single consciousness. This separation of the three mental qualities also occurs whenever one is 'exploring' higher realms.

How this manifests is usually that you find your thinking-life becomes looser, so to speak. For example, earlier on, a certain thought quite naturally followed upon perceiving a particular object, then other thoughts followed, as if attaching themselves to the first thought. This now tends to be replaced by a feeling of uncertainty, and instead of confidently coming to a conclusion, to an assessment of something, one is not sure quite what to think. The ego must now consciously exercise its thinking faculty. Likewise, with emotions and the will, one can feel less in charge of them.

They tend to respond to events too immediately, without the ego having assessed whether it is appropriate to respond in that way. Why is all this happening? Because in this way, we are encouraged to become more responsible for our triune soul-faculties. That the meditant is now left more to his or her own initiative is part of the wise guidance of the angel; who does not depart from its human charge, in the full sense. That is, one is encouraged to take on responsibility for the further refining of the soul-forces, and hence how one lives and responds to life. Rudolf Steiner is also recorded as saying to his esoteric students that sometimes we are even given minor illnesses, to help us become aware of the imperfections in the soul, which are now more liable to manifest.

Disturbingly odd experiences
Earlier we noted that the ether forces are to be drawn up slightly upwards, and hence out of the body. The Esoteric School students were informed this can cause the odd, but only temporary result, that in meditation you may become aware that you seem to be no longer seeing, hearing or aware of other sense impressions. (1909/13) They were told that this brief state of being disconnected from 'everything' (everything physical) can occur shortly before the phase is attained wherein consciousness opens to the higher worlds. An additional experience is that of sensing a heaviness in the brain and indeed throughout the body. It is as if these have become a heavy weight, instead of being more or less unnoticed; and together with this sensation you gain the impression that your body no longer is part of you.

Rudolf Steiner pointed out that gradually your awareness moves from the body, which is losing its normal aliveness as the ether energies slightly withdraw, to the soul. Then you become aware of what is happening to the soul, rather than what the body is undergoing. I feel that this experience has a similar cause to that which happens when one is leaving the body at night in sleep, and is able to be somewhat conscious of this process. For a moment, you seem to perceive the body falling, when in fact it is not. It is actually that your soul is rising up towards the ceiling, as Rudolf Steiner, explains this is the cause of the sensation of a sudden jerk.[48]

However, a kind of bi-location of consciousness occurs at that moment, wherein you are partly in your body, and partly in the astral body. The result of this is that you experience the illusion of falling. Secondly, another aspect of this may be awareness of the astral body hovering somewhat vertically near the bed, but with bi-locational consciousness, you seem to sense a stranger standing near the bed.

Although it is unlikely, you may experience whilst in meditation another odd thing, a kind of unpleasant 'quirk'. These rarely occur, but in the case of a person with a healthy, integrated personality, they are normally due to a traumatic event of the past. An example given in Rudolf Steiner's esoteric lessons is that a person may become aware that, whilst in meditation, he or she is faintly hearing a howling or meowing of a wounded dog, or cat. If this does happen, and it is only an example, it is caused by the fact that when you were a child (or in a very sensitive state) you witnessed a horrible scene, such as a dog or cat being killed in an accident. Its cries of pain were heard by you, and they were, of course, imprinted powerfully into your ether energies. As your soul becomes more exposed to your ether forces, through the process of meditation, the sense-impressions that are stored in the ether-body become perceived.

For the soul interweaves itself into the ether-body by imprinting its own chakra structure on it. In other words, since all sense impressions are stored in the ether-body, including the accident scene involving the dog, this becomes registered by the soul. (1913) It could possibly even happen that you realize in meditation that your voice itself is softly producing some of this howling. That is of course unpleasant, but not in any way harmful; and it will generally stop soon. For the sake of clarity it is important to know in this connection that the kind of meditating described in this book certainly does not in any way link you up to animal forces. Incorporating lower astral forces into one's aura by invoking those of an animal or its group-soul (power-animal) is **not** recommended in this pathway.

It is simply that during meditation, when this interweaving process is actually occurring, any outstanding memory-picture (including its associated noises) is registered by the soul. This could even be expressed by the physical body, for example through the voice. The ether image presses into manifestation, so to speak. That is however, very rare and unlikely, and would mainly apply to such an old stored

---

[48] R. Steiner GA 143 page 69.

memory-picture from a traumatic incident that you have forgotten or repressed.

The second cause of experiencing something unpleasant whilst meditating – which is not caused by any soul flaw of one's own – is connected with the decadence of modern civilisation. If whilst you are meditating, someone in a nearby room is viewing a so-called 'adult' video or a violent/horror video or reading a book of such a kind, then you may find truly disturbing images and words reverberating through your mind. Such entertainment activity will disappear when a spiritual wisdom governs society, and that which invokes lower beings, and strengthens their grip on people, is no longer legally protected. The meditant becomes susceptible to such potent astral thought-forms in the vicinity, for you are in a much more sensitive state in meditation. (1909)

Further, such negative influences, in so far as they are physically manifested, for example in the sound-track, can be detected by your ether-body, and whilst in meditation, you encounter them in your ether-body. This may cause dismay until you realize that the lewd uncleanness did not originate from your own being. This perception by the ether-hearing can occur even though the sound is too faint for the ears to detect, or rather for the brain to resolve into distinct words. However, for the developing meditant, this phenomenon means that a psychic associate who detects these thoughts in one's aura could gain a skewed impression of one.

Another cause of a negative image or thought occurring is when you are meditating in an environment which is antagonistic to spiritual matters. Especially when the antagonism has been specifically aroused, either against you or your group or because of a recent controversy. (1911) Then the thought-forms of 'anti-spirituality' are active and this can lead to a meditator hearing inwardly a phrase like; "The idea that we live on after death is drivel". In today's coarse world, the words you perceive may be much less polite than that, in fact very indecent. (Remember the words do not derive from you!)

These antagonistic, impure thoughts can in fact drift towards a source of spirituality (someone in meditation) to express their inherent hostility, for a certain hostile elemental force lives in such dynamics. I am pointing out these negative matters so that you are not put off should they occur. In the main, meditation does not lead into such things, on the contrary, as I have repeatedly indicated, **it is an activity that confers profound joy**.

In Chapter Seven a method of defence against such problems is given, as well as other practical hints. Further, in meditation one could have a puzzling vision of an image that seems strangely familiar, associated with a sense of disquiet. As the initiate Steiner explained to his students in Germany, this kind of vision can be caused by the effect of a painful illness that you underwent in the recent past, perhaps when an operation was necessary. The suffering is imprinted in the ether-body, and retained there, as another memory image of one's life. In meditation this will also be registered by the soul as in the traumatic accident scene mentioned above.

However, and this is a tenet in anthroposophical psychology, if in meditation you encounter this memory in the ether-body, its vibration will activate other such traumatic memories of **similar type** that are present in the ether-body. Now those other memories may be from your childhood, and will include the nightmarish inner quality which a child's soul experiences in suffering. This additional unpleasant mood merges into the primary recalled memory image of the recent operation; the result is perhaps a vision which one experiences as quite unpleasant. (1912) Yet it is simply your own inner emotional stresses and stored memories merged into a unity; nothing 'objective', about which you need to be concerned.

Ethereal clairvoyance: seeing etheric life-energies
Finally, we need to note that as meditation continues we may discover that a form of higher vision is developing, bringing perception of radiant ethereal energies around one. You may then wonder just what is happening, whether your eyes are playing tricks, for it is not as if you are perceiving the actual soul or spiritual realms. In this phenomenon, you do not have intense visions that rivet your attention in the way that classical astral clairvoyance does.

Instead you become aware that ever so tenuously and shyly on the edge of your consciousness some remarkable glowing points of light or lines of energy are being perceived. These seem in fact to be almost physical or perhaps due to a defect inside your eye and being so faint they are easily ignored.

Actually, this faculty is of great importance because it has been developing in people since early this century, quite spontaneously. It is more clearly developed through the pathway described here, but it is simply also developing as a new faculty - a kind of sixth sense - in the course of evolution. This new dynamic is described by Rudolf Steiner in lectures in 1910 about the new clairvoyance.

In fact one of the tragedies of modern times is that precisely this faculty of seeing into the ether world which is happening on a wide scale is being generally ignored. This means that a potent force in civilisation for the overcoming of materialism, with its often damaging technological schemes, is being neglected. In an effort to address this situation, as well as to help those people who are experiencing, or wish to experience this, I will describe etheric vision further on. We shall see that this phenomenon is connected to activity undertaken by Christ.

Changes in ethical values and habitual attitudes
This refers to psychological changes caused by the transformation processes invoked through meditating. However, we will defer a discussion of this until the next chapter, when further secrets known to the esoteric path concerning the threshold will be considered. The threshold is the boundary between our physical consciousness and the higher worlds.

CHAPTER FIVE
The dark night of the soul

"The veiled statue of Sais" (In a temple of Isis at Sais, long ages ago)

...The acolyte, full of wonder, noticed a large veiled statue, and asked; "What is it, that is hidden behind this veil?" "The truth" came the answer. "What !?" he cried, "I am striving solely for the truth, and it is precisely this, that one covers from my gaze? "Arrange that with the goddess", responded the hierophant.[49]

Friedrich Schiller (1795)

Crossing the threshold into the spiritual world

In this chapter we will consider the spiritual dynamics active in a meditator who is beginning to experience higher realities. This will be followed by an exploration of the chakras from the perspective of Christian initiation knowledge. An important part of the training for success in deeper meditation is knowledge of the esoteric truths about the lower-self. Earnest meditating will at some time result in one experiencing what earlier mystics called 'the dark night of the soul'. This is a phase that a meditator goes through in the process of attaining to union with the higher-self.

It involves encountering and removing any residual lower qualities in one's soul. Until that is done, progress must not be too rapid. There is a kind of boundary or threshold which one has to cross to gain **cosmic-spiritual** consciousness, and this can only be safely crossed when the lower self has been met and subdued. So, impatience is very ill-advised, the process takes time, and various barriers unsuspected by the neophyte have to be dealt with.

A guardian of the threshold

"If one enters into the higher worlds, without the self-knowledge that the Guardian of the Threshold mediates to the meditant, then one can be overwhelmed and disoriented by the experiences of this realm. Then these experiences can later push through into normal physical sense-world consciousness as illusionary images and be taken as correct and accurate images."[50]

---

[49] From Friedrich Schiller's poem, "The Veiled Image at Sais", which Steiner regards as deriving from a genuine far-memory by Schiller of a too hasty acolyte seeking initiation, in ancient Egyptian times.

[50] R. Steiner, "The Threshold of the Spiritual World ", chapter 'Concerning the boundary between the sense-world and the higher worlds'.

We assume at first that meditating is a personal private matter, something that we undertake and strive to achieve as our own personal life-goal. For example, it is natural to assume that if deeper spiritual insights are achieved or visions occur, this is something that we have brought about by ourself. We have raised our consciousness above the mere material sense perceptions, and become free to extend our experience of life into the spiritual spheres. However, this assumption is only partially correct, for when a meditator does 'cross over the threshold', a certain being who protects the threshold has given permission for this to happen, so to speak. The old saying, "no person is an island" is especially true when spiritual matters are involved. In this chapter we shall explore the nature of this protector being.

As I indicated in Chapter One, we are not alone in the activity of seeking the spirit. It may at first be astonishing to consider the idea of a protector guarding the entry to the spiritual world, but some reflection will show just how valid this idea is. For example, why is it that each time we leave the body in sleep, we lose awareness of our environment; why is there no perception of some higher reality? It is because if one were then to have direct awareness of the other worlds – and the full extent of our interaction with this would include the lower self – this would be deeply disturbing, for the personality is not ready for this.

The personal self would encounter the real truth behind the subtle intellectual materialism that can permeate our thinking, or earth-bound desires, and this would be disturbing, considering that the personality can be reluctant to give up traits that belong to the ego-centric illusory self. However, if we reflect upon the interweaving of our own soul-life with the spiritual, we can become aware that precisely when we are falling asleep, and as we gradually awaken, some kind of spiritual experience does tend to occur. This phenomenon is mentioned by Steiner in lectures on awareness of the interaction that occurs, subconsciously, between the incarnate and the discarnate.[51]

We really do have an interaction with the worlds beyond the physical plane, at this time. For example, we may seem to hear a voice placing a question to us, or have a faint picture of a past epoch or some other unusual scene before our mind for a second. There are two occasions when a transitional state occurs, as we separate from the body; we leave it in the evening, and we return to it in the morning. So, at these times, we are neither fully in the body, nor in the spiritual world. It is then that the 'doors of perception' are slightly ajar, and we can have a brief awareness of the beyond. Yet only a brief glimpse, because that is all we

---

[51] For example, see his lecture, "The presence of the dead in our life", 25 May 1914".

can assimilate. At these two times, we are crossing the border or threshold between physical consciousness and the higher worlds.

But **a meditator is** in effect, **someone who is requesting that the blinkers be fully removed from the inner eyes**. So that they may be permitted to enter consciously, gradually and gently, into the spiritual world. The wisdom behind the world order has arranged human life so that we generally have no encounters with that which is beyond until we are ready for it. Although this is not strictly true, for there exists this faint interaction with the spiritual world as we enter and leave sleep. Secondly, because humanity does have free-will, it is possible for a person to 'rush past' the guardian and plunge unprepared, into the other realms.

The main way in which this improper process is carried out is by hallucinogenic drugs. The negative results of doing this will be clarified later. The Old Testament allegory of the spiritual being with the flaming sword at the gates of paradise stopping Adam and Eve from entering could be applied to this very real inner dynamic of the human being after the Fall. It refers to the guardian of the threshold, whose task is to prevent people from a premature encountering of the full hidden extent of their own being.

The threshold, where we meet the spiritual world
In ancient times, the threshold or the lower sill of a doorway was a sacred place, a place that was also dreaded. At the threshold of great temples that served as the mystery centres of antiquity, various protecting statues were placed. These depictions of fierce monsters or powerful gods who were placed at doorways were originally guardians of the threshold. The threshold is that place which is the border between the physical world and beyond; these statues are now seen only as intriguing ethnic art. To stumble when walking through the door-way was regarded as very bad luck, a serious omen, and in some primitive societies to tread on the threshold of the dwelling place of the chieftain meant death.

In the Old Testament, it is most significant to see that the Lord - or His agents, such as mighty cherubim - was met by His prophets, **at the threshold of the temple**. This is where the clairvoyant prophets of the Hebrew mystery schools met the divine. This border between the outer world and the inner world, is the meeting place of humanity with the spiritual realms. This fact, of a protector who seeks to prevent people from being influenced by the forces and beings "over there" has a far deeper significance than we at first realize. For there are implications in just how a person develops higher faculties, both for oneself and for the community in which we live, and also for the spiritual realms.

Why is it that, as I stated above, we are not ready for exposure to the higher worlds? There are several reasons. For example, deep meditation that provides a way of connecting with the spiritual and all the joy it brings, does require inner transformation. Because our imperfections are real, and when one's consciousness enters into the astral realm, then one meets with these lower qualities. They take on a certain elemental aliveness, so to speak. Naturally, this is only a minor challenge to the earnest meditant who will be developing high ethical qualities.

Hidden flaws: acknowledging the shadow side of the soul
The pathway to enlightenment and spirituality demands that we face our inner reality with complete honesty. **When any intuitive insights arise about one's imperfections they are to be received with deep gratitude, not with resentment**. The emotional, intellectual and will forces all have a shadow side to them, but we don't normally think about this aspect of our being. This shadow-side has quite specific elemental powers within it, which possess a certain kind of life.

This shadow side is after all, not really an intrusive part of life, but it is there, and is connected to that which is active in seriously unethical behaviour. So, if one really wants to develop spiritually, using esoteric meditation, then some consideration has to be given to this subject. A technique that I found useful in my seminars to clarify the situation is to view the human soul as if it were a quantity of water in a glass, say the kind of glass tumbler that has a band of colour around the lower part. Looking at such a glass, it appears that the water is really clear. However, hidden by the colour band is a layer of sediment.

Normally, parental upbringing, education, religion and one's ethics keep the sediment right out of the picture; rarely do people who are **genuinely** on the spiritual path manifest revenge, lies, violence, adultery or other such behaviour. One strives to live an upright life, and one feels at ease with who one is. However, an acute observer of life can sense how many good and decent persons live in a state of inner tension concerning evil or immorality. This matter of unethical dynamics also includes more subtle forms of behaviour, namely jealousy of those who are regarded as more spiritually advanced, or allowing oneself to become convinced that one is far more advanced than the reality.

The dark night of the soul
This dynamic, of striving to maintain an ethical behaviour against the constant promptings of the lower self, must become intensely unsatisfactory to the meditant. It must above all be an affront to one's sense of freedom. **Freedom in this context means, the ability to act from impulses arising from the higher-self**. This is the real meaning of

freedom; it was this kind of the 'urge for freedom' that was meant in an earlier chapter. It means to manifest the impulse to be naturally ethical because that is one's inner reality, and not because the trapdoor to the basement is so firmly locked. The contents of the cellar, beneath the trapdoor, must be cleared away, rather than keeping an eye on the lock.

This subject is very important; the meditant must realize that in striving for a lofty spirituality the sediment layer has to be removed. This is known to our guiding angel, and so it happens that in the karma of one who seeks union with the spirit, the glass of water is shaken up, making tangible the potential for unethical impulses.

We experience to the full whatever lower qualities have been hiding away in corners of the soul, the clear water takes on a dusty cloudy colour. In other words, as the effort is made to really become a vessel of the higher-self and manifest the higher spirituality, the spiritual powers which regulate karma, bring to our attention the presence of whatever imperfections are in our soul's inner being. This in turn leads one to a determined effort to reduce as much as possible such qualities from one's being. The final intention is of course, to ensure in this way that the water in the glass becomes clear; however, several life-times are required to complete this. Morality from then on derives from a centre within our soul – from the presence of the higher-self – not from obedience to external laws, ethics and traditional morality. In addition, an uneasy suppression of the shadow is no longer required.

However this is not to imply that the meditant is then utterly perfected spiritually, for a complete perfecting of the soul, that is, merging of it into the human spirit, is a process which of course, only a tiny handful of people have achieved. These are referred to in religious literature as 'redeemed saints' or initiates, and indeed such persons no longer incarnate on the Earth, as the have achieved the transformation of soul into Spirit-self, and hence have conquered their lower self. It should also be mentioned that such a spiritualizing process is not actually achieved alone, it involves the activity of what in Christianity has become known as the Holy Spirit.

Further, it was forecast by Steiner that this dynamic of the lower-self becoming somewhat intensified would become a widespread phenomenon in modern times. He explained that this was not going to occur because of large numbers of people becoming interested in esoteric meditation, rather because there is a tendency psychologically now for the shadow side of the mind to become a little more active. One reason is that, as of the twentieth century, people are starting to experience a tendency towards a loosening of the soul, ether-body and physical body from each other.

This brings about a slight development of a psychic faculty, which was mentioned as causing etheric vision in the last chapter. As we have discussed, this results in increased exposure to the forces within the lower self or shadow side. Hence humanity is entering a phase that gives increased possibility for negative anti-social behaviour, **but** — and this is the main over-riding fact — **it is a phase which bestows an increased possibility for spirituality.** The consequence of encountering one's double is an intensified urge for spirituality.

The guardian of the threshold
For the meditator, the process of encountering an intensified lower-self, is much more conscious and graphic than the meeting with these forces which civilisation in general is encountering. The meditator must come to a clear realization, (as too does humanity, but at a slower rate), that in each human being a potential for evil exists. This potential derives from primordial times when the human soul life contained a destructive and fiercely self-seeking power. A fitting image of the human being in remote primordial times would be that of an anthropoid dragon on the ground, whilst above in the astral realm an innocent angelic being is hovering. Gradually over long periods of time, these two extremes have become less polarized, creating a tolerably pleasant human form, and soul with many good qualities, but hidden within there lurks a lower-self – the power of this is of course much less potent if much spiritual work has been undertaken in previous earth-lives.

Upon each return to the Earth, this force enters into the person, varying in intensity according to the degree of spirituality attained in the past life. It also varies according to the local geographical forces, that is, the elemental powers in and below the Earth at the birth place. Spiritual development could be defined as a process through which this shadow-being is greatly diminished in one's soul.

The guardian of the threshold has the task of preventing people having premature exposure to the power of the lower-self. In addition its task is to prevent premature access to spiritual secrets and powers, for this is dangerous if the higher-self has not been born within. However, when the meditant is ready, the guardian eventually reveals the lower-self to the esoteric meditant, because this is a vital factor in the process of perfecting one's being. It appears as a form which graphically expresses the lower qualities.

This protector also guards the portal to the higher worlds. Hence the soul is either permitted to have conscious spiritual experiences or is not permitted to have these, according as this being decides. That is, if one is illicitly crossing over the threshold, then by contrast the knowledge so gained is unreliable, if not completely incorrect, often personally flattering, and perhaps tinged with a malignant quality. As I mentioned earlier, a person with an insatiable thirst (an un-purified, self-centred urge) for direct higher knowledge or indeed occult power, can forcibly by-pass the guardian, via drugs for example. This however is achieved with the help of opposing powers; but then such a person becomes subject to their influence.

In the following public lecture, Rudolf Steiner, echoing a central theme of his teachings, emphasized that a serious meditant must strongly develop higher spirituality, in order to enter into the spiritual realms. That is, whether one is starting to have more meaningful dreams or working with determination on the various inner exercises experiences distinct clairvoyant 'glimpses' during the daytime, these will only reflect back subjective experiences to that person, if one is lacking the enhanced morality. "Indeed certain things in the spiritual world will speak to him, but all this that is so conveyed to him, will only be an echo of his own being...he hears his own being as 'tones' or 'words' reflected back."[52] Steiner goes on to explain that eventually the meditant who is about ready to be given access to the higher worlds, does encounter in a vision, his or her own astral reality;

> ...this all appears outside oneself as another being, not as oneself....when one experiences this, one also experiences just how strongly effective are the magnetic forces, which draw one towards one's own {not yet refined} personality. One realizes that these astral forces {despite this magnetic pull}, have to be abandoned....one observes in this experience of encountering the double, which one has been manifesting up to now, that it does not want to let one go...one feels, the more one wants to be released from these forces, the stronger is the pull back to them....Therefore it is the truth of the spiritual realms that anyone in the night, or in a meditant state, can indeed arise as far the guardian – but only those can pass by him {in a conscious state, or at least a state that will result in some conscious experiencing of the spiritual}, who pass by him through the power {engendered in their soul} of an enhanced spirituality.[53]

Two very important truths of developing higher consciousness now emerge. Firstly, this guardian is the only avenue to valid conscious spiritual knowledge, secondly, the meditant can only be validly granted access to the spiritual realms by this being if one has developed an

---

[52] Lecture 3rd April 1913, "Die Moral im Lichte der Geistesforschung"; in GA 62, page 431.
[53] Ibid., pages 436/8

enhanced spirituality. Such an encounter with the lower self presented by the guardian who adopts this form of our lower nature, may seem a daunting experience to the meditant, and indeed it is. However, it does not occur in the beginning phases of the meditative life, it does not happen until one is inwardly strong enough to cope.

From my experience of the threshold, and from my work with the thousands of pages of notes from Esoteric Lessons, and the First Class lessons, it becomes clear that there are actually three distinct ways of experiencing this being.[54] Firstly, the direct clairvoyant experience, memorably described in a fictional work by Bulwer-Lytton, and then made famous by Rudolf Steiner's book, *Knowledge of the Higher Worlds, how is it attained?* This being appears to one in an experience of which one is fully conscious, and it depicts in a pictorial form all that which is still un-spiritualised in one's soul. When we think about such a powerful encounter as this, we need to realize that such an experience requires, as indicated above, a substantially developed clairvoyance.

So this type of encounter presupposes that the meditant can perceive both the form and the thoughts that this being wishes to manifest. It is known that in his book, *Knowledge of Higher Worlds.* Rudolf Steiner was anticipating that a number of his students would achieve a more empowered spiritual development than was actually the case. This conclusion is confirmed by reports from his students to that effect. In any event, it appears unlikely that more than a tiny number of souls have progressed to this stage. A more likely experience for students on this pathway is of a preliminary nature; a brief glimpse of this being, or even a not-quite-visual, but distinctly sensed 'encounter'. From either of these considerable insight into one's 'double' is gained. The full experience, which consists of a sustained vision, with communication occurring, and tends to be ongoing, even if subtly, is a rarer experience.

The preliminary encounter happens whilst in meditation, one dimly perceives the shadowy form of this being, and indeed one can become aware of the intensely earnest admonitions coming from it. Although these admonitions are not precisely heard in the sense of a voice, yet they are intensely clearly cognized, and they make you aware of factors preventing you from entering that night more consciously into the spiritual realm. This is a deeply moving, enormously earnest experience.

---

[54] The "First Class" lessons are intended for people with a substantial background in anthroposophy, and a satisfactory outcome with these texts will require the student to actually be on the meditative path, and to understand its rigours; an understanding which is not so prevalent. This volume provides such a background.

Later, as one develops the ability to have some consciousness of – and subsequent recollection of – the night-time, one can experience oneself moving, and also beholding an abyss deep beneath oneself, with unpleasant creatures lurking in it, as one moves across it. This is not a disturbing experience, as one feels secure and more aware of some higher goal, up above, towards which one is moving.

Such experiences belong to this preliminary, less daunting encounter of that guardian that the non-clairvoyant meditant experiences at an earlier stage. These are granted by the guardian without the need for this potent vision of one's lower-self. It is my conclusion that it is normal in the process of self-initiation, for the encounters at first to be fleeting, and to occur prior to entering sleep, or in a more conscious dream experience. A direct encounter requires quite an advanced stage of inner development, a stage in which **psychic-image** consciousness has definitely developed.[55]

Now, this entire theme of encountering such a protector of the entry into the higher realities is usually quite confronting for the student in this pathway. For most meditants, the encounter will be of the second type, described above. If however, one does really strive towards the lofty goal of entering into an eternality of consciousness, that is, of merging the personality with the eternal self, then there is a third aspect to experiencing the guardian. If such a lofty goal, in all its earnestness, is not your direct concern, then this does not have to be a problem to you, but to know about these matters is important, even if one is not intending to have such potent experiences. This third aspect to encountering the guardian concerns the fact that this encounter can become a long-term and challenging process which is woven into the karma of an aspirant to self-initiation.

As Rudolf Steiner once cautioned his listeners, the normal type of encounter (the preliminary type) is only a comfortable, elementary experience. He cautions that the real encounter "…is a life struggle, a sad, tragic nuance in one's life, in respect of all concepts concerning higher knowledge, and concerning one's connections with the spiritual word, with Lucifer and Ahriman."[56] With these words, he wished to point out, rather solemnly, that the lower-self is empowered and actively seeks to pull the aspirant down into a lower ethical state than he or she had at the beginning of this life.

Many bitter lessons about one's unsuspected flaws occur, and in addition, the potential in all human beings for serious misdeeds – the

---

[55] R. Steiner, lect. 27/Aug/1912, in "Von der Initiation:von Ewigkeit und Augenblick".
[56] R. Steiner, Lect. 6th August 1918, in GA 181, p. 426

existence of which the meditant was previously oblivious – are encountered. This is a potential which does not normally intrude into the dynamics of decent people, but in the deeper striving towards spirituality, certain qualities of an undesirable kind, which have accumulated from lives on the Earth in the remote time-cycles, become activated.

Eventually though, as such qualities begin to signify their presence in oneself by creating inappropriate thoughts, desires and attitudes, the aspirant can decisively conquer them. This triumph is achieved by remaining steadfast to the discipline of meditation, with the knowledge that such a deterioration is precisely one of the temporary 'trials' through which one has to go. Gradually, the sad-tragic element in life recedes and is replaced by one of triumph.

The guardian is a complex theme, and I strongly urge the reader to study the primary texts from Rudolf Steiner, the only modern initiate who taught really clearly about this being.[57] There are actually several aspects to the nature of the guardian. The double or the lower-self, which the guardian brings to one's awareness as subtle personal insights, and eventually as an earnest vision, is slowly revealed to be an extension, almost a vestment of the guardian itself, which acts as a kind of barrier to the guardian. However, the germinal essence of one's higher-self is also closely associated with this dualistic being.

As the spiritualization process continues, and once some clairvoyance has been attained, the guardian, of whose appearance the advanced meditant will from time to time be made aware (this is really a portrayal of what is not yet transformed in one's own soul), changes for the better. For the divine higher-self works with this guardian, and oversees the inner work of the meditant; eventually, when the 'Earth-dragon' is subdued, one beholds one's higher-self in its glory.

Such esoteric truths as these were taught in pictorial fashion by those who created the fairy-tales and myths of old Europe. For example, the story of the maid encountering a bear at the doorway (this is actually, the threshold), and she sees through a rip of the bearskin, that underneath the bear is wearing a beautiful costume. But, as mentioned above, it is important to note that a really conscious encounter with this being – as a noble, independent entity that directly admonishes one, is not attained for a long time.

---

[57] In particular, "Knowledge of the Higher Worlds; How is it attained?" and "The Stages of Higher Knowledge" and ,"A Way to Self-knowledge of the human being".

As part of its helping work, the guardian permits the lower self, with its various lower forces to manifest a little more strongly when meditation is undertaken. These forces, which have an elemental life of their own, can externalize themselves occasionally to the advanced meditant, and appear as an ugly replica of one's being. Hence the lower-self can also be termed, 'the double'. That the term 'double' is used in esoteric wisdom for the shadow or evil side of the soul can be confusing. For, as many people are aware, in normal mystical literature this term only means some kind of vague second self. There are various kinds of "doubles", one of them is the rare phenomenon in which all the lower forces in one's soul steps outside the aura. You then see it as a figure, in a vision for a moment.

This rare experience which occurs normally only at an advanced stage of meditation is important because it really makes the meditant far more aware of his or her soul-blemishes. As a result, they are acknowledged and transformed speedily. However, again, this is rare, normally the meditant is simply aware that the lower qualities are somehow more real and thus demanding to be met honestly and removed. There is also another being involved, called by Steiner 'the greater guardian', the reader is referred to his Knowledge of Higher Worlds, How is it Attained? for further information.

Seeing the double – other phenomena

However it is important to note that one can see a double that is **not** an image formed by exteriorized lower qualities; there are various other causes of this phenomenon.[58] For example, Rudolf Steiner explains that in order to deliver 'a message' to a person the angel can cause one to see a double, this means in this context, simply a replica of our physical appearance. The reason for a person being given such an experience is to alter their pending actions. Unless one is definitely able to function consciously on the astral plane, that is, one is strongly psychic, the angel can only do things that will impinge on your emotions or will. For example you may be saved from an attack because, upon seeing the apparition, you then decide not to go to where you where going. (1912) The angel can also deliver a message by causing a picture to fall from the wall with a loud noise; this need not be caused by malignant poltergeist activity. (1912)

A second cause of seeing a replica of yourself is not connected to the angel, but is due to damage done to your own ether-energies. An internal organ that is extensively demanding on the life-forces may be ill. The result of this can be that a portion of your own ether-body for a split second is unable to stay properly integrated in the physical body.

---

[58] All specific statements here about the double derive from R. Steiner, especially from his esoteric schooling lessons.

This abnormality can, for complex reasons, cause a view of yourself to flash to mind, from outside, so to speak. (1913)

This is a rare occurrence, and not something to worry about. Yet another cause of seeing a replica of yourself is that the ether-body is briefly but substantially freed from the physical body; one cause of this can be a sudden shock. As it flits out, one is given a glimpse of the physical body. (1913) That's what the common expression, 'to be knocked out' means; out of one's body.

Since one of the aims of meditation is to bring about a gentle and partial separating of the life-forces from the body, it is especially possible that you may then have this experience. It is now necessary to bring the threads of the above important disclosures about the double and the guardian together, and form a clearer picture about the experiences which the meditant may have. In seeking to develop real sanctification of the soul, one is in effect asking that initially at least, the mud in the glass of water be stirred up. Before the water in the glass becomes clear, the meditant may well experience increased lower desires, and other forms of egotism. According to brief notes, Rudolf Steiner told his students that it can and probably will happen that the wise powers who guide human destiny may arrange opportunities for decadent behaviour to possibly occur, as if out of thin air, in the daily life of the earnest spiritual seeker. This is done to test whether one has developed the integrity to resist (and eventually to lose interest) in satisfying such desires. (1905)

Naturally these experiences of the lower desires in both inner and outer life reduce as one succeeds in taking charge of the double and removing such qualities from the aura. During this phase it is **vital** that one focuses with real sincerity on sacred truths and also strives to be engaged in good and creative deeds. Otherwise the personal ego might drift down into the temporarily strengthened lower qualities, empowering them, whilst undermining one's potential to develop further in this life. There is in fact the danger of the empowered lower-self becoming more potent than the similarly empowered higher-self. Rudolf Steiner describes this as the 'separating of the ego': the astral body does tend to develop and manifest some polarisation, into a lower and a higher-self.

This process does occur to some extent in every meditant, hence there is also a real possibility of the more central lower elements becoming stronger, subtle spiritual conceit, ego-centric behaviour and sexual lust in particular becoming strong. One can become ensnared in a lascivious obsession, and for the male meditant especially, this could lead to improper sexual activity. Steiner warns his students especially against this possibility. However, it is not inevitable, and is not a serious danger so long as the intense effort to maintain selflessness is not forgotten, and above all, if one has worked intensely on the preparatory Four Moods exercise.

Rudolf Steiner also advised an active involvement in artistic experiences as an antidote to this problem. (1910) It is here that one must realize that freedom from this very serious danger is as easy as it is close to hand; it is a matter of making the effort to actively divert one's ether energies into a specific developmental process.

Either one encounters the hidden lower potential, and thereby dissolves it, or one fails to rebuff it, and becomes, for a while, ensnared. The tarot card of the devil becomes relevant here; this depicts a passive devil with chains around the necks of a naked man and a woman. But the chains actually end in very large loops, so the two people can easily lift them up, and remove them. It simply requires the use of the will. The will power needed here is obtainable by **ensuring that the self centres itself in the higher, nobler personality**, not in the temporarily empowered lower drives. Not that one has any need to be unduly anxious; it is a matter of remaining earnestly true to one's intention to 'walk within the light'. In particular, Rudolf Steiner also urged the meditant, precisely in the context of being troubled by the lower self, to strive to develop humility. A particular exercise, which was recommended was the contemplation of the following idea (not in an intensely emotional way):

> "I am an egotist. The sacrifice of the cosmic Christ, on Golgotha hill, was due to such impulses existing in my own being, in so far as I am part of humanity" (1910)

He also recommended an intensified, specific striving towards impersonal love; love which is a profound good-will for all beings. In allowing this aspect of one's spirit to flourish in the soul-life, the lower self is more effectively dissolved, and the double is weakened or rather, transformed. When such love is present, one will also have a natural impulse to be involved in a form of selfless activity. The advanced meditant, when dealing with the residual echoes of these lower forces, can experience certain images of the sacrifice of Christ as a vision, that help one in this process, and also, paradoxically, testify to the loving help that the spiritual realms are offering to one in this time.

Already as a 28 year old, Steiner wrote a private document, a kind of position statement about this need for selflessness....

> There are four spheres of activity in which a person can devote themselves to the spirit and in so doing dissolve the self-centredness; (spiritual) knowledge, art, religion and loving

service to another person (or noble cause)....knowledge is the most spiritualized form of devotion to the world; and selfless, loving service is the most beautiful form of selfless devotion to the world. For love is a truly divine radiance in daily life. **Pious, truly spiritual love refines our being into its innermost fibre, it ennobles all that lives in us. This pure, pious love transforms the entire soul-life into another which is attuned to universal spirit...**[59]

For souls who ignore the obvious signposts on the journey, there is a real possibility of being enmeshed in increased sexual desires, arrogance and ambition for power over others. This state can encourage negative forces to draw near and intensify the uncleanness. Regarding the matter of sexuality, little can be said as to how an initiate views this, owing to the need for strict objectivity by the student in concerning this or any other subject before an initiate will speak about it. In addition, the activity of negative powers has in recent decades sadly weakened the once innate understanding of this vital matter.

It is very important to note that Rudolf Steiner emphasized that it is especially incorrect to meditate - in the special esoteric sense described here - if one is in a sexually aroused state.(1910) This has a very negative influence in the higher worlds, by spreading a certain force, present in one's aura into those higher realms. This is not to imply that every meditant has to overcome all such desires totally before commencing a life of meditation, for that is not possible (but see the note at the end of this Chapter).

However, normally in this process of having the cloudy water become pure, there is simply a heightened awareness of the lower self. Various qualities like jealousy, exaggerating, slyness, seeking power over others, etc manifest in this phase. We do have to consider such matters, because in meditation a person may well experience, to their dismay, that subjective antipathy to, or liking of, other people becomes much stronger. These are times when the lower self is becoming stronger, as it feels its reign is ending, but it does not last long.

The students in Steiner's Esoteric School were advised to read and ponder the Lord's Prayer, the Sermon on the Mount or the beginning of St. John's Gospel during such times. And also only for those who have read beforehand his lecture cycles on the Gospels, he suggested also certain lectures about the life of Jesus, given in late 1911.
Experiencing inwardly the double when meditating

---

[59] From his private creed or statement of life principles, written in his 28th year; see also his lecture, "Love and its meaning in the world"; 17/Dec./1912

Further it could happen that potent sensual attraction to, or sullen angry dislike of, someone arises during the meditating. These are feelings which one would not normally allow to come to mind; and yet now do, and they seem justified and valid. Here it is vital to realize that, as the students were told, "All hindrances to the goal of higher spirituality that arise on the path are signs of inner progress", this is reported from many esoteric lessons. The karma-guiding powers, acting in harmony with the guiding angel, are now allowing the shadow-side to be encountered, that we may conquer the dragon within. Indeed, a person who has already developed a certain degree of higher vision can still have some of the double left in the soul. Sometimes, it happens that the meditator may go through a phase wherein even use (or think) various indecent expressions which they would never ever normally use. (1913)

Such an experience need not last long, and when it is over, a great step further along the path has been achieved; a deep seated negative force has been removed from the soul. In this connection these forces which the meditant in the first instance stirs up are not only removed from his or her soul in this process; they also have their role in the economy of the cosmos, that is, in the processes and dynamics of the cosmos.

Rudolf Steiner is reported as saying that these unwelcome forces have a certain important role to play in the future of one's evolution. He did not elaborate on this (or at least the notes made afterwards by a listener do not say any more), but I conclude that once these forces have been 'brought to the surface' and experienced and then honestly resisted, they may be transformed in future lives, into useful energies. We could say then, that when any previously unsuspected imperfection manifests – within the soul-life of an earnest meditant – this shows us that it is 'on its way out'. Continued earnest work on ethical development will ensure that it disappears of its own accord permanently.

There is another important perspective that the meditant needs to know about the lower-self, with its 'baggage', the shameful, impure thought-forms and emotions 'energies'. In response to a question about whether we have to carry these energies from all of our earthly lives **for ever**, Steiner emphatically answered in the negative;

> That would be terrible, to be eternally bound to the insignificant, the erroneous! No, all that which is not of the eternal, of the spiritual, all that which is not relevant to that soul who is now freed of the lowly, falls away from that soul. In the cosmos, there is the yawning bottomless pit of 'Orcus', and it is this which receives whatever finds no place in the progressing life and ever more radiant beauty of this life.

> Everything that can find no place in the divine, sinks down into this Orcus, this bottomless cosmic-abyss. The shadows of dark deeds descend into its depths, from which they can no longer arise into the radiant eternal worlds of the soul who has achieved moral freedom.[60]

To the guiding initiates of the pathway represented in this book, it is a matter of direct perception that evil powers seek to destroy moral perception in modern humanity. This influence has been exacerbated because contemporary lifestyles have so alienated us from those wholesome influences in the natural environment that offer protection from them. The meditant must strive to remain free of such influences (Steiner speaks of us "being in daily, nay hourly, danger of absorbing such influences"). Hence the meditant does not use unclean words, such as those which refer to that which is putrefying. This is important despite the decadence of today causing obscenity to also merge quite comfortably into the background of normal conversation. For the mental picture that corresponds to the word (and every word has its mental image) can allow evil powers to have access to the aura of the speaker and of the listener.[61]

Steiner also cautioned in this context that 'thoughts are things' and any negative thoughts which a person sends out will eventually come back to them. As sensitivity to astral images strengthens, eventually becoming astral vision, one will experience this process in images. Images like burning arrows which are imprinting a distinctive form onto one's house for example. (1904)

It is vital to realize that any such negative conditions have been brought about to help one on the path to the divine, for the result is that one then sets about the task of correcting the situation. Rudolf Steiner's recommendations for the following are: if vanity and ambitiousness seem to be strengthening, then rather than focussing on one's own reality, it is advisable to take up an intensified study of the spiritual-psychological nature of the human being. In particular, the complex details of the inter-working of soul, life-forces and spiritual tendencies, as portrayed in the basic texts recommended in Chapter Three.

---

[60] This answer is given in the words of his student, Frau Emmy von Gumpenberg, in her unpublished memoirs. The date of the occasion of the conversation is not recorded by her. 'Orcus' is a term in ancient Greek mythology for the subterranean hell, that is, for the ruler of this, **and** his kingdom.

[61] The truth behind these words is well known to those who know of the existence that the dead in the lower soul world have; souls soon cease to use such terms because of the inner astral reality which manifests directly when they do, it is not pleasant. The opposing powers are working intensely to ensure that what is evil or obscene becomes regarded as 'alright'.

If jealousy seems to be developing a life of its own, then seek out experiences of beauty, whether in nature or art or in the noble, inspiring deeds of outstanding people. It is not recommended to attempt to 'make good' by thinking nice things about a person of whom we are jealous. Trying to directly fight a palpable mood by substituting nice thoughts is not advised, better by far to actively immerse the soul in beauty, as in classical and some modern art. (1908)

This exercise is not to be confused with the fourth exercise given in Chapter Two about tolerance. There it was a matter of replacing instinctive jealous or critical thoughts with a positive one, so that the soul's very being changes. Here it is a question of acknowledging that this is not yet the case, and that certain autonomous elemental powers are temporarily getting stronger, and thus one immerses the mind in art, which has the effect of dis-empowering these forces. A very important point here, is that one should never focus on any such bad, intruding thoughts as this can lead to them developing a life of their own, that is they may become more intense.

Imagine what this would be like if these imperfect qualities were consolidated into a caricature of one's face. This is actually what can happen at a certain time in esoteric development; one sees this 'face'. It is important that you know these secrets of real initiation wisdom, as it can happen to a meditator, that 'out of the blue' you see a somewhat ugly countenance. It is rather upsetting because you seem to recognize yourself in this vision. What is happening is that we are being given a very valuable experience. Namely an image of our own 'shadow' still lingering on in the aura is shown to us; it is this that needs to be transformed (so it's a type of guardian experience). By seeing these inner qualities moulded into a distortion of one's face, the meditator perceives what work still has to be done before the negative tendencies are overcome. Gratitude towards one's guiding angel for giving the experience is called for.

The double in the ether-energies
Secondly, the life-energies are also being 'shaken up' by the process of meditating; from these energies, or our ether-body, we have our deeper seated background predisposition, or the temperament. Particularly long-standing deep-seated emotions and attitudes gradually take hold of our life-force body and form our background mood of soul, or so-called 'temperament'. The four kinds of energies which make up our life-forces are connected to the four elements, and since our life-force body determines our moods, our temperament can also be affected by the more intensive esoteric development.

Our temperament determines much of our semi-conscious habitual attitudes and responses to life. Within the ether energies are elemental forces of 'fire' with a connection to fiery impatience, and of the 'air' with an airy-changeableness, of 'water' which engender a watery-placid inertia, and fourthly of 'earth' which can bring about a rigid, duty-bound even depressive earthiness. We have a connection to the four elements, they are intimately involved with our ether energies.

One reason that the birth chart is so valuable for understanding oneself, that is, our personality, is that it shows what kind of elemental energies, as well as zodiac energies, we have in our aura. The process of esoteric development does involve one in experiences that are connected to influences from the ether energies behind fire, air, water and earth in our own elemental qualities.[62] In the ether-body there are also negative tendencies; so the double or shadow consists of negative ethereal energies, too, not only negative soul forces.

So one's habits, predisposition and general everyday relations to the environs can go through some confusion or temporary worsening. This can lead to a bad habit becoming worse, or a difficulty in remaining truthful. Truthfulness and lying are in fact connected with the life-forces, not only the soul. Here, the meditant simply has to recognize that the truth must be upheld even more rigorously. For example, it is most unfortunate for an earnest meditator to limp away from upholding and clarifying the truth, perhaps in the face of a sceptical friend or relative. For example, if in some important social setting sceptical relatives challenge to affirm whether you really believe in a specific spiritual truth, it is important to affirm your truth (of course with sensitivity to others, and an offer to discuss it at a suitable time).

In the Esoteric School it was explained to the students that when a person lies, then the negative forces engendered in the soul-body flow on into the ether-energies, causing some inner lameness within it. This can gradually increase and create the tendency towards untruthfulness, as these negative energies which cause untruthfulness can have access to the life-energies. The degree of untruthfulness that the meditant still possesses can be measured by how strongly or weakly a breathing problem arises in the early stages of meditating. This phenomenon is a feeling that one can not breathe so well, as if the air is blocked at the throat. This may be so faint as to be scarcely perceived, or quite strong, in either case it is due to the activated influence of the lower self in the life-forces, the ether-body. (1913)

---

[62] See "Knowledge of the Higher Worlds, How is it attained" for further details on various trials and challenges that initiation requires.

Now, what significance could such untransformed qualities in the ether energies really have for a meditator? As I have pointed out, in effective meditation the soul and the life-forces extend themselves out of the body to some degree. These 'exteriorised' energies are permeated by our inner qualities, and these have an objective reality in the astral plane. If there are serious moral defects lurking in the meditant, then these forces draw negative beings into them; a common result of this is that one sees a vision, but a false vision. One may see delightful forms that act temptingly on the soul, reinforcing one's ego-centric desires and attitudes. In other words, false visions are conjured up in astral substance by opposing powers who can utilize false attitudes living in the meditant's aura. Therefore initiation knowledge proclaims: **untruth hidden within results in untruth seen or experienced without**.

Motivation from the tempters

In general terms, there are two fundamental kinds of dynamics that live on in the soul, or in the 'double', until much hard inner work has been done. One of these is to become enchanted by the sheer blissful delight of being free of the body. There can be a yearning to be able to wander through exquisite scenes of an enchanted paradise. Such motivation may appear to be apparently only a faint, harmless thing – until one is free of the body. Then, it takes on a much stronger nature. Often such a yearning is one of the motivations behind the decision to take up meditating. This same impulse can often become present in a less obvious way, namely, **as an unreal attitude to the world**.

One feels the urge to get away from various duties and demands of life, and dissolve away into higher realms. It is owing to this same urge that we can be afraid when standing at the edge of a cliff, that we might just throw ourselves off, in order to somehow fly. This dynamic can also lead to a naively egoistical attitude to the world; for example, the meditant gets the idea that he or she 'has a special mission'. These phenomena living in our soul-life are connected to a class of spiritual beings that actively seek to encourage such 'flighty' or self-indulgent attitudes. These beings are responsible for the strange urge to fly that can be felt when on a high building or the edge of a cliff. The way to remove the cause of such problems, and indeed a general tendency towards nervousness of various kinds, is to consolidate the sense of self, this can be achieved as described earlier through the six parallel exercises and a study program.

These beings could be called "the tempters". They wish to lure the meditant with visions of a 'false Paradise'. In the everyday world, they instil a subtle irresponsible egotism, especially in the emotive life. In the higher worlds there are realms formed by beings who are intent on staying out of the real balanced cosmic evolutionary process. They tend to imbue the human soul with the same kind of antipathy to the world of challenges and growth, both physical and spiritual. They seek to influence meditants, and their effect could be summed up as causing the feeling of "let me ascend and dissolve into the light". It is these beings that also conjure up in astral light the visions of oneself in some grand impressive state in a past life, such as an ancient Egyptian Pharaoh, or a Master of an esoteric order, etc. Any 'meditation' system that offers a way to be separated from the necessary involvement with earthly reality becomes very appealing; such systems owe much to the inspiration of these beings.

This class of spiritual beings is designated by Steiner as belonging to a being called Lucifer. This is a tragic, fallen being whose influence is responsible for this yearning in human beings to avoid full involvement with Earth. Lucifer is regarded as a being who fell from a state of blessedness through conceit and pride, and the hosts of Lucifer use those qualities in the unaware meditant. Naturally, for the prudent and sincere meditant, they can not do any real direct harm, except to try to intensify any such tendencies in the soul.

Their power is broken when the ethical development process outlined in this book is taken up - this process is described in detail in Steiner's work, as is the nature of these beings.[63] In particular he urged his students in the Esoteric School to strive incessantly towards genuine humility and selflessness, for these in particular keep the self-centred indulgent moods away.

One result of intensely meditating in which one transcends brain-bound consciousness, yet has not made the necessary effort to gain enhanced inner ethics, is that one may see false visionary images. This could only happen (in a prolonged manner) if the meditant ignored the various inner warning bells about various ambitions and indulgent attitudes. However, false images are a phenomenon that need to be taken very seriously. These are images that are real in the astral world, they are really perceived around one in meditation, but they are not truly part of the objective spiritual 'environment'. So, where do they come from? As I indicated above, they derive from the personal ambitions and vain desires living in the aura. These are drawn out of the aura and paraded brilliantly before our soul by 'Luciferic' beings, hence they are convincing and strong.

If you think that this theme of spiritual beings is absurd or too fantastic, just reflect that you don't really expect to enter into cosmic

---

[63] See his "Knowledge of the Higher Worlds; how is it attained?". You can also read about this Luciferic force in the Bible, in one passage, which refers to both the Being involved and its influence in the Earth's political dynamics; this is Isaiah Chap 14; verse 12-15 etc; the King James version is best here.

heights of meditative insight, and yet discover no other intelligences. Then why should not the preliminary process, of actually beginning to develop higher awareness not also bring about an interaction with other beings? There are indeed many spiritual beings, and some of these have an intimate connection to us that derives from our shared, intertwined evolutionary history. Much of what we feel 'inside' our hearts that we find disturbing derives from these beings. Substantial witness to this fact, and to the 'dark night of the soul' can be found in those earlier and quite interesting manuals on the inner life by Underhill and Poulain.[64] The famous painting, "the Temptation of St. Anthony" in the magnificent Isenheim Altar, by Matthias Grunewald depicts this situation. A common area of mischief for these beings concerns past lives. They make much effort to delude the meditator about his/her past lives, about karma research in general.....

> One believes one is viewing the past lives of various persons, but if the ethical development has not been fully undertaken, no truth-filled research can be undertaken. Instead one sucks up (with oneself) into the higher states of being these hidden vain desires, then one sees them in astral substance as if objective, and then brings them back down, but this is only an illusion. An illusion formed from that which one has thought and pondered about on Earth... [65]

Many a novice in meditation does exactly that, and sets about convincing younger people of his or her greatness and their greatness too. Many valuable initiatives have been lamed by having such unhealthy dynamics in the background. It is very common for a meditant to be exposed to flattering ideas and visions which lead one to assume a past life of great importance. Following is a brief extract from the fascinating dramas wherein Rudolf Steiner graphically portrays what happens to a person who crosses over the threshold. He wrote four such dramas, called 'Mystery dramas" because their purpose is similar to the dramas performed in the ancient Mysteries of Greece. The thoughts which Lucifer tries to instil in someone at the threshold are presented by describing the experiences of an advanced meditant, crossing into the higher realms consciously.....

Lucifer's words from a scene in the drama, freely translated: (Sc. 4)
>"Human being, you sought yourself in the confusion of earth life -- to find your (real) self was your reward and proved to be your fate. You found **me**! Other spiritual beings tried to place

---

[64] Evelyn Underhill, "Mysticism", first pub. 1911, and R.P. Poulain, "The Graces of Interior Prayer", 1910. Rudolf Steiner's guidance as given here provides further expert advice on these themes.
[65] From a lecture of 31/May' 1913

the veil over your senses, but I tore this veil apart ! Divine spiritual beings sought to follow their own will within you, but I gave you your own will....maintain your own self through spiritual daring, as you will find only alien being-ness in the expanses of spiritual realms; and this will condemn you to mere human fate, it will oppress you.."

One sees here how the false tempting attitude is conveyed that the divine-spiritual powers are restrictive; and not really worth revering ! This is an influence which seeks to enhance emotive egotism, and which leads to spiritual irresponsibility and self-indulgence. The full text of the play called the "Portal of Initiation" is very deep, and well worth studying in detail.

Motivation from the adversary
On the other side, there is the tendency in the soul, including in those who want higher development, to seek power in this world. Rather than fleeing from this earthy world, one yearns for power and influence. In other words, the urge is felt to empower one's own personal ego, and to establish authority over others. This is usually accompanied by the wish for occult powers that will give one a great 'superiority' over other people, the ability to manipulate them.

This is the other dynamic to which one is exposed; note that it is the polar opposite to the first. The fact that one is exposed to these two extremes is a matter that requires serious attention. The first tendency is a dissolving away into self-centred enjoyment of bliss, which seeks to separate one from karmic necessities, the other is a dynamic that hardens the soul, so to speak. It has a tendency to reinforce any egotism that may be in the will-energies, and this results in a wish to dominate others.

The dynamic is due to a class of spiritual beings more malignant than the former. These beings are under the control of quite an evil entity, which Steiner referred to as 'Ahriman', a Persian equivalent to the Biblical term, Satan. (The terms, 'Devil' and 'Satan' although normally regarded as interchangeable, actually refer to different classes of beings.) This is a sinister fallen being whose influence is responsible for the urge in human beings to empower the untransformed ego, so that it may become dominant. What results then is the esoterically aware 'Napoleons' who seek to impress and then to control people by various means, perhaps setting up an "esoteric order". Their influence causes the ambition: "I will develop occult powers, for I must have authority".

These two polar dynamics are very real, although only someone who ignores the signs of imbalance in the pathway outlined here, and whose motivation was not genuine, has any possibility of being seriously harmed by these extremes. In the same Mystery Drama the influence of Ahriman (known in the Hebrew Scriptures as the Father of Lies) is described like this; (Portal of Initiation, Sc. 4)

> "Human soul; you have fled from darkness of the spiritual realms, and found the light of the earthly realm. Spirits wished to tear you away from the beauty of the sense-world, but I make the ground more solid and secure.. this solid ground, which you could also lose if you try to arise into the spiritual realms... so seek the **power** of truth from the firm dense quality of my energies, for I lead you into your true being....you might only dissipate your spiritual energies in those light-filled heights...."

These words indicate a reality, for this being tries to stop all humanity escaping from materialistic thoughts, but if that battle is lost with a meditant, then this being seeks to encourage the meditant to harden the normal egotism by focussing on an Earth-bound goal. These words, which I have freely translated here, have immense depth, for this is the spiritual power that condenses matter into existence from the ethers; these words are not meant to be mere poetic metaphor.

Fortunately, this second class of beings is repelled vehemently from the soul when effort is made to **think** spiritually, besides having a warm and caring approach to life. So, precisely through the foremost characteristic of the pathway presented here, that is, the requirement to undertake regular study, the influence of these beings is kept away. Let us be really clear about the following fact, the best form of 'occult protection' is to develop the highest and most enlivened spirituality that one can. As Rudolf Steiner emphasized, developing real purity of heart, overcoming desires attracted by illusory glamorous flattering temptations, protects the soul from the beings that live in the unrealistic, flaming radiance of false paradises in the astral realm. Whereas striving to develop the new form of spirituality - thinking with real spirituality - is the foremost protection against the subtle malignant influence which is the polar opposite of the other, the one that seeks to produced cold, hardened selfishness. That is, to strive to develop spirituality in the thinking, this happens when for example, the meditant can really 'think the thoughts', that is, really understand, transcendental truths, and not just vaguely 'feel' them.

An example of such thinking is the thought that the 'substance' of the true spiritual realms has no material element to it, at all; it does not consist of refined matter. Even a refined, more rapidly vibrating matter is still material, so it does not exist beyond the physical plane. One needs to comprehend the idea of existence in spiritual realms as consisting of that being-ness of which the mind consists; namely thoughts, emotions and will-impulses. This is just one such example of spiritual or sense-free thinking; there are many more in the books mentioned in the Appendix to Chapter Three.

The light enkindled in the aura of the soul, which rays down into it from the spiritual aura, through such thinking, repels these beings. In addition, as further protection, it is important to develop strongly the attitude of acceptance of one's karma. This means to be appreciative of what is given to one, and not to regret what one can not attain. It does not mean fatalistic acceptance of life, nor non-resistance to an abusive relationship. Rather, to accept the blows of fate with equanimity, and to find a way towards fulfilment within the reality of one's life. It is obviously important that the meditator is protected from such influences, by not prematurely opening the soul to the influences from beyond the threshold, described above.

These qualities of seeking to flee the reality of the world and one's karma, or to enhance personal authority and gain occult powers whilst still thinking materialistically, really do exist as a part of one's soul. Naturally, there are also other qualities that constitute the lower- self in the aura, too, such as the well-known vices, but it is these other problems which the meditant needs to focus on. Of these two influences, however, the powers which seek to harden the heart, and pervade thinking with a coolness, are a more serious problem especially in the Western and European countries, as they can stir up the urge for occult powers, within a materialistic framework. For the urge towards cold superiority on the basis of occult powers is itself a materialistic idea, since it ignores the spiritual foundations of the cosmos.

Naturally the results for those who seek to strengthen their egotism in this way are unpleasant. This includes the inevitable suffering in the after-life within the lower soul-world realms, and the consequent darkening of one's inner being in a next life. One result of having insatiable curiosity for spiritual experiences, and disregarding the stern requirements of the guardian for ethical development, is that this offers these powers an opportunity. They can step in and present vivid, attractive, ego-gratifying images to the errant meditant, based on his or her current ideas of what they think they should 'see'.

The result is a subtly materialistic vision in which everything has a remarkable similarity to the physical world, it follows the general pattern of the earthly world. The images are really there, in astral substance, they are not illusory, in that sense; however, they are especially conjured up for the person to observe. To make it even more daunting, the person may well have had a glimpse of higher matters, this glimpse is then taken and materialistically distorted. To give protection from a premature opening of the 'doors of perception' is the task of the guardian of the threshold.

Anyone who reflects on the sinister side of esoteric occult activity which occasionally gets reported in the news, cannot help but see how real these matters are. In particular, the tendency of self-centred desires, emotive conceit and flightiness, and on the other side, the tendency of power-seeking and inner coldness. What is very important to note is, that these influences only have the power to cause some problems if their corresponding dynamics **are not overcome in oneself.**

Hence the fundamental first law of meditating for real spiritual development: work ceaselessly on one's own ethical development. Any system of meditating which offers shortcut techniques is exposing the acolyte to both these influences which then approach so subtly that they can not be simply avoided. The earnest meditant is not in danger of either of these two dynamics if the pathway that is presented in detail in literature mentioned, and outlined here is followed. For there is a golden rule that applies here: whatever force 'opens the door' for us influences what we experience. Naturally there is nothing to fear from the pathway and meditative exercises given here; they are not designed to suddenly plunge you across into the other worlds prematurely.

You may think that all this is just a theoretical idea, or an exaggeration of the facts; but in my counselling work I have experienced cases of people initiated into misguided esoteric activity, who then experience difficulties caused by lower beings. One such experience was caused by a direct raising of the mysterious kundalini force, which in this person's personal life caused severe and ongoing stress.

Motivation from the guiding angel
The esoteric pathway elucidated in this book is based on the attitude of seeking sanctification of the soul first and foremost, and ultimately the gaining of psychic powers and astral clairvoyance is of secondary importance. It can not be said too often, that the spiritual faculties are attained **through developing spirituality**, and not via occult techniques which directly stimulate the chakras. By following the pathway explained here, the guiding angel is able to draw closer, and begins to inspire one with a motivation that is attuned to the spiritual worlds. The angel was with us in spiritual realms before birth into this life, when the next phase of our karma was being formulated, and it then guided us down to the Earth for this life. The guardian angel is our link with the ranks of divine-spiritual beings into whose realms we yearn to enter.

When the right motivation arises in the soul and works within one then I would suggest that the motivating factor could be summed as: **may wisdom and selfless love from the Light of the Cosmos Spirit (God),** the being of divine love, now incarnate in the Earth's soul, through the cosmic Christ, grow within in me as a result of my meditating. The guiding angel nurtures within its wings, so to speak, each person's higher spiritual qualities and seeks to help the earthly ego to become a vessel for these qualities.

With such attitudes as this for our motivation, conceived in genuine and deep humility, there is little to be concerned about, for then our guiding angel works with us in the great quest. The angel beholds the guardian and knows what its attitude is to our inner reality. Hence, when the higher experiences and insights occur, these are in accordance with the wishes of the guardian of the threshold. In the next chapter we will consider a beautiful pastel drawing by Rudolf Steiner showing the spiritual beings who work with a meditant, especially the guiding angel, and in Chapter Nine, a meditation for attunement with the guiding angel is given.

It is reported that the ancient Greek initiate Pythagoras once said that, "He who stumbles against the threshold should turn back", a saying which I conclude has an esoteric meaning. If we consider that the threshold was regarded as a symbol of the border between this world and the beyond, then the words of Pythagoras have a second meaning. Namely, if you find that you are coming across some problems when trying to rise to a higher state, then the guardian is indicating that you are not ethically developed enough. It is best to desist for a while, and focus on acquiring greater spirituality.

If one is earnest in the wish to meditate and live so as to reach the higher-self, then one must be able to confront the real issues. For the wish to really meditate does not mean that the lingering negative tendencies are simply going to evaporate. They have to be actively worked upon. Until these qualities are dissolved by inner effort, they can manifest during meditation. Unless the shadow side is overcome, the goal can not be reached, in the fullest sense. As we noted earlier, the double, is in effect the shadow side of human nature, the shadow-side of the three qualities of the mind; namely, thinking, emotion and willing. This is depicted by Rudolf Steiner in his extraordinary building, designed to be a home for spiritual and artistic conferences and performances, etc in Switzerland. This building, which he named, "The Goetheanum" in honour of Goethe is located near Basel and shows the superb organic architecture style that he pioneered back in the early 1900's.

At the top of the stairway, at the threshold to the great hall, he incorporated a huge window of red glass, revealing in a fascinating scene, the spiritual dynamics involved in the initial stage of meditation. (see **Illustration 3**) The glass is inches thick, and was carved by using a device he invented especially for carving into glass. On the left side, the three shadow realities of the human soul, have been portrayed in the form of symbolic monsters.[66] These are more clearly reproduced in **Illustration 4**. I have taken the liberty to colour them, even though, as part of the red window, they are all red. The colours I have used are taken from specific indications on these three entities given by Rudolf Steiner on this theme in advanced "Class" meditation lessons, given in the last year of his life.

The three beasts or monsters of the shadow
We see depicted in the red window a tall mountain upon which a seeker is walking, but not in a very empowered or clear way. The person's gaze is downwards, they appear unable to look in the direction of the light - in contrast to how she or he appears on the other side of the triptych window. Furthermore, below this confused seeker are three unpleasant 'creatures'. Very significantly these three are portrayed as part of the underlying stratum on which the seeker is walking, as if they are part of his or her being. Without focusing too much on these, I feel it's valuable to see what they are representing.

Underneath the text reads "it manifests", this means that the real truth of the lower self is now being confronted by the seeker. This is a time that is called in classical mystical literature "the dark night of the soul". The three creatures portrayed in this window are a depiction of the three autonomous, malignant powers that live within the lower self, that is the negative forces in our thinking, feeling and will. They are not merely abstract ideas, as Steiner admonished one student, who asked if they were representations of the distorted thinking feeling and will.[67]

On the left, in dull red, we confront the shadow side of our thinking, which is that which holds us back from acquiring spirituality in our intelligence. If thoughts are able to fly, to soar up to the heights, then a bird, especially an eagle is a good symbol of thinking. Here however, we see a dumpy, earthly **flightless** bird! It has a tiny brain and the typical un-nerving glassy, 'unresponsive' eyes as well. The lesson here is that the meditant needs to overcome materialism in the thinking, not just in

---

[66] There is an error in this current window - but not in the special form of it as reproduced here, namely the endowing of the middle monster with an eye (even if closed). It actually does not have an eye, neither in the sketch by R Steiner nor in the coloured drawing made from this sketch by Asssja Turgenieff, to help her carve the first Goetheanum windows.

[67] Steiner's caution about being so theoretical has lead some of his students to falsely conclude that one must not even consider them to be the Three Beasts, as these are known, following his choice of terms in esoteric lessons from 1924. These students are perhaps unaware that the scenes carved into the red window considered as a single window, were given the name "Initiation" by Steiner himself (in his notebooks.)

the emotions. This is a really subtle challenge as we discussed in Chapter Three. In effect it is a question of overcoming **doubt about spiritual reality, and thinking materialistically about higher realities.** How? By energetically applying the mind to grasping the higher truths and by doing the exercises in Wonder and Awe, then this 'doubting Thomas' quality is eventually overcome.

Higher experiences become subtly distorted in the soul if the mind-set is alien to the transcendental nature of the spirit. Many people make success in meditation difficult by not resisting this subtle materialism; especially by

> ...thinking that the spiritual realms are like the physical world, only finer, more pervasive. This is a great obstacle, because then one does not sense the delicate and tenuous indications of the awakening to the spirit. Such materialistic attitudes must be pared away. Those who have these are like a person who ascends into the atmosphere in a hot-air balloon and believes that he/she can at any moment disembark and step onto some mountain peak and rest there. (1914)

This example from an esoteric lesson, shows graphically that one must have gained through study a really non-material concept of the spirit, or one simply will not recognize the higher realms as they begin to draw near. This problem in the thinking is overcome as it becomes spiritualized (holistic), because it develops an inner warmth. When one's world-view incorporates spiritual realities it fills one with enthusiasm and happiness, and it also enables a form of empathy with other people to arise; even if it is more in the mind than in an emotional form. The meditator has a warm, empathetic quality in the thoughts now, they are no longer alien to the living world, and abstract. It is as if the head now lets the heart share in the process of forming thoughts. Then the doubting and resisting of spiritual ideas is overcome. This monster represents doubt about the spirit.

On the right, in yellow, with grey patches, is another monster. We see the head is greatly over-sized, whilst the middle section of the body is rather shrivelled up, as are the limbs. The hair is mostly gone, and appears rather hardened; the teeth are very prominent; generally a somewhat deadened, exaggerated head-like quality, rather than an emotional quality. Here we see a portrayal of the shadow-side of feelings or emotions, or rather of the effect on a person's heart if it has 'shrivelled up'. It represents metaphorically the appearance of a person who is unable to manifest the deeper emotions, the finer feelings. One can imagine that such a being would experience real **antipathy to the spiritual realities of life**, perhaps because they could appear somehow threatening, or too restrictive on personal desires, etc. In any event, the intellect becomes gravely over-emphasized if the emotions are ignored, one becomes very clever, but not wise. The teeth represent the most hardened part of our body, and if one suppresses the true emotional potential, then a kind of hardening can occur in one's heart.[68] This monster represents hatred of the spirit. Although the head is so enlarged, it lacks any sign of real life within. One may conclude that the thinking life for such a person must become earth-bound; fearfully clever, but inwardly dead.

The meditant is here told, at the threshold of the temple, that the heart must be en-filled with enthusiasm and love for the selfless qualities required by the spirit in the heart. This in turn implies that part of the lower-self which must not be harboured, are elemental energies who resent those fine qualities in whose presence egotism can not manifest. An imbalance in the mind, namely of intellect at the expense of the emotions is common in the modern world, and means that this shadow aspect could be stronger than one suspects. There exists an elemental power within all self-centred desires that deeply resents the very existence of the spiritual reality, and which mocks and scorns at spiritual ideas and ideals. This elemental power becomes activated when the self through meditation seeks to eradicate such tendencies.

The most self-indulgent desires are those which detest and resist the spiritualization process the most. In the middle of the group of three monsters is the most prominent of these creatures, a tall figure, which I have coloured a dull blue, this represents the shadow-side of the will, the most powerful of the shadow-forces. Here we see a powerful image of the dynamics in the will, our volitional force, in so far as it is not inclined towards 'doing the good'. To understand the mystery of an 'anti-will' we need to consider the question, what are the organs of our will?

Our limbs are our will organs; for we walk with the legs, and carry out all our deeds by way of the arms and hands. As the fifth will-limb, we have the jaw-bone: through this we speak. Speech itself is the expression of a very significant volitional power in the human being. It is a kind of crowning glory of the human race, it lifts us above the animal. So we have five limb-organs; two legs, two arms, and the jaw-bone.

So, regarding this third creature, what does its limb system reveal? Its legs and arms are four legs – the signature of an animal; and they are

---

[68] The student of anthroposophy may now be confused in that the explanation of these three figures, as given by Wilhem Rath in the portfolio; "The Goetheanum Glass Windows", assigns shadow-emotions to the tall central figure in this part of the window This however, I have concluded differently, as my following text shows.

tiny, weak things. As for the fifth limb, it is in fact here fused into the rest of the head, so it has not really been developed. Likewise, it has no eyes (the depicting of eyes in the later, the second Goetheanum, as noted earlier, is incorrect). So, here is a portrayal of an anti-will; that is, the absence of any real human-divine will, it is replaced by a kind of animal will.[69]

It is especially fascinating to observe that in this figure, the speech limb-organ is stunted, for this indicates that a very high aspect of human volition - the urge and ability to form language as a vessel for ideas - is missing.[70] It is the natural quality of will to be active, and to seek to rise to the heights of spirituality with people who are on the quest for spirituality, so here we have depicted a rejection of the impulse to be actively expressing the potential of the human being, and to explore the spiritual possibilities of life. Further, since it is the characteristic of will to have courage, to yearn for activity, one may assume that this rejection, this non-will or anti-will, derives it strength from **a fear of the spirit.** This is the manifestation of the shadow-side of our will; a kind of numbness to possible initiatives and opportunities in life for higher development, as well as a certain fear of the spiritual dimension of one's being.

The exercises of the Four Moods given earlier, are effective techniques to overcome this fear; especially in developing the mood of awe and reverence. In the esoteric guidance as given in 1908 and 1912 it was taught that when these qualities live in the heart, then fear dissolves, it is metamorphosed into the necessary awe and pious reverence. These are precisely the qualities that were described in Chapter Three as vital for success in meditation. The attitude of wonder is a preliminary to this; it provides a basis from which reverence and awe can develop. The meditant can in this way overcome anxiety about experiencing the higher realities, or else, like a caged eagle that has lost its courage, he may decide it is too risky to leave the cage. Moreover, what we don't do in any lifetime, because forces of fear are too strong, is an opportunity lost to our future. Whereas what we do dare to try, and dare to carry out, becomes a basis for further development in the next life.

---

[69] The illustrations in the windows of the Goetheanum are invaluable for the process of self-initiation and for understanding the Class lessons; the esotericist who has entered into this process can discover many priceless secrets in them.

[70] Esoterically this means that the subconsciously working cosmic Logos power is absent. It is this power which, as St. John indicates in his Gospel, 'spoke' the world into being, in the beginning, and which over the ages has manifested in humankind as the faculty of intelligence and language.

As reverence and awe develop, the irrational fear element fades away. This subconscious antipathy to the actual encountering of higher spiritual reality is quite strong. The antipathy is connected to the fact that such imperfections in the soul have to be encountered. The major reason for delays in acquiring higher experiences, for lack of progress in meditation is this semi-conscious antipathy. (1912) It induces a feeling of discomfort in the soul as the ether and astral organisms start to be drawn slightly upwards in meditation. In particular Rudolf Steiner pointed out that there is nothing so opposed by the shadow-self as the withdrawal of the ether forces from the body. It is virtually a reflex action, in that it tries to draw the auric energies back in, as soon as any slight withdrawing upwards is noticed.

In this connection, the cult of horror-films needs to be avoided. This peculiar phenomenon reinforces the subconscious fear of the hidden and unknown realities. The film images live in the ether-body for the rest of life, they do not evaporate away, there they become a fertile basis for the intensification of this inherent fear tendency. Anthroposophical psychology does not see in this activity an expression of a desire to challenge one's courage. Rather, it seeks oblivion to the efforts of the fear-enhancing beings, who inspire the horrific images. These images are preserved in the ether-body in full intensity, and work as obstacles to eventual 'threshold crossing' in meditative activity.

Some very important indications (from lessons given in 1911/12) follow about the kind of annoying 'quirks' in one's soul-life that can occur as the inner cleansing process gathers pace, and the three-fold lower-self is conquered. I have garnered all of these from the 220 lessons to students in the Esoteric School. However, when reading them, remember that these difficult symptoms only apply to those who really pursue meditating with earnestness. They are only temporary problems and usually occur only very subtly, not as severe problems. They are felt in the morning, usually as subtle inner dynamics upon awakening and re-entering the physical, ethereal and soul bodies.

Temporary problems mentioned in the Esoteric School

* A feeling of having heavy weight on you, as if you could be in chains, or a feeling of being in a small jail cell. For a meditator this is due to being unwilling to accept and work with one's karma; apart from many other non-esoteric causes!
* A feeling of the throat being restricted, almost like a force stifling, restricting you there. One needs to seriously consider just how much dedication is there to the pathway. How much of the interest in the inner work is just from a wish to float around in the enjoyment of the prettiness and ethereal-ness of it all. How deep are one's motives for

such meditating? Secondly, how genuine are we about our own motives? We can do something for an egotistical reason, but persuade ourselves that it was for a noble reason. This kind of self-deceit re motivation also causes the above problem.

* Awakening with a nausea feeling – if this is being caused by the meditative process, it is due to not having succeeded sufficiently in tearing out feelings of jealousy or envy deep in the soul.

* A feeling almost as if one is vaguely half suffocating or half drowning – this is due to not being really earnest with the effort needed. One is only just playing around and not taking it seriously.

* Dizziness spells occurring (anytime) – this can be due to being too dreamy and aloof from life in one's spiritual endeavours. This can manifest also as not wanting to be really involved with the social dimension to life.

* Sweating during the night is, like sensual night dreams, an indication that some deep earth-bound forces of an 'elemental' nature, are still embedded in the lower aura. Yet as with all these symptoms, the forces behind these are 'sent' to the earnest meditant, so that the corresponding imperfection is eradicated. It may be very unsettling to consider the trials through which the advancing meditant has to proceed, but, as the famous New Testament quotation indicates; "For whom the Lord loveth, he chastiseth." (Hebrews 12:6). So, the Lord's 'destroying angel' and his hosts are not only despatched to evil-doers! [71]

These symptoms occur only rarely, but it is important to know about the possibility.[72] It is only by meeting these hidden flaws, which have been gathered up along the journey of many lives, that the great goal of union with the higher-self is achieved. We must not let a reminder of this part of the process blind us to the fact that through meditation the over-all result is one of great inner peace and happiness. Every worthwhile spiritual path includes, at the earlier stages, some sorting out of personal 'baggage'.

Note: obviously these 'symptoms' could also indicate a medical condition, therefore you are advised that you should see your health practitioner if they occur. Do not simply assume they are due to inner soul changes.

---

[71] In sinister occult circles of antiquity and today, the effort is made to actually encourage lascivious dreams in an occult context; the egoistical pleasure is bought at a cost; the sleeping soul is made prey to low entities in the fallen astral planes, and then at death, if strict effort at reversing the process has not already been made, one must meet these entities — now one's masters. This theme like many in this book can only be elucidated so far in a book; the deeper aspects are discussed in the author's seminars or private consultations.

[72] It is my conclusion that the further indications given by the initiate as to the various types of malignant beings involved, do not belong in the public domain.

Success: Reaching the divine light!
On the other side of the red window is represented the development in the seeker's soul, after successful meditation, through which higher faculties are acquired. See **Illustration 4**. We see the person now reaching up triumphantly to the light from the spiritual sun. The seeker is being supported by three pairs of angelic beings, and as you can see from their colours (which I have added), they are a higher, clearer form of the three creatures. This indicates that the divine potential in our thinking, emotion and will has been accessed and is now manifesting itself. The text underneath reads "it has manifested", this means that the spirituality within the meditant has manifested itself, so the shadow side of the soul or lower-self has at last had its day; it is finished.

The three monsters are now virtually vanquished, what is left over has subsided deep into the abyss. In their place is the divine spirituality inherent in the threefold mind. That these three soul-qualities, now spiritualized, are shown as three pairs of angelic beings upholding the meditant is a wonderful and significant indicator. This proclaims the wonderful truth that our inner being is intimately interwoven with the divine beings who live in the higher worlds, and their consciousness is starting to have presence within us.

Rudolf Steiner taught that our holistic-imaginative thinking is connected with the angels, whereas our emotional and feeling/sensing qualities are connected with the archangels. Finally, the will is connected with even higher beings, namely the principalities. That is, the **good** principalities; St. Paul's famous declaration about fighting 'against the principalities' (Ephesians 6:12), was in reference was to the evil fallen ones. In the ancient Grecian Mystery Centre of Delphi, above the threshold to the great Mystery temple, these words were written: "O, man know thyself". Here at the entrance to this great modern temple to the spirit, the red window portrays some of the deepest secrets of the quest for self-knowledge and spirituality. We are now ready to consider the much more positive and indeed sacred realities of the path to the spirit.

Appendix

If one is being troubled by one's double, or just has just entered a new relationship, it is a substantial fallacy to keep up the meditating, 'as a matter of sacred duty'. The advice given by Steiner in the situation of a new relationship, especially for young or newly married people, is to wait two years before getting seriously into deep esoteric meditating. Some other form of spiritual activity that is **not aimed at separating the three bodies**, is recommended. Concerning a mature person, an experienced meditant whose double is temporarily strengthening, especially a male in mid-life who finds his lust nature intensifying, the advice given was to stop meditating and to find a way to generally maintain a spiritual soul-mood.

Certainly this does not mean that one simply stops all inner work, but rather one ceases the meditating which is designed to form the chakras, thus separate the subtle bodies. The initiate taught his students that meditating whilst a person is in a sensuous state, results in the incorrect energies being activated in the aura, and in the astral world. Regularly cultivating a spiritual mood helps ensure that a spiritual influence is maintained in the astral body. Another suggestion is to read descriptions of the higher worlds, such as from books on life after death.

CHAPTER SIX

Sleep, dreams, the guiding angel and the three auras

Earlier in Chapter Four we saw that the first signs of actual enhanced spirituality occurs during sleep, when one is dreaming. Steiner points out the obvious, yet not often realized fact, that when we sleep we leave our body and enter into the spiritual realms. So we are as a soul actually in the higher worlds at night, without the encasement of the flesh around us. The more the organs of perception develop in the soul (the chakras) the more likely it is that one will first be able to perceive the soul world during the sleep process. That is, the more likely it is that one will be able to cognize (to consciously perceive at least for a little while) the non-material environment.

Most sleeping souls are predominantly in a dreamy state when out of their body, or when at times they are quite conscious, they are unable to retain awareness of the experiences upon re-entering the body. This is especially so if the mind is attuned to more material and earthly interests rather than spiritual themes. Likewise after death such souls discover they focussed during their incarnation on will o' the wisps which now are of little value.

But as one's life focuses on the spiritual realms and constant practice of experiencing transcendental thoughts/truths in meditation is undertaken, then the soul at night can begin to 'look around' and cognize just where it is and in what reality it is functioning. And if the chakras have been imprinting their image on your ether-body, then upon awakening you will retain at least some memory of the wonderful realities of the spiritual world. However one need not worry that meditating will all too soon plunge one into a world too alien and remote from the known, comfortable earthly world and current ego-hood; for any such awakening in the dreaming state will occur gently and gradually. In fact it won't progress beyond the occasional wonderful dream or inspirational message unless one really works hard at the inner development.

To be as attuned as possible to the immersion into the higher worlds at night, preparation is needed. Before sleeping, do your meditation, and the Evening Review - as explained in earlier chapters. Don't go into sleep after seeing a video of unpleasant scenes, etc - for the last experience of the day lives on in the soul as it begins its journey each night. The advanced meditant will enter sleep with clear memories of the last evening's dreams re-echoing in the mind.

Well, where are we during sleep? What are dreams? To answer these questions in detail would require many pages; to keep this book to a concise length, we will consider this subject only briefly. Dreams can often derive from mundane sources, such as matters of concern in daily life, or suppressed fears, desires, ambitions etc. But some dreams can be an expression of an objective encounter one has had with the guardian angel or a deceased friend or with other forces and beings in the higher worlds. However when such dreams occur they are often confused and jumbled. Through meditative activity, these dreams can become coherent and therefore deeply instructive.

We actually journey during sleep right through the soul-world and the twofold spiritual-world. It is during the journey through the astral plane that our consciousness has the interaction with the spiritual environment which is able to be recalled as a dream. It is here that deceased friends are most likely to be encountered, and many kinds of spiritual beings. Then in the dreamless sleep phase we have journeyed further from the Earth and entered lower spiritland, where the sublime hierarchical beings exist. And then later in deep dreamless sleep we are in higher spiritland, and very near to the origin of our own spiritual reality.

But the higher we journey at night, the less possibility there is for the soul to assimilate experiences consciously in those realms. Therefore it is rare that dreams occur which manifest anything of the experiences that the sleeping soul has whilst in the two stages of the actual spiritual realms. For in those remote realms the nature of existence is so different from what we understand of life here on the Earth, and so transcendental that perception and understanding of it is difficult.

In the morning it is important to avoid harshly breaking off contact with the higher worlds. There is an after-echo of the spiritual realms resonating in the soul as it fits itself back into the body. This should be sensed and maintained as long as possible. To achieve awareness of this after-echo avoid using harsh types of alarm clocks or radio-alarm clocks, for the discordant jangle these make is very harmful to this exercise of maintaining the link with your own higher-self. Such sudden loud noise, in bringing you so abruptly into the physical world, effectively ruptures the link you could have with the delicate spiritual after-echo. The subtle moods and images which are present in the soul each morning derive from the higher-self or other sources of wisdom.

If you really can not awaken in time for work without an alarm, and perhaps this is because you are especially getting up earlier to make time for meditation – then try this. Affirm strongly and clearly in a simple phrase, three times, using exactly the same words each time, that you need to wake up at such-and-such a time. But also set the alarm at first, if it is vital that you are not delayed for work; gradually you may find that at the stated hour you simply awaken. It really can work very effectively, unless you are ill or very over-worked. If however this technique does not work for you then make the effort to purchase a musical alarm clock, this brings the soul back to the body gently so that the delicate after-echoing is not obliterated.

Once you are aware that you are waking up, then close your eyes and be still, try to sense what mood you have, and then try to remember the dreams. Keep a dream diary wherein you write down your dreams as soon as practical after waking up; do not try to analyse them before writing them down. Include all the details and impressions about the dream, do not censor a detail because it seems too silly or obvious or irrelevant. The very fact that an obvious detail is being emphasized in a dream is itself of importance. Later on, at the end of the month for example, go back over the dreams, you will be amazed at what insights you gain from them. To enter ever more deeply into the dream experiences is for the meditant of very substantial importance. For once serious esoteric meditating is under way dreams take on a deeper symbolic meaning which is intimately connected with the higher worlds.

This was elucidated in 1904 in a lecture (unpublished) upon which the book, "Knowledge of the higher worlds; how is it attained" was based,

> "The dreams become less chaotic as the exercise for control of thinking is taken up seriously. The life which unfolds for the soul in sleep is entirely different for those who are training and improving their spirit-body, as compared with those who are not involved in this...The dreams become coherent, having little actions that develop on into something quite orderly and meaningful, because then our true inner spiritual being is active in us. As this happens, you will notice that you are remembering your dreams during the day-time {this is rare in normal life, but furthermore with the meditator the dreams are remembered in} a quite different way to how it normally occurs. You remember them in such a way that you are yourself an object amongst other objects in the dream. This is in fact how the **continuity of consciousness** manifests, which occurs ever more as the person develops spiritually. So long as a person identifies themselves with their body they can not acquire self consciousness when out of their body at night. Continuity of consciousness occurs slowly, this is the state wherein you are in fact awake to yourself when in higher worlds.."

One kind of dream which can occur for a meditator and which has a spiritual origin is that kind wherein someone appears and solves a difficult situation for you. This other wiser person is, according to statements made by Rudolf Steiner in esoteric lessons, one's own higher-self. This is how the increasing attunement or nearness of the soul to the higher-self manifests for the acolyte in the dreaming phase. Another example given in the Esoteric School of a dream symbol which the meditant may experience, was a vision of a radiant angelic figure offering a chalice towards one. Such a vision {or semi-awake dream} in this context is communicating that before we return to our bed we are experiencing that higher powers are again now offering conscious life to us in the physical body as a gift of grace.(1913)

As we noted earlier, the term 'chakra' is Sanskrit and means 'wheel'; it refers to circular vortex-like centres in the astral body, through which the soul can perceive in the spiritual realms. As the chakras develop, and the normal ego is in the process of transforming into its own higher archetypal truth, then more and more consciousness is gained in the sleep state. This brings its challenges at first, but then wonderful experiences are bestowed on one. In the early stages of this process you may awaken with some discomfort, feeling that you have just fled from some unpleasant reality, or you may find yourself awakening yet **already** involved in reaching for the lamp switch. These are signs of progress, but also signs that one was confronting some lower astral reality (internal or external), and perception of this caused one to return back to the physical world.

If this is happening there is no danger; do not let irrational feelings of fear triumph, just keep the curtains a little bit open, so that the room is not in total darkness. Or have a torch or lamp within easy reach, that way you can see some physical light and awaken to a secure environment. But if this all seems discomforting to you, remember that this actual beginning of interface with the hidden realities does not occur unless one has really invoked it by intense meditating. This does not have to occur, and one can just remain quietly and securely with the Rose-Cross meditation and the Foundation Stone meditation; these are given in a later chapter. [73]

Later on, if the meditant really perseveres in meditation and reaches towards tangible results he or she will be able to experience, and carry over into awakening, impressions of his or her nightly journey back through the cosmos to the Earth. For example a star constellation, magnificent in the night sky will be seen, and superimposed on this a

---

[73] I received much more impetus towards such experiences through having access over 20 years to the German originals of the more potent meditations given by the great initiate in 1924. These texts are not dealt with here.

zodiac symbol or the sound (and glyph) of a letter of the alphabet will resonate through the image.[74]

Later on you can then learn in studies of Steiner's works, that indeed the consonants are derived from the zodiac energies, raying into the aura; and the validity of your experience is supported, especially if the glyph you see is the correct one for that sign. Later on this experience may include inner feelings or images about an insect species or internal body organs, and one may start to realize that these are also related to that zodiac sign. This is a beginning of what the modern initiate may experience of what in the ancient Mystery Centres was called, "The journey to the gods above" (as distinct from sensing the divinities **below**, that is, within the soul).

One notes now how much more profound this is than an astral projection journey in which one remembers the outer landscape such as the large clock in the church tower down the road from your house, and the gleam of the moonlight on the gutter, as you float along, back to your house and into the bedroom. (See next chapter for an esoteric clarification of the nature and limits of astral projection). From the nightly journey through the cosmos when asleep, and the ability to more consciously 'dream' and recall this upon awakening in a clear and meaningful way, one is enabled to gradually understand the cosmos in which we are journeying. It also enables profound insights from the guiding angel to be received and retained.

The guiding angel and the meditant
The guiding angel of the meditant has the task of integrating into the soul-spiritual nature the dynamics which we have mentioned above. That is, to what extent our personal karma/destiny can accommodate the time for inner development, and the encountering of higher forces, as well as the opportunity to redeem some further past negative events. These live on as a part of the lower self or double, as well as occurring as a 'tension' with other persons, which has to be eventually balanced out.

The angel also has to be more involved in guarding the meditating person, whom it is guiding, from negative forces, and yet at the same time assisting the person to be more receptive to the influence of higher spiritual beings. For the meditant is gradually given intuitive glimpses into new esoteric life-tasks, small at first, designed to help other people and the Earth itself in various ways. These glimpses have to permeate through to the meditant's still somewhat clouded

---

[74] As my ability in this aspect of esoteric activity developed, I discovered that some of the planetary angles (aspect) in a client's chart could be known, without referring to their horoscope.

consciousness, and here the guiding angel is in the strongest position to ensure that such insights are registered.

The guiding angel is of course fully conscious throughout the night, caring for the soul in its care as it is carried by cosmic currents through the planetary spheres into the zodiac and then back again by morning. The guiding angel is active in the night, weaving the essence of our previous day's experiences into the tapestry of world karma. It also converses with us each night, giving really clear and relevant advice for the next day. As Rudolf Steiner taught, it may well 'say' to you, 'At 2.15 tomorrow afternoon you will encounter the following opportunity; you should respond in this way, if you wish to avoid negative consequences for your future destiny....'

There are two really important aspects to the matter of one's relationship to the guiding angel. Firstly, when we will to walk through life consciously with our angel, it is really of the greatest possible importance in this 'working' with our angel to realize that we **must ask** specifically for its help. This is not necessary for those specific actions which the angel itself has decided to undertake, nor for much of its work with its human 'foster-child', but for a task which we can see is necessary, and of benefit to the community, (not of benefit to our ego-centred longings) we need to directly ask for help. This activity is different from deep meditative prayer which is more correctly directed to much higher powers.

However because the activity of the guiding angel becomes so important, it is anyway important each day to attune oneself to one's guiding angel and seek its help for that day. The experienced meditant will start to discover that again and again a conscious reverential request to this being at moments of difficulty, will bring a discernible result, even sometimes tangibly, like a little miracle.

This being is also intimately involved in the ultimate goal of the inner pathway, namely the arising of high spiritual qualities within one's soul, the sum of which constitutes the spiritual self. These sacred spiritual forces derive in the first instance, cosmically speaking, from the real heavens beyond the astral plane; more specifically considered, they derive from the hierarchy of the angels. Hence for each individual they are held and nurtured by the guiding angel. It is the angel's task to encourage us to seek spirituality and then to let the 'substance of spirituality' merge into the human soul (aura) in proportion as the lower self is extinguished. So the inner experiences and outer 'accidental' events that occur to the meditant are an expression of the will of the guiding angel. Naturally such nurturing guidance has to be in accordance with the necessities of one's own past karma.

To assist the meditant to become attuned to this activity of the guiding angel and to awaken in us the holiness of sleep, Rudolf Steiner gave the following meditative text;

> "I go to sleep. Until I awaken my soul will be in the spiritual realms. And there it will meet the higher being who guides me through this earthly life. The guiding angel who is ever present in the spiritual world, who hovers above my head. My soul will meet there the guiding spirit of my life. And when I awaken this meeting with the guiding spirit will have taken place. The wings of my guiding angel will have drawn near to my soul."[75]

As the soul journeys on towards union with the eternal higher-self, and spiritual 'substance' becomes ever more present in the aura, then a link is forged with the guiding angel. This begins to manifest in various wonderful ways. In particular, a kind of inner dialogue begins, in moments when we place a question before our own consciousness, a still silent 'voice' is perceived, it is not a tangible voice of any kind, but rather an answer to the question, the dilemma, is registered. (If it is a voice then a being of some kind on the astral plane is contacting one – not always a good sign).

Gradually, one learns to take up dialogue with this 'voice' perceiving it to be an aspect of the self, namely the higher-self, but this is brought to an interrelationship with the earthly self by the guiding angel – until it is totally integrated into the meditant's consciousness. This stage of communion with the angel reduces the need for external counselling and advice, whether from the oracles like the I Ching or from various people to whom we turn in times of need. At a later stage the angel can inspire the earnest meditant in sacred meditative activity with insights that announce themselves to the interior mind, imbued with an aura of holiness. And the experiencing of these insights brings profound joy.

Once the meditant has achieved the beginning stages of self-initiation these moments may even bring those same sacred experiences that occurred to advanced spiritual seekers in earlier centuries. For example, when in deep contemplation of holy truths, seeking to bring into conceptual form high spiritual truths, a process which is usually regarded as scarcely possible, a task of the highest value to contemporary humanity, which is so caught in intellectualism, a physically perceptible 'sign' of the presence of an angelic being can actually occur.

---

[75] In German there are several terms for guardian angel, one of which is 'genius', which means in German a non-human spiritual being. It has been placed untranslated so to speak, in the published English version: this is erroneous, for in English it means a person with a high IQ.

A specific example of which I am aware is that of an exquisite perfume of some unknown flower, that permeates one's meditative space when in special moments of deep focussed contemplation of sacred truths, an exalted state of **cosmic-spiritual** consciousness is reached. In achieving this, the higher self becomes at least momentarily stronger, allowing influences from angelic beings to pervade the aura. This is not a subjective phenomenon, another person entering the room, can detect the exquisite perfume too; such a sacred experience imbues the soul with a deep and joyous peace.

The matter of our interaction with the angels is not an abstract subject, for as Steiner revealed, much depends in the near future destiny of humanity, as to whether humanity does respond to the inner prompting of the angels. For we are now due, in the cosmic evolutionary scheme of things, to develop some sensitivity to them, to prevent a serious decadence engulfing modern civilisation.[76] Indeed part of the responsibility of the meditant is to understand that many unexplained 'divine' events in human life are the work of the angel, (as heralds of the will of God).

Certainly God is very close to the inner core of our being, and is the foundation of our existence. It is however the angel that sends a telepathic 'watch out' message saving us from walking too far towards the edge of a cliff, thus falling over into the yawning chasm, or impels someone to open up the old disused 'fridge' door only to find a frightened child locked up in it by accident, etc.

The second point is much more esoteric, it concerns the fact that although our higher-self is a very real entity in the higher worlds, an entity with awareness of all of our past lives, the higher self, from the viewpoint of our human consciousness, is in essence germinal, it is like a bud seeking to unfold and become empowered. Until our consciousness is lifted up to merge with the higher-self, or human spirit, this exists as part of the spiritual being-ness of the angelic hosts, in particular of our own guiding angel.

For those with a deep focus on the Christian concept of the Holy Spirit as the bringer of spirituality, I suggest recalling an earlier point mentioned, namely that the Logos is the same being as that known as Brahma. Now it is clear the Holy Spirit is the third aspect of the Trinity, however, as Steiner taught, the most holy of the angels as the vessel in that hierarchy for the Holy Spirit, is also meant by the term, "the Holy

---

[76] See his lecture, "What does the Angel do in our astral body?" 9th Oct 1918 R. Steiner Press

Spirit". So, impulses from this angelic being will naturally involve our guiding angel.

Now the implication of this is, Steiner taught, that as higher consciousness develops, we actually begin to have the same sort of consciousness as our angel has. That is, as Image Consciousness occurs, we will perceive higher realities just as does our angel. The implication of this is that our 'seeing' or consciously experiencing transcendental realities involves, to some extent, the merging of our consciousness with that of the angels.

The reader is well-advised to contemplate the further implications of this reality, for example with regard to Spiritual Enlightenment and the archangels, by studying the text referred to earlier, "An Outline of Esoteric Science." Such a consciousness is unlikely to be achieved through a pathway not derived from genuine initiation knowledge, of which Rudolf Steiner was the leading representative in recent times. In this text, it is explained that the incarnation of the cosmic Christ is of pivotal importance in making possible such an advanced state of being.

Our knowledge of the world derives primarily from our sense-organs, from what these report to us about the environment around us, and the thoughts that we consequently form in response to these. If higher knowledge and actual Spiritual Enlightenment is to occur, then we have to develop the ability to use 'other 'see-ing' organs, namely the vortices in the aura, often called, 'chakras'.

Once these are active in the meditant, they extend the ability for perceiving into the realms beyond matter and thus acquiring knowledge from this realm. But to develop them requires the various ethical qualities considered in the next chapter, and the inner strength that is attained by encountering and subduing the lower-self, as explained in the preceding chapter. Further, one needs the courage to actively explore beyond the senses' boundaries.

This perspective is beautifully expressed by Steiner in a meditative verse, entitled 'Pentecost'. He gave the text this name because his research showed him that it is the subtle activity of the cosmic Christ in the soul that sustains the meditant in these processes. The Pentecost festival refers to the day in the Church calendar which commemorates the outpouring of the spirit upon the first people to recognize that the cosmic Christ had come to the Earth.

From that time forth those people experienced a higher consciousness which was not damaging to their normal self-hood. To progress as a conscious person beyond the portal that stands at the boundaries of the sense-perception, is the great challenge for the meditant.

Pentecost

Where the senses' knowledge ends,
there first arises the portal,
which opens to the soul's being
the realities of life.
Its key is formed by the soul
when it empowers itself through the battle
that cosmic powers wage
with human forces
in its own inner depths:
when through itself, it drives out the sleep
that envelops in spiritual night,
at the boundaries of the senses,
its faculties of knowledge*. [77]   (* that is, cognition)

Since it is only whilst we are alive on the Earth that the ego can in freedom find the will to achieve the union with the divine light, contemporary initiation knowledge discourages the urge to flee from the Earth. Rather it advises one to consider transcending the Earth only after the necessary link to the cosmic Christ (or Brahma, or cosmic Logos), the source of spirituality, has been achieved. This requires a number of incarnations. The reason that it is possible only on the Earth is because here we have such an independent ego-sense, through which we may in freedom choose whether to align with the source of human spirituality. This involves also meeting our lower-self and transforming it, something that is not really possible in the full sense in the higher worlds.

It has a 'future-oriented' goal, seeking to be of assistance to the Earth in the future, rather than wanting to end one's series of incarnations, which is almost always a premature wish for most spiritual aspirants. It is a question of not being premature with this goal, overcoming the need to incarnate is not, in itself, incorrect.

The three auras and how they change as spirituality develops.
The ennoblement that the meditant is granted by earnest inner work on the initiatory path is very clearly portrayed by considering the three auras of the human being. It is generally known in esoteric circles, that we don't just have an aura of our soul, but two other auras as well, which are a manifestation of our spirit. It is important here not to become confused about these two spiritual auras, especially if your

---

[77] The German text of this verse is copyright to Rudolf Steiner Verlag, Dornach, published in Wahrspruchworte, 1969, page 105.

reading of anthroposophy has made it quite clear that we have a triune spiritual structure. As the initiate explains, the spirit is threefold (which he designates as spirit-self, life-spirit, spirit-man), but these manifest as two, not three, distinct auras.

Descriptions given by Rudolf Steiner[78] (there are similar descriptions to some extent in theosophical literature) of these other two auras, indicate how the human soul and spirit appears to the seer in an unevolved state, and also after spiritual development has been undertaken. In the drawings of the various auras of the human being presented here, the intention is to portray the typical colours which the seer sees in the auras, and which indicate our soul and spirit qualities.[79]

No attempt has been made to 'paint the aura', since it is impossible to portray the chakras and the intricate, living, metamorphosing variations that occur. The actual aura is of course three-dimensional and full of energies in constant motion, and also changing slightly in colour and form.

These drawings nevertheless are a valuable guide to realizing just how real is **the effect on the soul of spiritualization exercises, especially meditation**. The substance of colour-patches in these diagrams are not composed of substance, they are the colour equivalent experiences registered by a seer endowed with Image Consciousness, of the corresponding soul quality.

Illustration Six represents the typical 'colour experiences' of an aura of the undeveloped, un-ethical soul. It does not represent precisely how such an aura would appear, rather the most common qualities. This picture was painted from the indications by Rudolf Steiner as to the colours of such a person.

The colours of the unevolved aura

Top left: An area of greyish stripes, this is how fear appears.
Top right: An area of muddy brown-red, this is how sensual lust appears
Middle left: Dark blood-red, this is indicative of unintelligence

---

[78] These descriptions were given to his esoteric students in 1905, and in his book "Anthroposophy" {"Theosophy"}, and in an article in an esoteric journal (1904).
[79] As Rudolf Steiner carefully insists in his "Theosophy, the inner qualities in the soul are seen by a seer as something which **corresponds** to what we know as colours in the physical world. There are no 'finer substances' of different colours in the aura, there is only astral reality.

Central: Darkish unclean green, this identifies injured dignity, self-centredness
Middle right: Indigo, this reveals an inner laziness, unwillingness to work upon oneself, but can be quite happy to do external work of any kind
Lower right: Orange-yellow, the lowest kind of self-centred hardened egotism
Lower left: Grey-blue patch, cowardice
Bottom: Red and blue intermixed, intelligence used for personal pleasures

Diagram 1 gives some understanding of the proportions of the auras to the physical body; as Steiner described, these extend about a metre from the body, in all directions. Now, if we want to compare this to an aura that is somewhat more evolved, one would notice that the general colour tone has lightened, the brownish-red colour has gone, and the orange yellow has cleaned up and become smaller, the green will be much cleaner, showing more capacity for empathy with others. If this person is for example, anxiously waiting then red-blue stripes, raying out appear. There can be patches of red with orange flecks; a sign of inquisitive curiosity. Flecks that change from blue over to green indicate absent-mindedness.

Cleverness which still clings to sensuality appears as green and brown mixed through each other; if there is more green showing, and less brown, there is real helpfulness, and considerateness. Red nodule-shaped forms, with root-like extensions indicate anger; if there are small but strong arcs of brownish-red, these reveal retained grudges.

As the effect of a spiritual lifestyle, in which meditating, in this deeper esoteric sense, begins to manifest in us, our astral aura changes, and the lower of the two spiritual auras becomes much more structured and radiant. As Rudolf Steiner describes:

> As love and enthusiasm for the great spiritual ideas take hold of the person, everything in the aura becomes quickened, and the outcome of this higher life of thought is that the aura is cleansed. All earthly desires and materialistic attitudes, which do come to expression in the aura, now form into small globular shapes and condense with advancing spiritual work, becoming ever smaller and then are dissipated and expelled by the purifying light of the spiritualized consciousness.[80]

The astral aura of an evolved, spiritualising soul

---

[80] Lecture of 5th June 1910, in GA 125, page 67.

Now consider **Illustration Seven.** This shows the astral aura which has been spiritualized. In this the seer experiences much more attractive qualities, which register as finer 'colours':

Top: A pleasant yellow, indicative of clear healthy thinking
Upper left: Purple (and mauve), indicating piety, reverence with real religiosity
Upper right: Viridian green, showing understanding of life, and compassion
Upper left: Paler green, indicating intelligence
Upper right: Orange, revealing tendency to pride, to vanity
Middle left: Bright reddish-pink, showing presence of natural selflessness, especially mother love
Middle right: Rose-pink, benevolence, affection
Lower left: Pale blue, indicative of piety, religiosity
Lower right: Indigo, showing an earnest person, with idealism
Bottom: Red and blue pleasantly intermixed, showing capacity to place intelligence at the service of others
Also (not shown in sketch), pleasant yellow-green, this shows a good memory.

Now we come to an important point; if the aura, the soul, becomes 'spiritualized', then it is from the human spirit (which is intimately linked with the higher divine beings) that the spiritual energies or 'substance' is coming. And if the human spirit is able to come into life within the soul (personality), then it is also **itself** becoming more developed and consolidated.

That is, from the effort of the meditant, and of the angel, the human spirit or higher-self is becoming more tangibly developed and empowered for the meditant, and this is to be seen in the beautiful improvement in the soul aura. However, this in turn means that the spirit or spirit-body (and hence its aura) must have developed; and indeed it has.

Diagram 1: The relative size of the soul aura to the physical person.

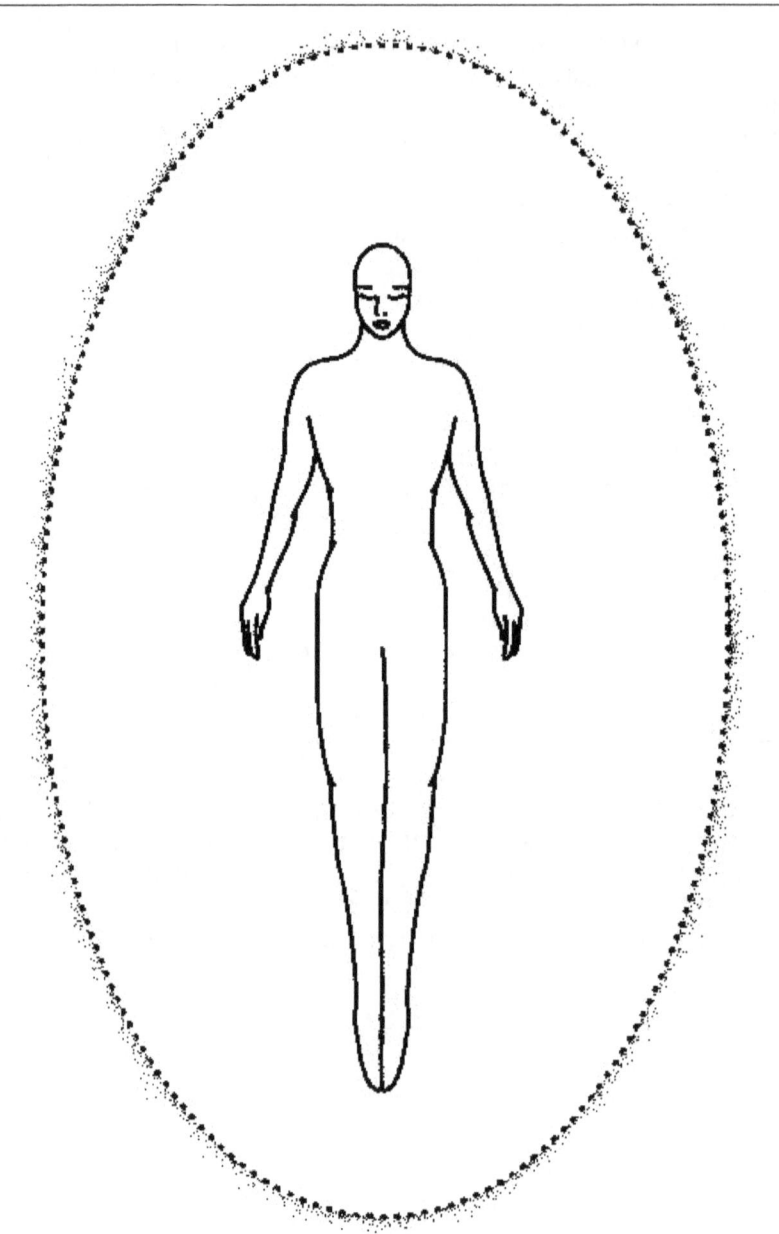

Before we consider the colour (that is, the colour equivalent impressions) experienced by the seer of the human spirit, it is important to note that the human spirit is two-fold with regard to auras, the nature of these are explained in Steiner's book "Theosophy", see my appendix to Chapter Four. Briefly, he explains that the lower spiritual body or aura is an expression of our spiritual thinking and feelings, whilst the higher spiritual body is formed of the selfless will, in which divine energies from heights of spiritual reality are present (or from God, in normal language). Here it is important to note that our spiritual bodies or auras consist of that same 'substance' as selfless love, as inspired thoughts, and its origin is from the consciousness of the divine spiritual beings that sustain and evolve the human life wave.

Illustration Nine shows the first, or lesser of these two spiritual auras in its unevolved state; this is also known as the mental-body aura. Rudolf Steiner taught that in previous millennia this appeared as an unimpressive small auric oval. Its colour then was brownish, and within it there is not much more than greenish patches and patches with both red and blue, all of a dull nature. In modern times, it has developed finer 'colours', and it has enlarged to almost the size of the astral aura (space has no reality in the spiritual realms, but nevertheless there is a spatial impression gained of this aura when observed with incarnate people). In fact, when those finer qualities have arisen in the astral aura that we considered earlier, then the first spiritual aura has also gained these same 'colours' – for it is from the spirit(aura) that these qualities have permeated the astral aura.

Diagram 2 shows the relative size of the evolved higher spirit aura to the physical person. It is clear from the above, that the reasonably developed **first** spiritual aura will have a close similarity to that of its consequence in the astral aura – with the exception that the 'colours' are much more alive and scintillating (and of course the substance of them is of the spiritual realms, not astral). In other words, the colour experiences of the ennobled but lesser spiritual aura are very similar to the ennobled astral aura, except that they are formed of higher 'substance' and hence much more radiant.

Illustration Eight: The 'colours' seen in this first spiritual aura. These have a similar implication as in the developed astral aura. As with illus. 7, no attempt is made to represent the chakras in the aura. It's a case of trying to gain an impression of the spiritual-energies that constitute these auras, by indicating the colour-impressions they give to the seer. A pleasant yellow is indicative not only of clear thinking, but also that the person is someone with a spiritual-holistic thinking ability;

Diagram 2: The relative size of the evolved higher spiritual aura to the physical person.

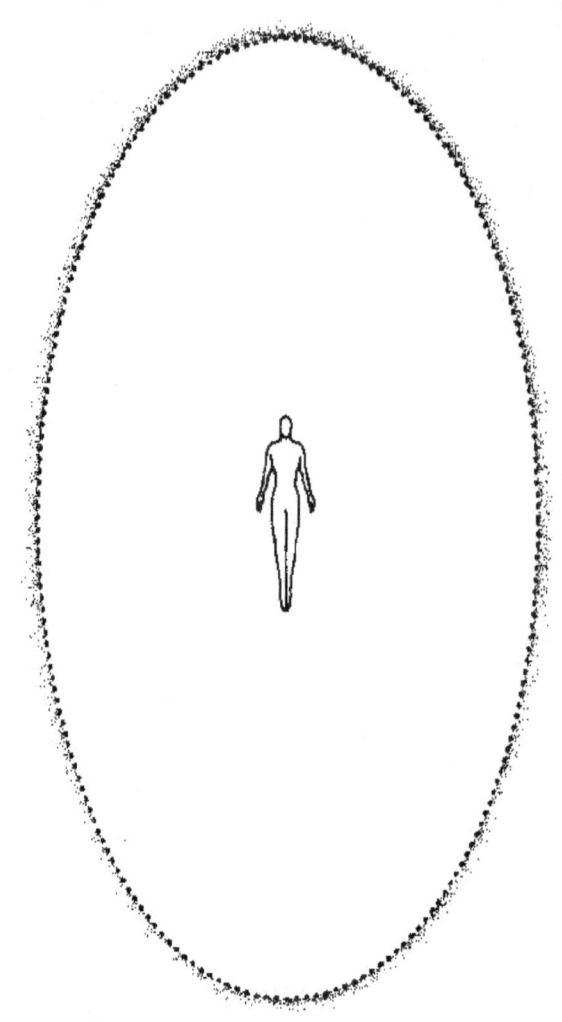

purple shows piety and reverence with real religiosity; viridian green showing understanding of life and compassion; orange can still be there, revealing a tendency to pride. The bright rose-red, showing the presence of natural selflessness in the astral aura, is somewhat different here.

Steiner describes thoughts which derive from devoted unselfish love as raying forth in "glorious rose-red", whilst rose-pink indicates benevolence and affection. Pale blue is indicative as before of piety; the presence of indigo shows an earnest person, with idealism. Purple shows piety and religious fervour, and the ability to selflessly serve a sacred ideal. Gone is the small brownish oval, with its dull colours; it has become a radiant and beautiful spiritual-body (aura), and has imprinted its qualities onto the astral aura, which thus resembles it.

However, we also have a third aura, that of the higher aspect of the spirit-body. Within it lives the eternal core of **cosmic-spiritual** consciousness. This aura is not so developed in humanity, and amongst people of little evolvement it appears in its undeveloped form; namely a small brownish oval with stripes of dull indigo and stripes of dull green. It is shown in its unevolved condition in **Illus. 9** (the upper aura), and is also known as the causal-body or ego-body. Rudolf Steiner also refers to it as the spiritual-body. This aura or spiritual-organism is slowly developing; the indications from Rudolf Steiner are one of the very few sources about this aura when it is well developed, as few seers even have perception of those spiritual energies of higher spiritland from which it is formed.

The well developed higher spiritual aura is shown in **Illus. 10.** Like the other drawings, the effort here has been to indicate only the colours and general nature of the aura. No attempt is made to indicate the chakras, but it is very important to realize that they are now there in all their glory in the developed, empowered spiritual-aura. It is also important to note that this illustration is included, like a number of other esoteric themes mentioned briefly in the book, in order to give some orientation as to the wonderful future that awaits evolving humanity. The fully developed higher spiritual body or spiritual aura shown theoretically here, is described by the initiate in a lecture about a high degree initiate, and obviously will not develop in normal humanity for millennia.

The evolved higher (second) spirit aura
This aura presents the effect of a rich viridian green, indicating a deep compassion, towards all beings. It reveals also a gentle pink, indicative of the capacity for devoted love. It also has heavenly blue, showing the presence of self-sacrificing selflessness as a constant mood of the

heart. As Rudolf Steiner writes, "As this self-sacrificing intensifies, then the blue metamorphoses into a pale purple, showing the presence of self-sacrifice as a will-force, in other words, active service to the greater good." Thus there is also much purple, which Rudolf Steiner describes as indicating "love-filled devotion to a task that helps the world" and "self-sacrificing will". There could be some orange present, revealing that a personal egotism can perhaps still be subtly present.

This aura's outer area commences with a magnificent golden-yellow, showing the capacity not only for **cosmic-spiritual** consciousness but also for **high-initiation** consciousness. Around this golden area, there is encompassing layer of a exquisite rose-pink, the colour of feeling unconditional love, and this rose-pink passes over into a magenta tone. Finally as the outermost layer, this aura rays out into its environs in violet, a spiritual colour. Such a person has become an initiate with **high-initiation** consciousness. Rudolf Steiner described violet as a colour reality in the aura as indicating the ability in the spiritualized human being to revere, to express reverence. Whereas violet, as a colour reality perceived elsewhere (in a sacred cloth, or appearing in a vision), speaks of "the soul resurrecting within the spiritual".

In these simplified drawings then, we have a depiction of the actual changes that occur as spiritual development takes effect on the basic 'tones' of our soul and our two-fold spirit. **Diagram Two** indicates the approximate proportion of the developed higher spiritual aura to the physical body. An audience in a lecture in Berlin in 1904 were informed that the higher of the spiritual auras was equivalent in size to a typical three-storey house in Berlin.

It is important to realize that one should engage with colours, to seek to feel them sensitively, and therefore to realize that there is much confusion regarding colours that arise when red and blue are mixed. There are also incorrect translations of German terms for a colour into English. It appears that especially the actual nature of the colour "violet" is unclear to many people; violet is the exact colour of the flowers called 'violets'. Some anthroposophical publications refer to the third set of windows in the Goetheanum as 'violet' for example, unaware that the colour is actually purple.

The chart from Winsor & Newton paint-makers shows a form of purple as violet. Winton oil colours card only shows a 'cobalt violet' – which is purple. It also shows cerise (or magenta) as a form of burgundy-purple. You often cannot actually correctly see violet except in natural sunlight. Using an electric globe will often distort the violet into purple. Chromo oil pastels make a true violet.

So, in an evolved soul, who has taken up the meditative life earnestly, the astral aura will have the appearance of **illus. 7** and the lower of the two spiritual auras will have the basic colour qualities shown in **illus. 8**. The higher spiritual aura will not be as magnificent as **illus. 10**, but it will have improved way beyond the basic state shown in **illus. 9**. Now if this stage is reached, then the meditant will be gradually gaining awareness of, and eventually merging with, the higher-self, or human spirit, with its two-fold auras.

Having considering the aura of the ennobled human spirit, it is appropriate here to conclude this chapter with some indications from the Esoteric Lessons about encountering the higher-self, through meditation. Furthermore, since this also involves the theme of the so-called Masters, or high degree initiates, a brief overview of this theme is included also.

Encountering the higher self
Two different perspectives were given in the Esoteric School, on the profound theme of the nature of the higher-self. The actual encounter of this higher-self involves experiencing the full scope of our self, as an aspect of God. The attaining of such a sublime heights of consciousness is in effect, to experience the divine-spiritual hierarchical beings that make manifest the uncaused God. Normally we only vaguely sense the indirect presence of our higher all-enveloping self, for example when we feel awe at the wisdom guiding our steps through an unfolding karma, or at the sheer wisdom that is interwoven in the symbolic language of a dream. Such a deepening of consciousness is in many respects, the goal of meditating, as indicated in the Introduction.

Our consciousness undergoes an important change in meditation, and this can remain beyond the actual meditation session. As we have indicated earlier, our thoughts begin to be experienced as they really are; living spiritual insights, not simply somewhat lifeless mental images, which constitute a large part of earthly thinking. There is a vital difference between these mental representations that we make when a thought is registered by the brain, and the actual thought-insight itself.

The former is but a shadowy silhouette of the latter. Consciousness (thinking) becomes ever more refined and ethereal, and this enables one to experience spiritual thoughts independently of the brain. A major theme in the early years of the Esoteric School was that of the higher self, as a great macrocosmic reality. The students were taught that as one attains to this, one begins to have the feeling of, 'it thinks' rather than 'I myself am thinking'; as if something else, some other aspect of my higher being is thinking within me.

It is as if a 'thought-body', a coherent organism which produces real thoughts, (that is, spiritual insights) is now actively present. One is now experiencing this inner activity which originates in the human spirit, rather than simply the mental images that we form after becoming aware of the thought or insight. This living inter-weaving activity of the 'intuitive spiritual thinker' within us is always present, but usually not detected, it is the supra-conscious, so to speak. It is through such subtle, but significant, spiritual development processes as this that consciousness becomes ever more body-free. In other words, the ego accesses this transcendental higher 'thinking' that exists in the soul.

This gives rise to the feeling that some higher spiritual presence is living in the thinking-consciousness. Eventually, this same kind of enlivening of consciousness can also be felt within the emotive forces and the will. This is how the earnest meditator first meets with the mysterious higher-self, the divine spiritual essence of the human being. This is obviously a deeper process to that of just stepping out of the body by various astral travel techniques.

Important notes from one esoteric lesson (1906?) record, "Above all, the esotericist should keep in mind that the entire purpose of one's striving is to reach the higher-self, and therefore one should constantly contemplate what this higher-self is. The meditant is not to think that one should bring something towards the higher-self, but rather await in patient humility for the higher-self to draw near. An indication that this is occurring can manifest in a new and wonderful experience when we are dreaming; it is known as the 'doubling of the ego'."

The students were taught that, if in a dream someone appears before you and advises you what to do, and the advice is indeed wiser than your own conscious intelligence, then this is often a sign that your astral body is becoming receptive to one's own higher reality, or higher-self. A second indication Steiner gave is that which involves hearing a subtle voice giving advice, just when you are in a really difficult moment. This can occur when you have made a decision that seems appropriate, but then you become aware of this inner voice advising against the decision, and it turns out to be right. Thirdly, during meditating another subtle experience of encountering the higher-self in the preliminary sense will occur, which later becomes ever more substantial.

In a lesson from 1909, the ways that the mysterious higher-self manifests were explained. The initial experience is very subtle and hence hard to describe; one knows that it has drawn near, only through its after-echo. It leaves a mood of holiness which lives on and enriches one's day, pervading it with a meaning and nearness to divinity, in the midst of mundane activity. It is rather like suddenly seeing the sun appearing from behind the clouds on a dreary overcast day.

In my experience, it is similar to the experience of almost remembering an exquisite dream, but only catching a mood, not any images. Again the reader should contemplate the point mentioned earlier, that our higher eternal-self is intimately interconnected with the divine-spiritual hierarchies.[81]

Concerning the Masters
Much speculation is to be found in New Age writings about the individuals who are thought of as Masters or Adepts, or what I have usually called, initiates. Such advanced souls are generally extremely discrete and do not disclose themselves to more than a tiny number of students. Rudolf Steiner said very little about this subject, but it is important that some remarks about the true initiates are mentioned here. The first point is to know that earnest meditating, in the sense of this book, has the effect "that the meditant participates in the work of the initiates". (1907)

That is, we can help these great individuals whose will is merged, in a certain sense, with the hierarchies or divine-spiritual beings, by making active in us our spiritual potential. Also, Rudolf Steiner taught his esoteric students that during meditation, these great persons let their wisdom stream down upon the earnest meditant, and that indeed divine beings also can stream down, and help the spiritualization process. (1907) [82]

It is clear from the view of human nature and the spiritual world, as elaborated in Rudolf Steiner's teachings, that 'channelling', meaning a process for which the receiver requires no genuine esoteric development, is not the method for communicating to a person which is preferred by a true initiate. It may be used at times, but it is also used by many other

---

[81] Very much about this profound subject can become disclosed to the earnest seeker who contemplatively studies the cosmology chapter in Steiner's Outline of Esoteric Science.

[82] The writer has had some small affirmation of the reality of this process of meditation bringing about interaction between the earnest meditant and the divine hierarchical beings, namely, the lesser of them, the angels. In particular the meditant, when seeking earnestly to become enlightened concerning initiation insights, itself a process of real sacredness, can become aware of exquisite scents of heavenly flowers.

beings and deceased people, with naturally psychic people. But there are also malignant initiates, and some of these seek to influence our thoughts through alluring occult-esoteric writings, channelled by a variety of persons. Unfortunately, most of these 'channellers' are unaware that intensive esoteric development along the lines elucidated in this book is essential for insights of real integrity and depth to be experienced.

Regarding the deeper communicating of a Master, Steiner taught that when the Master speaks, the student may hear nothing directly, however the student will subtly hear the wisdom of the initiate resounding within their own thoughts, if they can become attuned to their own inner being. (1907)

Another passage from Rudolf Steiner concerning the great initiates emphasizes this point that the greater self is outside of the normal personality. The student should not consider that the wisdom they are seeking is within the current personality, but rather one must be slowly imbued with wisdom, from without...

> "I should no longer will to use {as a basis for the quest} that which is in me, which is only the effect of the past; rather I should hollow out my personal egotistical nature and become a vessel for the wisdom of the initiates. Only after this is attained may I receive the wisdom which allows me to gaze into the future of the human life-wave.
>
> Thus it is that for the seeker, self-knowledge is living existentially in a humble listening to those who have already learnt what she or he has still to learn, and this of course will normally be the case for the student. It is for this reason that the esotericist reveres any true initiate or advanced disciple on the path, if such are encountered, and does not seek to find the Master or advanced disciple **within** himself or her self, but rather finds the self in the other, greater self which is outside there in the world." (1905)

From a lecture in 1904, the following valuable general remarks about the Masters.

> ....when some one believes that they have nothing to learn from anyone, then that is a sure sign that a person is **not** so advanced. The more advanced is a person, the more certain they become that human beings stand at different levels of development, and that at all times there have been present

those who have been the spiritual leaders of humanity, people who have advanced ahead of the rest of humanity. These are they who are most difficult for the less developed sector of humanity to understand, they have at most only been recognized.

The Theosophical [Anthroposophical] movement was founded by such difficult-to-understand, difficult-to-recognize individualities. It is often asked just why these highly developed persons do not show themselves; why they make themselves only slightly perceptible. The answer is to be found in one of the deepest of the theosophical texts, a small book, which at the same time encompasses a world of wisdom: Light on the Path. What is said there, is that these leading beings, that are so far ahead of normal humanity, are highly evolved individualities; they can be present, without being recognized. It is said they can reside in St Petersburg, London, Berlin or Paris, without anyone recognizing them, or at least, only by a tiny handful of people, and this is true.

There are certain reasons why these persons remain discrete, why these leaders of humanity must remain hidden. It is necessary for these beings to have a kind of wall around them, so that only those who are prepared for the experience of meeting them through an appropriate life-style encounter them. Such beings have, in addition to their infinite goodness, at the same time a great power, and much that occurs in human evolution proceeds from these beings, without humanity knowing this.

For those to whom in moments of inner stillness the voice speaks, for these the social organizations {Theosophical/Anthroposophical Society} are only the outer instruments of these beings.....these great adepts can not be placed within such a society, their activity transcends organizations. The outer organization is not the main thing, yet we still do want to care for such societies, not because we over-estimate them, but because we would be disturbed and hindered in our spiritual work without such an organ of the {spiritual} activity. That is, if such an organization or society encompassing Europe, America, Asia, Africa, and Australia did not exist,{the activity would be hindered}.[83]

A society dedicated to the impulses of these great individuals is different to other societies, the people therein wish to be united

---

[83] Yes, he does specify Australia.

to each other not through dogmas and concepts but through the heart; through developing a heart dynamic in which the feelings can comprehend truths, a heart imbued with wisdom. We wish to feel filled with a common spiritual life, this spiritual life or power should flow wherever our souls are together in such a way.

Such a society seeks, in that it seeks to develop such heart qualities, to build a middle point, a centre of a vortex, in which the spiritual qualities of a group are gathered together, and it thus seeks to allow this concentrated light to flow out in all directions into the world. In each gathering this is the important thing, not so much what is said, what is taught, but rather that the people feel themselves en-filled with this right spiritual life, which then streams out into the world, enabling other people to gradually comprehend this light."

Obviously such great people as the high degree initiates have a tremendously developed spirit-body, which would be perceptible in their two spirit auras. Within these auras, the chakras would be fully empowered, radiant and scintillating. In the next chapter, the actual esoteric nature of the chakras and how they are developed in an esoteric manner is explained.

CHAPTER SEVEN

The chakras

In this chapter we will consider the spiritual dynamics active in a meditator who is beginning to experience higher realities. This will be followed by an exploration of the deeper secrets of the chakras, that is, aspects which are not dealt with in popular New Age books. Above all else, in this pathway the wholesome development of the chakras is recognized to be due to the development of higher spirituality in the soul. It is the presence of virtue, of purity and wisdom, which causes the chakras to form.

But, furthermore, the process of spiritual esoteric development, as I have emphasized earlier, is not a solitary human reality. It occurs in tandem with the help and inspiration of the divine beings of the higher worlds. This is not just a 'pious' attitude, it is, to the initiate, a statement of specific fact. The chakras develop **not only** as our soul is purified through our effort, but also as spiritual energies stream into our aura, helping this process.

Illustration Eleven is a pastel drawing by Rudolf Steiner, called "The human being in the spirit" (Der Mensch im Geiste), shows some of the fascinating secrets of the deeper meditating system presented here. It indicates something of the cosmic forces that stream into the meditating person. The meditant is seated on a stump or clump of rock, deep in meditative thought on St. John's Gospel.[84] The golden quality about the head indicates the presence of cosmic thoughts (spiritual holistic truths) in his or her aura. For such thoughts have a 'substance' in the astral world, they are a reality. When the meditant attains to the thoughts experienced during meditation, especially the deep spiritual insights attained in **cosmic-spiritual** consciousness, these cause an intense radiance in the aura.

Above, in the middle of the picture, in a green-blue colour, is the guiding angel, whose arms are receiving a heavenly golden radiance, and then letting this beautiful light flow gently down onto the meditant. Beyond the angel is a remote spiritual light-source, with four arms, slowly turning, from which the divine light is emanating. This represents the sun, not the physical one, **but the spiritual sun**. Higher up, and within the orange-red colour field, is a bright orange being, which seems to be lacking any lower part to its form. This is a dubious entity, which can be identified, in anthroposophical language, as a Luciferic angel, which is similar to what is known as a 'fallen angel' in Christian traditions. Steiner describes that this is how such beings

---

[84] The letters "Joh" are an abbreviation of the German name, "Johannes".

appear to the developed seer; they lack a lower part, and have 'wings' which originate from the larynx area.[85]

One feels that this being would like to influence the meditant, but is prevented from doing so because the guardian angel is actively intervening. Naturally, this dynamic is true only if one is meditating with the right motivation. It would be the reversed situation if one were to seek to **simply experience freedom from the body** by some other kind of 'meditating' technique. For example, those techniques which strive to separate the meditant from the Earth, perhaps by conferring the ability to float in the air, or survive on almost no food.

The chakras in the advanced meditant
We shall now consider in detail the significance of the so-called chakras and the kundalini in esoteric wisdom, by referring to the central panel of the red window. It is important to realize that the chakras in the aura of the soul (astral body) **can not be developed by simply having a wish for this**, or by carrying out a mental 'chakra-balancing' exercise from a New Age book, because they do not exist in the aura, except in a rudimentary form. Certainly, some healing work and 'balancing activity' with regard to centres of force in the ether-body can be carried out, as these vortices do exist there, but they are not the chakras of the astral body.

Refer again to **Illustration Four,** especially the central panel in the Red Window. It shows a human face enveloped in a number of extraordinary things, some symbolic, some real. Underneath this panel are the words "**I am beholding**", that is, the meditant has succeeded in raising his/her consciousness above the material world and attained to seer-ship. The carving depicts some of the fascinating processes that occur in the aura of the meditant when this stage is achieved.

Rudolf Steiner designated this panel as **"Initiation"**. Firstly, underneath, in the heart area, a dragon and a spiritual being are engaged in battle. This being appears to represent the great archangel Michael, who seeks to assist humanity against the dragon of the lower self. This scene indicates that the meditant has become more aware of the imperfections of the human soul, and of its potential for both good and evil.

However the gaze of the archangel is directed to the spiritual, **not** at the evil, and this is an important lesson for the meditant to learn! For the acquiring of higher wisdom also brings deeper insight into the mystery of evil, **but the meditant realizes that her or his gaze should be firmly**

---

[85] R. Steiner private notebook, published in Beitrag (Supplementary journal) to the Complete Works, No. 19, 1967.

focussed on the light. If in the Chapter Five the theme was the need to transform the shadow-side of the soul, now the beautiful and uplifting mysteries of the perfecting soul and its blossoming 'lotus flowers' are our focus.

The third eye or forehead chakra

Before attempting advanced meditative activity through which the chakras become active, there is the essential task of consolidating our self or ego. This is achieved by establishing an independence of thought, an ability to assess life situations ourself from our own ego, not influenced by general opinions and attitudes. This is done by the **program of spiritual study**, mentioned earlier, including learning to **discriminate between truth and illusion** in many different ways, and by the kind of **meditating** described in these pages.

These exercises have the vital effect of stimulating first of all the forehead chakra into activity, before the other chakras are influenced into activity. This is essential if the experiences of the higher realities are to be assimilated rightly; in other words, it ensures that one is capable of maintaining one's ego-sense whilst in the higher experiences. Consider again **Illustrations 3 and 4.**

On the forehead is depicted the two-petalled chakra, also known as the 'third eye'. We see that the face has two angels hovering at either side of the forehead, from whom energies stream out, nurturing this chakra. The deep initiation knowledge behind this red window is depicting here the role of spiritual beings in human esoteric development. There is an interweaving of spiritual influences with the human being in meditation. The chakras do not develop 'by themselves' just through the effort of the normal personality. We receive help from the spiritual realms. These two beings near the forehead are pointing towards the two-petalled chakra, radiating spiritual forces into it.

This indicates that as enlightenment from the angels in the higher worlds is grasped by the meditant, the chakra is stimulated into life. One of the angels is near a circle from which curved rays of energy sweep out, the other from a crescent centre from which straight rays emanate. These represent the sun and the moon respectively, the moon angel represents the past karma within which, the meditant has to work. Whereas, the sun-angel represents the future possibilities.

To the soul on its journey after death, the sun-sphere has special importance, for it is here that a particular aspect of karma is developed, namely the significance of all efforts made on Earth towards spirituality are integrated into the stream of our earthly karma for the future. When a person resolves to enter the quest for their higher eternal ego-hood, then new dynamics are invoked into one's karma by the angels in the sun realm. This can manifest for example as significant meetings with people who influence and assist one's new life situation. Furthermore, the **sun angel represents our higher-self** which brings forces from spirit realms (symbolized as a spiritual sun in esoteric traditions) into the aura, assisting the third eye to develop.

The **moon-angel** however, **depicts the past karma** and especially how this is incorporated into our current heredity and environmental factors. Therefore she is looking backwards to the past, from which of course our karma derives. Whatever degree of higher consciousness is achieved through meditation has to be in harmony with one's karma, with the present life situation. In addition, it is only through working with one's karmic circumstances and learning how to harmonize this for spiritual advancement, that the meditant can progress.

Furthermore, the moon is in many ways the door into the spirit. For example, if one considers the moon to be a symbol of the night-time when we are immersed in the cosmos, then the moon-angel represents the acquiring of more real dreams, of more consciousness in one's dreams. This very important subject is dealt with in more detail in the book, Knowledge of the Higher Worlds.

The forehead chakra or third eye confers, once it is active, the faculty of astral clairvoyance. How does it do this? As it becomes active it also becomes radiant, in the original sense of this word. Namely, it has a glow that is especially out-raying. It is this inner radiation that illumines the astral environment for the meditant. It sends out two rays of light beyond the meditant's own aura, illumining the inner worlds for her or him. Whilst developing, it causes an odd sensation of coolness in the centre of the forehead, because this process involves the mysterious pituitary gland. The two rays of inner light then begin to rotate. As meditation proceeds these two astral rays intensify and broaden out, illumining the inner planes around the meditant. The notes from a lesson in 1908 indicate this..

> "...in meditating, only after perhaps some years, one should begin to sense that one's inner being is illumined, glowing. Oneself becomes a lamp, and illumines the spiritual world around you.... in moments of deepest inner peace, it is as if an inner sun, not the outer sun, is rising over your inner horizon..'

This text then, gives us an important meaning of the 'spiritual sun'. This forehead lotus flower or vortex in the astral aura is especially developed where effort is made to learn to discriminate between illusion and reality. All study that requires one to develop thoughts that correspond with spiritual reality assists this centre to form. As Steiner comments in these two paragraphs,

"Within the western world the developmental process (for spiritual faculties) must primarily consist of so-called thought-control. We can more easily control our thoughts (as distinct from will and emotions)...despite the fact that they are by nature instinctive and chaotic. I have pointed out that one must acquire the sensitivity for perception of thoughts that are illogical and poorly directed. The normal human being will feel pain when the sense organs are affected {by exposure to a jumble of stimuli}. However those people are rare who feel pain when encountering uncontrolled, incoherent thoughts. And yet it is impossible to achieve spiritual vision without having acquired this sensitivity for a kind of pain when someone speaks an uncontrolled thought in your presence." (1904) {This kind of training of the thinking life is achieved by the exercises in spiritual study mentioned in Chapter Three.}

It is not a question of **understanding** the deeper thoughts in a meditative text, but rather of those thoughts becoming more and more living in you. These deep thoughts will live and weave in your being, they will show how other thoughts can arise out of them, of a most fertile kind. {This is what I described in Chapter One as sensing insights whilst in meditation.} Then you will experience just what has to be overcome within. For this is where you will need the sensitivity to invalid thoughts, as if you have been pricked with a needle. One has to learn to think clearly and to recognize and love true ideas (of a spiritual kind). If you believe you have understood an insight which came to you in meditation, then you must not let it go out of sight, but continually work with it."[86] {That is, extend the meditating if you have the time, or return to that theme in the next session.}

The constant challenge **to discriminate or judge for oneself regarding important life questions** helps one achieve this too, that is, as distinct from having a guru decide all such matters for one. Failing this initial process, the vital matter discussed in Chapter Three of keeping one's mental faculties ready to interpret and assess experiences will scarcely be possible. So, one may not be able to competently analyse the experiences, nor would a healthy balanced connection with the Earth and one's karma be easily maintained.

For example one may wish to sever ties with the Earth. It is very important to note that before the heart chakra is developed, this forehead chakra **must be at least partially formed** before that next

---

[86] From an unpublished lecture: "Knowledge of the higher Worlds; how is it achieved?" 1904, 2nd Feb., Berlin

stage occurs. Otherwise, deep meditation will lead only to mystical experiences, which are not as desirable as esoteric spiritual experiences, because of their generally vague, and unclear nature. An excellent example of the unclear, yet delightfully alluring nature of mystical higher experience is to be seen in the early poems of St. John of the Cross....

"I entered in, I know not where,
And I remained, though knowing nought,
Transcending knowledge with my thought.
Of when I entered I know naught,
But when I saw that I was there,
(Though where it was I did not care)
Strange things I learned, with greatness fraught,
Yet what I heard I'll not declare.
But there I stayed, though knowing naught,
Transcending knowledge with my thought....
So borne aloft, so drunken-reeling,
So rapt was I, so swept away,
Within the scope of sense or feeling
My sense or feeling could not stay.
And in my soul I felt, revealing,
A sense that, though its sense was naught
Transcended knowledge with my thought..."[87]

Later on in his life the experiences of this great saint matured. His early experiences indicate clearly the results of impelling oneself, by intense emotional impulses, out of the normal consciousness without having trained oneself beforehand. That is, without having prepared oneself to maintain ego consciousness in higher realms through holistic thinking exercises. Rudolf Steiner refers to this kind of purely **cosmic-spiritual** consciousness as 'sense-free' thinking.

A developed forehead chakra confers the ability to behold in the astral and ether worlds, hence the words in the middle section of the red window; "I am beholding". Eventually the developed forehead chakra confers the blessed ability to commune with the higher-self consciously; this is nothing less than gradually attaining to eternal consciousness. This same process therefore also means that the now clairvoyant meditant gradually communes with the divine-spiritual hierarchies. Here we approach a profound aspect of the inner life concerning the ego. Rudolf Steiner taught that an earnest meditant will repeatedly contemplate the tremendous mystery of the innermost self,

---

[87] "Poems of St. John of the Cross": transl. by Roy Campbell, published by Penguin Classics

or ego. However, on this path, this is not done in order to convince oneself that it is an illusion which should be surrendered. There is indeed a certain illusory quality about our personal ego and our concept of self, but within the ego there are influences from the eternal higher ego. These influences derive from the cosmic Christ/Brahma, it is from these spiritual energies that a new spiritual condition came into being for humanity. This momentous event that has made possible a substantial change in human inner life, happened in Palestine some centuries after the insights of the Buddha were formulated. Through meditating, the personal ego or self becomes ever more aware of, and indeed an expression of, the divine higher-ego. The important theme of our eternal-self is taken up again in the next chapter and is an important theme in this book.

One result of this process, as it gradually develops, is to begin to relate to one's thoughts as if to one's ego itself. Normally, we say "I" only to our innermost being, we can not call "I" any other thing or person in the world. (See 'Theosophy'.) Now, as spiritual study deepens and practise in insightful thinking is undertaken through meditating, one may begin to formulate one's own thoughts from the very centre of one's being...."When a person through conscientiously persevering in meditating brings it so far that she or he has such a direct and immediate relationship to their thinking-life – and not just their own, but the thought-world as such – then they are an **intuitive** person. Then your thoughts arise from the centre of your being, {and no longer stream in from the periphery}." (1904)

This idea may seem vague and 'intellectual' but it is not. Rather it is our every-day mentality which is vague and intellectual, and hence unable to livingly grasp transcendental ideas. Just imagine how exalted and free one's mind would be if instead of just experiencing thoughts coming from nowhere, one consciously conceived each thought. The immediate experience of the spirit implied here is clearly seen when one realizes that the "thought-world" refers to the Platonic realm of Archetypal Ideas, or, in anthroposophical terminology, Devachan. That is the sublime realm in which the divine hierarchies produce the Ideas from which creation is maintained.

In other words, the self is then able to consciously experience and formulate spiritual-transcendental truths as an expression of its innermost reality. This is enlightenment in the best sense, wherein one's ego, at the heights of meditative attainment, is retained, although in a spiritualized form. Higher consciousness in this pathway is not some kind of blissful state that requires you to surrender the self. For one remains intensely alert and conscious, capable of assessing what is occurring and even expressing afterwards higher experiences as holistic thoughts.

The spiritual thoughts or insights are experienced as an aspect of one's higher ego. In a further, deeper stage, one's thoughts may be experienced as a living expression of the creator, or rather of the divine hierarchies whose cosmic consciousness (or spiritual thoughts) pervades the cosmos. Such a state has been called 'thinking the thoughts of God.' It is perhaps the deepest and most potent of all results of meditating, that one discovers - or rather it is inwardly announced to one's maturing sense of self - that we are intimately interconnected with the living cosmos. The human soul and spirit are connected to the vast numbers of divine-spiritual beings who together constitute the body of the cosmos, the manifested being of God. However this book is not intended to explore in depth these realities, nor the deeper secrets of the way to initiation.

When this very advanced stage of development is reached, the third eye which at first influences only the pituitary gland encompasses the pineal gland as well. This only occurs when the consciousness rises from **psychic-image** consciousness to **cosmic-spiritual** consciousness. At that stage the ether-body has become greatly transformed as well, with access to a source of ethereal light and life of great significance. This process can continue on over lifetimes, and reach an almost unimaginable development, which bestows magical powers on the person, at which time the pineal gland becomes enveloped in golden threads of energy.

To achieve this takes several life-times, but when it happens, the meditant, now an initiate, has become chaste and then develops the extraordinary powers of an adept. Such a person becomes a source of inner cleansing and healing of the Earth's aura itself, communing with the soul of the Earth as it moves along its pathway through the cosmos.

Throat chakra
In the scene carved onto the red window, we noted at the beginning of this chapter that there was a battle scene depicted, between a dragon and a spiritual being in the heart area. Above this, is depicted the 16 petalled lotus flower at the throat area. The 16 petalled chakra already has eight of its petals (its rays or channels of force) developed in the normal human being. The development of the remaining eight petals is achieved in the pathway described here by various exercises in spirituality. Since this chakra is connected with considerable occult power once it is fully active, **it is essential to become harmless in speech and thus in mind.** This stage of inner development is mentioned in the inspired booklet Light on the Path... "Before the voice can speak in the presence of the Masters it must have lost the power to

wound".[88] Completely overcoming the urge for vitriolic criticism and making aggressive spiteful comments is required. Moreover, the fifth exercise in Chapter Two about learning to be open-minded in one's world-view is a potent force towards developing this chakra.

Meditative study of the eight **Beatitudes of Christ** also develops this centre. The Beatitudes are those sayings found in the fifth chapter of St. Matthew's Gospel (verses 3-12) which start with the words, "Blessed are". There are nine sayings, the ninth being a further development of the eighth statement. They portray deep secrets of the process of spiritualization of our earthly human nature. These immensely deep meditations focus on how the ego spiritualizes our being, provided its empowerment derives from the higher-self, not from personal ambitions.[89] The throat chakra is also developed by living and contemplating the **Noble Eightfold Path of Buddha**. Rudolf Steiner has offered a modernized version of these wonderful spiritual exercises for daily life, as well as of the eight Beatitudes, I reproduce his version of these in Chapter Ten.

The esoteric Christian wisdom, of which anthroposophy is a significant expression, contains much deep wisdom, and is entirely capable of instructing in the mysteries of the chakras, but its approach is different to the classical Eastern approach. It is necessary that at least some aspects of this are given here, and yet it may appear as something very odd if you are new to esoteric matters. What is mentioned in these pages to a great extent derives directly from, and all of it can be supported by, Rudolf Steiner's teachings. **The ego is at first an egotistical reality, but rather than casting it off, one is advised to spiritualize it by absorption of the spiritual essence given to the world by the cosmic Christ.**

As this being became 'incarnate' in Jerusalem, the old method of initiation, or attaining to a union with this spiritual essence through a three-day 'sleep' was rendered obsolete. Instead it is now achieved via meditation and adopting a suitable way of life. This spiritual 'substance' which is an aspect of the divine spiritual world, was known as 'the dove' in ancient times. In meditation, when undertaken with the some understanding of these mysteries, the expanded ether-body actually becomes receptive to absorb precisely the energies given to the Earth by the cosmic Christ. These spiritual forces now circulate through the planet's aura.

---

[88] Mabel Collins wrote down the profound texts that were shown to her by an adept, which were published as "Light on the Path"; it is usually available in Theosophical bookstores. It has similarities to the much more comprehensive esoteric teachings of Rudolf Steiner.

[89] See Chapter Nine for a more accurate translation of these sayings, derived from esoteric insight, with a brief commentary.

As we noted earlier, this throat chakra confers perception of thoughts rather than emotions, it also brings perception of the archetypal Ideas (or 'Imaginations') in the cosmos – that are living in divine-spiritual beings – through which they maintain the cosmic order. It is also from this centre that a new kind of enveloping sheath forms around the ether-body. For eventually the ether-body also becomes metamorphosed as a result of inner development.

As a result of this process an advanced meditant may develop from this centre certain creative powers of a magical kind. This chakra is developed by learning to overcome the 'wounding by the voice', that is, voicing spiteful thoughts and wishes. This is attained by living the Eight-Fold Path, contemplating the Beatitudes, and by working intensely with **the exercise in open-mindedness** (given in Chapter Two).

As a result of such inner work, the divine hierarchical beings are enabled to counter the influences of malignant powers. In particular, to moderate decadent forces in the human astral aura which seek to make the reproductive forces a focus of lust. Striving to develop the soul qualities necessary for making active the lotus flower of the throat invokes the help of the most recent Buddha, Gautama Siddharta. He strives to inspire compassion in human souls, not only through the teachings he gave whilst on Earth, but also now, spiritually. As Rudolf Steiner reveals, from the viewpoint of the cosmos and its structure, Buddha has undertaken a particular work for humanity involving the refining of these Mars forces as they stream through the solar system, and are absorbed by the soul on its way down to incarnation. This Buddha is regarded here as a very high initiate in whose sacred being forces from the cosmic Christ exist.

A different approach to the chakras

The scene carved into the red window also teaches us that if higher vision is conferred simply by various occult techniques, then these processes involving the higher-self are thwarted. There are techniques such as gazing into a mirror or focussing on the centre of the forehead, which in certain occult quarters have been instituted to replace the three-day trance process. But although at times effective, these techniques thwart the fundamental dynamic of uniting with the higher-self. Thus the gradual attainment of holiness, of sanctification and of wisdom, is not involved. Instead, the current personality becomes able to access spiritual powers without having undergone the ethical changes, **hence any clairvoyance so gained may be untrustworthy**.

For example, the ether-body will not have a replica of the astral chakras and hence the resulting visions will be subject to all manner of fantasies. One's own personal delusions and dreams will create a gratifying, tempting fantasy-world. The reader can see that the chakra centres are approached quite differently in this pathway to that put forward in popular books. The detailed suggestions about using certain kinds of food or colours for chakra enhancement are regarded in this pathway as quite irrelevant.

The reason for this is that although there are special techniques which can be of use to quicken the process, such techniques are regarded as harmful. For the chakra rays or petals that then form are usually malformed, and in this state, they bring distorted visions. Such speeding up techniques are only valid if the fundamental approach of enhanced ethical development has already produced considerable results.

Another source of confusion is the fact that the astral chakras are already partially in existence in the aura, they do not have to be **fully** built up from nothing, so to speak. In each person's aura, a part of them exists already, for example at the throat area there are eight rays of force already in existence. Only the other eight rays need to be developed in order for the centre to become fully empowered. Likewise with the heart centre, there are already six petals or rays present. Some dubious occult techniques can stimulate these partially formed latent chakras which are another source of untrustworthy visions.

The heart chakra
The approach to chakra development in this pathway is general rather than specific; one does not focus on them, but rather on the soul-qualities needed for their development. Once they are developed it will become clear to the meditator just how to work further with them. You learn for yourself how to do this, and such knowledge is best kept private. Until then it is more important to understand the underlying reality of the so-called chakras, this is especially true of the heart chakra. The basic literature referred to provides invaluable knowledge of these underlying dynamics; for example, the connection between the heart and the astral body. Since it is important to properly develop the heart chakra, it is important to learn what relation your emotional life and heart have to your aura, and to the heart chakra.

For example, as the embryo is growing in the womb, the incarnating child hovers near, and energies stream into the tiny heart from the child's aura.[90] Now, the astral body is in effect, the soul, and the soul has of course emotions, intelligence and will; the heart is the central organ of human life processes, so the ancient attitude that '**the seat of the soul is in the heart**' is completely correct. Our heart physically is

---

[90] The process of the soul forming the embryo is described in various lecture cycles by Steiner, e.g., The Theosophy of the Rosicrucians.

the primary expression in matter of the creative activity of the incarnating soul, which is of course an intelligent and conscious entity.

The seat of our intelligence or the site in the body wherein our soul is primarily expressed is therefore the heart. Admittedly the intellectual qualities are expressed through the brain, but this intelligence must also derive from our soul in the first place. It is simply manifested by the brain. The most alive immediate responses to life occur in the emotions, and it is only possible for us, so long as we are living in the body, to be aware of emotion through the fact that we have a heart. That is, the emotions and feelings are expressed by the incarnate soul because of the existence of the heart. It is the organ of our emotive life, just as the brain is the organ that makes thinking perceptible.

The meditant must grasp such truths, for all esoteric development requires some knowledge of anatomy in the holistic sense. Rudolf Steiner pointed out that the brain can only be an instrument of intellectual activity because there is a channel of energy raying up into it from the heart area. This special channel of forces from the heart area of the aura constantly bathes the pineal gland with its powers. If our soul was not constantly permeating the brain from its heart area, we could not experience thoughts. The other internal organs are also permeated by forces from our aura, but to a lesser degree.

So, since the heart chakra is in the centre of the astral body, it is not surprising that, when it is developed, it brings perception of the **emotions and feelings** of people and other beings such as nature spirits. It is also the **'soul-eye'** or lotus flower that brings the ability to perceive etheric energies in minerals and plants; that is, it inwardly senses the living elemental moods and dynamics of mother Earth. During meditation, if the heart chakra has begun to develop, it can happen that one feels as if from every point of the body's periphery, energies are streaming in towards some central middle point; this middle point is the heart. (1910)

There is a further development of this experience wherein one feels as if these energies are now streaming out, into the environment. The heart chakra brings to the meditant the kind of clairvoyance that consists of sensitive empathy with other beings, as distinct from perceiving their thought-forms. Now, when we sense some subtle elemental quality, perhaps when walking near a flowering bush at sunrise, we sense it in the heart area rather than the head. So what does that tell us about the heart chakra?

It indicates that the heart chakra uses the **feeling** and **sensing** abilities as its mode of psychic consciousness. Of course when this centre is really developed the sensations it conveys are much clearer and more conscious than the vague feelings we normally have. In other words, a person who succeeds in developing this lotus flower discovers the ability to be experiencing a union with the feelings and moods of other beings or nature. This is a psychic or clairvoyant faculty, for then our emotional forces take the meditant right into the inner life of other beings. It confers empathy with their emotions.

Therefore the special physical organ of this same chakra, the heart, will in normal circumstances manifest the same quality of sensitivity, but somewhat dulled and muffled. The presence of the physical heart, which has been formed from the aura at that area, enables us to experience emotions; our own and those of others. However, until the astral heart chakra is activated we are not able to clearly register the emotions of other beings, especially invisible beings like nature spirits and divine spiritual beings.

Why are emotions and feelings normally not psychic, that is, why are they unable to sense what is occurring in the environment? Because the self is immersed in a flesh body, which muffles the soul's awareness of what the aura is perceiving. Secondly, it is also the case that our emotions are focussed incessantly inwards, concerned primarily that which satisfies our wants, wishes and desires. Once they become released from this they become open to union with that which lives and weaves around one in the environment. Then our desires take on a quality that is in harmony with the dynamics in the heart chakra, which is to seek empathy with the world of living beings around us.

As this state of emotional selflessness and purity is attained, it creates growing interest in the inner reality of one's environment. Such attitudes stimulate the heart chakra and thus clairvoyance is not far away. Once the psychic empathy faculty of the heart chakra is developing it can be empowered through exercises that restructure the ether-body energies. Through these you form a subtle sensory system that brings direct awareness of the environmental energies. These exercises are given in Steiner's "Knowledge of the Higher Worlds", which is as mentioned earlier, an essential text to study.

The ether heart and the 'etherealization of the blood'
We are now coming to a more difficult section of the book, for readers who are new to Steiner's works. But some knowledge of the interaction between body, soul, and also the life-energies, is essential. Without this it will not be possible for anyone who wants to go beyond the basic stage of meditating, to understand what is happening. The points mentioned here are mainly derived from a lecture by Rudolf Steiner published as, "The Etherization of the Blood", Oct 1st 1911.

The spiritual forces in the central area of the astral body, work in unison with a person's ether-energies. The heart, like most other organs in the body, has its specific ethereal counterpart, hence there is also an **ethereal heart.** It is from this ether heart that our physical heart is formed, just as the other organs are formed from their ether archetypes.

That is, in the ether-energies at the area corresponding to the heart, there exists a vortex of ether energies that have approximately the form of the physical heart. There is a constant interaction between this ether heart-form, the blood flowing through the heart, and the astral aura. For as our blood passes through the heart, on its way to the lungs, it is not only just physically purified, it also releases some of its subtle energies, its ether forces. The heart chakra's deepest significance is only grasped when one knows of the existence of its ether counterpart, and of the etherization of the blood.

Before considering these matters further, we need to view the **body-soul interaction** in a much more holistic way than is usually the case. In particular, the mechanistic model of the human being has to be discarded, even though this is at first results in some very new, unfamiliar conclusions. Rudolf Steiner insisted that **the heart**, as the expression in matter of the soul is incorrectly looked upon as a pumping machine. His research found that it is **the full power of the soul, exerting its efficacy in the blood stream** by utilising etheric energies, which is the actual power behind the pulsing of the blood through the body. The blood circulates through the body with the help of the heart's rhythmical pulsing; should physical factors cause the astral-etheric activity to be less effective in its 'impulsing' of the blood, then the blood can be pumped through the heart with the help of a mechanical pump.

We can say then, to achieve the wonderful phenomenon of the life-beat pulsing in a conscious human being, **the soul needs to be active in the ether heart**, with its powerful energy streams. The physical heart's valves and chambers assist the surging pulsing motion given to the blood in the first instance by the soul. These ether energies 'behind' the muscle substance of the physical heart help to circulate the blood tirelessly. The two processes together resemble a pumping mechanism, and achieve the same result, but it is the extraordinary fact that it is actually the intimate and direct influence of the soul that makes blood circulation possible.

Just consider the work of the physical heart as a muscle. It is involved in an enormous work and it works very powerfully, constantly assisting the blood flow, which in parts moves at one metre per second, beating some 2.6 billion times in a lifetime, helping pulse 6 litres of blood through some 60,000 kilometres of capillaries; and yet the heart **never** rests, never tires. It is therefore the only muscle that never becomes tired. It is also directly speeded up or slowed down in its 'pulsing' by the emotional condition of the soul. Emotive states immediately cause it quicken or slow down.

The actual reason that it never tires is that it has such a concentration of ether-astral forces within it. But therefore, on the other hand, negative emotive states in the long term can be deadly to it. What may help the reader to grasp this radical perspective is the description by Steiner of how during pregnancy, the incarnating child hovers over the mother, and energies stream into the embryo from the child's aura, forming the heart. As this process continues on, and the physical heart takes shape, the seer can observe how the soul aura loses some of its fine geometrical patterning. **The heart is linked symbiotically to the core qualities of the soul**.

So our blood is an expression of soul qualities (or, our "astral forces"). But it is also permeated by ether energies. On the physical level the heart receives blood that is full of fresh oxygen from the lungs. This is then distributed into every cell in the body, and then the blood takes into itself the carbon dioxide breathed out from the cells, back up to the heart. However, the distribution of oxygen molecules in this way is a material expression of the fact that the blood has been permeated by prana. Prana is a Sanskrit term for an ether energy absorbed from the Earth's atmosphere, which streams in continually from the sun. As the flow of blood with its ether energies streams throughout the body, it releases the Earth's prana into our body cells. But equally important it also **absorbs into itself something of one's own ether forces**.

However, the blood is permeated through and through by the astral body, that is by the auric energies that constitute our soul, indeed to some extent all of the body is so permeated. It is the presence of our soul forces in the blood that cause it to rhythmically pulse throughout the body. Our blood coursing back to the heart has then our own ether and soul qualities within it. These intermingle in such a way that the soul qualities we possess fuse with the ether-energies present in the blood stream.

To understand further aspects of this interweaving of soul, life-forces and body we need to now consider a key passage from Steiner. It explains how the subtle ether forces that permeate our blood are carried back up to the heart area, and there...

> "If you observe a person clairvoyantly, something constantly streams out from the heart. When you observe the blood clairvoyantly pulsing through the body, you see how in the heart

it 'thins out' to use a figure of speech (i.e. it undergoes a dematerializing). You see how the finest, most tenuous constituent elements of the blood dissolve and return to an ethereal state of being.

Just as, long ago (during the forming of the material Earth) the heart and the blood condensed out of the ethers, so now we have in contemporary humanity the reverse of this process. **The blood etherealizes itself, and thus within the ether-body ether-energies constantly stream forth from the heart up towards the (throat)**. {That is, our own soul qualities, weaving within our blood, pass over into the ether-energies of our ether-body.} In this way the ether-body is becoming re-formed through that which lives within the bloodstream. In the area of the human heart a continual metamorphosing of the blood into ether energy-substance is taking place. It occurs so long as the person is awake, and it ceases when they fall asleep."

(Lect, The Etherization of the Blood", Oct 1ˢᵗ 1911)

The heart chakra and the sacred mystery of the Holy Grail
There are many different ways of understanding the mysterious concept of 'the Holy Grail'. In the following section, it's meaning will be explored from an esoteric point of view, which is directly relevant to meditation. To comprehend the deeper significance of the process of the etherealization of the blood, we need to consider this question: what actually happens to those ethereal energies from the bloodstream, in which our soul qualities are interwoven? To answer this, we need to consider in a really conscious manner, the question **how does the soul walk the 'Way to the Sacred'. How does it becomes a chalice for the source of the divine spirit.** This theme is central to religious and spiritual groups, but how does it really occur? Not just in terms of higher moral qualities, but in terms of the soul as a substantial reality amidst other tangible realities of the astral plane?

To the initiate, good and also evil soul qualities are substantial actual 'things' in the astral world. There are cascading, surging streams of light-substance in these other realms, which are what we recognize as virtues, and there are dark, lower streams, which are vices. If this seems odd to you consider those drawings of the human aura, which is in effect, the soul. Within the aura there are various patches of astral 'substance' – in the form of clouds, fine currents, or swirling masses.

These are the mental qualities of that person, for on the astral plane these have a tangible existence. So, in what way does the divine spirituality considered now as tangible light-substance in the higher worlds, actually become part of the human soul? How does the soul actually receive such light? An unusual question perhaps, but of great importance, because union of the soul with God, and therefore union with the eternal higher-self, derives from this.

This is naturally a vast and complex theme, but from the perspective of this chapter there is a specific answer. As the 'etherealized blood' streams upwards towards the head, some of it accumulates in a centre in the ether-body near the throat chakra. **That is, as the soul qualities or astral substance in the bloodstream unites with one's ether energies, these accumulate in the vicinity of the throat chakra**! As explained earlier, all the spirituality which one develops through conscious effort and meditation exists not only in the aura, but also lives in the its astral counterpart of the bloodstream. These soul energies enter into our ether energies (or 'etherealizes') and streams up into the throat area of the ether-body, and there, as the Initiate taught, **it accumulates**.

It is this process that enables the throat chakra to become so powerful in a saint, an adept or initiate. Their voice possesses the power to heal miraculously, to command spiritual beings, and to bring enlightenment to an acolyte. Before we consider this aspect of esoteric physiology, it is important to remind ourselves that esoteric Christianity regards many religious streams of the past, such as those of ancient Egypt, Persia, Celtic lands, etc as all intimately connected with the **central divinity** of our solar system, and that this being is the same as the cosmic Christ, which is now united to the Earth. It views the purpose of such religions or 'mystery cults' of antiquity as being a preparation for the descent of the cosmic Christ to Earth. It was well known centuries before the events of Palestine in the Mystery Centres of various countries that the cosmic Christ, the foremost of the sun gods, would one day unite with the Earth. This being had been the most revered of the spiritual beings worshipped in the rituals and sacraments of such ancient centres.

The leaders of such Mystery Centres knew that this being had inspired great avatars of the past; Zarathustra, Krishna, Moses, Sig (a north European avatar) Gautama the Buddha, Mithra and certain other avatars. Then in Palestine in AD 33 through Jesus of Nazareth, the momentous spiritual event occurred. It was not 'only' one of these sacred avatars that united to the Earth then, **but the divine essence of the human spirit; the cosmic sun-god**. It is this being which became known – or unknown – in the Christian cultures as 'Christ'. After the Resurrection this highest spiritual force merged with the Earth's own aura or soul. In Jesus who had been the vessel of this divinity for three years, this sacred spiritual reality also became eternally present, hence His name, Jesus the Christ.

As the meditant earnestly strives to re-vivify the primal spiritual qualities of infancy, this results in those etherealized soul-qualities that are rising up from the heart, acquiring energies of an exceptional spirituality. When the meditant attains the ability to stand in awe before the starry heavens, to become immersed in wonder at an autumn leaf, to revere truth, beauty and goodness, to experience real spiritual insights, and to become selflessly loving, then a source of spiritual renewal is forming within the heart. Such inner exercises, together with the constant effort at thinking spiritually – both in study exercises and through intuitive thinking (i.e. meditative activity) – **is creating a chalice to receive the divine light-substance into the aura**.

It is a central message in Rudolf Steiner's teachings, that this process of spiritualization, of finding the way to the sacred, has become possible for every person because the spiritual light of the cosmic Christ (united to the soul and spirit of the person, Jesus) **now exists as an ethereal life-essence in the Earth's aura**. Prior to the events on Golgotha hill, only a few select acolytes could attain to this.

The mention of the human vessel of the sun-god, Jesus of Nazareth is necessary here, because when he became united to the cosmic Christ, he became the archetype of the fully sanctified (or initiated) human being. And it is essential that an archetype exists of the fully spiritualized human being, because once the archetype exists, then millions can follow. For then the correlation of higher-self or human spirit to the personality (soul) in the incarnate person, once achieved, allows a manifestation of this divine pattern in all other people.

Rudolf Steiner said of Jesus, "**It may be said His being has all the love which the human soul can ever attain**". His descent to birth at Bethlehem from the heights of the spiritual-world, was His first (and last) life on Earth. He was kept away from malignant influences for long ages; until that time, he was "in the nest of the dove" as the ancient Hebrew initiates said.[91] This is a significant expression, indicating that His own inherent spiritual energies provided the Earth's aura with life-energies of unique purity and creative power. These energies had not been available on the planet since the so-called 'Fall of Man'.

As this book is not an exposition of esoteric Christian wisdom, I will just briefly mention that His soul has become permeated by, and then after three years eternally united to, the light of the cosmic Christ. Thus in the aura of our planet there are radiant streams of divine love and a purifying, healing light that emanate from His being. Moreover, these forces are the quintessence of the divine potential within each human spirit. For it is precisely the wondrous secret, which is a reality not limited to any specific religion, but a relevant fact for a person of any

---

[91] This expression occurs in some obscure esoteric Kabbalistic-Zoharic treatises.

religion, that in His being, perfect human spirituality is united with the higher human ego or higher-self, itself deriving from the logos-enfilled cosmic Christ.

It was the knowledge and the mystical experiencing of this wonderful spiritual fact that caused the Manicheans, the medieval Knights Templars and the Knights of the Holy Grail to be so devoted to esoteric Christianity. It was also knowledge of this coming event that so inspired the Essenes, the Hebrew prophets, as well as members of the Mithraic esoteric religion and Zarathustrian teachers, amongst others, to help prepare for this. Remember, the babe Jesus was actively sought for and recognized by "Magi" who were actually Persian Zarathustrian astrologers ! This fact of 'pagans' proclaiming the birth of Him who would become the vessel of the Christ is not emphasized in exoteric Christendom.

At this point it is necessary to emphasize the perspective given by Steiner; that this being is definitely not the exclusive property of European or Western Christianity. **This being is the source of divinity within every human being,** therefore it was entirely normal for Zarathustrian Magi to be awaiting the birth of the soul through whom It would enter the world. It was revered across the world and across millennia, ever since the ancient Atlantean Sun Temple was established. Christianity however, after the fourth century lost much understanding of the cosmic nature of the cosmic Christ, the foremost spiritual divinity of our solar system.

The heart chakra – receptacle for the light of the spiritual sun.
The full significance of the above complex truths were understood by the ancient Manichaean Christians with their exceptional wisdom.[92] In a hymn to Jesus by Chinese Manicheans, who also revered Buddha, are the following words that indicate the profound significance His being has for the quest towards higher spirituality...... "He is the leader (on the path) and also the treasure (which we seek). He is the (source of) deeper knowledge of the jewel-bedecked people....He uplifts and heals those who remain spiritually inclined; and He vivifies again the light-substance in all..."[93]

---

[92] The Manicheans were those people who in the 4th century responded to the teachings of Mani, a high initiate born in Persia, who understood that the Christian Saviour was the Cosmic Christ. He also knew that reincarnation and karma were a reality, even if in a different way to the classical Oriental view. But only fragments of his teachings survive. According to Steiner, an erroneous idea of these people is given by Augustine of Hippo, because the order by then had corrupted its teachings.

[93] The original text is a long-dead Chinese language, a German translation of which was passed on to the author by a Professor of Linguistics in Munich who worked with this material.

The reference to people 'bedecked with jewels' does not refer to external signs of wealth, rather to those advanced souls in whose auras the chakras are empowered and spinning. **Once the chakras are activated, they have a beautiful appearance similar to living jewels**, a multi-coloured radiance sparkling and moving. The core of the mystery is that the spiritual forces permeating the Earth from the Sun's aura were poured out so people may absorb this into their soul. More specifically, it could be said that those who seek spiritual development may receive this into their heart-chakra, and also into the ether-body.

The essence of human spirituality present in the Earth's aura, from the cosmic Christ, can actually merge with our soul, because it has been united to the forerunner or archetype, Jesus of Nazareth. The divine light and love can merge with our own finest soul-qualities as they etherealize out of the blood in the heart area, permeating the ether heart. By the path of the Four Moods, and the spiritualization of thinking, a spirituality is able to blossom in the human being which can receive from the Christ-light its own quintessence.

However the 12 petalled astral heart-chakra is intimately connected with the ether heart, so its radiance permeates the spiritual core of the human being. Here certain esoteric words of this cosmic being in the Gospel of St. John take on another meaning.... "Abide in me, and I in you. As the branch can not bear fruit of itself, unless it abide in the vine, nor can you, unless you abide in me." (St. John 15:4)

It is significant that when these previously secret truths of Christianity were revealed by Rudolf Steiner, it was also made clear that the meditant needs to study such truths abut the cosmic Christ, and contemplate them deeply in times of prayer and meditation. **For it is the conscious contemplation of this sacred process that enables the union of divine and human hearts to fully occur.** In other words, those human beings who seek to attain this in their earthly life - and **only here on Earth can this be done** - need to undertake a contemplative study of this.

These esoteric teachings are in fact a modern form of the ancient Sun-Mysteries[94]. So far, we have considered the nature of the spiritual heart and the accumulating of our spirituality into the throat chakra. Also, the spiritual energies which are now in the planet's auric sheaths are of the same 'substance' of the awakened spiritual self. So they are in essence now, what humanity is intended to become in future ages.

---

[94] These derive from the religious life of the pre-Flood Atlantean culture.

It may be seen now, that this future goal of a perfect spirituality, which is attained within the context of an empowered ego-hood, is the precisely same goal as this meditative path. It is that which the meditant is seeking to acquire. When one realizes this, namely that the divine spirituality awaiting us in the course of our future lives now permeates the planet's astral energies as a kind of spiritual 'substance', and is incorporated into the being of one remarkable sacred human, then one is taking the first step towards the quest for the Holy Grail.

This quest could be defined in modern terms as living so as to enable this light to permeate one's own ethereal and astral being, during this life (and in lifetimes of the near future). To do this through the way of living which arises from the Four Moods exercise, and in study and meditative activity. In addition, the quest for the Grail requires that one knows that the way to attain this spirituality is by absorbing the divine spiritual essences from the incarnate cosmic Christ.

It is clear by now, that this process is not restricted to any specific creed or religion, and indeed the implication from various of Steiner's teachings is that this is a global impulse. This cosmopolitan spontaneous possibility of spiritual renewal is closely associated with the majestic archangel 'Michael'. This being is a kind of regent of the new cosmopolitan esoteric schooling of humanity, it is for all humanity.

So the heart is the centre of the soul. Naturally, the meditant needs to evolve a life-style that encourages generally the process of spiritual development. The etherealized soul qualities imbued with the Christ-light then proceed to flow from the heart chakra up into the area of the throat chakra. It was such truths as these which acolytes in the Holy Grail mysteries once learnt from their teacher in remote forest glades of old Europe. This was due to their souls being permeated with experiences of such holiness that they could find the inner strength to keep true to their spiritual goals. As is well-known, the Holy Grail mysteries are associated with the theme of purification of the sensual desires. The final outcome of this striving for high initiates of the Holy Grail is to achieve celibacy.

The reason for this emphasis amongst those who represent the Holy Grail wisdom is associated with the etherealizing process in the heart. For they know of the connection between the blood's etherealized life-forces and the ether heart. It is this process of empowering and spiritualizing the ether-body that is affected by sexual activity; hence the advice to strive to moderate, but not forcibly repress, these desires. **This perspective has nothing to do with the profoundly wrong forced repression of sexuality,** which, although deriving from some vague perception of the above matters, produces only harmful effects for all concerned.

An overview of the chakras
"...listen to the words of Him who holds the seven stars in his right hand, and who walks amidst the seven golden lamp-stands..." Rev. 2:1.

The first of the remarkable changes that the meditant brings about in his or her soul is the **provisional** development of the two-petalled lotus flower or chakra in the forehead. This process is assisted by the study program mentioned in Chapter Three, that is, by the persistent attempt to develop spiritual thinking, spiritual insights. This includes the ability to see through materialistic intellectual illusions. Once active it bestows perception of the higher astral realities, including, eventually one's own higher-self and the divine hierarchies.

However, before this centre is made fully active the heart centre starts to become active. The development here is assisted by the quality of seeking spirituality in the emotive-life, in essence, a strong and un-compromised search for freedom from desires and emotions that undermine spiritual integrity. Compassion becomes a hallmark of the soul. The six Parallel Exercises develop this too, especially the control of thought exercise. Once developed, this chakra bestows perception of the emotive forces in other beings (visible and invisible), as well as perception of the elemental powers within plants and stones.

The throat centre (the 16 petalled chakra) then begins to develop, and this is assisted by contemplation of the eight Beatitudes. It is also assisted by practising the six Parallel Exercises, especially the fifth one, which focuses on open-mindedness. It also requires the virtue of not having a capacity to harm others by voice (or deeds, of course). This centre bestows further perception, beyond that of the forehead centre, of the thoughts of the gods, or the 'cosmic thoughts' (which we humans designate as 'laws') that sustain and develop creation.

The chakra below the heart area, the '10 petalled centre' requires the meditant to have such a sovereign presence of the higher ego within the soul, that attitudes, opinions and feelings are not subject subconsciously to subtle astral forces in one's environment. The ability to process sense-impressions (without which one can often make materialistic assumptions about life and creation), is also needed. This centre bestows deep perception of the elemental qualities in the three kingdoms of nature, and their connection to cosmic forces. The reader is advised to look into Steiner's Knowledge of the Higher Worlds from which I have taken some of the indications in these paragraphs, for further information. Regarding the lower centres, the six-petalled and four-petalled chakras, these have their dormant existence in the territory of the lower-self, and it is dangerous to seek to activate these until the higher ones have been developed. Little information is available about the seventh centre or star within us, the 1000-petalled crown chakra, as it is the last to develop, and brings about a potent empowerment of the meditant.

Once the higher-self has begun to manifest within the ego, then the lower centres along the spinal column, can be developed by the now empowered ego itself, safely in the course of time. There are considerable dangers associated with this process, if carried out incorrectly. When eventually the crown chakra above the top of the head is developed, then the power and light of the spiritualized soul becomes awe-inspiring. This crown chakra is indicated in the red window by the symbol of Saturn above the initiate's head. At that highly advanced stage, the initiate can release potent spiritual forces from his or her soul, and carry out remarkable 'miraculous' actions. For by now the entire process of how the cosmic forces interweave with one's soul can be regulated at will.(1904)

When the chakras are developed, and are set like a series of vortices in a row, and when from this row of vortices a kind of bridge forms across to the (ether counterpart of) the spinal column, then the mysterious kundalini-power becomes fully expressed in its superhuman power. Rudolf Steiner did not disclose the details of this matter owing to its potential danger, and taught that this stage of development will not be fully achieved except in extraordinary cases for some 20,000 years. (1904)

Now, a very important point has emerged from the above material, about the chakras, namely that they are **developed by enhanced morality**. There is one other important point that needs to be clarified; as I have mentioned earlier in this chapter, they do not form by themselves. Spiritual forces flow into our soul to help them develop. As I indicated briefly earlier, Rudolf Steiner taught his students that intensive earnest meditating, as described in chapter one, causes vortices to form in the astral aura, which work out towards the aura's periphery. As higher spiritual qualities form in our soul,

> ...vortices of energy arise, "travelling outwards to the edge of the aura, and there, **these developing centres meet spiritual forces flowing in from the higher worlds, and this results in the forming of the chakras or lotus blossoms.** Then, during meditation these lotus flowers begin to spin, and in this way to transmit perceptions to the meditant. (1912)

This meeting of personal and cosmic forces at the periphery of the aura is a very important truth. On this very important matter of the interconnectedness of our soul and spirit with the macrocosm, it becomes clear from the other passages of Rudolf Steiner's works, that the forces to which this initiate is referring are planetary forces. These which flow in towards the periphery of our aura, merging with what is intensifying and moving outwards in our astral body.

As the seven chakras start to form, they each have a specific correlation to one of the planets, as indicated in a drawing in a note book of Rudolf Steiner, preserved in his archives in Switzerland. In this the planetary forces are linked to the aura, and the symbol of the planet is placed at the chakra position. The arising within our aura of our finest soul forces and their raying outwards to the periphery of our aura, via the half-formed chakras, constitutes a sevenfold emanating of energies that are planetary. These planetary forces were originally absorbed by us from the planetary spheres, before birth.

As our soul has its inherent sevenfold spiritual energies stimulated into a higher activity by meditating, our chakras form, and forces from these begin to stream outwards from our aura. These energies then **encounter their own macrocosmic (planetary) origin, streaming into towards them** ! That is, we have planetary forces already integrated into our soul before birth, and these microcosmic planetary energies now encounter these planetary energies out in the cosmos, attracted towards our auric qualities.

It is as if our spiritual striving invokes a response, a strengthening from the (spiritual counterpart of the) solar system. **It is as a direct result of this meeting that the chakras form.** Do note however that the chakras eventually form further in, in the area occupied by the physical body, that is, not out at the periphery of the aura. It would make this book too large to elucidate the nature of these planetary forces. A study of astrological wisdom about our psychological connection to the seven planets, is very helpful here. To help clarify this dynamic, I include a simple diagrammatic illustration of the chakras in connection with these planetary rays, based on the above quote, [95] see Diagram 3.

In this connection, one notes that moreover, as many of Steiner's lectures explain in detail, the astral body is composed of energies from the seven classical planetary spheres, these enter the human being as it descends down to re-birth. Other lectures refer to the planetary alignment of a chakra in our aura to a corresponding planet.

Furthermore, one also notes that the involvement and consequent response of the human being to these energies is a primary element in the anthroposophical view of the human being. For example, Rudolf

---

[95] It is a valuable help to think of this mystery in terms of the initiation manual called the Book of Revelation; chapter 2, verse 1, "the one holding the 7 stars in his right hand".

Steiner explained how in the infant, speech and language arise in direct response to the registering of the planetary energies in its aura, and in adults the timbre or inner quality of the voice is directly related to the birth chart's planetary 'aspects'. That the chakras are actively sending our astral qualities out into the macrocosm, emerges from another lecture, where he speaks of the currently existing – even though only half-formed – chakras emanating astral energies into the cosmos, and that we encounter these after our death.[96]

This initiation wisdom is hidden in the Book of Revelation, which contains the words of St. John, inspired by the risen Jesus. This text indicates to the insightful reader that as we enflame into light the normally slumbering lamp-stands (the chakras) within us, a response arises from the seven planets (or 'stars'). The enormous significance of the solar system for our soul-life, and for our spirituality is thereby indicated. Steiner's research has made possible an extraordinarily valuable deepening of 'astrology', but it is not possible here to elucidate that.

---

[96] Lecture 12 March 1918 in G/A 181.

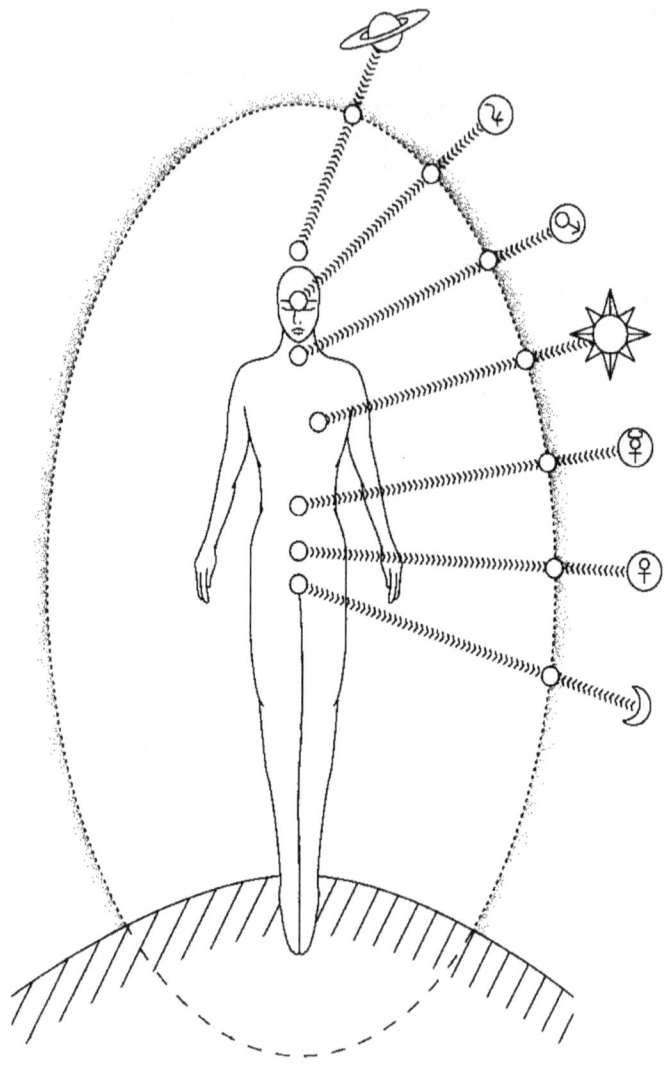

Diagram 3
The seven planets co-forming the seven chakras : from the top downwards; Saturn, Jupiter, Mars, Sun , Mercury, Venus, Moon

Concerning the chakras then, it is my conclusion that references to chakras in popular books are in fact to the inherited half-developed ones, or to various ether vortices, and thus deal with the use of ether energy to impact on the astral aura. For an experience of the developed chakras is only possible when they have been arduously developed, whereas etheric energy-centres occur in everyone. Secondly, our ether-energies can be influenced in such a way as to have an impact on the aura. These inherited vortices (which may perhaps be called 'etheric chakras') can exert various influences, including that of stimulating whatever rudimentary astral chakras currently exist in the aura. Indeed Buddhist esoteric meditation texts of nearly 2000 years ago refer to this technique of stimulating the astral chakras from the ether-body.[97]

But such techniques from ancient times are now obsolete, and quite useless for developing the spirituality of the soul. The essence of Steiner's teachings here is, that with the incorporation of the cosmic Christ into the Earth's soul, the normal ego can always find a way to become a true, eternal ego; in other words, the 'I am' is born in humanity. It will be from the power of the ever-deepening ego, that the aura becomes transformed into a wonderful complex set of chakras or organs of perception, not by manipulation from the ether-body.

Steiner taught that if the meditative activity is followed by real effort at Contemplation, as described in Chapter One then, "...this forms the lotus flowers further and also strengthens them. These centres are sensing organs of the soul, they are undergoing their developmental process also." [98] The emphasis is on ethical development, rather than occult techniques to stimulate these centres, perhaps by visualizing energies there, whilst intensely repeating a mantra. According to the Initiate, these external techniques can indeed cause the centres to develop their rays or petals, but then the petals become malformed. They appear non-symmetrical, and this induces distorted visionary perceptions. The idea of selecting foods of a certain colour to develop a chakra is likewise a way to externally affect it, thus by-passing the vital fundamental inner approach. This was recommended also in the Esoteric School of H.P. Blavatsky, but to this author it appears only to

---

[97] The ether-body has zones in it which are connected to the elements; and which has a particular ether force in it. This is implied for example in the ancient Uiguric Buddhist scroll "T 11 Y 21" from Yar-Choto in Turfan:.....along the lower legs is the element earth, an ochre coloured ray one must visualize here...from hip to breast-cage the element fire is predominating, one must visualize an orange coloured ray from here....from shoulder to forehead the air element is predominate, a bright violet ray one must visualize from here....once you have visualized these five rays one must visualize within (their combined radiance) a 1000 petalled lotus, in the midst of which is the syllable "shi"....."
[98] In a lecture on "How is knowledge of higher worlds is attained"? from 1904 (unpublished).

have minor relevance to the **ether-body** centres. Vegetarian foods however, are of advantage to the refinement of the aura and therefore to the forming of the lotus blossoms.[99]

Kundalini
The term kundalini is Sanskrit and refers to a powerful force concentrated in the astral body. This force is said to be near the base of the spinal column, and can be raised up by esoteric techniques. However, this subject is seen very differently by Rudolf Steiner. The esoteric wisdom of Europe is informed about this 'infrastructure', even if references to it are rare in old European literature. One example of this the symbol known as the caduceus of Hermes. This symbol, also known as the staff of Mercury, is a rod which is intertwined by two serpents, one black, the other white; this is amongst other things, a symbol of the kundalini force.

Rudolf Steiner taught that the kundalini is the full, but latent, power of the energies within the astral body.(1904) In contrast to practices in some movements, which derive from ancient times when circumstances were different, in this esoteric pathway the meditant is strongly advised **not** to seek to bring about any so-called raising of the kundalini, until the spiritual development process has given one the ability to spiritualize the full power of one's own astral forces.

It is especially emphasized that one is not to use techniques that stimulate the kundalini, causing it to 'rise up', that is causing it to commence a movement upwards from the sacral centre. For a cardinal rule in this path is that development of the soul's own 'infrastructure' must start from the **forehead downwards**, not from the base of the spine **upwards**.

That is, this development and activation process must be the natural outcome of developing higher spirituality, and with modern humanity, this starts with the thinking life ! It is then very soon focussed on the heart, the full power of our emotions and desires. That is, the pathway begins at the head area (i.e., the forehead chakra), and then the heart (i.e., heart chakra). Then later on, probably in a next life, the more hidden and elemental layers of consciousness that are connected to the solar plexus, and to the lower part of the body are illumined. Only then can centres in the groin area with their, as yet untransformed fire-forces, be involved in an activation process.

Hence it is emphasized that only after most of the seven chakras are well developed, does the full power of the astral body arise, quickening

---

[99] Vegetarian foods generally assist the soul to spiritualize itself (see next chapter).

the forces inherent in the astral body, along the astral-etheric spinal column. At that time, with some advice from a teacher and the expertise one has by then acquired, the matter of the kundalini that is, of fully activating the creative energies in the aura, may be taken in hand. So there are several profound reasons for this approach. It has been well documented that to stimulate the astral forces at the base of the spine is to risk serious danger to the acolyte's mental health and morality, since in that area both the ether-body's full reproductive power and the lower self has its home.

Even if no permanent ill effects are experienced the process itself as described by Indian meditants, is often one of psychological trauma with serious personality disorders involved. It can cause such disorders as priapism which is extreme and uncontrollable lust. Even with yogis who later become highly regarded gurus, priapism or other disorders, such as attempted suicide may occur. These problems are not limited to unguided acolytes.[100]

As I mentioned earlier, the author knows a specific case of an improper occult kundalini-raising act which left the person in a very painful and disturbed state, both sexually and emotionally. So in the pathway described here, the goal is to ensure that the acolyte is on their way to becoming their own higher spiritual self, and then naturally, the full power of the then spiritualized ether-astral energies can be made use of correctly. However the primary damage caused by having the full power of one's astrality incited into activity by the base centre is that the entire process of acquiring **cosmic-spiritual** consciousness by transforming the conscious (thinking) process, and of acquiring sanctity in one's heart, is by-passed.

The kundalini then, is in essence the fullest expression of the soul's power, of its light and fire. The kundalini is not a separate force from the soul, it is the unrealised or untapped (or coiled up and waiting) full power of the soul, a power that should only be manifest once the higher-self has been empowered, and thus the soul purified. Any stimulating of the base chakra which leads to a so-called 'kundalini experience' is actually an ill-advised activating of astral forces in conjunction with the non-purified fire-force of the ether-body, which is associated with reproduction.

Thus Rudolf Steiner refers to the kundalini as identical with the spiritual energies that start to develop in the chakras. (1903) So the wonderful radiance of the purifying aura and the enhanced energies in the developing chakras, are all kundalini; but kundalini that has begun to spiral throughout the entire aura, so to speak. New Age literature

---

[100] From the memoirs of Swami Muktananda and Ramakrishna.

erroneously defines only the finest and most powerful energy of the fully awakened soul-body as kundalini. However, the famous silver cord that keeps the human soul attached to its body during the night, is another aspect of the kundalini (1903). This cord is capable of infinite extension, taking the sleeping soul up into the stars.[101] Yet it is also capable of extreme compression, returning a person in less than a second. In the pathway explained here, as the 'kundalini force' gradually becomes active through the meditative process it is under the direct control of the now purified meditant.

Atavistic clairvoyance, and newer forms of clairvoyance
Rudolf Steiner taught that human consciousness has not always been the same, it has changed over millennia, in the past **all humanity had a natural clairvoyance**. It was due to the fact that people were less strongly bound to their physical bodies. This condition existed naturally for humanity from time immemorial, and whilst it existed there was very little capacity for individual rational thought. The implication of this harmonizes very well with his other discovery concerning human consciousness over the ages, namely that there was **little individual ego-hood present in earlier millennia**. People had more a group consciousness in earlier epochs. The natural psychic state began to end about 2500 years ago, as far as the classical civilisations of the Mediterranean and central Europe are concerned. It faded away at different times in history for different groups within this culture; earlier for the Romans and Greeks, later for central Europeans, and still later for the Nordic people.

The atavistic psychic condition is a clairvoyant condition which has not been developed on a foundation of spiritual study, but it is simply 'there'. This state is a throw-back to the earlier condition of human history, when a psychic state was normal. The term 'atavistic' implies here an unusual state that derives from the past, from a past situation living on into the present. It is a clairvoyance that is able to manifest because of an unusual condition prevailing in the person's subtle bodies. A person who manifests this, has their ether-body incorporated into the physical body and the soul in a different way. It is this condition which triggers off an inherent psychic ability.

There are still certain groups amongst the European peoples whose subtle bodies are so related to the physical body that the condition of atavistic clairvoyance is often present from childhood onwards. A life of this psychic kind in modern times, requires one in the next incarnation, when others are progressing with the **new clairvoyance**, to focus

---

[101] The silver cord and the ether-body is referred to in the book of Ecclesiastes 12:6 "Lest the silver cord be severed, or the golden bowl be broken....and shall dust return to dust.."

especially on self-developed ego-hood, to the exclusion of clairvoyance. This will be achieved especially by acquiring a clear conceptual understanding of life, without any psychic ability.

Those people who are born with a psychic ability – which therefore has not been achieved by inner transformation of the aura (the soul) by the ego in this life – usually represent this past state. They embody the past dynamics, wherein awareness of the greater subtle nexus in which we live was present, but not so much focus on individualism and individualistic rationality. Amongst the many fascinating people I have met in my life, was a Scottish Romany gypsy. She was born into one of these special groups which retain an atavistic clairvoyance, and, during my time in Scotland, she volunteered to give me some interesting, quite clearly clairvoyantly gained information. She was however totally unable to read or write, and hence had almost no experience of the thoughts that underlie modern civilisation. It may be a help for that person's evolution if in this life the psychic faculty is actually brought to an end, however, this is a general observation.

There are also people who are given by the gods this unusual condition, in order to be an instrument of divine help in the world. People with such powers can undertake to help others in a kind and caring way, and they may possess healing abilities, but their psychic ability is not the result of strenuous inner work. Such atavistic clairvoyance is not as controlled by the person's ego as the kind that is now spontaneously developing. Where the ego is unable to be fully present and assess the soul's experiences, the possibility of error or deception creeps in. Some people actively yearn for a vision so much that they take up mediumistic clairvoyance by various means of manipulation of the subtle bodies. In this state, the ego is usually weaker, and may even be absent, as in trance mediumism.

There are many caring and kind people who are mediums, and the information they 'transmit' back to this plane can be accurate, caring and informative. However this activity is harmful to one's spiritual being, and often to one's physical body, and as Steiner taught, can lead to channelling of nothing more than discarded astral auras of souls who have left the soul-world, and entered into the true spiritual realms.[102]

This does happen; I know of a medium who contacted the deceased relative of a distressed lady in Australia, and proceeded to channel various very accurate typical expressions of interest and memories from this person. However, the lady actually had just experienced two

---

[102] See lecture cycles such as The Theosophy of the Rosicrucians, for an explanation of the 'discarded shell' of the soul.

dreadful traumatic events in her life, but the 'relative' obviously did not have a clue that this was her current situation and could not be informed of it – for this 'relative' was merely an astral after-echo of the soul, who had moved on to higher realms.

Mediumism is in effect a psychic state in which the self is becoming ever less in charge of its own astral body. Such mediumistic psychics are manifesting the old clairvoyance. It is not recommended that a non-psychic person forces mediumistic faculties on their being. It is far better for such a person to take up the process described here, through which the self becomes master of all the processes involved in clairvoyance. Then the higher realities are livingly perceived, rather than transmitted to one by a third party. The exception to this dynamic is the person, who in their past life, developed themselves in such a way, that a predisposition for higher faculties blossoms in this life. As a consequence they have some psychic tendencies early in this life. But even so, clairvoyance is unlikely to persist (or emerge) in their **adult** life without some effort by the person now. However such a person might already have in early adulthood a slight clairvoyant sensitivity, and a childhood filled with enchanting, special psychic experiences.

Solar plexus clairvoyance
One form of powerful clairvoyance, similar in its dynamics to the old type, may be termed "abdominal clairvoyance".[103] It is **not** the result of the specific, deliberate spiritual development process, as with the above condition, it is simply there. Rudolf Steiner explains that it is due to a disturbance in the forces associated with the solar plexus, a mysterious focus point in the physical body and also in the ether-body. In the physical body it is virtually a subsidiary nervous system in its own right. This centre can bring up into consciousness powerful astral 'waves' living in the soul, and this triggers off visions.

For example, powerful 'waves' of ambitions or desires can then appear as convincing visions. However for this to happen, such waves of energy would have to be unhealthily suppressed for some years for them to build up enough pressure to force these visions into existence. This abdominal clairvoyance in its weaker mode is like 'a gut feeling', wherein someone senses a fact that could not ordinarily be known.

Rudolf Steiner describes that this same centre can also produce powerful images, spread out before one's gaze, of the internal organs and their dynamics. Hence a person with this faculty can predict

---

[103] R Steiner's various indications on solar plexus psychism, summarized in the above material, are in G/A 161, lect. 27/3rd + 1st May 1915; G/A 208 Lect 2/10/21; G/A 125 Lect 21/Nov/10.

illnesses and give worthwhile advice on healing. It can also transmit some remarkable images that represent ideas and realities that exist in the astral world; ideas which are not usually accessed by humanity. This nerve-centre is in a much more intimate relationship with the environment than the nervous systems in the head and spinal column. In trance conditions, the latter nervous systems (which the astral body uses to convey impressions to consciousness) become inactive, thereby causing the solar plexus system to be activated. This somnambulistic psychic faculty puts its feelers out far over the environment. So it is much more encompassing.

If we were to empathize through this centre, rather than our normal nervous system and sense organs, we would experience an intimate unity with the world around us. In fact invertebrate creatures, such as sponges, star-fish, snails, many insects, and worms, have a nervous system that is the equivalent of the solar plexus. The result is that these creatures are in a state of such intimate at-one-ness; thus Steiner describes for example that a caterpillar munching a leaf experiences the leaf or blossom as existing within itself ! [104] However, remember, these creatures have no **self**-consciousness. The old atavistic clairvoyance uses this centre, which can provide glimpses of the future, although these may not be too reliable.

In contrast to the powerful and immediate visions mentioned above, the visions experienced by a meditant who works with patience and effort at the study and soul attitude exercises, are faint, delicate and subtle for quite some time. Only gradually do they become colour-enfilled and strong. In contrast to this, the visions seen through the 'abdominal clairvoyance', right from the start, are powerful, fully coloured and impressive. If they are not concerned with medical-healing matters though, they can be very unreliable and subjective since the conscious ego is not there to assess the situation. Hence one may experience a resplendent display of one's own suppressed wishes.

The spontaneous new clairvoyance
What is meant by the term 'the new clairvoyance'? As we have noted briefly before, **a person may begin to experience a 'new' clairvoyance that bestows a certain limited awareness of higher realities in a wholesome manner.** Since early last century, a faint clairvoyance has been developing naturally in humanity. Steiner explains in various basic texts, that this is a result of the fact that we have entered a new time cycle in evolution. This cycle is bringing about a slow ascent out of the physical plane for all humanity, whereas until recently humanity was still travelling on a path which took it ever further into matter. This

---

[104] R Steiner's abilities enabled him to research the consciousness of such beings, in an esoteric lesson of 1906, he mentioned this.

phase of entering ever more deeply into matter commenced in the remote Lemurian epoch, which preceded that of the Atlantean epoch.

People have been incarnating ever more densely into the body since then. The last phase of this cycle brought about materialism, for we no longer possessed any real psychic faculties. But, since 1899 a new phase or age has begun wherein people are incarnating less deeply into the body, with the result that quite spontaneously a psychic faculty is re-emerging. This is causing 'the new clairvoyance' to develop. In this phenomenon, one does indeed have inner ego awareness during a vision, without odd medical or psychological side-effects.

Etheric vision, a major part of the new clairvoyance
As Rudolf Steiner taught, and many people can now affirm, a new clairvoyance is developing. This brings in particular, awareness of the ether world or ethereal life energies. This is one of the most important facts for people today to know. If humanity could become aware of this etheric clairvoyance it would have great impact on the efforts being made all over the world towards a spiritual renewal of civilization. It was explained earlier that humanity was endowed naturally with a slight clairvoyance until about 2000 years ago. This is what Rudolf Steiner terms the 'old clairvoyance'. This has died away, but since the beginning of the 20th century, higher faculties are redeveloping. The reason for this is that the ether-body is no longer being so tightly bound to the physical body as a soul descends to incarnate; in other words, the soul is no longer incarnating as deeply into the material, physical body.

This means that we are starting to have perception of realities beyond the sense-world, since the physical sense-perceptions are no longer completely blocking out awareness of ethereal objects and energies. Such a process is connected with cosmic influences active in the evolution of humanity, and it is not due to specific spiritual striving by the individual. It manifests very subtly, and therefore it is very easy for us to ignore. In fact the signs are as subtle as those which occur when meditation brings its first results. And the signs are also very similar, because meditation brings about a clairvoyance, which is of the same kind as the spontaneous sort, except that it is stronger and able to be gradually deepened. **This fact is really what lies behind the idea that we are currently entering a New Age. It implies that if people undertake meditation from the twentieth century onwards, it will be easier for them to achieve higher faculties, because the cosmic conditions are now favouring a spiritual renewal.**

But **it is extraordinarily important that people become aware of this process**, for otherwise all of the above signs are simply ignored as they hover fleetingly near the threshold of awareness, only to disappear if not affirmed. Then, the opportunities of this colossal spiritual event, namely **the bestowing of a new clairvoyance on humanity** will be futile. For if it is rejected people will remain bound in the snare of materialism, even whilst actually perceiving (but not consciously cognizing) a cosmic realm, namely, the etheric world. Perception of this realm reveals how untrue is materialism, for it is composed of energy of a higher finer kind than physical energies such as gravity, electricity, magnetism, ultra-violet/infra-red light, micro-waves, x-rays etc.

Some of the signs of the new clairvoyance that Rudolf Steiner gives include the following. You may discover that after having completed a particular deed of some significance you become focussed inwardly for a few minutes. You are aware of an unusual image or scene in your consciousness; so you become a little dreamy for a while. You may perhaps become aware that the scene is puzzling, it is not something you have witnessed or have otherwise been involved in.

However, it is very likely that such a subtle event in the inner life is simply not registered. That would be unfortunate, for the picture is a proclamation of the future karmic (destiny) result of the deed you have just carried out. The pictorial scene which one sees, portrays oneself and the others in a situation which is the effect of an earlier cause, namely a deed recently carried out. That is, this phenomenon reveals in pictorial manner, a cause and effect dynamic, which is in fact, the karmic consequence of significant deeds.

The karmic result may occur later in this present life, or in a next life. The scene will indicate the way that one will be called upon to balance out the deed. **Once we have been made aware that this process is actually happening, we are empowered to become much more conscious of it, and can work with it**. One will be able to notice these tenuous images and to then focus on them; gradually this technique enables one to recognize more quickly that this is going on, and the images become clearer. The destiny consequence of our deeds, the forming of karma, creates an image in the soul-body and this is reflected into the ether-body. The new etheric clairvoyance brings one into contact with these images.

Another sign is that of seeing an image which depicts a scene from normal life, but a scene which you know has not happened. It is a bit enigmatic, until perhaps the next day or three days later, the event occurs. Perhaps you don't at first experience a picture, it may be only a hunch, a feeling about the coming event. This is the same phenomenon in a weaker form. This remarkable preview of one's future events live in the aura, and are imprinted into the ether-body.

Now, some of the more potent events of a **past life** have a presence in our aura, and these too can be reflected into one's ether-body. By perceiving these, the new clairvoyance therefore also brings memories of our past life; even if fragmented and slightly confused at times. The advanced esoteric meditating taught in these pages also brings recall of the past life, but in a much more clear and controlled manner.

Another sign of the presence of a new ethereal vision which Rudolf Steiner forecast would occur, is what he described as the perception of "...a bright layer or strip of light around other human beings. Around the human physical body, people will start to see the delicate sheath of the ether-body glowing".[105] He indicated that as of the 1930's such access to ethereal vision would occur. I can certainly confirm from my own experiences and from the comments made by seminar participants that this is now happening. Many people report that when they reflect a little on what they really see when looking at a person, that there is a bright radiance shimmering around the outline of that person.

Seeing 'faces' everywhere
Some of my readers may be familiar with the eerie phenomenon of seeing faces everywhere, embedded in the forms of common everyday physical sensory objects, such as a tea-towel or a pile of papers or toys. What was at first just an innocent haphazard collection of forms, is suddenly seen to resemble a face; this is a real phenomenon, and does not indicate any form of mental ill-health, nor does it mean that you are in any kind of a danger. It arises when a slight etheric clairvoyance develops – and hence is bewildering, as we do not realize that we are crossing over the threshold between this physical world and entering, as it were, the ethers.

Such slight etheric perception can develop through the very ill-advised practise of taking illicit drugs, as one young woman commented, "After I took marijuana, I started seeing faces everywhere, so I have a nervous tick about faces being depicted in a subtle way in graphic work." Rudolf Steiner spoke briefly of this phenomenon to a trusted student, "Nature strives everywhere to make faces. That is its goal. And when I go outside, I constantly see faces, which are trying to come into being, everywhere..."[106] So, in effect nature spirits seek to create countenances wherever possible, and this is what we see, in the ether. Although it is eerie, it is quite harmless, and presents a challenge for the meditant, to be more courageous. One can thereby prepare for the more challenging experiences of seeing actual beings, when one's higher faculties have developed further.

---

[105] See lectures on "The Reappearing of Christ in the Ether".
[106] Reported by Assia Turgenieff, in "Erinnerungen an Rudolf Steiner" (Vlg Freies Geistesleben; Stuttgart, 1972), 99.

The self-achieved clairvoyance
In contrast to the spontaneously developing new clairvoyance, there is of course also the new self-achieved clairvoyance. This description is simply a way of referring to the attaining of the three higher states of consciousness which esoteric meditation confers. These are the states which we have discussed in detail in earlier chapters, namely, **psychic-image** consciousness, **cosmic-spiritual** consciousness and **high-initiation** consciousness. Through striving to attain these, the meditant today is in effect, developing a new clairvoyance, it is not an atavistic nor a spontaneous condition. The three clairvoyant higher states possible each have a preliminary mode, that is, a vague, weaker way of manifesting, which many people experience even if some do not like to admit it.

Differences between the old clairvoyance and the new
We noted very briefly that there is also a 'new clairvoyance' developing. That is, a form of elementary psychic perception which is spontaneously occurring. We need to note here that there is also a **third type of clairvoyance**, and that is the specifically self-achieved higher faculty, the outcome of meditative exercises. So there are three types of clairvoyance; **the old** which may occur atavistically, i.e., is simply there, secondly **the new**, which is spontaneous, and thirdly the (new) **self-achieved** clairvoyance achieved through meditation.

The old clairvoyance is not as easily controlled as the clairvoyance that is developed by one's own ego forces, or the spontaneously developing new type. The old can dominate a person. In the new forms, any dialogue with other spiritual intelligences is entirely wholesome. But most importantly one has the ability to inaugurate and to stop this oneself, and certainly one has the ability to 'read' (perceive) an aura by oneself, without the need of a guide. With this self-achieved clairvoyance, one also has the ability to assess the inner reality of an approaching being; it is an ego-active state. In this sense, the atavistic state is by contrast a passive one which requires some suspension of critical faculties. At best it brings experiences which one can only assess indirectly, afterwards.

The atavistic clairvoyant vision usually has the character of making one unfree through the **insistent** way that it appears. If in doubt as to just which condition is applying, the above criteria of self-awareness and assessment will show the truth; in addition the facts of the person's inner history will provide substantial indications.

In Chapter Four we saw that the self-achieved, ego-controlled higher consciousness produces visions that are at first fleeting and ephemeral. The atavistic state (which can be at times an ego-weakening state) is the opposite. Its visions are from the start strong and hard to forget. However, it is important not to confuse a strong and unforgettable vision which is bestowed upon one by a good higher being, as a unique experience, with **ongoing** strong visions of the atavistic faculty, which is derived from one's constitutional qualities. Atavistic people – in the cultural areas defined above – have not focussed in a past life on inner processes that consolidates the ego-sense. Hence their connection with the other worlds is one that all too easily dominates the potential of their ego.

There are also several other distinct features of the new clairvoyance, especially the self-achieved clairvoyance, in contrast with the old type. One difference is that with the old clairvoyant state (whether in earlier epochs, or surfacing as an atavistic power today) the chakras revolve anti-clockwise in a person's aura, when seen by someone else looking at them. Whereas, as the initiate explained to his students (1906), the chakras in the self-achieved ego-endowed clairvoyance, and the new clairvoyance, revolve in a clockwise direction.

There is an additional important distinction between the two types of clairvoyance, which is ascertainable to normal consciousness. This difference is that with atavistic clairvoyance the person is not able to observe their own consciousness every second of the experience. In other words, with the old clairvoyant experience the person is in a trance, or semi-trance or unable to fully exercise their self-awareness.

Indeed in the earlier ages when what is now regarded as atavistic was the norm in the contemporary situation, people often entered a state of ecstasy. The ego-state is greatly dimmed, but the feelings enhanced. The ecstatic conditions loosen the connection between the body and the subtle bodies, and imbues the person with other influences, but seriously reduces the presence of self-hood. That is, the thought life can not assess, or monitor the experiences, let alone become consciously and deliberately a vessel of the higher-self, with its transcendental higher awareness. Such people may become a vessel of a lower or neutral entity of some kind, such a situation also harms the mastery of the astral body by the ego.

The atavistic condition is also indicated when psychic faculties develop without the person having first learnt to comprehend spiritual truths conceptually. For it is precisely this activity that endows the self with the inner strength and the inner spirituality necessary to form the chakras in the aura. However, it is also true that a developed soul may well require only brief inner work to have the self-achieved ego-based clairvoyance manifest. So hasty judgemental attitudes are not advisable here.

In the old clairvoyance, too, other beings become excessively influential. The 'guide' could become an all controlling and authoritative figure. It is atavistic when one leaves the actual task of perceiving in the higher realm – perhaps of medical matters or aura reading – to 'the guide', whose communications are then transmitted to you. Likewise when one receives from a spirit guide communications about one's daily life and inner realities in all details, and 'recipes' for behaviour and attitudes.

Again the parallel of this natural higher vision with esoteric development is clear, for we have seen that meditation gradually confers the faculty of what I call **psychic-image consciousness** or image-clairvoyance (etheric-astral vision). As was pointed out to the Esoteric School students, one of the first higher realities to be seen by the meditant as they start to activate the chakras will be their own ether-body. This is to be seen glowing in the shadow cast by one's physical body. (1911)

What is seen with ethereal vision ?
To start the profoundly transformative journey into actually seeing the ethers – the life energies that sustain all physical life on Earth – it is first necessary to allow yourself to accept that this is possible. Then, as your meditative activity proceeds, remain alert to the subtle things that appear on the periphery of your consciousness. I will give some examples, drawn from my own early experiences on the path to self-initiation, in the 1970's. It was after commencing meditation on the cosmic Christ mystery as elucidated in Rudolf Steiner's lecture cycles that a first phase of this occurred for me.

As I moved a hand whilst standing in a door-way, beyond which was a darkened room its ether-counterpart glowing like pale mauve smoke became visible against the dark background. It is when an object is moving that its ether-counterpart can be more easily seen, as it tends to trail delicately behind the physical one like a feather, catching up and snugly fitting into it as the movement stops. This same phenomenon means that watching a group of dancers on stage takes on an additional dimension of interest.

However, before you see this, it is much easier to develop perception of the Earth's own ether energies, which are present everywhere. The air is filled with various kinds of ethereal forces, a brief description of these forces in various levels of the atmosphere is given in my first book.[107] So, make the experiment to determine whether or not you have already some etheric vision. Simply gaze quietly into the blue sky (not at the sun of course, and not with the intention of self-hypnosis); just rest and look at the apparent blue nothingness of the air. Now, what do you see?

---

[107] "Living a Spiritual Year – seasonal festivals in northern and southern hemispheres".

Do you see really just blank uniform blueness? I doubt it ! Because in my experience, most people can see a certain ether force in the air, but they just don't cognize it.

That is, they fail to recognize what they are seeing, because they have not been given the concept 'ether'; that is, ether energies shimmering and dancing in the air. Lacking this concept, they can scarcely find it possible to acknowledge what they are seeing. (Hence the enormous value of esoteric knowledge. It provides the concepts, the thoughts upon which the spiritualization of the Earth depends.)

If you keep looking calmly, not staring, you will begin to see that the air is filled with a multitude of small bright spots of light which are in rapid motion, darting and gliding everywhere. They may appear to have little tails like miniature comets; they also give the impression that they are semi-conscious, i.e. somewhat alive. There is another ether force that looks like rain, indeed you think at first that it is lightly raining, because of its similarity to the typical pattern formed by raindrops falling ceaselessly at an angle.

However, it is not rain, but a curtain of in-raying of energy from the sky forming a delicate pattern, which is more easily seen in dim light against bushes and trees. These are perceived by the new ethereal vision, whether achieved through inner effort, or are naturally occurring. However the advantage for the meditant is that one can proceed to attain to higher capacities than simply that which is given to people in the course of evolution.

These darting energy-points and shimmering curtain of life-forces exist and if you can not yet see them, you certainly will after some time of earnest meditation and adoption of the corresponding life-style. These are not caused by defects in your eyes, note that carefully; they are actually there in the ether plane. They are not the same as the medical condition called 'Muscat volantes' or specks inside the eye which move around as your eye moves. They are to be seen just as clearly on a cloudy day, against the grey background of the clouds. In fact, as the meditant develops more skill in using etheric vision, this phenomenon can be seen just a few feet from you in most environments.[108] And amidst these semi-animate energy points there will occasionally appear a more intense, powerful point of energy. This indicates the presence of entities which are active in the ethers. This may all seem at first to be some kind of self-induced fantasy, but it isn't.

---

[108] Advanced meditants seriously involved in this self-initiation pathway will discover that they can interact with these etheric forces.

It is important to note that a form of internal etheric vision may also occur, as explained in the following.....

> "It can happen that a meditant sees in the air, a conglomeration of tiny points or vortex-like whirls. They may then go to an eye specialist who declares this is occurring in the eyes, and it is then some form of vision impairment....but the actual cause of this is that the ether-body begins to make new kinds of movements, because of the meditating. These are carried over onto the physical body and manifest as such. This does not mean that the health is being impaired, for after a while the ether-body corrects the situation, and the odd images disappear".(1913)

Tragically, knowledge of such matters is still very limited, despite the spread of New Age literature. It was however Rudolf Steiner's intention that a number of his students, already decades ago, would have ensured that such knowledge became a significant influence in the cultural life through books like this and spiritual centres, but for various reasons this has not happened. This is itself a tragic thing, for ignorance of the ethers at a time when ethereal vision is spontaneously developing causes obvious psychological stress.

The author knows of a man in New Zealand who voluntarily committed himself, with his wife's consent, to an asylum for the mentally ill, after he developed the capacity to see etheric entities and forces. He simply had no concepts of such things, and could not find such a concept amongst mainstream counsellors, and certainly did not know that higher faculties are spontaneously developing. As the cultural environment was so spiritually barren, he assumed he was mentally ill. Rudolf Steiner in 1910 foresaw precisely this situation, teaching it would happen more and more to people if knowledge of the existence of the ethers did not become widespread.

The realization that one has this ability to sense at least simple ethereal forces, bestowed on humanity through the grace of the powers behind the evolution of the world, is very important. For then as a meditator you will be able to empower this process, stimulating the chakras further through meditation. This enables doors to open onto new and beautiful experiences. You will be able, as the chakras strengthen, to go beyond the spontaneous psychic experiences. For example, one can contemplate the moon, but now seeing it etherically. The moon then becomes a brilliant white-glowing orb, (no trace of the dark spots!) and this is surrounded by an aura in shades of mauve and red. Later you may decide to observe its inner life-qualities throughout the seasons. This becomes a fascinating experience. For one then discovers how the moon shimmers in a dance motion as the spring equinox full moon approaches.[109]

A similar research can be undertaken with the majestic and vast ether-aura of the sun, but that requires caution – on **no account** may one ever gaze directly at the sun etherically or physically. The sun must be shaded off from your eyes by the hand or by positioning oneself behind a friendly tree-trunk. Its ether-aura extends across a large portion of the sky, in orange shades. One of the fascinating experiences also possible is that of gazing inside a sun-beam, that is, of observing the sparkling etheric forces within the sun's rays, which can be seen in safety by observing a ray of light through the leaves of a tree.

Walks in nature can then become a time of great solace and uplift, because then one knows from direct experience about the existence of the ether realm, and as a consequence, the existence of the astral and spiritual realms become more real. One feels oneself becoming part of the living cosmos, and can sense the necessity of harmonising one's deeds, wishes and attitudes to holistic spiritual truths. Then theoretical-intellectual spirituality gives way to full soul-centred spirituality. Furthermore, as knowledge that such a phenomenon is actually happening, ever more people will perceive the ethers, then the damage to the environment by technology can be greatly reduced. Then ether-energy systems can be developed to replace the nuclear energy and polluting fossil-fuel energy systems.

As a final theme to contemplate on this topic, this process of sensing the ethers is connected with the profound mystery of the 'Reappearing of Jesus'. Although this is not our main topic, yet so significant is this theme, that a brief mention is necessary. Rudolf Steiner teaches that Jesus has made it possible for humanity to encounter Him in an etheric form, as from the early 20th century, for He will never incarnate again into a physical body. So the capacity of perceiving in the ethers also means that people may actually see this most holy God-Man in an ethereal form, or at least receive an inspiration from Him. This theme with its remarkable implications is of immense importance and I recommend that Steiner's texts on this subject be read.

Messages from spirit realms

It is important to note that there are beings in the astral world who seek for converts or 'instruments' here on the Earth amongst persons who are psychic. It may be an entity which is compelled to effect changes on Earth in a particular nation or group of people. Such beings

---

[109] Why this happens, and what is so important about the springtime moon of either hemisphere – which is when esoterically the Easter moon occurs – is explained in my first book about the seasonal festivals.

can easily feel that 'the ends justifies the means' and manipulate acolytes in ways contrary to their best interests. This seeking of an agent (channel) can be sometimes for a good, or at least neutral, reason, but it often has disregard for the agent's own freedom. Such beings can also stimulate into action an atavistic clairvoyant condition, in a suitably passive person. Then the person is directed and controlled as regards their spiritual experiences, not by their ego, but by the other being.

There are many entities, including deceased persons, who have an intense yearning to remain an active force in the human world. These beings use atavistic persons or souls just acquiring ego-based higher sensitivity for their own purpose. This may include impelling their 'agent' to take up 'propaganda work' amongst a certain ethnic group or nation or adherents of a spiritual order.

The entity has a potent urge to see that the respective group of people is given a certain 'message' in the form of a spiritual philosophy, etc. A worse situation occurs when lower beings whisper messages to the seeker. Such messages are often believed because the existence and active involvement of malignant spirits at the threshold is unknown or ignored. A person developing wholesome new faculties, but not yet freed from subtle personal egotism, can also become a bearer of a distorted message, rather like an atavistic seer who can not inwardly monitor the messages.

In the Esoteric School the students were taught that the crucial question here is; if you give the message to people, would it be a pleasure for you, or would it entail some pain, some sadness? If there is a certain pleasure, derived from a subtle egotism and the sensational aspect of it, then it probably is not appropriate to speak. If the message or perspective has a certain wisdom and truth within it, then it is not only valuable, it must also have entailed some earnest re-examination of life, or even some inner suffering for the person who communicates an insight to another. Naturally this is but one aspect of this complex matter, but it is important and relevant especially for the beginner.

On this matter of pain, as the old wise saying says, 'all wisdom is crystallized pain'. The spiritual teacher will have suffered and learnt much on his or her pathway, thus refining the inner being, and have become capable of relaying truthfully wholesome new perspectives. This advice about caution in relaying apparent messages, was compared (1911) with the humour of a comedian or clown. Those humorists who have suffered, and bring to expression their sadness and their poignant reflections in their humour can provide a deep contribution to society.

Astral projection

Astral projection is an occult practise wherein one removes one's soul from the physical body by a certain technique, in order to be free to wander in the astral realm. It has a strong appeal to those who find the idea of flying through the night sky fascinating and tempting. That is, the idea of remaining the normal earthly personality, but being free to float and fly like a bird. Astral projection is regarded as an inappropriate activity for students on this esoteric path; although for experienced meditants, it may occur, under special circumstances without jeopardising the process of union with the higher-self. The reason that it is not recommended is that in astral projection, the person is basically not involved in the process described in this book.

It is precisely in the nature of the esoteric path to the sacred inaugurated by Steiner, that strenuous personal development through which the higher-self enters into the increasingly selfless ego, bestows awareness of the higher spiritual realities to the person. In other words, the deeper meditative activity enables one to develop the ability to raise one's awareness beyond the physical plane **whilst in the flesh**, that is, whilst functioning as an incarnate person.

This requires consistent inner work and slowly leads to sense-free consciousness, or spiritually intuitive thinking. In other words, when higher faculties begin for the meditant it is because his or her actual consciousness is now lifted to that of the higher worlds, and thus the aura has formed the chakras. The meditant's consciousness is then inherently functioning in the astral and perhaps even spiritual realms. This is by-passed in astral projection. Instead one's matter free consciousness is only so non materialistic because the body has been deserted.

The practise of meditation brings a far superior form of interaction with the great cosmic nexus that we enter at night than does astral projection. It enables the soul as it leaves its body to retain a sense of self-awareness whilst immersed within the spiritual realms, and hence to both more profoundly experience the divine reality, and to remember this upon awakening:

> "When we awaken each morning we often have a tenuous memory of the spiritual realms. It is from these realms that spiritual strength flows to the meditant, and it belongs to one of the most beautiful experiences of the esotericist to remember that world from which we have drawn inner strength. A realm in which we found the source of this strength. In this remembering, it may also occur that some spiritual energies from a deceased loved one are inter-woven. Those who may experience this subtle communing should regard this as an especial act of grace." (1910)

However, each person at night-time in the normal course of going to sleep, journeys into the other worlds and this is a similar phenomenon to astral projection. However the difference is that in going to sleep, people do not enter this condition deliberately through occult techniques. So although we do not artificially exit out of the body, we are as souls released each night from the body and therefore in a position to go a-wandering, so to speak. Most of the night, the soul is not wandering at all, in the sense of a person strolling along a street; because the soul, unless we are speaking of that of a meditant, tends to merge into the cosmic nexus through which it is journeying, and hence loses to some extent its separated-ness.

For some of the night, there is a more separated self, which can undergo a spectator experience; otherwise, it is more a matter of somewhat merging with the divine reality in which we enter. Regarding the fact that we do undergo a journey, in whatever degree of consciousness it may be, Steiner taught that the more advanced one is, the further one can go in the astral body at night, and that one can also have a degree of self-consciousness then, but "you normally can not remember these most remarkable wanderings." (1903)

However a very advanced meditant can remain self-conscious in the process and therefore the next day will be also able to remember the night time experiences. But there are limitations to such journeys.... "You can visit someone in Asia for example, and ask them questions, but you cannot experience whether they are at that time writing a letter or at the meal table; however you can learn from that person and then later write down what you learn." (1903)

So astral travelling is a reality, it is not excluded from activities for a seeker after purely ethical spiritual transformation; but on the other hand, it is not sought for. It is simply a specialized esoteric activity, which does not necessarily depend on real spirituality to be achieved. In astral projection, one wills to separate the astral body from the physical body, whilst maintaining self-awareness as John Smith or Susan Simpson, so that one may explore the environment. Naturally if this succeeds, then the awareness, the kind of consciousness that the person has, is not much different to their normal earthly kind.

Hence their experiences are not any more revelatory of the astral world than those of a traveller in a foreign land who does not speak the language, and from whose sight the inhabitants are hiding or only seen as silhouettes. The astral traveller's mind-set has not in any way developed up to the state of the astral world. All thinking and attitudes will be profoundly if subtly oriented to the world of time and space and matter. Therefore the environs are perceived from the standpoint of the three dimensional world, and this again can lead to visionary experiences which are intensely materialistic delusions.

A famous example is that of an American guru who declared he 'had a cup of tea with the Buddha in the seventh plane', and when he was criticized, he pointed out that, of course it was 'a **spiritual** cup of tea'. This is exactly the delusion of materialism to which the astral projector is subject. For the same reason, when the astral projector falls asleep, he or she loses self-consciousness; for they simply can not be conscious in a world where there are no physical sense-stimuli coming in. They do not have the means to stay self-aware in higher worlds when entering it in the normal way, at sleep. But through this unusual process of ejecting one's astral body out of the physical, their normal ego-state is, sometimes, able to be maintained.

For the ego has not yet developed the ability of thinking about the spirit in spiritual terms, in spiritual concepts. It can not yet see spirit (spiritual realities) in the mind's eye, let alone behold it directly in astral light. Only a meditant can do this, or a soul whose earthly life has ended, for then, as Rudolf Steiner explained,[110] its aura is re-oriented to functioning with consciousness in the astral light.

Whereas astral projection is like a materialistic person who, through an accident, which resulted in an out-of-body experience, now realizes that the soul exists, but has no inner attunement to merge into the divine reality that **is** there behind the illusions that tend to fill the astral world. Such attunement is needed to put this discovery into context. This intuitive **cosmic-spiritual** consciousness needs years of study and meditation to achieve the required orientation for such an experience. So the astral projection experience does not enable the ego to absorb the truth of the spirit right into its core, to become one with transcendental **cosmic-spiritual** consciousness.

When such spiritual consciousness does exist, through one's thinking life one can, for example, explain the concept of 'spirit' to another person. Through actually being self-aware out of the body, one can certainly know that there is an astral world, which is indeed a powerful experience. But one has little ability to put into context the real significance of that, except of course in the elementary way that a child can convincingly say that faeries exist, having seen some. But such a child can not possibly conceptualize just what these beings are or what their own inner nature and evolution has been. Of course, the path to esoteric development must begin somewhere, and awareness of the

---

[110] See various of his lectures on life after death, e.g., "At the Gates of Spiritual Science", lect. 4.

soul as a reality may then lead the astral projector onto a spiritualization of their conscious mind.

In the state of astral projection, a person may soon lose the ability to stay self-aware and be drawn back to their body after a little while, or perhaps seek to awaken in the body because they have begun to feel uneasy. Or they may fall into sleep, and awaken later with or without memory of their experiences. So they have passed from ego-endowed, or awake consciousness over to sleep consciousness outside their body; this is a remarkable, odd situation. The soul as it enters sleep has its being interwoven with the living reality of the higher worlds. In the astral projection process, confused recollections of various kinds are possible, especially since the falling asleep occurs in an irregular way, when one is actually out of the body yet still in the normal earthly ego state.

It then becomes very likely that materialistic illusions within one's soul are seen as visions upon awakening. When however the ego is progressing in its ability to transform the soul, it may indeed go on special journeys in the astral plane. However that then occurs in a more natural way, during normal night-time activity.[111] Should a person have attained the ability to have astral and even Devachanic consciousness through meditation, then he or she may propel their soul out of the body at certain unusual times.

For example, certain initiates, usually known as saints, adepts or holy men, have been known in an extreme situations, where demonic powers are attacking, or when other people are in dire need of help, may find it expedient to deal with these situations in an 'out of the body' condition. But usually such astral travelling activity is chosen on rare occasions for certain esoteric instructions, as indicated by one of Rudolf Steiner's most advanced students, whom he occasionally instructed through certain experiences that could be called astral journeying.[112]

---

[111] More about this is said in the last chapter when dreaming is discussed.
[112] Appendix 3 has some further details about this, and her encounter with the guardian of the threshold. Countess Johanna von Keyserling is the student, she had out of body journeys as well as the ability to raise her consciousness to the higher worlds from within her body. In an unpublished manuscript given to this author she refers to this.

Appendix 1

The archangel Michael

The reader who is new to anthroposophy is advised to read Rudolf Steiner's works about the archangel Michael, an immensely important being for spiritual aspirations of modern humanity. One notes in the teachings of this initiate, that spiritual beings themselves are also in an evolving process, they move up to higher ranks over time. According to Rudolf Steiner, Michael is now gradually moving up to the rank of principality, and under his auspices, there is another archangelic being, who helps those who seek to develop the new spiritualized consciousness. This being has the name "Vidar" in the Edda, which contains the mythic texts from northern Celtic Europe. This being is closely connected both with the nature-spirits who maintain the life-processes in each hemisphere, and with the cosmic Christ. This being is also closely involved with the mysteries of the Holy Grail, and anthroposophical initiation wisdom is specifically intended to offer the opportunity for spiritual seekers to move towards the Grail castle, so to speak.[113]

Appendix 2

Uniting with the archetype of the spiritualized human being.

The remarkable revelations concerning the absorbing of the finest forces of the spiritualized soul, and the incorporation into these of spiritual reality from Jesus are at first very striking. But this is because modern materialism is so far removed from the holistic truths of life. In earlier ages similar ideas were scarcely discussed, because they were self-evident. For example in the ancient Egyptian initiation wisdom, it was known that after death the soul becomes one with Osiris; Osiris being the sun-god. This is in fact an Egyptian name for the cosmic-Christ. For if the deceased person's name was 'Ani' then he becomes 'Ani-Osiris' after death, hence such passages as this appear in the Book of the Dead... "shine thou upon the countenance of Osiris-Ani, who is now victorious.."

---

[113] This being, is a regent of the new self-initiation process. Prokofieff (in "The Cycle of the Year as a path to initiation to experience the Christ being", p. 338 German edit.)falsely identifies this being as the "The Angel of the Lord" of the Christian Scriptures. Whereas Rudolf Steiner revealed (1923) that this archangel was not involved in the Biblical events, but spent several centuries converting itself to the Christ-impulse, from its home within the faerie realms of Scandinavia.

Other passages reveal an even more intimate symbiotic link between the human soul and the light of the sun sphere; "Behold I have come forth this day and have become a being of light, Horus the son of Osiris hath made for me a spiritual body from His own being..."[114] Earlier we noted that precisely those processes which occur after death, occur during life for the serious meditator. So, if from modern initiation knowledge we learn that the incarnate cosmic Christ from the Sun-sphere permeates our soul – the heart chakra area – with Its light, so we in a certain sense become one with It, is this not virtually the same process as referred to in such ancient texts about the nature of life after death? The union of the Christ-light with the astral heart, that is its finest qualities, accumulated in an etherealized form, is then quite in harmony with ancient classical spirituality, although they used different names for this divine being.

---

[114] The Book of the Dead, transl. E.A. Wallis-Budge, chap.78:25, p253.

CHAPTER EIGHT

The two pathways: above and below

This chapter explores some of the major issues that confront a person who is seriously interested in meditation, and wants to put into context some of the experiences it brings. We start with a brief over-view of the two fundamental dynamics which every persistent meditant encounters sooner or later, described by Steiner in various lectures. These two were well known to the spiritual fraternities of antiquity, but usually an acolyte experienced only one of them. The ancient initiates (known as a "heroes" or avatars) of earlier civilisations were therefore of two kinds. Those of whom it is said they **descended** deep into subterranean evil realms wherein they eventually found their way through to divine beings.

Secondly, there were those of whom it is said they **ascended** into cosmic heights, perceiving the causative forces from the cosmos at work in the Earth. When it is said in mythology that a hero like Perseus or Orpheus descended down below into the Underworld, then this refers to the initiation stream of the first kind. That is, these seekers were in fact entering into their own double or lower-self. Their journey involved learning how to overcome the evil egotistical beings which are active in the lower-self, in the triune double, in the shadow side of thinking, emotions and will. They sought illumination from the 'gods below'; this refers to the divine forces from which the soul's spiritual transformation derives. To achieve this inner illumination, the hidden subconscious tendency to evil had first to be consciously encountered.

In contrast, the second kind of initiates were the heroes who ascended into celestial heights, like the ancient Persian teacher, Zarathustra, and the Druids. They sought to become attuned to the cosmic forces within the stars and the planetary spheres. They ascended to the 'gods above'. In other words, such an initiate experienced the ranks of hierarchical beings active throughout the cosmos. They became aware from direct experience that life on Earth originated from and is maintained by zodiac and planetary influences. It is from this kind of initiation, that creation stories and also what we now know as astrology had its origin. (This is true of the non-decadent spiritual streams, but bear in mind that there were and are also occult streams of a sinister kind, and these also exerted an influence, and seek converts.)

Their inner achievements were described as outer deeds, and became the basis of a mythological story. If one was living in an area where the Mystery Centre offered a path that led deep into the inner soul-life, then it was only possible to undertake the journey up into the cosmic spheres by travelling to another Mystery centre where that pathway was taught. This fascinating 'localization' element is well-attested to by various authors in antiquity, and by Steiner. This situation existed for millennia, and ended about the time of Christ. However, in modern times, it is vital that **both** pathways are taken, or rather that the path we take encompasses both elements. That means the meditant needs **to strive to ennoble the soul, and also to become sensitive to the planetary and zodiac forces**.

The meditant who really undertakes the study and meditative pathway outlined here will find sooner or later, that they are encountering the dark corners of the lower self. This is a bracing, sobering experience, but it also bestows eventually a wonderful and inspiring gift. One discovers an inner purity, a chasteness and an integrity developing; with this comes a deepening of whatever level of inner peace you have attained. The way to the sacred is not of course entirely achieved by the meditative efforts, rather the meditant has enabled the source of sanctification in realms of the spiritual to imbue the soul with the spirit-self. **There is little that can bestow such deep tranquillity and happiness as the knowledge that one is on the pathway to banishing one's potential towards ignoble acts and thoughts, as one's endeavours against the lower self and towards sanctification begin to make some headway.**

A major cause of nervous conditions today is the suppression of the sensing of the lower-self, especially when the individual is resisting the process of personal growth. A spiritual path should build a bridge between the spirituality in oneself and the spiritual reality in the cosmos, which is 'behind' the illusory material world. Hence this pathway will also lead to more and more insights into the interconnectedness of the human soul and the cosmos. The meditant gradually becomes aware of a symbiotic link between the soul with its various qualities and phases and the movements of the planets, and the sun and moon through the constellations. Astrology becomes re-born through the insights of such a person. These are then the two aspects of the path which the soul must take on the way to higher consciousness.

Why am I not making progress?
We live today in difficult times. Never before has such a materialistic earth-bound consciousness existed and imposed its arid and malignant influences so strongly, invoking its allied decadence. It is clear from Rudolf Steiner's research into karma and history, that many people have had a higher spiritual awareness in a previous life than they now possess. One reason for this is the effect of incarnating in bodies that are subtly 'hardened'. This hinders the person in it from awareness of higher influences. For the body is now influenced by hardening influences prevalent today, such as materialistic thoughts, and

chemicals allowed by the state to be used in food-production and processing, and in the water supply.

The term **'materialism' means here an intellectual attitude, namely that matter is the sole reality in creation**. This is a relatively recent soul-illness. It is not ancient, and it has the effect of coarsening the body because it lames the ether-energies which maintain the body's structure. There is also in today's cultural life an immense strengthening of ego-centric earth-bound desires; lower forces achieve this via the entertainment and fashion industry of today. There are also the numerous artificial, often toxic, chemicals in food. The meditant obviously needs to take some trouble to minimize such influences.[115] There can also be an inner reason for a person not being in this life as capable in spiritual matters as in the past;

> "it could well be that someone was far more developed in a past life than they are in this life. This is perhaps because in this life through factors affecting the physical body that {spirituality} which was within them in a past life has not been able to manifest. For the soul-forces developed in the past must be drawn out {and made manifest} by the spiritual forces of the current life. For example, someone could have been a wise priest with magical powers; but now, perhaps the physical body is not sufficiently malleable to the spirit to enable this previous condition to re-occur. However, it could also be that in fact now other spiritual qualities are lacking, for example, love and goodness. If this is the case then one can not in this life draw out those prior spiritual qualities." [116]

The implication in these words appears to be that, although one was a highly placed religious person one did not maintain during all of that life one's spirituality with enough earnestness. So in effect such a person was living on their laurels during the latter years of the past life. Or one has not struggled hard enough in this life to re-acquire the purity needed. However the reverse is also true! **One can be really very close to developing higher spirituality and its attendant clairvoyance, but not realize the subtle inner signs of its developing within one.** Whether a person almost immediately has results from a program of earnest inner work, or still has no apparent success after decades depends upon several factors. Namely, what did one actually do in the

---

[115] The choice should be for bio-dynamic food (the enhanced organic method, called 'bio-dynamic' is the world-leading system of organic agriculture developed by Rudolf Steiner; reject those organic foods which use cleverly-processed sewerage as one of the components of the compost materials).

[116] R.Steiner; from a more intimate lecture, given 4th Dec 1905 (untranslated).

last life as regards the inner path, and how sensitive is one to the signs of developing spiritual insight, so that it is possible to work with them?

The first question is of course unalterably in the past, but regarding the second question, we dealt with this matter of the signs of developing higher consciousness in an earlier chapter. Whatever one achieves in this life is carried over and bestowed upon the next life, even if no obvious results occur now. And much indeed can be achieved in the way of cleansing and strengthening the soul-life, without any apparent signs of this occurring. It is for this reason that Rudolf Steiner emphasized that the **effort** which one makes is of paramount importance, not so much the results! The more effort is made, the greater will be the inner potential to continue on the spiritual path and to achieve results, in the next life. With regard to this matter of the progression of the soul from life to life, his following words are of considerable value;

> It is of course a question of where a person stands in the spiritual evolution of humanity as to how quickly meditation leads to inner results. The person can be much more developed than they realize. Inwardly a person today can already be in a position of (potentially) using his her will and spiritual powers in the spiritual world. Thus it takes longer with one person than someone also in the esoteric path to achieve the goal". [117]

Here we should also note again that efforts by the meditant can ultimately only bring results if the beings in the spiritual world affirm the efforts. Such affirmation causes stream of spiritual light to permeate the soul, forming the spirit-self. Many aspects of the divine beings are involved here, but perhaps the more readily sensed is the activity of the angels, whose activity in the human life-wave focuses on transforming the soul (astral body) into the spirit-self. In having this influence the angels are representatives of the most sublime angel. This foremost of the angels is itself a vessel of what in traditional Christian terms is referred to as the Holy Spirit.

In addition, the mediant is invoking the assistance of the next higher rank of divine beings, the archangels, whose influence for humanity is focused on the ether-body. Their activity is involved in the process of spiritualizing the ether-body into what in anthroposophy is termed the life-spirit. This process is especially important with regard to the capacity to be actively compassionate, that is, to attain to a source of spiritual reality in the Devachanic realm from which life and healing proceed. It is also this activity which enables the attainment of **cosmic-spiritual** consciousness, or consciously functioning in realms beyond

---

[117] From an unpublished archive lecture of Dec 1905.

the astral plane. According to Rudolf Steiner, this process is what is actually meant in (some of) those passages in the New Testament which refer to 'receiving grace'.

The full implication of this is beyond the scope of this book, but it is important to just note here that the term "grace' has two aspects to it. In Christian thought one refers to the kindness of deity, in allowing humanity to become assisted, despite being imperfect beings. The other meaning is more subtle, and refers to the dispensing of the capacity for the life-spirit to humanity. As we noted in the first chapter, the over-all capability of a spiritual transformation is owed to the deed which occurred on Golgotha hill, so this is grace in the usual use of the term, and secondly, it is through the sublime life-spirit powers of the sun-god (the cosmic Christ) that humanity will be able to develop their life-spirit, and this is grace as well – in the esoteric meaning.

Note that the physical body is a potential cause of inhibiting spiritual attainment of the past from manifesting now. Through subtly refining and etherealizing it in this life, such a potential barrier in the future is less likely to have an influence. The body, now and on into the next life, is influenced by various soul activities. Making the effort to think spiritually, undertaking meditation and also becoming a person of ethical initiative, and responding to an intuitive insight, are the most important influences. There is also a special esoteric breathing meditation which assists in this, which is considered later. With the decadence of the current times, this is not easy, and furthermore there is a lack of amenities for the development of spirituality, whereas, in ancient cultures there were magnificent temples or Mystery Centres.

However it is also true that many people are consciously replacing the negative influences with positive new ideas designed to enable a spiritual renaissance to gradually occur. It is really a question of will; if one can summon up the will to keep on going with regular meditation, many subtle negative influences to which we have been exposed from the childhood years can be overcome.

The tendency to 'slacken off' is a notorious problem with meditating, this is due to esoteric reasons that are discussed in Chapter Five. If we can only maintain some awareness of how fulfilling it will be when the goal is attained, then this problem is reduced. I am including some words that I found inspiring about the Kingdom of the Heavens. These are from a deceased artist, who was able to stay in touch with his psychic sister even as he entered into the spiritual world, beyond the illusory astral plane.[118]

---

[118] I have translated this from a German text, pub. by Vlg Die Kommenden, Germany 1971: part of which has been published as "Bridge over the River" -

"The nature of spiritland is a wonderful refreshing tranquillity. Amidst the millions of streaming, weaving rays of light, sparkling colours, tones of music and thoughts which flow and surge through each other, there prevails a profound peace...magnificent, powerful currents of thought flow softly throughout and around everything here....the last veils have fallen from my eyes; seeing am I ! And this seeing is also somehow the highest kind of feeling, and within this feeling-sensing, I am hearing !"

Recalling the past of this life and a past life
Another wonderful result of regularly meditating is that it brings gradually, a much fuller and deeper knowledge of ourself, by giving us a powerful panorama of memories of earlier times in our current life, right back to infancy. By genuinely seeking to attain **cosmic-spiritual** consciousness in the various ways pointed out, one will also eventually gain awareness of a past life, that is, memory of the previous life on Earth. Although that is a more difficult and longer-term process.

But it is important to note that in the pathway taught here, the theme of recalling a past life is closely interconnected with two other themes; developing awareness of karma, which eventually grants us an inner guide as to what decisions to make in one's life, and secondly, with the fact that it is not beneficial to actually get knowledge of the past life except through expanding the present 'I am' to include perception of or merge with, to some extent, the higher-self. When the meditant continues in meditating faithfully, then there begins to develop what we mentioned in Chapter Three, namely the memories of childhood.

What is actually happening now is that **psychic-image** consciousness is becoming stronger, and so images of one's early years — stored in the ether-body — that one lived in unconsciously then, are being accessed, together with their inner ambience. Eventually, these delicate, enhanced memories become a majestic powerful tableau or panorama of one's entire life. To arrive at this stage takes months or years, depending on how well you succeed in entering into deeper meditating. You begin to recall, without any apparent cause, scenes from your childhood; or perhaps you simply remember a mood or atmosphere which was experienced during one's life as a child.

Yet these are not just normal memories, because they are not really simple recollections of the past, there is more to them. It is as if from

---

by an anonymous author. R Steiner read the early section of the manuscript, and declared it genuine.

the core of our being, something of profound significance is brought to our adult awareness. Namely the interweaving that actually occurred all those years ago between our child nature and the spiritual reality 'behind' the world of the physical senses. In other words, you sense (or more accurately re-experience) within the scene that is being recalled, the spiritual ambience that pervaded that scene for you when you were a little child; a wonderful, enchanting, hauntingly vivid 'presence'.

It begins to happen in a manner that provides intense joy and uplift to the meditant, providing the first of many rewards for all the years of devotion to the inner work. I will draw on my own experiences, in describing this more closely. When you recall a past scene, it is often triggered off by some sense-impression you are currently registering. This gives way, and merges into a recalled memory, wherein a similar sense-impression is being registered very intensely by you in your childhood. Perhaps you are perceiving the odour of new-mown grass or perhaps the floral-pattern on a tablecloth, or even the particular shade of colour on a food wrapper. Perceiving this, you suddenly find that you are remembering a scene from early childhood which you had forgotten, but which has a colour or odour similar to that object which you as an adult are now seeing. The crimson stripe on a food wrapper is the same as that of some childhood object, perhaps a toy car or mother's apron.

However, it is not a neutral remembering, nor simply a noting of a particular event. No, it is much more than that; you are recalling perhaps the toy car, or the favourite glass marble, the parsley growing around the old garden tap, but permeating this pictorial image, and enveloping the recall experience, is an exquisite, divine ambience. The entire experience is joyously uplifting, an almost exhilarating sense of being in communion with the very source of all human joy; an enchanting atmosphere imbued with a spontaneous communing with the divine. It is in this way that the process of self-initiation can bestow a profoundly insightful child psychology, for eventually one can enter as a conscious adult right into the soul of a child.

The experience may occur as you walk in a park during autumn. Apparently the experience is simply remembering yourself, as a young child, walking across a moist autumnal lawn, adorned with red-brown leaves. But, suddenly and subtly, you become aware that you have entered into your childhood's own secret inner world; the exquisitely alive at-one-ness with the odour and texture of the leaves; all experienced in a wonder-filled innocent happiness. The memory then starts to move laterally, one becomes slightly aware of other events and dynamics that constituted your life then and of which you had lost all memory until now. When this starts happening then you as an adult truly know what otherwise is virtually unknowable: the gloriously enchanted, innocent immersion in a spiritual environment that nurtured us in our infancy and early childhood.[119]

These experiences are not artificially created, they are spontaneous. Until you actually experience this, it is difficult to credit the joy that it brings; this is one result of meditating which also teaches the meditant another life-lesson: learn to become capable of experiencing 'joy', in contrast to seeking sensual pleasure. When this inner illumination occurs, one begins to have a profound insight, concerning pleasure and pain. The meditant begins to perceive that some pleasures are actually painful for the soul and spirit, but they **appear** to be pleasurable to non-spiritualized consciousness. But the painful nature of the experience is concealed, for as long as it is possible for the person to get gratification of the desire.

These memories which you experience are in fact different to a normal recall of a past event in the ordinary sense. They have this very fine, subtle spiritual element in them. As Rudolf Steiner described these recalled memories with their direct granting of a spiritual ambience; it is as if you are walking across a paddock, over the grass, when from time to time, you notice some flowers blossoming amongst the grass. What this means is that in the course of normal spiritually subdued adult living, one becomes aware that some subtle, beautiful interacting with the higher worlds is occurring.

Namely the mind is becoming freed from the limitations of body-bound thinking, and is sensing the images retained within your ether-energies. Above all, these 'memories' are to be distinguished from normal 'remembering' because you eventually begin to recall scenes which occurred before you had any real self-consciousness, that is as an infant.

Most people find that in trying to recall childhood years, their memory stops in the third year of life, in other words some time after the second birthday. What then does this spiritual experience mean? It means that you are really starting to become attuned to your ether-body, wherein memory images of all these events are spontaneously stored, even the ones with which as an infant we have no self-conscious involvement. As this stage is reached, consciousness is transcending the physical plane, it is etherealising, we are accessing the images in our ether-body.

Recalling the past life

---

[119] Of course, the experience of this environment would have been obscured if one was subject to traumatic circumstances in childhood.

Now, once this stage has been reached, then the next stage can be undertaken, through the Contemplation activity that follows the first phase of meditating. As the meditant attains to **cosmic-spiritual** consciousness, then gradually awareness of the time before birth, that is, before conception, occurs. It is through **cosmic-spiritual** consciousness, the second state of higher awareness that real past life recall is achieved. For such recall is an earnest and remarkable extension of consciousness, which eventually takes us back to the higher Spiritual realms, to that time when that personality of which you are the current outcome, has died, and is therefore entering into those high realms. (What can be experienced as psychic impressions, of this time, by the lesser state of **psychic-image** consciousness, will be considered below.)

As **cosmic-spiritual** consciousness develops, it gradually leads to a recall of the last days or even the last minutes of that preceding life; in fact, to 'your' last death. This experience is not grotesque, one is a spectator, and not directly emotionally involved, and furthermore, the death is experienced from within a spiritual nexus. When a recently deceased person looks back to their passing, and now sees the event as if shimmering with an ambience derived from an awareness of the other worlds; so too, for the meditant who has attained to this level of consciousness. But in addition, the experience widens out and deepens, to include an awareness of the journey made into the ever higher realms of the spirit after that death.

This process, unlike many of the quick ways to past-life discovering, unveils a true reality, not a false picture caused by various subjective 'agenda', which are still in the subconscious. Why is this way to past life discovery regarded in this path as the 'most appropriate' way? Because, with regard to this past life recall, it is very important that **this unveiling of the secret** occurs within the context of our own efforts to expand our current self-awareness to include our true higher-self. **This also means that it is occurring with the agreement, so to speak, of the spiritual realms.**

For when we strive to achieve some further stage of inner development, such efforts are always inter-woven with various spiritual forces; forces that could be called, karma-directing powers. These are intimately involved in arranging our every-day karma, and also what kind of response shall be granted to the inner work. Therefore, when any such insight into our past life is given, it is integrated into one's own mental processes. Therefore it is **not grafted onto** the bewildered or gleeful John/Sally Smith, but rather **merges into** John or Sally's consciousness in a most natural manner as he or she becomes ever more attuned to their own higher-self.

In the higher-self, an awareness of our past lives is present. It has been gradually merging into our consciousness for some time prior to an actual vision occurring. Hence the meditant feels no trauma or unbalanced response to the revelation. So, one's ego-consciousness grows to encompass one's own past life's reality, and perceives how it has metamorphosed into the present reality. Once this stage is achieved, the meditant is enabled to work consciously with his or her karmic potentials and challenges, as well as developing gradually into an eternal higher consciousness. This theme is powerfully expressed in the dramas, referred to as "Mystery Plays' by Steiner.

This is the way to **cosmic-spiritual** consciousness; and this is one meaning of the words of Christ; "You shall know the truth, and the truth shall set you free." (St. John 8:32) The current personalty then transforms itself, and becomes the transcendental higher, true ego, which results in a growing-beyond-oneself. Consciousness becomes imbued with an eternal quality, so one no longer identifies oneself as the sum total of the current personality. Therefore one has gained knowledge of one's past lives, as one's self grows to encompass awareness of and memory of those earlier incarnations; the ego has become those past lives; it has become all that one was and is. [120]

In these circumstances the materialistic objections that genuine knowledge of a past life is impossible, loses whatever validity it may have had. This is because here we are considering the deep, esoteric path to the sacred via meditating, not a short-cut or dreamy time of imagining past events. Usually the objection is that all such higher experiences are simply naive responses of the seeker to unknown subconscious yearnings and ambitions. The esoteric Christian path, born of initiation knowledge in the truest sense, opens doors to a thorough self knowledge which provides protection against self-deception. However, there are always possibilities of quite real astral images, which convey falsehoods to the not yet purified meditant.

As mentioned above, it is also true that, quite apart from **cosmic-spiritual** consciousness experiences, one can gain some isolated images, or at least impressions, about one's past life at the stage of the newly developing lesser stage of **psychic-image** consciousness. During or shortly after meditation, impressions will tend make themselves felt, and indeed these are fascinating. However as explained in detail earlier, such experiences may be erroneous, that is they may truly mediate to one an astral image (reflected in the ether-body) but the image may simply be a thought-form that embodies what one has oneself been wistfully fantasizing about. For those who take up a serious

---

[120] In the late esoteric lessons of 1924 the initiate placed a veiled method of developing the ability to recall one's past life.

engagement with Steiner's work, there are indications to be found in his 'karmic relationship' lectures of 1924 as to meditative activity that assists one to develop insights into the karmic influences that are active between oneself and other people.

Breathing exercises and meditation

In the ancient East various breathing exercises are an integral part of the meditative striving for higher consciousness. However, almost no emphasis is placed on breathing exercises in the path presented here, as this approach is not regarded as advisable. But there is a special breathing exercise in the esoteric stream inaugurated by Rudolf Steiner, which is designed to subtly etherealize the body. There are however, other reasons for undertaking breathing exercises, which are quite valid; for example for relaxation or special medical purposes. But, as Steiner explained to his students, in ancient times the oriental yogi who undertook breathing exercises of a meditative kind was really entering consciously through the emotions (or sentiency) into the breathing process. He entered into awareness of what is happening spiritually as one breathes, whereas usually awareness of this exists only at the subconscious level. He could therefore experience some spiritual processes within his being that are normally quite hidden from the mind.

Amongst other things, it is possible to sense how the deeper levels of consciousness are interwoven with breathing. The essence of our auric energies (our consciousness) permeates the breath as it is inhaled and exhaled. The air is a carrier of prana or etheric energy, so the ether-body is involved here. The yogi could thereby become aware of the deeper insights which exist behind our normal awareness or thinking, whereas normally we only sense the mental representations of our thoughts. He became aware of his Spiritual Enlightenment to the extent that these become interwoven with the air, the breath-stream.

However, as Steiner explains, when the yogic technique of merging with the body's breathing dynamic brings awareness of the past life it is, as if one **remembers** what one was prior to birth. Whereas in contrast, through this path which derives the esoteric heritage of Europe, it is more the case that one releases the soul from the influence of the body (and the body-connected breathing process). Consciousness is thus able to merge with the higher worlds and then **directly perceive** whom one was in the past life. For our past reality is preserved in these higher worlds; it is preserved in the so-called memory of nature (also called in Theosophical terminology, the Akashic Chronicle).

Naturally this kind of perceiving can be achieved in the yogic path by applying **other** techniques, but that is not the point. The point is that instead of crossing the threshold by hitching a ride on the breathing process, the mind is to grow its own wings that carries its consciousness up to intuitive-cosmic awareness. The alternative method, based on the breathing forces, is to strap on a pair of wings, so to speak, and fly with those – which is possible so long as one breathes in that special way. As we mentioned earlier in modern times individual thinking has strongly developed, whereas it was scarcely present in ancient times. **Now that same ego-consciousness needs to make the effort to spiritualize itself, rather than connecting to the spirit by immersion in the breathing energies.**

Therefore in the path presented here, those who seek to become aware of this higher 'thinking', this cosmic archetypal consciousness, are advised to do so through normal meditation. It should not be achieved by a breathing technique but by a more individual effort of the soul to reach enlightenment. That is through directly awakening the higher mind by meditating in the way described in Chapter One.

In the words of the modern initiate, Rudolf Steiner,

> "When the person {meditant} can develop an inner love for thoughts and insights {which occupy the mind as one attempts meditation} then, one is able to move from normal conscious-thinking to meditation. The meditant needs to experience just such a love {good-will} as one normally brings to another human being. When we can really merge right into these insights through this loving attitude, then our thought-life receives an inner empowerment. An empowerment which is indeed quite different to that which the yoga-breathing techniques bestow.
>
> It does have a similar influence, but the result is quite different from that of the yogic-breathing technique, for this seeks to send the breathing-process {and the awareness of the yogi} up into the head. {In the head area we are much more conscious than in the chest area of the body, where breathing occurs, so if its forces can be raised up to the head area, the person can use these consciously.} There the yogi seeks to inwardly probe, illumine and gain knowledge of the soul-spiritual nature of the human being.
>
> Whereas we gradually attain a deep, true power of thinking {i.e., **cosmic-spiritual** consciousness} through which one achieves, in quite a different manner, a similar inner probing, an inner illumination. In this way, through the conscious strengthening of the life of the soul {i.e., its thinking ability} modern humanity can invoke a precise and accurate clairvoyance, whereas in older

epochs of human evolution, a more dreamy kind of clairvoyance was striven for in a way which is more body-dependent." [121]

So the modern meditative texts in the pathway presented here are actually designed to **prevent** the breathing from having involvement in the state of higher cosmic 'thinking'. An additional reason for people taking up breathing exercises is to induce an odd state of consciousness that can trigger off psychic experiences, this attempt to experience "movies" is contrary to the basic principles of the pathway presented here.[122]

The fact that astral clairvoyance or **psychic-image** consciousness can indeed be attained through meditative breathing exercises is not denied by Rudolf Steiner. In one lecture he comments....

> "As the meditant gradually lives consciously into this breathing process, which previously he or she had done unconsciously, but is now undertaken in a conscious way, this enables new worlds to open all around one. In a manner which is similar to learning to appreciate music and awakening to the experience of melody, there is an awakening in the spiritual world, for the meditant via the breathing process. One then experiences new worlds. If one lives consciously into the breathing process then Imaginative consciousness {i.e., what I term **psychic-image** consciousness} begins. Imaginative Consciousness enables a person to awaken {to awareness} of images in the mind, images which are not simple visions, rather they are images which originate in the 'primal foundation of existence' {Urgrund des Daseins}." [123]

However, as mentioned above, Rudolf Steiner does **not** recommend attaining to astral perception {**psychic-image** consciousness} through meditation which is connected with breathing.

There is another dynamic involved with breathing exercises, namely the stimulation of the ether-energies so as to alter the prana or ether currents. Such activity can have fascinating effects, but this really only has a valid place in certain metaphysical pathways which can use this in

---

[121] From a lecture of 31 Oct 1922, not translated, not yet published in the "Gesamtausgabe", (the German Complete Works) of R. Steiner; publ. in Blätter für Anthroposophie, Stuttgart: 1996, Nov. No.11.

[122] Obviously in cultures where this esoteric Christian path is not active, it may be the karma of an acolyte there to strive to attain to psychic experiences under the guidance of a guru, in the context of the traditional yoga path or through shamanistic practises.

[123] Lect. unpublished; "Yoga", 4th Dec 1904.

healing techniques. It is a medical technique not relevant to the theme of specific spiritual development through meditation. So, do breathing exercises have any place at all in this meditative pathway? In the sense of striving for enlightenment through a meditative exercise, drawing on the occult effect of special breathing exercises, the answer is, no. Rudolf Steiner did however give a meditative breathing exercise to more advanced students, from 1904 through to 1923.[124] But, he insisted that no student of his could do such a thing, unless he personally advised them as to the precise details as to what to do.

It is very important however to note that the breathing exercises that he gave to students were **basically different** to those used classically in the East. The text which accompanied the breathing exercise is designed to direct consciousness to profound spiritual truths about the nature of the higher-ego or about the transformation of the physical body. The mind is not directed to immerse itself in the energies involved in inhaling and exhaling. He maintained consistently over the years that it is ultimately best to achieve this transformation of the body without using breathing techniques.[125] But there is one breathing exercise which the earnest meditant can use which has a very specific purpose, and which is undertaken in a different way to that of the ancient orient.

This purpose is to achieve a subtle refinement of the physical body; which in turn is connected to the attainment of **high-initiation** consciousness, the highest of all clairvoyant states. It is important here to note that this theme is not an introductory theme, it involves some remarkable, esoteric truths. The attaining of the highest state of initiatory consciousness is obviously a challenging theme to discuss. For those who are new to anthroposophy, it is probably best to just skim over this section.

Now, what does it mean that a special breathing technique is used in conjunction with a meditative text, in order to achieve "refinement and redemption of the physical body" ? Furthermore, how is this in turn connected to the attainment of **high-initiation** consciousness ? This has to do with the fact that, as we breathe, ethereal energies such as prana, flow in and out of the body; and if we breathe in a special way, then the potential power of this ethereal force can be somewhat activated to refine the matter of which the body consists. The following quote from an esoteric lesson illustrates this idea:

---

[124] In 1904 he gave various such meditative exercises to his students, and in 1923 he also gave such a meditation to Fred Poeppig, an advanced meditant (described in his autobiographical "Schicksalswege zu Rudolf Steiner" 1995 Germany).
[125] In 1904 in "Occult Science - an Outline", p.278 and in 1922 (27/May) he taught that such development should ideally be achieved without using the breath.

The human being needs to bring order and rhythm back into its astral body. A part of the work involved in the inner life is making the breathing rhythmical. This is connected with very deep spiritual dynamics that exist between the human being and the cosmos. The human being breathes in oxygen and exhales carbon dioxide. The plants do the reverse, {they inhale carbon dioxide and exhale oxygen.} There exists in the evolution of the world a connection between the plant and human kingdoms. Plants, beautiful flowering rose-bushes, and other such blossoming plants grow rhythmically according to nature's laws. They are also entirely pure, chaste; because they possess no astral body.

Plants on the one side stand higher than the human being, on the other side they are lower, less evolved. {That is, they have no lower self and evil desires, but they are of course incapable of self-consciousness.} In respect of their inner purity, they exist before our gaze as an {inspiring} ideal {of purity}. The human being's inner soul-life – its desires and wishes – must gradually become similar to a flower, to a flowering plant by making the breathing process rhythmical, {that is by deliberately introducing a specific rhythm in one's in-and out-breathing.} When one inhales and holds the breath longer, one in this way develops carbon dioxide in oneself, and exhales oxygen, one's human nature becomes similar to the plant nature in this way. (1905)

These mysterious words become much clearer when study is made of his more detailed lectures on this theme. What emerges is this – by undertaking a specific breathing exercise combined with a meditation the meditant develops in the ether-body the ability to 'alchemically' transform the carbon dioxide, so to speak. The oxygen is released from the carbon dioxide and used, but some of it that is not needed is also exhaled. As this process occurs, the carbon in the carbon dioxide is retained in the bloodstream. It is then subject to one's own prana, or etheric energies.

In future incarnations as one continues to make the effort with the inner life, one will then find that the retained carbon helps to form a refined, etherealized body. In fact, as the medieval alchemists were aware, eventually in the distant future, as the higher-self becomes more manifest in us, it will be able to fully manifest in such a body. This concept is not as odd as it at first appears, it is simply saying that in future time-cycles, the human life-wave will have evolved a more ethereal body. The body will by then be almost non-material, it will have spiritualized; so the initiate refers to this body as the 'diamond body', because it will be imperishable, translucent and consist, chemically, of not much more than carbon. Perhaps we could think of this as a 'soft diamond' organism, this is in fact the famous "Philosopher's Stone" of the alchemists.

Meditative breathing exercise: For spiritualization of the physical body.
Because this breathing exercise was designed by Rudolf Steiner in approximately 1904, for the Esoteric School students, specifically to help in the spiritualising of the body, and is not at all a meditative breathing exercise in the sense of ancient Eastern practise, I am including it here. This consists of seven breaths, during which you focus on the mystery of the pure life-forces in a plant, and how these contain the solution to the overcoming of the death/decay process to which humanity is subject. A breath consists of course, of three phases; inhaling, exhaling and also retaining of the air within the body, or abstaining from inhaling for a while.

This is the process: you inhale, then exhale; and then you abstain from inhaling for a while. During these breaths you visualize a beautiful, blossoming rose-bush or similar, a plant which is well known to you. It should be as if this plant is right there in front of you and you are seeing it constantly.

Concerning the length of time for each phase of the breath, **it is essential that you do not try to achieve maximum possible time spans** !! Do not try to excessively retain your breath. Just aim for a comfortable length of time. You can at first look at the second-hand on your watch, but soon you should just be able to reckon the time involved, it need not be precise.

For the first three breaths
You inhale and then slowly exhale over **twice** the time it took to inhale. Then you refrain from inhaling for **three** times the period of inhaling. For example: inhaling over 3 seconds, exhaling over 6 seconds; and then refraining from again inhaling, for 9 seconds.
So the ratio is: Inhaling =1 Exhaling = 2 Holding the breath outside = 3
During the inhaling, think this thought **to the plant**; "your death, my life". {That is, from the living and dying of the plant, oxygen is given to the air, from this I as a human have my life.}

During the exhaling, think this thought towards the plant; "my death, your life". {That is, from the decay/death processes in my being, deriving from my fallen soul-forces, from their impact on the Earth's ethers, you have life, for you gain my exhaled carbon dioxide.}
Whilst holding the breath outside, try to have no thoughts, just be relaxed and receptive to any insights which might be experienced.

The next three breaths
Remember you still have that plant before your mind's eye.
It is the same except you hold the breath after inhaling. So you inhale, **then** hold you breath, then peacefully exhale. Hold the breath for **three** times the inhaling time, exhale for **twice** the inhaling time just as before. As before when inhaling think: "your death, my life", whilst holding the breath think of nothing, and during the exhaling, think as before; "my death, your life."

The seventh breath
Now, for the last breath visualize that you have left your body and entered into the plant, become one with its spiritual reality, and from it you gaze back at your own body. The same ratio applies as before.
During the inhaling; think this thought to your body (remember you have become now in an instant at one with the plant), "my death, your life." {That is the plant's dying yields up life-forces for the human body.}
During the holding of the breath; think of nothing.
During the exhaling; think this thought to that human body you are gazing at as a plant-being, "your death, my life."

Then return to normal breathing and consciousness; but enter into a state of inner peace and spiritual upliftment for as long as you comfortably can. Do this by focussing on a sacred truth, a spiritual reality which you always find special. Then finally as a way to end this or any meditative session, immerse yourself in what you understand to be the great divine ideal, the future goal of human destiny. It is not as complex as it at first seems, although as with any genuine spiritualization process it requires some effort; a meditative system which is easy, like flicking a switch, can not produce long-lasting results.

And to counteract the abhorrent decay processes in the body, set in motion by the effect of the lower desires since Lemurian times, is not easy, but will obviously confer much joy for humankind living in future bodies when it is achieved. The time to start to build such a future is now !

CHAPTER NINE

Practical advice about meditating

We start with various brief key-note passages on aspects of meditating, these are drawn from the notes of students in the esoteric school instruction lessons. These will clarify and summarise various points considered in earlier chapters.

Caution
As I mentioned in Chapter Three, it is important to avoid falling asleep when doing this kind of meditating. Strange as it may sound, Steiner emphasizes that lower spiritual beings could temporarily strengthen their influence on the soul, if the meditant allows himself/herself to fall asleep in the activity, or is lax about this process. In other words, exercise real caution, do not meditate in bed; unless you are certain that you shall not fall asleep in the process of meditating ! It is much better before getting into bed to sit on the meditation chair, and energetically apply yourself to the meditation. It is better not to meditate than to do it half-heartedly, for not only must one not fall asleep, but the process must also be earnestly and intensely undertaken, to avoid negative outcomes. Secondly, on no account should meditation be undertaken if flesh-desires are a strong factor in the soul-life.

Thirdly, Rudolf Steiner cautions against this energetic deeper meditating if one has not attained some soul transformation. For example a genuine selflessness and an atmosphere of sanctity when taking up a sacred text begins to be sensed. For if the soul is still suffused with many egocentric qualities, then during meditation some lowly thought-forms may be created in the aura (such as those derived from grandiose, conceited ideas or self-centred ambitions), and these can attract negative beings. In that circumstance, one is cautioned to stay with the study program or inspirational attunement exercises, or creative artistic activity.

This caution is **not to be confused** with the phenomenon whereby negative thoughts, of perhaps the very same kind, appear to one whilst in meditation; this is entirely different, these arise from within, because the lower-self is fighting against our effort to meditate. I could also add, from my own understanding, that if you are just about to begin for the first time to really meditate, and it is a day or night when a solar or lunar eclipse is occurring — visible from your part of the globe — then you may like to wait a day before starting. Rudolf Steiner had originally advised his students not to commence the very first efforts in meditation during the waning moon, but he dropped this cautionary advice after a couple of years.

Attending religious services

Rudolf Steiner explains in his lecture of Dec 31st 1922, that the esoteric meditative path is intended to be used by those people who have outgrown the need for a religious mediator-ship by organized religion. That is, a service in which the priest serves a mediator between the divine and the congregation. In conversations Steiner pointed out forcefully to the senior priests of the church he assisted them to found (The Christian Community), that people who were ready for esoteric meditation activity were not to be participating in the Act of Consecration of Man (the name given to the form of the Eucharist in this church).

The same principle applies to the central sacrament in the Christian Churches of other high-liturgy hierarchical denominations, namely, the Mass/Eucharist/Divine Service. However this stricture on the esoteric meditant does not apply to attending such services for social reasons, such as accompanying children, etc. Nor does it apply to being involved in other sacraments, such as marriage, nor to Communion in congregational style services, where the pastor is regarded as one gifted member of 'the priesthood of all believers' and hence is not acting in a mediating role.

Regarding traditional high-liturgy church services, in contrast to meditation, Steiner taught that there is an essential difference between esoteric meditation and the purpose of ecclesiastical ritual. The liturgical ritual seeks to bless the laity through its **"bringing down"** of a spiritual reality into the feelings of the people; this is possible because the very essence of the church's authority to do this derives from the understanding by the laity that the celebrating priests become a vessel for Christ.

Whereas by contrast, esoteric meditation has the effect of **"lifting the person up"** to an increasingly real and transformative encounter with the divine, when the individual makes intense, personal, solitary effort. This solitary process (in human terms) is also one in which the meditant is subtly assisted by divine realities (in traditional language, the Holy Spirit) which have an affinity to the spirit-self, which has been able to become active in the meditant.

Meditating raises the meditant up in terms of attainment to empowered transcendental thought-insights, to direct clairvoyance. It also lifts the ether body slightly up literally in the sense of lifting the ether-body up out the physical, so that the chakras can be formed in the aura. Hence Rudolf Steiner pointed out that active involvement in these two modalities (the ecclesiastical and the esoteric) in the sense of personally seeking an interface with the divine through them is incompatible, each will cancel out the effect of the other.

If however as a family member one accompanies one's children to a liturgical service, and does not seek to merge into the traditional cultic process of the descent of blessing, then naturally, no inner conflict arises. The esotericist also finds that the experience of the esoteric truths, as they become fully embraced by the heart and the will, begins to directly mediate awareness of the spiritual realities, and interest in authoritative formalized high liturgy modes of religious activity fades. These comments do not apply to forms of simple ritual that are derived from artistic and sensitive celebrating of various of life's blessings, such as observing the seasonal festivals, nor to non-liturgical church gatherings.

This entire matter has never been clarified in anthroposophical circles, owing to the slightly confusing fact that the main six sacraments (such as marriage, confirmation) are valid for all persons, including the esoteric meditant (or her/his family), whereas the seventh sacrament (the Mass, Eucharist and Act of Consecration of Man) is not valid for the esoteric meditant. This dualistic nature of the ritualistic ecclesiastical life has caused confusion.

Evidence that confirms this perspective is to be found in the material kept confidential by the church; namely the collated memoirs of various founding members of the Christian Community, Friedrich Rittelmeyer, Emil Bock and Rudolf Frieling. This book, *Erinnerungen und die Begründungsereignisse der Christengemeinschaft*, was privately printed in 1984, and edited by two priests. It records the following words of Rudolf Steiner on this issue:

> "...but anthroposophists, especially if they are older....should become advisors to the priests, and not the priests to the anthroposophists." Ibid. p. 176.
> "I myself (Emil Bock) had mentioned to Rudolf Steiner that, according to a statement from Mr. Werbeck, in Hamburg one hundred anthroposophists had participated in the Service {the Act of Consecration of Man}, and also three other persons who were not members. 'If that is so', he (Steiner) said, 'Then we must in fact see to it that this {numerical} proportion is reversed' {3 members, 100 non-members}." p. 296, a report by Emil Bock.

Rudolf Steiner also energetically admonished the priests against allowing the laity to do esoteric meditative activity {the priests in their confusion, had been giving to their laity esoteric anthroposophical meditations}: "Rudolf Steiner attempted to explain to us that this was not to be done, because whoever does that, works against the effect of the religious service..." Emil Bock, ibid., p 68.

For readers who are unaware of this, the above statements may be quite surprising, they are however, quite in accord with all other statements made by the initiate on this subject in his lecture cycles and foundation address to the church. Lack of knowledge of these important remarks, and insight into this issue has lead to a crossing of the boundaries in many instances, after the death of the initiate, and is continuing in the present day. See the Appendix to this chapter for a further note on this subject.

Perseverance
What does one do with the problem of failure, or the lack of will to keep on going? Parallel Exercises given in Chapter Two will help you to overcome the problem of giving up. In addition, I recommend having some text handy that inspires you with ideals of what the future could be and will be as enough souls take up the inner path. When you are in the meditative session, keep on returning to the content of the meditation, but do not fight directly against interfering thoughts (mental images); rather use your will to keep focussed on the theme as best as possible.

When a person constantly does this action of continually returning to the theme, then, the initiate informed his students in Germany, it is as if one eventually creates a sphere around one within which the interfering thoughts can not proceed.

Advice from Rudolf Steiner concerning initial difficulties:
One may experience a kind of lack of inner peace which seems to be right in the blood, it seems to be prickling and scratching the soul. This of course interferes with the inner peace that we are so determined to have right then. But eventually it fades away or is no longer a bother. It is described as just one of several ways in which the lower self manifests its opposition to meditating. (1913) Secondly it could happen that you feel weak and even begin to have perspiration.

The initiate is reported as explaining that this is caused in the meditant by excess eating. When the body has too much food the ether energies can not expand out beyond the body - an essential part of the meditation process. (1911) Thirdly if one goes into a dreamy condition all too easily, whilst in meditation (especially in the morning, when you are not tired) this indicates that one may not be willing to really enter into social obligations and interaction in life, but would rather repeatedly live out fanciful ideas. (1911)

To be involved in forming this clear strong space around one's consciousness (not physically) is to form ideal conditions for higher experiences. But note that this technique is only effective if you are actively persevering with the exercises in thought control described in Chapter Three. On the theme of perseverance it is very important to note a very significant hint which was given in the 1924 lessons, that the student must try to realise how significant it is when one solemnly vows to keep on meditating faithfully without giving up – and yet only after a short while one does actually give up.

In particular, it is serious when additionally, one is somehow quite unaware of this negligence. It is as one is **incapable of noting** or recollecting that this has in fact happened. The implication of this phenomenon is that exercise of consistent meditating is the door to inner freedom, and hence immensely important. However, the further implication is that there exists in the hidden recesses of the soul, subtle enemies of such human freedom.

Protection
Consistent meditation, on the basis of really working with the six parallel exercises (of Chapter Two) produces results which help guard one from any lower forces....

> There are people whose {auras}, to clairvoyant vision, look quite remarkable. They seem to be enveloped in a crystal, or a crystalline vessel, in the centre of which they live. All inappropriate thought-forms from other people rebound when they reach the edge of this 'crystalline' sheath. Such people are those who have learnt to live a meditative life, people who have learnt to regulate and direct their life from a centre within their being." (1904)

In addition, in 1910 he gave a simple but effective formula to protect oneself. I strongly recommend that you use it before every meditation session until you feel naturally secure because your aura is acquiring its own integrity. By now the reader will be aware that for these valuable exercises to work, and for the practise of meditating to be effective, **a definite commitment to meditation is necessary,** including the study of Steiner's basic texts, and a life-style that helps the over-all process. The protection then, is as follows: visualize strongly and clearly that the outer sheathing of your aura is densifying or forming a shield, and mentally speak these words, as you visualize this...

"The outer sheaths of my aura are 'condensing'. These layers now surround me as an impenetrable shell against all unwanted, impure thoughts and feelings. It opens itself only to divine wisdom."

Now, after the meditation the aura will of course be open to the normal astral interactions between people, but it is important to realize that during meditating the aura blocks off all other influences. Secondly, it was recommended that one should also visualize that the space around you is filled with a delicate heavenly blue light. Remember when visualizing the light and your auric sheath that you must think of the area **below** your body, as well as above. Your aura extends out on either side of the body about as far as you can reach, and it extends about a yard below your feet and above the head.

Further in one esoteric lesson, the brief, obviously sketchy notes of one student record that "should you at some time have a virtual tumult of visions, of forms appearing and causing confusion, it was recommended that you focus strongly on these words from the New Testament, 'I am the light of the cosmos, whomsoever follows after Me shall not wander in darkness, but will have the light of life'. Then the visions dissolve away and true visions emerge.(1913) Naturally this activity would not be effective where there is a psychological disturbance, which requires therapy. In addition, the Rose-Cross was recommended as protection. The meditant was advised to immediately visualise it. Notes from the same student record that "then evil powers must give way and yield." (1913)

All such notes from the meditants in this great Esoteric School in Germany, wherein the re-establishing of the initiation process for modern humanity was being attempted, are brief because written notes were only permitted when the session was over. The above Biblical words from the cosmic Christ, spoken by Jesus, are from the Gospel of St. John (8:12). This Gospel is regarded in this esoteric stream as the most sacred Christian text, because it conceals within it especially deep initiation teachings, and an especially deep perspective on the Christian mystery.

The reader can begin to gain some idea of the esoteric depth in the quotation being referred to here, by considering that the term "I am" in this sacred text refers to the deity, the cosmic Christ, not to the human being, Jesus. But the Greek text also implies that the self (higher) of individual human beings is the subject of the sentence, thus indicating a symbiotic link between human beings and the cosmic Christ.

Reliability of a higher experience
When a person sees even the normal physical world, images are seen; everything seen in the physical world is after all an image. The images which appear through the inner path must be stimulated in the soul in the right way if they are to be reliable. What is important regarding the realm that then dawns upon our inner eye is that it is a **truthful** world of inner images. This is precisely the difficulty in meditative training.

As long as the person still has personal desires and wishes one can not tell the true from the false images, and false images are likely to occur. Thus there is the vital necessity of being self-less, rather than egotistical. In this regard, Rudolf Steiner mentioned that in the schooling of the Pythagoreans, this truth was expressed, for pedagogical purposes, in the following way. 'That you will only really know something about life after death when it is entirely indifferent to you as to whether you live on after death or not'. (ca. 1907)

What the ancient esoteric teachers were wanting to convey here is that when subjective wishes are excluded in the process of the soul attaining to Imagination (**psychic-image** consciousness), then that which is expressed in the images seen will be the truth. Such truths as these, conveyed in astral images, then bestow freedom on the seeker. This means freedom from bondage to the illusion of the every day self, from the forces of egotism. This is implied in another immensely deep text from the gospel of St. John (8:32); "You shall know the truth and the truth will set you free", that is, enlightenment releases the person from the chains of intellectual and ethical uncertainty.

Obviously the question of being sure that a spiritual experience is actually a genuine experience, e.g., a vision is from a truthful source, not a deceiving one, is immensely important. It should be really clear to the reader by now, from all that has been explained in earlier chapters, that the entire way of living and training oneself for meditation, and the method of meditating that Rudolf Steiner has put forward, is designed to prevent the meditant from plunging herself or himself into a sea of deceptive visions and the consequent unhealthy attitudinal problems. That is, if the meditant really does conscientiously put into practice the advice given, with regard to attuning the heart through the four moods, and the six parallel exercises, then only minor problems occur.

There will still be the challenges of being exposed to illusions that do not pose a serious threat, such as visions that are expressions of as yet not purified dynamics in the soul, about which the meditant has been informed, and which he or she will be anticipating. So, what is given here in these brief comments are refinements to general advice, and they refer to more advanced experiences that the successful meditant may have. In a lecture from 1912,[126] Steiner specifically explains how the really advanced meditant, who has developed the ability to behold spiritual beings, can deal with the very important theme of how to know whether the entity from whom one may receive some 'insights', is a good or an evil being. Now, this is not of concern to most meditants.

---

[126] Lecture 27/Aug/1912, in the cycle, "Von der Initiation-Ewigkeit und Augenblick."

It obviously only applies if one has developed far on the path, but it is important to know the approach used.

He explains that the seer then undertakes immediately an introspective search, that is, really focuses on the soul-life intensely, and with uncompromised humility identifies qualities that are (still) self-seeking. If this is a familiar inner exercise, and thus effectively carried out, its effect in the astral world is such that a deceptive entity is unmasked and becomes harmless. On a lesser scale, the same principle applies to the normal meditant; active nurturing of purity and high ethics protects one from deceitful experiences.

Group meditating

There are various kinds of meditating which can be done in a group and this is a valid and beautiful activity that enters the karma of people who take up a spiritual life-style. Group meditating was also part of Rudolf Steiner's approach to the inner life. However it is most important to note that the kind of deep esoteric meditating that is taught here is the solo kind, it **is not suitable for group meditating**. He instructed that this is **never** to be practised in a group, because this kind of meditating is specifically designed for solo activity. Otherwise you may well have some unpleasant experiences that are potentially harmful, namely that the double of the other person, or of your own being, may become stronger and try to influence you.

So the kind of 'meditating' which is valid to undertake in a group is the kind which seeks to uplift and inspire the group, or to unite the group for its common goal. For example Rudolf Steiner, gave a group meditative text designed to prepare a group for study and dialogue on spiritual issues.[127] To strengthen the dynamics of a group of his students in their esoteric striving he directed that each member of the group individually every Sunday morning at nine o'clock was to send forth into the world a simple thought; such as "within the spiritual being of humanity I feel myself united with all other esoteric meditants." (1912)

Esoteric meditating certainly does not offer involvement in social activity and group-soul or group-entity activity. Solitariness is its characteristic, but one should be able to experience this as pleasant, not painful. It is only in such private activity that the deepest meditative

---

[127] From the spirit's luminous heights,/ May there stream God's radiant light Into human souls/ Who will to seek /The spirit's grace/ The spirit's power/The spirit's being. /May it live in our hearts in the inner being of our souls,/as we feel ourselves gathered here in His name." German text published in: Verses and Meditations by Rudolf Steiner Press, London, 4th impression 1985, p.194.

states are attained, and to develop the ability to endure such isolation brings very considerable spiritual advantages when entering into higher worlds or states of consciousness.

Earnest studying and discussion of deeper spiritual realities in a group has a quite specific influence on the soul. When, during the night-time, the day's activity lives on in the soul, it echoes on as a spiritual energy, so to speak. As a result of the interweaving of the soul at night with the divine beings in the cosmic spheres, all such deeper human conversation actually strengthens the conscience of the individual.

Loneliness
Rudolf Steiner also advised that the advanced meditant can find, when they cross the threshold, a condition which creates an acute sense of loneliness. He gave the following helpful explanation,

> .. what one experiences at first, in that one releases consciousness from the body and enters into one's own inner soul-life – now **consciously**, for the first time, for normally we are unconscious of this – is a feeling of total loneliness. One does not have this experience of loneliness in any other situation. A condition in which one is completely and totally dependent upon what at this stage is one's soul and spiritual reality. One becomes aware that because of this intense loneliness feeling that one is able to maintain the sense of self, one's ego-hood in the spiritual realm.[128]

But, the positive side of enduring this sense of isolation is that our inner being is greatly strengthened, and consequently the ego is empowered. Group meditating, of the right kind, and the studying of spiritual matters in a group can be an important counter-balance for solitary meditating. However, in addition such group activity is also important in the spiritual environs in which we live, for it enables a connection to form between Heaven and Earth.

Certain divine beings in the spiritual realms seek to 'incarnate' or, as one would say in normal language, to 'envelop themselves' within such dialogue and such group meditative activity. Their subtle participation has a value to the cosmos in the intended goal for humanity in the future. However, this is not a kind of participation that leads to 'channelling' or mediumistic messages, it is more subtle than that. It enables a greater interaction of divine and human realities, without necessarily any specific definable local result.

Clothing

---

[128] Lect from 1/12/'21 "Self-consciousness".

Going barefoot habitually is not recommended, as subtle energies can enter the aura via the feet, and indeed negative energies are attracted to the feet. Also, in meditation it is very important to wear shoes; otherwise your own freedom will be slightly or strongly undermined. (This does not apply to those other non-meditative occasions when one feels it is good to feel the soil or sand on the feet, especially in places of fine 'vibrations.') For example, I know an atavistic clairvoyant who worked with the nature-spirits in her garden, but found that she was often 'bossed around' by them. She found it hard to resist their demands, which were sometimes very inconvenient, and urgent, at least to them. Once she decided to always wear garden boots, she still saw and spoke with them, but she now had the ego-strength to determine whether or not to do what they wanted her to undertake in the garden.

Secondly if negative influences try to enter a human aura they actually do so through the feet area. Shoes with natural leather soles (or better, strong plant-derived soles) are better than synthetic shoes, as these cause an insulating effect between your ether body and the Earth's energies. A kind of vacuum occurs around the soles then, and this can allow unpleasant energies to have access to your ether-aura. A black robe or largish garment draped around one in meditation is a good idea, for it gives protection and assists the centring of one's being. It is worthwhile to learn something of the inner quality of colours. There is confusion regarding black.

This is actually not a colour, but an absence of reflected light. When you are clothed in black, the light and the ether energies within it do not radiate out from you. Certainly in grief or in negative and depressive states the aura takes on a darker appearance, hence black is associated with sadness and brooding/negative attitudes. However that is a separate issue to that of its helpful effect for people involved in meditative activity. In this context, it is regarded as appropriate by Rudolf Steiner (see the Appendix).

As spirituality is acquired, an increased sensitivity to coldness will develop; you will value woollen underclothing and a warm hat during the colder days. This is because the same spiritual force in our self that eventually creates the condition for **cosmic-spiritual** consciousness also works the magic of nutrition, forming heat-giving sugars from our food. The subconscious power that underlies the attainment of **cosmic-spiritual** consciousness is the same power that works the miracle of digestion and consequently bodily warmth. The more this mysterious force has to generate warmth for an inadequately clad body, the less soul-energy will exist for success in meditation, or experiencing any kind of creative insights. Such truths are not as odd as they may at first appear; we already know that to study and concentrate when you are freezing cold is exhausting. Here we are simply revealing that this fact has a further side to it.

Glowing coronas and technological devices for seeing the aura
Students in the Esoteric School were informed that if one strives excessively for clairvoyance through soul exercises for seership it is possible to cause some harm to the eyes. This would include the 'seed' meditation given in 'Knowledge of the Higher Worlds, how is it achieved?'. The students were cautioned that they could begin to see everything as if enveloped in a sort of aura; if this happens, and you will feel intuitively that something is wrong, the advice was to stop meditating and return to simple inspirational readings. With regard to 'seeing the aura', using some form of optical (electronic) device, Steiner cautioned that these are harmful to the eyes and should be avoided. (1912) They anyway only reveal the finer physical aura around the body; for it has an aura of infra-red energy and some electromagnetic energy.

Whether to speak about one's experiences
Consistent meditation brings a subtle deepening of consciousness, and this in turn can cause a problem of a social kind, namely people you know may find it difficult to relate to you, with your deepened inner being. This needs to be regarded as a blessing, not a burden. Eventually you will learn new, more spontaneous ways of communicating and the problem will lessen. If you are fortunate (as I am) to have a profoundly empathetic and compatible life-partner you can certainly try to have a dialogue on your inner experiences but even this is sometimes not possible. To live daily life whilst 'carrying' such insights can become a special joy, not a burden, especially as these develop and deepen, heralding the approach of the higher-self to the personality.

In any case, to learn to be silent about spiritual insights, when it is inappropriate to speak about them is an important part of the inner discipline. It is important regarding your actual threshold spiritual experiences to avoid chatting about them, as about the weather, or to impress others. If this is done, then as brief notes from a student record, "these results of esoteric development that are pawned off to others, disappear from the meditant." The initiate explained further that to refrain from speaking about personal inner experiences, in this sense, is to build up ever more spiritual ego-strength. (1912)

However his students were also told, "that it can be enriching for one's inner life to earnestly discuss such experiences with a small group of friends who are at about the same level of experience. But if one does discuss such matters in this way, considerable effort must be made to have the right mood of reverence and humility." (1911)

It is also relevant in this context to refer to advice from the initiate to his students about habits which require the expenditure of mental forces undermining the process of developing the higher consciousness states. It was emphasized that (1904)

> Through the exercise in thought control, the faculty is developed which enables a person to behold in the astral and spiritual realms...It is a process similar to storing up a power like steam in a boiler. For example, habits like greedily reading a newspaper out of curiosity, or idly speaking when there is no need to speak, need to be mastered. ....overcoming the urge for meaningless communicating stores up forces in us; overcoming vanity and curiosity prevents the steam escaping from the steam-engine boiler...[129]

Obviously, this advice is going in the direction of a really disciplined life-style especially developed in order to attain to actual clairvoyant capabilities. One also needs to differentiate between reading newspaper for orientation about events, news and entertainment, and what Steiner is meaning here, namely using the mind only for worthwhile pursuits. An early Steiner lecture records that the strict rules of silence enforced in the Trappist religious order has the effect of storing up substantial powers in the astral body, soul-powers that will consequently be available to that person in the next incarnation.

Mantra
By now it will be clear that meditating requires considerable inner effort and ego-presence, although it is not strenuous once you have practised for a while. The repetition of words, or a sound, more or less rhythmically is the main feature of a mantra; and here care is needed. For repeated activity of any kind after a while 'takes over'. It continues to influence us, even when we are hardly present in the activity. This is exactly what this path seeks to avoid because it is aware of the ego's potential for spirituality; a potential which the sun-god through the sacrifice on Golgotha has gifted to humanity. Such resonating from a mantra is not harmful so long as the self is consciously present in such an influence.

The reason for this emphasis on the encouraging of the personal self to strive for spirituality has been explained in detail earlier. It is only necessary now to point out, as Rudolf Steiner explains, that in earlier ages when mantras were used, people were much more exposed to their inherent power, because words were less intellectual (even less

---

[129] From a lecture, untransl., unpublished, on Knowledge of the Higher worlds, 1904.

conceptual), and therefore more 'cosmic'. Hence a mantra had a power almost unknown in modern times. Further, a strongly developed ego-sense, which seeks to attain to higher reality through human earthly experience, was uncommon in earlier ages. The tendency was more to withdraw from the physical plane. The mantra were used to immerse the less ego-endowed soul into the ocean-nexus of the spirit. But this process is no longer helpful for modern humanity, in whom the self or ego has developed. However, when the mantric qualities are allowed to be occur, this can still be of value today, providing the meditant refrains from allowing their self to be dispersed in such an experience.

How does a mantra work in today's world? It works by ensuring "a similarity between the vibration of the words - the sounds of speech - and the vibrations of the ideas in the words." (1910). That is words virtually always have a meaning, for they convey ideas to us. These ideas exist as subtle ethereal substance, and these ideas also cause a certain unique 'energy' or vibration or 'signature' to arise in the ethereal realm. By choosing words with certain vowels and consonants, a similar vibration is created in the speaking of the words, as that which the ideas contain. If the initiate is of high degree (and they are very few, despite claims by various teachers!) then he or she can formulate these ideas in words that have a particular metre or rhythm; this metre corresponds with, or harmonizes with the vibration of the ideas. So a real mantra is a powerful reality, to be used carefully.

So long as the meditant is **consciously dwelling** upon the transcendental ideas or images that the words convey, then the text can be recited to experience its metrical properties, it can be used as a mantra. But if the conscious ego-based effort of esoteric meditating is omitted, and then the 'hypnotic' metrical effect is invoked, the mantra has an effect which is definitely not recommended in this path. It may well cause 'results' but such results are simply grafted on to the current personality.

It is interesting to have some knowledge of the view which prevailed in earlier times when mantra were the norm. As Rudolf Steiner commented in regard to the wonderful old maxim, "Aum mani padma hum; the person undertakes something cosmic. Their soul oscillates in harmony with the highest pulsing vibrating in the world, the meditant's individual tone resounding in harmony with the entire spheres of cosmic being." (1904)

How often to meditate?
Usually in the evening and then again in the morning, but perhaps just once a day; the main point is to be consistent with the time when you meditate. Steiner did give a meditation to young people which was to be

used three times a day. As was explained to the students in the Esoteric School (1906?),

> If I meditate each day at a definite time, say 6 am, then I bring a rhythm into my life. But when I meditate at 10 am the next time, the rhythm is damaged. And if a person undertakes to meditate at 6 am, then at midday, and then before sleeping, those become three definite points that also can bring rhythm into life.

The soul will be effected adversely if the meditative activity is spasmodic and irregular, once begun it should be maintained in the same rhythm. Naturally if one is ill or under severe stress, then the routine need not be maintained.

Since meditating, in the sense described here, is an activity which is so especially free of influence from the lower-self and associated beings, the more often and more sincerely it is carried out, the better it is, of course, for general spiritualizing of the soul.

Necessary conditions for meditating
Firstly, establish a thought or higher truth in your consciousness, that is, to be able to focus your attention on it, to become one with that thought, become really attuned to it, but not in an analytical way. This was described in Chapter One. Rather, one strives to be sensitive to the images which that the verse conjures forth. One is no longer aware of your body or a ticking clock or the distant traffic noise outside, etc. But one is fully aware of one's self, one is not in an "ego-dimmed" condition. Finally, Contemplation is practised by dismissing the verse or image from your mind, but remaining for a while absorbed in the after-echo of such meditating; which is in effect becoming open to sensing more subtle spiritual truths, through developing the capacity I have called **cosmic-spiritual** consciousness.

Another purpose of Contemplation is to strive to become aware, in the after-echo of the meditating, of the creative forces coming from the higher-self, which form the images experienced during meditation. One has been intensely forming images, and focussed on them and their consequent insights; this is a creative activity partially caused by the higher-self; to become more conscious of what kind of spiritual faculty is involved in this is an important part of understanding one's inner being.

When living into the imagery of a text, it is good to form thoughts or images inspired by the text as vividly and full as you can, because spiritual beings live within the forms and colours of the higher worlds. Hence the word, 'light' needs to be experienced as an out-raying brilliance, etc.

A mood of prayerful gratitude and reverence is essential when preparing for meditation; there is simply no point meditating 'cold'. The soul-state must be lifted up to this reverential mood beforehand. Gradually such a mood will prevail at other times in the day, such as seeing flowering bushes, listening to deep music, and so on.

Doing meditation and some difficulties one may encounter.
To meditate practically you simply take a seat with your back reasonably straight, and with your body as comfortable as possible. The aim is to become oblivious to your body as well as to your environment. The room should be not too warm nor too cold; feet should be covered and warm, and the head comfortably cool. You may need wax ear-plugs to block out noises, and of course a darkened room to reduce the focus on the physical environment. It is best if you can have a special chair or part of a room, or even a small room, set aside for meditating, in which hectic or earthly activity is minimal.

It is also advisable to have little or no electrical or electronic devices near you, or at least unplug or switch them off at the wall. Then after the attunement phase you simply focus your attention on the text or image (use an electric light to read the text at first until you know it from memory, don't use a candle, as that strains the eyes). The actual inner activity was explained in Chapter One. Here I wish to just emphasize the pragmatic aspects, and to point out that there are a few other phenomena which may arise in addition to those mentioned in Chapter Four.

How does one actually bring to mind the words of the text? Once you know them from memory, you can repeat them to yourself. But once you have some experience – and this is important – do not murmur or mumble or even **silently** voice the words! Do not use your throat even in a subtle way, at least not for the deeper meditative work. For then your inner being is spending part of its energy in producing that activity, and is diverted from full attention to and absorption in the insights which are trying to get your attention. Naturally if there are verses of great beauty and mantric quality, and your meditative session is designed to enter into this aspect of the spiritual, these can be softly spoken in the session. Otherwise, for most meditating, one focuses on the text without any 'speaking', and you will be able to experience its series of images hovering before your inner mind. That is, all of its content, its images and concepts, will simply live in your consciousness without you having to have the actual words before you, either on paper, from memory or recited.

Instead you will be able to focus on one or other of the image-thoughts of the text, and from this activity, various deep insights will unfold. Before you get to that stage where you inwardly know the text, the advice given by the initiate was, as an alternative to silently murmuring them, to try to visualize seeing them appear on a 'misty curtain' before your mental eyes (1904), sentence after sentence, as you are ready.

Pictorial meditations: A few suggestions regarding more esoteric images to meditate upon or to have as inspiring background images in a private meditative room/space.

The Caduceus of Hermes
This is a vertical column, broadening out towards the top, which is intertwined with two serpents; one black, the other white. This symbol, described as having the power like the Rose-Cross to dispel malignant forces from one, depicts the deep mystery of the union of night and day consciousness. From this arises the fabled continuity of consciousness; one of the great goals of the quest. It is also connected with the kundalini and its two inter-twining energy streams, the Ida and Pingala, but as we discussed in an earlier chapter, one is not to attempt via a symbol to focus on the rising of the kundalini.

Quite a number of images of great value for attunement or for actual meditating, can be found in the artistic work of Rudolf Steiner; these the reader can obtain from a Steiner bookshop. But two are especially worth mentioning: the series of nine coloured glass windows in the walls of the Goetheanum, available in a folio from Steiner publishers. These immensely esoteric illustrations are of tremendous value for the serious meditant.

Secondly, the illustrations by the initiate for the Apocalypse of St. John, created for a theosophical Congress in 1907. These are of real depth. In addition, the Last Supper by Da Vinci is very special. This picture indicates the presence of the Logos within the cosmic Christ, from whom the zodiac system was formed, as well as the human dimension (response) to this being, and the nature of good and evil.

Isenheim Altarpiece
This is the altar painting known as the Isenheim Altarpiece-triptych by Matthias Grünewald, painted in the 15th century. According to oral traditions in the anthroposophical movement, Rudolf Steiner regarded this painting as depicting virtually what the advanced initiate may see when allowed to behold the resurrection of Jesus Christ in the Akashic Record. It also depicts elemental beings and babies waiting for incarnation, and it has an enchanting quality of astonishing power. It is

a truly magnificent esoteric depiction of the incarnation and resurrection of Jesus.

Shroud of Turin
The Shroud is regarded by this author as the authentic image of the face of Jesus transferred onto the cloth by etheric forces from His unique ether-body. I am aware of the debate about its authenticity, but my familiarity with etheric images persuades me that it is genuine. It is also the case that the Shroud was guarded by medieval initiates, the Knights Templars. These noble souls, regarded by Steiner as 'external members' of the medieval Order of the Holy Grail guarded a valid and holy artefact. However, so powerful is this image, that I am not suggesting that you have it always in view, and further it should be balanced by an image which presents the Resurrection.[130]

The Polish Rider by Rembrandt
This fabulous painting by Rembrandt painted ca.1660, is of the greatest value for the attunement phase, prior to meditating. Contemplation of this painting with esoteric insight, affirms the conclusion of Rudolf Steiner that this is a painting of the high degree initiate who assisted and spiritually 'counselled' Rudolf Steiner, the leader of the true Rosicrucian movement, Christian Rosencreutz. Furthermore, Rudolf Steiner once commented that in the background is 'the first painting ever made of the first Goetheanum'. My conclusion is that this picture resulted from a clairvoyant intuition of Rembrandt's.

Esoteric meditation assists the meditant to draw near to the highest of the sun-gods, the cosmic Christ, and within this sublime being is an aspect of that deity identified by the initiate as the primal Brahma of the Vedanta wisdom, or the Logos of ancient Grecian-Egyptian initiation wisdom and of St. John's Gospel. The Logos is thus understood to be the originator of the zodiac-cosmos, not just the solar system.

Appendix

One reason for the confusion on the issue of whether a person striving to undertake esoteric meditating with deeper texts, such as those from the Esoteric School or the Class lessons of 1924, is action undertaken by the Stuttgart-based anthroposophical-derived church. The Rudolf Steiner archives reported in the Goetheanum weekly newsletter (Das

---

[130] The research which establishes the deception is in at least two books, "The Turin Shroud is Genuine" by Rodney Hoare Souvenir Press 1994 which shows how erroneous the scientific tests were, and also "The Jesus Conspiracy" by H Kersten & E Gruber, Element Books 1994. This second book itself is not recommended as it seeks to prove a false exoteric theory, namely that Jesus did not die on the cross. Nevertheless the facts in the book about the cloth analysis are reliable.

Goetheanum Wochenschrift, 9 June 2002, No. 24,) that privately published, confidential editions of Steiner's lectures produced by the executive of the Christian Community (in the 1960's), contain passages in which Steiner's words about this subject have been altered. It is evident from the samples of altered texts presented in this article, that the editorial activity which created these modified texts, would result in the trainee priests concluding that all persons on the path of esoteric meditation should be participating in the Eucharistic service - a conclusion which is clearly regarded by Rudolf Steiner as false and harmful.

CHAPTER TEN

Meditations for different purposes

In this chapter you will find various meditative texts which derive from Rudolf Steiner, and which are designed for esoteric meditating. For you to meditate now, in order to find **'the Way to the Sacred'** for yourself, I have brought together here much of what has already been given throughout the book.

The meditation session
You are now in your comfortable chair, in a private space, not too warm nor cold, ready to begin at a predetermined time, which fits in with your personal schedule.
The **Attunement phase**: You seek to allow a mood of holiness to arise by focussing on a preliminary text or ideal or symbol/image (or all three in turn) which has this effect for you. This was discussed on page 292-93. Below are several attunement texts, which you may like to use. Next it is advisable, before entering into meditation to...
Consolidate the aura: This is done by using the 'protecting visualisation' technique, see page 281.
Meditating: Then proceed to the meditations. You may have chosen the Rose-Cross meditation and the Foundation Stone meditation, and also another esoteric text.
Contemplation: After the first phase of meditating, comes the second phase, Contemplation, which allows the state of consciousness in the true spiritual (Devachanic) realms to develop (**cosmic-spiritual** consciousness). See page 48.
Deep Contemplation: This is the third level of meditating, and relates to **high-initiation** consciousness. This was discussed on pages 56-58. Remember that this may not be fully achievable for many years.
Finishing the session: As you find the focus on the higher states gradually fading, then the initiate recommends that you tranquilly think of a theme, an ideal for your incarnation, to close the session. For example, consider how a particular virtue could enable a particular goal to be attained.
Journaling: It is also recommended that a journal and pen be kept nearby, because it is very important to write down special insights or subtle experiences which have occurred in the session.

Remember that in undertaking this activity, the main goal, at first, is to awaken into consciousness the inherent potential for wisdom. This means in effect to reach the stage of **cosmic-spiritual** consciousness, at least in its preliminary form. This process does not have to lead to potent encounters with the variety of spiritual realities revealed in this book, it may lead to some visions and associated psychic experiences, but now through the material presented, we are in a position to understand more clearly what is going on. We start with a solemn verse which emphasizes the extraordinary importance of meditation.

Meditative texts for attunement

In seeking, know your self,
Thus shall you become ever more your self.
But if seeking should cease in you,
Then you indeed still have yourself,
But existence removes you from
The truth of your own being.

The following text emphasizes that one can also find the path to the spirit by insightful observation of the sense-world, outside of the cloistered meditative time. This verse teaches that the sensitive observer may discover the imprint of the spirit **within** the dynamics of space and time. It is about perceiving the imprint of the spiritual as reflected in matter, through enhanced and sensitive perception:

The sphere of the spirit is the soul's home;
the human being reaches this
By walking the path of spiritual thinking,
By choosing as his or her empowered guide
the heart's capacity of love,
and by opening the soul's inner sensing
to the script which reveals itself
everywhere in creation.
A script which the soul may constantly experience
as a herald of the spiritual -
in all that lives and thrives there,
in all things too which, inanimate,
extend throughout space,
and in all that occurs in the
onwards flow of time.

This next verse is a polarity to the above, it teaches that truth is found when the higher faculties take one **beyond space and time**; it has a beautiful quality similar to the ancient Indian Vedic texts. It could be titled, 'Entering the eternal, beyond time and space'

Throughout the wide expanse of space,
Many beings and objects speak to human sensing,
And become changed in the flow of time.
But the human soul, stirring itself from slumber,
- not hindered by the breadth of space,
nor touched by the cycles of time -

Awakens within the flow of being and becoming
In the realm of eternity.

This translation encompasses the variations present in all three versions Rudolf Steiner wrote of this verse, which has implications similar to verses of St. Paul in 1 Corinthians 13:12.

This next verse has many elements of the above two verses. It is a contemplation on the current 'ego' or self as a reflection of the true higher ego. It presents a threshold experience, that is, an experience which can occur as one begins to cross over the threshold between this world and the astral plane:

I gaze into the darkness,
In it there arises light,
Living light.
Who is this light in the darkness?
It is I myself, in my true reality.
This true reality of the ego
Enters not into my earthly being;
I am only an image of this.
But I will find it again
When with good will towards the spirit
I shall have passed through the portal of death.

This verse presents the experience of a developing seer who glimpses at the threshold her or his own higher eternal self, and realizes that their current personality is but a reflected image, a part of the full glorious earnest truth of the human spirit. The person also realizes that they will merge with this wonderful reality at death. But, and this is most important, precisely the deep esoteric meditating encouraged in the pathway that Rudolf Steiner inaugurated, allows one to become one with this truth of one's full spiritual being-ness, **before** death. This important process is assisted by the following meditation which actually derives from the Theosophical Society (author unknown), and was used by Rudolf Steiner.

More radiant than the sun
Purer than the snow,
Finer than the ether is the self,
The spirit in my heart;
I am this self,
This self am I.

There is available a wonderful brief commentary on this verse by the initiate, published by anthroposophical publishers, in such books as, "Guidance in Esoteric Development'.

It is often said that the meditant is "Seeking the light", but from whence does this light derive? If the quest is a balanced one, then the answer is, from the spiritual sun ! The next two meditations introduce concepts that although really central to spiritual truths, are almost unknown in modern times. I have explained this to some extent already, in the commentary on the rose-cross meditations. This is the concept of the spiritual reality 'behind' the physical sun, the 'spiritual sun'.

Following are two versions of a meditative prayer by Rudolf Steiner on the sun-spirit-Christ and therefore on the existence of the inner spiritual sun. These appear to have a resonance with the ancient esoteric sun mystery wisdom, for example in ancient Egypt.

If you do not like the older style of language then simply substitute modern terms into the text. I personally experience this now archaic style as more appropriate, because it conveys more clearly the meditant's mood when sensing the nearness of Deity. (All such German texts have been translated by this author, unless otherwise stated.) These two texts about the spiritual sun may be used as attunement texts before or after meditating. These are published for the first time here.

Unveil, O Infinite One Thy countenance.
Thou who dost nurture the universe.
From whom all things derive and to whom all things return.
Remove from our eyes the veil of delusion,
Reveal Thyself to us, O Sun of wisdom!
Thou who art hidden in the shimmer of Thy golden light,
That we on the mighty path of the Ancient Wisdom
May perceive the Truth in the humble, living teachings of Christ
And thereby fulfil the purpose of our existence.
May Thou teach me that I can perceive the depths of existence.
May Thou instruct me that I can fulfil in truth my duties.
May Thou illumine me that I may behold my oneness in Thee,
For this alone leads to perception of God,
And to eternal peace. Amen.

This meditative prayer was also given in a second version, as follows: it is possible that the former one is to be meditated on in the morning, and the latter in the evening.

Thou who dost illumine the universe,
May Thou illumine me also, and remove
The veil from my eyes that I may behold the true Sun.
For it is still hidden from me;

Yet its shimmering radiance gleams through my soul,
Like a sea of golden light.
O grant that I may see it in full clarity, the pure truth.
Grant that in its light I may recognize what my life duties are,
And when my journey has ended allow me to reach its holy place.
O Thou comforter of all creation, give me the strength
to truly attain unto this place, the realm of the spiritual Sun.
O thou who art Love Divine, receive me into Thy purpose
And keep pure in me the eternal rays of faithful will.
Amen.

On the next page is a magnificent verse from Rudolf Steiner that is especially valuable for the attunement process, prior to meditating. It is a profound call from the heart for attunement to God.

Prayer To God Rudolf Steiner, 1905
(the same verse is given below, in more intimate language)

Infinite, ineffable lord of all,
You spirit of divine love, encompassing all, pervading all.
You who dwell especially within the heart,
And who has in my body your temple,
And in my soul, your throne.
I yield myself up to You, that the delusion of
My personal egoism may disappear, and
Within You I may awaken to real existence.

Give me the power to be always ready to receive
Your divine light for my self-knowledge,
And to let this radiance illumine my understanding.

Replace my limited intellect,
Which is led astray by sense-illusions,
And regards illusory sense impressions as reality,
With your infinite divine wisdom.
Grant that I may recognize your immortality
In my soul, and that I may learn to distinguish the
Eternal from the transient in me, and in all other beings;
And that I may allow the truth to prevail over lies.

Let me attain within You the strength, through your power,
To master my own nature and overcome its weaknesses.
Give me the will to ensure that the lotus-flowers of
Divine understanding will blossom in my heart,
And succeed in unfolding.
Grant that through your inner illumination, all hindrances

Which impede the awakening of this divine consciousness
in the depth of my being are conquered.

God, You who are in Your own being the profoundest tranquillity,
Let me through my inner guide, my own God, find my tranquillity
By relinquishing my unrest, and entering into your deep peacefulness.
Let me find my peace in your peace,
My strength in Your power,
My joy in Your glory!

Let my entire being be absorbed into Your being,
Just as the spark became radiant light in the flame;
That my self-delusion may disappear,
And Your wisdom become my knowledge.
May Your love become my love,
Yourself become me entirely,
And I entirely in You!
And in the Infinite may I know myself to be You,
And Yourself as me.
Amen!

In the second last line the term, 'infinite world', seems to me to refer to the deep mystery of the soul's life in the higher worlds, when the earthly sojourn is over. The question may occur, (and it is the experiencing of such questions that indicates approach of the higher-self), just to what being actually is this prayer addressed?[131]

Version in older style language.
Prayer To God   by Rudolf Steiner in 1905

Infinite, ineffable lord of all,
Thou spirit of divine love, encompassing all, pervading all.
Thou who dost dwell especially within the heart,
And whom hast in my body Thy temple,
And in my soul, Thy throne.
I yield myself up to Thee, that the delusion of
My personal egoism may disappear, and
Within Thee I may awaken to real existence.

Give me the power to be always ready to receive
Thy divine light for my self-knowledge,
And to let this radiance illumine my understanding.

---

[131] From a study of Steiner's cosmology, it may be answered that the foremost of the Principalities, active 'in the beginning' i.e., the first aeon (Saturn Age) is meant, in the first instance. But within this rank of beings generally the Father God, the uncaused primal being, has a presence, and hence through them a most intimate connection to each human spirit.

Replace my limited intellect,
Which is lead astray by sense-illusions,
And regards illusory sense impressions as reality,
With Thy infinite divine wisdom
Grant that I may recognize Thy immortality
In my soul, and that I may learn to distinguish the
Eternal from the transient in me, and in all other beings;
And that I may allow the truth to prevail over lies.

Let me attain within Thee the strength, through Thy power,
To master my own nature and overcome its weaknesses.
Give me the will to ensure that the lotus-flowers of
Divine understanding will blossom in my heart,
And succeed in unfolding.
Grant that through Thy inner illumination, all hindrances
Which impede the awakening of this divine consciousness in the Depth
of my being are conquered.

God, Thou who art in Thine own being profoundest tranquillity,
Let me through my inner guide, my own God, find my tranquillity
By relinquishing my unrest, and entering into Thy deep peacefulness.
Let me find my peace in Thy peace,
My strength in Thy power,
My joy in Thy glory!

Let my entire being be absorbed into Thy being,
Just as the spark became radiant light in the flame;
That my self-delusion may disappear,
And Thy wisdom become my knowledge.
May Thy Love become my love,
Thyself become me entirely,
And I entirely in Thee!
And in the Infinite may I know myself to be Thee,
And Thyself as me.
    Amen!

A meditation on God inspired by the Lord's Prayer
The next verse was inspired by the Lord's Prayer, and is valuable for ending one's meditative session. It is published here for the first time; there are three different versions in manuscripts, but each has only minor variations. This verse could be called 'A meditation on God inspired by the Lord's Prayer'. For those who know German the original

text is printed as an appendix to this chapter.[132] This verse may be used as a central meditative verse throughout one's life, in conjunction with the Lord's Prayer, so deep and uplifting are the truths about 'the God without and the God within' that it proclaims.

"Our Father, Thou who wert and art and wilt be,
our very innermost being.
Thy being is glorified and praised by all of us.
May Thy kingdom be extended by our deeds and our conduct.
We fulfil Thy will as Thou, O Father, hast placed it
in our innermost soul.
The nourishment of the spirit, the Bread of Life,
Thou givest in abundance to us, in all the changing conditions of life.
Thou allowest not temptation to come upon us beyond our strength,
for in Thy being no temptation can exist.
Because the Tempter is only illusion and deception,
out of which Thou, O Father, leadest us through
the light of Thy cognition.
Thy power and glory is active within us in
all the ages of the cycles of time. [133]
Amen".

Foundational meditative texts for gradual progress towards development of the spirit-self
If you do not yet feel ready to begin a 'crossing of the threshold', then by undertaking the study and some gentle meditative activity based on the Rose Cross and the Foundation Stone meditation, the soul will be gradually purified, enlightened and spiritualized. These two meditations are at the same time, essential parts of the meditative activity of the serious meditant, who is seeking to actively cross the threshold. As I mentioned in an earlier chapter, the actual 'substance' of the soul, the aura, is gradually replaced by higher astral 'reality', because the lesser of the two spiritual bodies starts to blossom. Absorbing the truths in this initiation wisdom is transformative.

To actively invoke a more direct crossing of the threshold by attaining higher faculties, and thus crossing the abyss and encountering the guardian, one has to intensify the effort, and strenuously undertake the Contemplation time as well, because some clairvoyance has to be

---

[132] It was called the 'Esoteric Lord's Prayer' amongst earlier members of the anthroposophical movement, however it is not a version of that prayer, but a separate text. The original Lord's Prayer is of infinite esoteric depth.
[133] (The word 'active' is more properly, 'efficacious' but this invaluable word, which means effectively active and correlates to the German, 'wirken' is not so well known.)

developed to encounter these deeper experiences. To proceed towards actual development of higher faculties, the meditant will be assisted by the meditative texts presented below, (and the so-called Class lessons).

Rudolf Steiner often recommended that the actual content of the meditation session be the Rose-Cross symbol with an accompanying verse (see below for two samples). Later on in his life he gave the great Foundation Stone Meditation. Both of these can be used in conjunction with the 1924 lessons, for those who are familiar with them. Another text can also be used from the selection offered in this chapter, or from an excellent selection of verses published in "Verse and Meditations" by Rudolf Steiner Press.

The Foundation Stone meditation was given by Rudolf Steiner in the northern hemisphere's Yuletide of 1923/24 on the occasion of re-founding the Anthroposophical Society. The winter-solstice (Yuletide) of either hemisphere is a time when exceptional spiritual forces are present. The following translation provides a more accurate translation than those normally printed, however I have not always found it possible to retain the metrical form of the original. This is the most comprehensive meditative text given by Rudolf Steiner, and therefore some commentary is necessary.

The reader is referred to my book, "**The Foundation Stone Meditation – a New Commentary**" in which a commentary is available, which makes many of the enigmatic phrases in this verse much clearer, and corrects some errors in earlier translations, which derive from the complex neologisms which Rudolf Steiner has coined for this verse. The meaning of the verse can only be ascertained by the attaining of esoteric insight, and in one case, by access to a private archive note from 1904.

My book on the Foundation Stone Meditation explains the meaning of these phrases, and shows the sections of the verse to be used on a daily basis. Through meditating on its very condensed statements most of his teachings can be discovered; it becomes a doorway into the central spiritual truths of the modern initiation wisdom. Through this process these truths become indissolubly linked to one's own being, they become one's own wisdom. In this verse is presented the essence of the teachings of Rudolf Steiner.

It is called the Foundation Stone meditation because for the meditant who seriously engages with it, it provides the opportunity to establish a foundational basis on which to become attuned to the spiritual stream deriving from the initiation wisdom elucidated by Rudolf Steiner. This stream draws its inspiration from the understanding of the sacrifice on Golgotha hill undertaken by the cosmic Christ, and the significance of this for the 'I am'. Meditating on this text draws the student near to the great spiritual powers nurturing the esoteric stream inaugurated by Rudolf Steiner.

It is important to note that Rudolf Steiner recommended only a part of the long four-fold verse be meditated upon each day, or rather that on any day the meditant is to focus especially on one particular section of it. Naturally one should contemplate the entire text at regular intervals, in order to have it livingly in one's mind. How often this is done is up to you, the individual is indeed treated as an individual in this path. There are seven extracts, each consisting of two parts, which he taught could be used, following the rhythm of the week. So on Monday for example one meditates upon two specific extracts namely, "Light divine, Christ-Sun" and "The Spirits hear this in East, West, North, South, may human beings hear it!" One links these two separate statement together, three times, thus forming one potent meditative text.

The Foundation Stone Meditation

Human soul !
You live in the limbs
Which bear you through the world of Space
Into the ocean-being of the Spirit,
Practise Spirit-Remembering
In depths of soul,
Where in empowered efficacy
Of the cosmos Creator
Your own I comes into being
Within the I of God;
Then you truly will live
In the cosmic nature of the human being.

For efficacious is the Father-Spirit of the Heights,
Engendering Being in the depths of the cosmos:
You Spirits of the Forces !
(... ... ...)
Let from the Heights resound
What in the depths is echoed:
This is spoken:
Ex Deo Nascimur –
'From the Divine, humanity has its being.'
The Spirits hear this
In east, west, north, south:
May human beings hear it !

Human Soul !
You live in the pulse of heart and lungs,

Which leads you through the rhythm of time
Into the sensing of your own soul's being;
Practise Spirit Contemplating
In equilibrium of soul,
Where the on surging
Deeds of cosmic evolving
Unite your own I
With the I of the Cosmos;
Then you truly will feel
In the authentic dynamics of the human soul.

For efficacious is the Christ-will from horizon unto horizon,
Bestowing Grace on the soul within the rhythms of
                                       the cosmos
You Spirits of Light !
(... ... ...)
Let from the east be enkindled,
What through the west is formed.
This is spoken:
In Christo Morimur -
'In Christ, death becomes life.'
The Spirits hear this
In east, west, north, south:
May human beings hear it !

Human Soul !
You live in the resting head,
Which, from the foundations of Eternity
Discloses for you the Cosmic Thoughts:
Practise Spirit Beholding
In serenity of thought,
Where the eternal aims of the Gods
Bestow on your own I
The light of Cosmic Being
That the will may be free.
Then you truly will think
In the foundations of the human spirit.

For efficacious are the Spirit's cosmic thoughts,
Invoking light into the being of the cosmos;
You Spirits of Soul !
(... ... ...)
Let from the depths be entreated,
What in the Heights shall be heard.
This is spoken:
Per Spiritum Sanctum Reviviscimus —

'In the cosmic thoughts of the Spirit the soul awakens.'
The Spirits hear this
In east, west, north, south:
May human beings hear it !

At the Turning-point of Time
The light of the Spirit of the Cosmos
Entered the earthly stream of being.
Deep darkness had lost its power;
Sun-radiant light streamed into human souls;
A Light,
That enwarms the simple shepherds' hearts,
A Light,
That enlightens the wise heads of kings.
Light Divine !
Christ-Sun !
Enwarm our hearts,
Enlighten our heads,
That good may come of
What in our hearts is laid down,
Of what in our heads we resolve.   Transl. Adrian Anderson

Note: The dots in the above text refer to the Greek names of the gods, (the so-called hierarchies) invoked by the meditant, and in English transliteration are usually written as:
  A :Seraphim, Cherubim, Thrones
  B: Kyriotetes, Dynamis, Exusiai
  C: Archai, Archangels, Angels

However, the original Greek terms are esoteric 'words of power' and are not to be used casually, hence when preparing the text of this verse for publication, the initiate himself deleted these terms from the text for publication. The reader who wishes to know the correct actual Greek text for these can enquire from this author.

The classic Rose-Cross meditation
This symbol was given to European humanity in the Middle Ages by one of the highest initiates in humanity, known by his mystery-name Christian Rosencreutz. It has a very important place in the meditation path developed by Rudolf Steiner, and the reader can find this in Steiner's book, "An Outline of Esoteric Science". The process involves the following; you begin, once quietly seated and relaxed, by visualizing a plant, a blossoming rose bush. One senses its life-blood, the sap running through its delicate foliage and its reproductive area, which is the blossoming flower. How pure, innocent and healthy it is !

Then you visualize a human being, with its blood stream coursing through the body, how we have lost our innocence and purity, how the red blood is permeated by lower desires and instinctive drives. Yet through this process we have developed an ego-hood, a conscious mental functioning and this bestows a potential for high spirituality. Now, these two images are dismissed and you visualize a cross of deadened, black wood – symbolizing the dying away of the lower self of a human being. Upon this cross, arising wondrously around it, you visualize seven lovely pink roses. The illustration is typical of the simple, unpretentious symbol that you are trying to visualize (**illustration Five**); to look at this symbol physically during this exercise may be of help to you in the initial phase, but as soon as possible you need to be able to create it in your mind's eye.

This is in essence, the Rose-Cross meditation; but see the fuller description in "An Outline of Esoteric Science" or other texts. The roses symbolize the purity of the soul in a meditant who has worked successfully towards spirituality. That there are seven of these roses indicates that the seven chakras are developing. One experiences a feeling of holiness when doing this meditation earnestly, as many deep truths are contained within it. The cross shape is vital, for it indicates to the meditant for example that it is through the power of the cosmic sun-god that spiritual development is now possible for humanity. The union of this being, whom Steiner referred to as the being of love, to the soul of the Earth has opened up this possibility. It is this being which was also revered in the highest mystery centre of ancient Atlantis, the Sun Mysteries.

The cross shape proclaims that the cosmic sun-god Christ is the source of the meditant's inner ability to overcome the lower self; and this being could also be called the spirit of the Earth, now that It is united to the soul of the Earth. This same cross shape is also indicating that our capacity to develop to a spiritual state of consciousness derives from this same divine source of light. As a result of what is known in the Christian religion (but not esoterically understood) as 'The Resurrection of Christ' this light now suffuses the Earth's aura, and is heard resonating in the Earth's ether-aura by various kinds of more developed elemental beings.

In similar manner, a sensitive soul can hear in the ethers a musical tone in ancient centres where initiation was carried out in earlier times. Although we have now described the Rose-Cross meditation briefly, there is still more meanings to this symbol, which gradually become perceived, so do not be lulled into thinking that its inner meaning is now all explained, see note of end of this chapter.

It is also quite important to clearly realize that symbols which are already completed and formed, available as published 'occult aids', are not recommended at all. They are totally incompatible with this pathway. The person must themselves form the image in their own mind, sensing what it means livingly as this is done. Otherwise, the symbol will exert its own influence upon the meditant, and this is a form of allowing oneself to be manipulated, of being influenced in a way that makes you inwardly unfree.

This influence may be quite dubious since many a symbol is formed by persons who are not at the stage of wisdom and purity which a high degree initiate attains. Of course contemplating quietly the cross or other sacred symbols, is quite wholesome. There are other quicker ways to develop than those Steiner gave, ways that bring indeed specific 'occult' development, but one must ask the question; do these techniques draw the meditant away from the light which guides the soul towards the source of inner purity and goodness?

I suggest that this meditation is used as part of your daily meditating; that is forming the symbol in your mind, after contrasting the flowering plant to the human being. Then proceed to use the Foundation Stone meditation. Then you may decide in addition to use another meditation which speaks especially to you. However, the above two meditations could remain the primary theme in your session.

Advanced meditation texts
The second aspect of meditation, namely what we described as Contemplation in Chapter One follows each of these two meditative activities. This is a shorter period of deeper inner quiet and emptying consciousness of the content one so intensely striven for in the first aspect of the meditative exercise. To bring the session to an end, one tranquilly contemplates (in the **normal** meaning of the word) an uplifting goal for one's own life, re-affirming what the purpose of the spiritual life is to you.

Rose Cross meditations
Evening:
(One visualizes the Rose Cross...)
Thou my soul,
gaze upon this symbol;
May it be to thee a sign of
The Spirit of the Cosmos,
Whose being fills all creation,
Who is actively present throughout the cycles of time,
And is actively present eternally in thee.

And then in the morning ...

(One pictures the Rose Cross)...
Let my thinking,
Let my feelings,
Let my willing
Be within this symbol.
May its meaning
Live in my heart's depths,
Live in me as light....   (remain in inner tranquillity for some minutes)
[134]

Note: The term 'actively present' is a translation of the German verb 'wirken' which means 'efficacious' or 'operative'. The term 'the Spirit of the Cosmos' as used here, refers to the high spiritual energies from the Sun-sphere, the highest of which are those of the cosmic Christ, who is active through an interweaving of spiritual light with other great divine-spiritual beings in our solar system.

Meditation text on the Rose-Cross: second version

This meditation, which was given in many different variations, is based on the following perspective. One is seeking to experience in the visionary light phenomena, not just 'normal' astral forms, but rather the presence of the sacred within this light. As one begins to have perception of the spiritual and astral realms, a divine radiant light, and a warm, spiritual energy of selfless love can become experienced. Within this light, if one can perceive with clarity and sensitivity, is the sacred spiritual reality underlying our part of the cosmos. That is, the radiant astral spiritual wisdom of the higher spiritual beings especially from the spiritual sun. Within the warm loving atmosphere, is the loving compassion and joyous blessedness of these divine beings.

In the evening:
The pure rays of the Light –
Reveal to me the Spirit of the Cosmos;
The pure warmth of Love –
Reveal to me Soul of the Cosmos.
Attunement to God
Be in my heart,
Be in my Spirit.
                              (remain in inner peace..)
And then in the morning:
(Picture to yourself the Rose-Cross...)

---

[134] [The German original of this text is copyright to Rudolf Steiner Verlag, and was published by this publishing house in Anweisungen für eine esoterische Schülung, p. 53, 1973.]

In my Spirit, In my heart,
Attunement to God.
The pure warmth of Love –
Reveal to me the Soul of the Cosmos.
The Light's pure rays –
Reveal to me the Spirit of the Cosmos.[135]

For those with an affinity to traditional Christianity. To contemplate one's inner connection with the cosmic Christ, the Being of Love.
Text One

In the beginning was Christ,
And Christ was with the Gods,
And a God was Christ.
And in every human soul
Lives the Christ Being,
Thus in my soul too, He lives,
And He will lead me
To the true meaning of my life.

Text Two   Another text of two sections

In the evening....

In the beginning was the Word,
And the Word was with God,
And a God was the Word.
And the Word,
May it live in the heart,
In the heart of thy being,
In thine I.

And then in the morning...

In thine I,
In the heart of thy being,
There may the Word live,
The spirit Word.
And the Word was with God,
And a God was the Word,
In the beginning was the Word.

Meditations on four great sacred texts

---

[135] [The German original of this text is copyright to Rudolf Steiner Verlag, and was published by this publishing house in Anweisungen für eine esoterische Schülung, p. 54, 1973.]

Aum
As we have seen earlier, the human being has not only an astral (soul) aura but also a two-fold spiritual aura. These two are referred to for the sake of simplicity as one single organism, known as the spiritual body or eternal self. In future time-cycles the higher of these two spiritual elements is destined to be developed. [136] Then this spiritual organism will be as complex in its structure and dynamics as the current physical body. Then people will be consciously living in a form of inner union with Deity, and hence also consciously using the will forces which are currently hidden deep in the subconscious; and which in our present age are often prey to malignant tendencies.

There is a wonderful meditation from ancient Indian spirituality, which has also become a central prayer for Buddhism and Hinduism, which is focussed on this deep mystery of the eternal self. Namely "Aum mani padme hum"; this Sanskrit sentence is usually translated as 'Hail to the jewel in the lotus, amen'. If the reader reflects on the themes mentioned in connection with the Philosopher's Stone in Chapter Eight, this expression takes on a deeper meaning.

The salutation 'Hail' is the famous word, Aum; and the final word, Hum is translated as a form of 'amen' or 'so be it.' Rudolf Steiner's elucidation of this sacred prayer refers to the higher-self within the normal self, although he does not recommend the breath-based meditative mantric activity invoked by the Aum. He explained this was intimately related to the breathing process, and to that unusual transitional state of consciousness between awakened and sleeping. But to gain understanding of the esoteric background to this formula is of value in a multi-cultural world.

The 'jewel in the lotus-flower' refers to the presence of the divine eternal-self which becomes present in the astral body as it flowers, that is, as the chakras form. However this eternal-self shall, as it manifests gradually in human evolution, transform the physical body, into the clear, radiant 'soft-diamond' body which I referred to in Chapter Eight. Hence the higher-self will have this 'jewel-like' presence in the current initiate or in future humankind.

So, the sentence has a meaning somewhat as follows;
Hail, primeval self ! Thou incorruptible spiritual jewel of light in my soul...higher-self of my future!

This version is then more in accordance to what the sentence conveys in its deeper aspect. This sentence in Sanskrit is of course a mantra, but

---

[136] Known in theosophy & anthroposophy as the seventh cycle of this current fourth aeon

that is not the aspect which we are considering here. The initiate referred to this concept of our personal self as a reflected image of an eternal real self, in an Esoteric Lesson as follows, 'in order to sense the presence of the divine in us, we permeate our consciousness with the following – that we are an image of the archetype from which God has created us. And only gradually can this image transform itself into the archetype.' (1910)

Meditations for the throat chakra

The Christian proclamation of the self-transcending ego
The Beatitudes from the Gospel of St. Matthew, 5: 3 - 11
These texts are powerful meditative texts for developing the eight as yet un-formed petals of the throat chakra. The commentary given below derives from Rudolf Steiner. A full elucidation of these sayings is not intended here, that would involve writing a lengthy chapter. I provide my own translations, and also the translations or paraphrases given by Rudolf Steiner. As he gave various versions, only slightly different in grammatical details, I have combined these different forms, to produce an accurate representation of his version.

"**Blessed**" in the context of the Beatitudes means to be joyous, and joyous because through the Resurrection, human souls shall start to experience a palpable, victorious presence of the spirit. That is, in one's normal earthly being or consciousness a higher spiritual quality shall manifest. These sayings are a proclamation of the effect that the presence of the cosmic Christ will have on the developing individualizing ego throughout the future.

1st statement (Verse 3)   [physical body]
"Blessed are the beggars for the spirit, for of them is the kingdom of the heavens."

This first beatitude concerns the spiritually poor (who to the extent that they are seeking to relieve their inner poverty, are beggars). Rudolf Steiner teaches that this is actually a reference to the role of the physical body in the maintaining of our human consciousness. Namely that it provides the sense of self-identity, but also tends to block spiritual states of awareness, and does this especially from the time of Christ onwards, as people will be incarnating ever more deeply into it.

For this reason, humanity would lose the old natural holistic perceptions and insights, and become actually 'beggars for the spirit". The natural awareness of the other worlds was dying, and Christ knew this would in the course of time lead to materialism and inner soul emptiness. But those who can sense this loss, who can actually be aware of it, will then strive to develop a meaningful link to their soul. Such people will find that through the coming of the Logos to Earth, a connection to their higher-self, to the spiritual realms, can be achieved. They will find a spiritual potential within their soul.

It is for this reason that Rudolf Steiner in his paraphrase, inserts the expression 'through their own self', or 'within themselves' into each of the Beatitudes. It is not in the original Greek, but it is an important aspect of these sayings: **"Blessed are the beggars for the spirit, for they shall find within themselves the heavenly realms."** This version by Steiner also puts a future quality into the sentence, emphasizing that the acutely self-conscious individual – to be developed soon after the time of Christ as a new factor in human evolution – will find the way, the truth and the life through her/his own striving, because the new spirit of the Earth will be journeying with maturing humanity, and providing this for each person.

2nd statement Verse 4 [life-forces]
"Blessed are those in distress, for they shall be comforted."

The inner meaning here is that the ego is empowered by a connection to its spiritual potential, and assisted by the spirit, will be able to deal with times of pain and suffering through an inner reserve of strength. People shall therefore be able also to access a source of healing from within. The emphasis in the Greek text is not on mourning for a deceased loved one, but concerns sorrow and distress in general. The cosmic Christ is proclaiming that people shall learn to listen to the destiny lesson implicit in the illness or problem, and find thereby the way to healing.

This is in fact an entirely new dynamic in healing, for as is well-known, in antiquity the so-called "temple sleep' was the means of solace and possibly healing for a sick person. That is, illness was often treated within the local temple by inducing an ecstatic or trance-like condition during which, according to Steiner, the healer-priest/ess could more easily gain access to the sick person's ether-forces. The healing priest would then intervene by applying some form of healing energy to the patient's ether-body. Rudolf Steiner's paraphrase is therefore, **'Blessed are those who engage with their distress, for they shall be able to find within their own self (a source of) solace.** (The exoteric interpretation focuses on another valid aspect, namely that those who are in distress will be spiritually helped.)

3rd statement Verse 5 [soul-body]

"Blessed are the gentle ones, for they shall inherit the Earth."

The meaning of this sentence is clearer in the second version, which is based more closely on Rudolf Steiner's elucidation of the Beatitudes. This second version however contains explanatory material which is not in the Greek text.

"Blessed are the gentle and harmonious ones, for the spiritual value of physical creation shall become incorporated forever within them."

This version does not contradict the spirit of the original Greek text, the main difference is the emphasis that the **spiritual-psychological** value of our lives on Earth, in the physical plane, is the focus, rather than the material globe as such. In this sense, we are taught that those souls who through their inner efforts subdue the lower soul-impulses, especially aggressive egotism, will have absorbed the essential purpose of life on Earth, during the time of its existence as a physical-material object. This is seen from the perspective of the future, implying this will be seen clearly when the physical Earth is no longer relevant to us.

This indicates that the soul-body (astral body) is the focus of this saying. With regard to New testament translations, the English in the King James is very archaic and based on inferior Greek texts. However the version itself is the most spiritually insightful. It has here the word, 'meek', "Blessed are the meek". This word in the 16th century meant a gentle, harmonious person, not a weak person. The higher-self has a far stronger presence in a person who has a mild harmonious predisposition, than one who is aggressive. The ego of such a person is much more capable of meeting real traumas and challenges than the person whose emotive forces dominate their being, giving a false impression of strength. Rudolf Steiner's concise translation is excellent: **"Blessed are those with a gentle spirit, for they shall inherit (from) the earthy reality."**

4th statement Verse 6 [emotions-conscience]

"Blessed are those who hunger and thirst for spirituality, for they shall be satiated."

This saying indicates that when a person becomes aware, as a general feeling, of the need to develop higher moral qualities, she or he will find it possible to develop such enhanced morality. It will occur through the gradual spiritualization of the individual ego; this will enable spirituality to manifest in one's emotive life. This is of immense relevance to Christianity since precisely this process of ego-spiritualization could be called the mission of the cosmic Christ. The processes involved here are connected to an enhancement of the conscience, an immensely important aspect of our spiritual nature which is often confused with acquired moral values. The conscience is not an acquired set of ethical values however, for it is the voice of our own higher-self intuitively active in our emotional being. Therefore Rudolf Steiner's translation is: **"Blessed are those who feel a hunger and thirst for spirituality, for this yearning will be appeased through their own self."**

The term, "own self" means the earthly personality with its new egoic capacity.

5th statement Verse 7   [mind: spiritual thoughts]

"Blessed are the compassionate, for they shall be given compassion."

Here we find the only occasion when that virtue in the first part of the sentence, is the same as that in the final part of the sentence. This can be seen in its deeper meaning when one understands that here the dynamics refer to the individual human intellect, as distinct from the emotions. These profound statements by Christ wherein He surveys the future development of humanity has in fact progressed through the nine-fold human being as Rudolf Steiner points out in his commentary. The statements progress from the physical body to the life-forces, to the general soul-body, then to the emotional capacity in the soul; and now in this fifth maxim, the focus is on the intelligence.

A person who manifests compassion has obviously developed their mind, they have acquired an understanding of spirituality and are actively manifesting that in society. In so far as humanity develops a compassionate and caring attitude, compassion (or in outmoded language, 'mercy') will start to become part of one's own life experience. That is, compassion will spread as a reality in human interaction, and we can then expect to receive compassionate treatment from others, when difficult circumstances arise. Therefore Rudolf Steiner's version is: **"Blessed are the compassionate, for through their own self they will attain compassion."**

6th statement   verse 8 [intuitive thinking]

"Blessed are the pure in heart, for they shall behold God."

As we saw earlier in this chapter, only that person actually sees into the spiritual realms who has developed a certain inner radiance. This is especially connected with the conserving and enhancing of the purest soul energies in the heart chakra. A radiance emanating from the purified meditant provides the means whereby one may be conscious and seeing in the higher worlds. But a person with such an aura also has the **intuitive** faculty developing; it is this faculty that enables perception of transcendental higher realities. It is not the personal desires and emotions nor the logical intellect, but rather the intuitive-thinking that is the faculty which brings subtle inward perception of the spiritual realities.

It is an achievement of the ego itself, whose highest soul quality is that of intuitive awareness. As we saw in Chapter One it is this same faculty which eventually becomes so empowered through meditation as to give glimpses of one's own spiritual nature. At first, these flashes of insight are brief and elusive but they are real, and gradually they grant insights into the nature of God. In the course of time the intuitive faculty is inwardly enhanced, making direct clairvoyant awareness possible. In ancient times however, the way to beholding higher beings was not so much through an enhancement of intuition, but through leaving the body in the three-day initiation sleep, during which time higher initiates would bestow such experiences on the person being initiated.

They would also take on a kind of guarding activity, to give protection for that person from untransformed lower forces in his/her being. But 2,000 years ago, that approach was dying out, so this Beatitude radically proclaims that the way to nearness to God is through one's own "inner work". The term 'god' in Greek can also refer to the divine within the human being, so the Beatitude has, as a secondary meaning, that aspect of God which is in the human spirit. R. Steiner's version is: **"Blessed are the pure in heart, for they shall, through their own self, behold God."**

7th statement　　　　　　　verse 9　　　　　　　[Spiritual-Self]

"Blessed are those who establish peace, for they shall be called the children of God."

The term 'peace' is often used in the New Testament in a quite special way: to refer to the profound tranquillity which a person may attain when the divine is present within them. For example, when appearing to the awed disciples after His resurrection, the divinized God-Man said, "Peace be with you" (St. Luke 24:36). It was more than just a kind greeting. The significance of this can only be fully seen when one understands that in the context of the esoteric life, 'peace' has an inner meaning. Namely it is that tranquillity which arises when a person's higher-self triumphs over the restless turmoil of personal desires in the normal earthly soul-body, like a star whose rays calm the restless ocean of the soul.

Hence the cosmic Christ, through Jesus, is also indicating that He not only wishes peace to humanity, but actually **brings** this peace (see St. John 14:27). This seventh Beatitude then is a meditation on inner peace as originating from the higher-self and its connection with God. It is a statement about the presence of the spiritual self in the soul. Exoterically, this Beatitude is rightly considered an affirmation that establishing external (social-political) peace is a valuable and noble deed. Rudolf Steiner's version is: **Blessed are those who establish peace through their own self, for they shall become children of God.**

8th statement verse 10   [Creatively-empowered spirit-self]

"Blessed are those who are persecuted for the sake of ethical integrity, for of them is the kingdom of the heavens."

This Beatitude refers to the fact that spiritual reality contrasts strongly with the inherent nature of the earthly world, and the illusory earthly ego. This strong contrast can draw hostile reactions to advancing souls from those to whom the spiritualization process is regarded with fear and resentment. Certain elemental forces in the aura of non-evolving souls, and elsewhere, can sense the presence of higher forces in the seeker from the spiritual-self and these may incite hostility. Should this be the case, then that person is here told that their inner being has now advanced to the point where the higher-self, an extract of the heavenly worlds, is present in their ego. Their self, or ego then has an eternal spiritual element functioning consciously within it.

This dynamic was especially relevant to the first centuries after Christ, when hundreds of thousands of people were subject to fierce opposition and torment because of their support for the cosmic Christ. It is also a truth for all time, always relevant to individual spiritual teachers, and in future ages it may again become relevant in one way or another. It is a profoundly uplifting assurance to seekers after spirituality, that in such spiritualized persons the sublime heavenly realms have (an extension of) their very existence. Hence R. Steiner renders this verse as: **"Blessed are those who are persecuted for the sake of ethical integrity, for in their self will be the kingdom of the heavens."**

This saying also has the implication, through the use in Greek of a past tense in the first part of the sentence, that such persecuted spiritual people, after their earthly life, become inhabitants of the higher heavenly realms. Namely; "Blessed are those who **have been** persecuted for the sake of spirituality, for of them are the heavenly realms". These spiritual souls are in effect the inhabitants of these realms.

Here the eight meditations on the development of higher and more empowered states of being finish. The next verse changes the direction of His words, it is no longer a case of addressing a particular dynamic in humanity generally. The next verse(s) in the Gospel contain more individualized statements concerning the duties moral guidelines and coming persecution of the soon-to-be established community of Christians.

Meditations for the throat chakra (2)

A version of the Noble Eightfold Path of Buddha
The following eight paragraphs were given to students in the Esoteric School. The text survives in the form of short, clipped sentences, but no original notes exist in the Steiner archives. They have a strict, some what impersonal quality to them, perhaps this is due to the person who wrote them down. They are meant to be worked on day by day throughout the week, with the eighth being a daily exercise. **They have quite a solemn quality to them, and no doubt they represent an ideal for strict discipline, but one should not adopt them in such a way as to become a dour and un-humorous person.**

Saturday
Pay attention to the thoughts/mental images. Think only significant thoughts. Learn gradually to discriminate between truth and opinion, between trivial ideas and deeper concepts, between eternal verities and transient matters. When listening to someone, attempt to be inwardly quiet and to objectively receive their words. Refrain from having subjective agreement and especially critical thoughts or moods about them.
This is the so-called 'right opinion'.

Sunday
Only decide to do something when you have fully considered the motivation. All thought-less actions, all meaningless deeds should be kept away from the soul. Have meaningful intentions behind all your deeds; and above all do not do anything which has no purpose. If you are convinced of the appropriateness of a deed, then be steadfast in carrying it out.
This is the so-called 'right judgement' exercise.

Monday
Speaking; only words which have meaning and purpose should come from the lips of a person seeking higher development. All speaking for the sake of speaking, in the sense of killing time, is harmful. The trivial kind of conversation wherein everything is colourfully mixed up, should be avoided. But one is not to thereby cut oneself off from conversing with others. On the contrary, one's conversing should gradually achieve a deeper significance. The point is, not to speak without reason! One considers all aspects of a planned answer or response. Learn to be gladly silent. One seeks to say neither too much nor too little. Listen carefully and then contemplate what you have heard.
One calls this exercise, 'right speech'.

Tuesday
External deeds. These should not be troublesome for our fellow human beings. Where one is impelled to act from deep within (from the conscience) consider carefully how one can best correlate the action with the welfare and happiness of the community. Where one decides more directly from out of one's own personality to do something, consider carefully the effects of the intended action very carefully.
This exercise is called, the 'right deed'.

Wednesday
The organising of daily life. Live in a manner which is both spiritual and in accordance with nature; not caught up in the trivialities of life. Avoid everything which brings haste and hectic disturbance into your life. Don't be hectic, nor lethargic. Regard life as a means to be able to work spiritually towards higher development, and live accordingly.
This exercise is called, 'the right perspective (on living).'

Thursday
Human striving. One ensures that nothing is undertaken which is beyond your ability, but nothing is omitted which is possible for you. Look beyond the every-day momentary concerns and formulate ideals which are connected with the highest human responsibilities. For example seek to develop yourself so as to be all the more able to help and advise others, even if this will not be possible in the immediate future.
This exercise could be considered as:
"ensure that the preceding exercises become a habit."

Friday
The striving to learn as much as possible from life. Let nothing pass one by without giving the chance to have experiences of use to the spiritual life. If you have done something imperfectly or improperly, this becomes a reason to do something similar in the future in a better way. Observe, in a kind way, the deeds of others for the same reason. One always looks back to earlier deeds before doing something, if these would be of help to you in the current situation. Remember one can learn something from every person, including children.
This exercise is called, 'the right memory' that is, remembering what one has learnt, from what one has done.

Summary
(The eighth exercise) Every so often look within, at the same time of the day, even if only for five minutes. You are to contemplate your own being; give advice to yourself. Examine and develop further your life-priorities and principles. Contemplate your duties and knowledge – or lack of – consider the actual content and real aim of your life. Consider your mistakes and experience real concern at your own imperfections.

Earnestly formulate the virtues that you must develop as part of your life-purpose. Find what is of essential permanent value in your being and life. (One does not fall into the error of focussing on what one really should have done, rather objectively strive towards a higher state of being.)
This exercise is called 'the right kind of inner-contemplating'

APPENDIX

The original German texts:

Meditation on the Spiritual Sun   (version 1)

Du, der Du das Weltall erleuchtest,
Erleuchte auch mich, und nehme von meinen Augen
Die Binde, daß ich sie sehe, die wahre Sonne.
Sie ist mir jetzt noch verschleiert zwar,
Aber doch in einem goldenen Lichtmeer
Durchschimmert mein Gemüte.
O, laß sie mich sehen im Bilde der Klarheit,
Der reinen Wahrheit.
Laß mich in diesem Lichte erkennen
Was meinen Pflichten sind, und wenn die Reise vollendet ist,
Laß mich ankommen am heiligen Ort.
O Du, Du Tröster des Alls, gib mir die Kraft,
Dort auch wirklich hinzugelangen,
O Du, Du göttliche Liebe, nimm mich auf in Deine Ziele
Und halte rein in mir den ewigen Strahl des treuen Wollens. Amen.

Meditation on the spiritual sun   (version 2)

Enthülle, O Unendlicher,
Der Du das Universum ernährest,
Von dem alles kommt und zu dem alles zurüruckkehrt,
Dein Antlitz.
Nimm hinweg von unseren Augen den Schleier der Täuschung,
Offenbare Dich uns, O Sonne der Weisheit,
Die Du im Schimmer Deines goldenen Lichtes verborgen bist,
Damit wir auf dem mächtigen Pfade der
Uralten Weisheit, in der demütvollen,
Lebendigen Lehre Christi,
Das Wahr erkennen,
Und den Zweck unseres Daseins erfüllen.
Belehre daher mich, daß des Daseins Tiefe
Ich erkennen kann.
Unterweise Du mich, daß meine Pflichten
Ich in Wahrheit erfüllen kann,
Erleuchte Du mich, daß meine Einheit in Dir,
Ich schauen kann, die allein zu Gotteserkenntnis
Und zum ewigen Frieden führt.   Amen.

Meditation on the Lord's Prayer

Vater Unser!
Der Du warst und bist und sein wirst,
Unser aller innerstes Wesen.
Dein Wesen wird in uns allen verherrlicht und hochgepriesen.
Dein Reich erweitere sich in unseren Taten
und in unserem Lebenswandel.
Deinen Willen vollführen wir, wie Du,
O Vater ihn in unser innerstes Gemüt gelegt hast.
Die Nahrung des Geistes, das Brot des Lebens, gibst Du uns in
Überfülle in allen wechselnden Zuständen des Lebens.
Die Versuchung läßt Du nichts über das Maß unserer Kräfte wirken,
Da in deinem Wesen keine Versuchung bestehen kann.
Denn der Versucher ist nur Schein und Täuschung,
aus der Du, O Vater,
Durch das Licht deiner Erkenntnis herausführst.
Deine Kraft und Herrlichkeit wirken in us
In den Zeitenläufen der Zeitenläufe.

Note

Working with the Rose-Cross meditation will lead you to discover further secrets associated with its counter-image. What do I mean by this ? When we look at a colour, for example pink, then its etheric counter-image is activated in us, in this case, green. As a psychic quality develops in one's consciousness develops, one becomes more sensitive to the after-images. One can actually look at something then close the eyes and for ten minutes follow a remarkable series of fascinating colour changes that the physical colours undergo, echoing on in the ether-body, before they fade away. Also the counter-colour of a flower appears whilst looking at it, as if hovering slightly above the blossom. That is, a bluish flower will have a yellow glow above it. When contemplating the Rose-cross one sees its counter-image. Many inspiring secrets are hidden in this seemingly simple symbol. It is really worthwhile drawing it in colour and having it in your meditation space.

Appendix
New perspective on the classical Buddhist view of the self:

The following text is a long meditative passage from a profoundly insightful lecture on the eternal higher ego. It gives a glimpse into the profound vistas on life which real initiation wisdom bestows. It is central to Steiner's view of human psychology, which greatly differs from the classical Buddhist view that the human ego is entirely illusory, being composed of skhandas or currents of astral impulses formed in the past life. The perspective in Steiner's teachings is that normal human ego although greatly lacking in depth and a definite central core, does have a central kernel. This kernel is admittedly not fully incarnate, but nevertheless it is effecting an influence into the personal self.

The existence of this supra-temporal, transcendent purely spiritual reality means that the human personality does have a connection to a genuinely eternal spiritual reality. More significantly, the somewhat illusory incarnate self can be gradually merged into this eternal, real selfhood, and indeed it is the will of the hierarchies that precisely this does happen. A major reason for Steiner concluding that personal self can be metamorphosed into its own archetype, i.e., spiritual eternal self, derives from his research of what happened when the incarnation of the cosmic Christ occurred into the Earth's heart chakra, at Golgotha.

In this process the cosmic Christ together with the indwelling ray from the Logos, actually became what Steiner terms "the Earth-Spirit". By this he means the highest spiritual being of the planet. The effect of this alteration to Earth spirituality is, that when human souls reincarnate, with their eternal self hovering above them, as it were, the human being can begin to experience the urge to develop within itself this higher spiritual kernel, and thus begin to merge into the eternal, true self, which in turn begins to manifest in the human being. The ego is then no longer only an illusory result of a past life's wishes, thoughts and will. Consider this passage of a Steiner lecture where the listeners are learning how the process of attaining to consciousness of, and union with, the true eternal self occurs, which is an excellent passage on which to meditate. In this extract, my added words are, without exception, clearly placed in such brackets like these { }; everything else is from Rudolf Steiner;

> "Here am I in the earthly world with my silhouette-ego, and {now through the development of higher faculties} I gaze far back in time to all which was the content of my preceding earthly life. But at the same time I see how my real ego was like an unwinding reality, proceeding through the higher worlds after the last life and then finally reaching into my current earthly life. **I perceive in the first instance my living true ego as if it**

were a separate being. And I recognize myself again in this being which at first appeared to me as something quite separate. In this sentence each word must be intensely contemplated, for each separate word in these sentences has a very specific importance.[137]

It is part of the entire experience that out of the perception of one's own real self as, in the first place, something alien, one wrestles through to the following realization - that which appears here to you as something alien and separate, that is actually you. So it appears to you as if in the past some other being had lived, but you yourself are this being. And then one becomes aware how this self in fact streams in from the previous earthly life, how it becomes somewhat covered over in this current incarnation.

One becomes aware also that it would only appear to one's consciousness if all the events which occur between going to sleep and awakening were consciously experienced. For in this {experiencing in the other worlds during sleep} there weaves and lives all that which comes from the past life, permeating through the astral and ether world then reaching us {as we journey through the night}.

You see, there is a world of earthly paradoxes and heavenly harmonies in this wrestling through to the realization that one is one's own true self. There are earthly contradictions in this way; that fundamentally on Earth one can not, {until highly developed anyway}, attain to this true self because of all that one has become from daily existence here on the Earth. In this Earth-ego however, there lives the first rudiments of {the true self, in the form of} spiritual love. And through this fact, life on Earth is given a special radiance, because indeed the power of love does ray into this earthly life. {Love, selfless compassion, as distinct from sensual personal desires, is a central strand of the true higher-self.} This kind of love is an expression of the real inner will. But this love must be intensified and enhanced so that higher faculties and spiritual awareness develops.

Then what lives in the person as egotism {earthly desires} which is the antithesis of love, can thus be conquered. **Yet this which lives as the antithesis, the opposite of love in the soul bestows on one the possibility to experience his/her own ego within earthly life.** {For within the earthly ego the higher ego is active, so one may experience the yearning to realize this higher-

---

[137] This last sentence is still the words of R Steiner, not mine !

self.} The higher spiritual love must become so strong that the meditant learns to look beyond, to ignore this earthly ego. For it could be said that the dynamic of love is the absorption of one's own being into the being of another. This has to be so strong that one really no longer emphasizes the every-day ego, as it lives in the earthly bodily existence.

Then the paradox occurs, that precisely through selflessness, through highest capacity of selfless love, one penetrates through to the true real ego, to that true ego which glows towards us from the distant future. Indeed one has to lose the earthly personal ego in order to acquire perception of one's own true self. And that person who does not will to lose their earthly ego, can not draw near to this true self. The true self does not wish to be sought out and queried as to when it intends to manifest, when it will appear. It hides itself if sought out. For it becomes found only in love, and love is devotion of oneself to another separate being. Therefore must the true self be encountered as if it were some other separate being.

But in this moment when the person begins to sense, to glimpse their own true self, one also begins to glimpse at this stage that which actually exists in the true spiritual world. Namely, one encounters the hosts of divine hierarchical beings; indeed the highest grouping of divine spiritual beings, the seraphim, the cherubim and the thrones."[138] {That is, not as objects 'out there' to observe, but as aspects of one's own spiritual being-ness.}

At this point in the lecture extract Rudolf Steiner moves to a closely related and immensely important theme, namely those divine-spiritual beings called 'the hierarchies' in mystical Christianity, that is, the angels and archangels, up to the sublime seraphim. In later esoteric sessions from 1924 this subject was dealt with in great depth; here I would advise the reader to read the basic study material recommended in earlier chapters. The full nature of the human spirit and higher-self can **not** be comprehended without knowledge of the intimate interaction and interconnectedness between the human being and the nine ranks of higher beings from whom our higher being has received its existence.

Rigorous contemplation of these teachings will reveal some discrepancies in the common Buddhist understanding of the complex theme of 'Anatta' or the illusory and real ego-hood, and the initiation teachings of anthroposophy. The difference focuses on the concept of

---

[138] These several paragraphs are from a public lecture in 22 April 1923 (G/A 84, untransl.)

the skhandas or current personality tendencies which are the expression of the past life's main dynamics. Rudolf Steiner is at pains to emphasize that the human being is not limited to an illusory ego, in so far as the higher eternal ego is always seeking to inherently vivify and deepen the earthly self. It is important to realise that these texts are meant for meditative study, don't be discouraged if at first the analytical intelligence is baffled by them.

A further meditation on the nature of the ego:

"It is said in Buddhism that only the karmic results of the illusory ego of the past life is alive on Earth. But the...initiate in the esoteric Christian stream...says this is incorrect, because that which appears there {as the normal every-day ego}, is in fact **the concentrating deed/action of the karma**.[139] And whilst all other deeds are temporal and are extinguished in time, that deed of karma which has led to the ego-consciousness of the human being, is not temporal...it constantly intensifies its own inner reality...karma and ego are **not** the same thing...my ego moves on from my present earthly state and will as such reappear in my next earth life and then connect itself to with the deeds of that future life... thus if I as an ego have done something, then **my ego** remains connected with the core of that deed, and moves on with that deed from incarnation to incarnation." [140]

Now it is very important to note when meditating on this material, a remarkably profound element in the spiritual psychology developed by Steiner is seen. Specialist knowledge of Steiner's psychological texts reveals that he often speaks of "the ego" in a way that **includes both** the personal and the eternal in the one entity. The term which in italics above is – *my ego* – is actually an example of this; logically, it **has** to refer to both egos at once, intertwined into a single entity, so to speak. If this were not the case, then he would be saying something quite inconsistent, because the **personal** ego can not remain with the deed, at least, not **unless** it is deeply interconnected to the higher eternal ego, because this is the only 'ego' that is able to "move with that deed from incarnation to incarnation."

---

[139] That is, it is an integral part of the focus, the purpose, the stream of further developmental possibility, in the karma. That is, **the karma** has brought it into being, as a consequence of the stream of evolution which flows from the past into the future, rather than it bringing into being the karma.
[140] Lecture: 21.03.1912 (untransl.)

CHAPTER ELEVEN

Influences of lifestyle

Vegetarianism and diet

Rudolf Steiner recommended that "if one is going to tackle the major goal of chasteness or conquering sexual desire, then a low protein (vegetarian) diet should be adopted. And in general, the eating of meat and fish is not advisable/wise."[141] The high protein diet makes this goal nearly impossible, because "by including animal meat in the diet, one is enjoying the animality or animal astrality" [127] hence any earth-bound desires will intensify. Vegetarianism in general was recommended by him as a way of life.[142] He was himself a vegetarian (although sometimes eggs were included), and as he commented most of the people studying his teachings were also vegetarian.[143] However, at no time did he ever suggest that other people were under an obligation to become vegetarian, and when such pressure seemed to arise for people in circles around him, he acted to counter-act this.

He mentioned that he could not have carried out the demands of his life's work if he were not vegetarian. This author has been vegetarian for thirty five years, since the mid-late teens, and can confirm Rudolf Steiner's comments that very substantial work-loads can be undertaken on this diet. He also spoke with compassion of the unfortunate nature of meat-eating, commenting on the superior attitude often found in Buddhism to that of the Christian cultures regarding this subject.

He did stress however that on a vegetarian diet one must be actively striving to be a thinker who really thinks through spiritual concepts, not just feels them. This kind of thinking is the activity that precedes actually having **cosmic-spiritual** consciousness and is of course usually found with people seriously interested in spirituality. Otherwise such a diet, especially veganism, would tend to lift the soul too strongly up away from the Earth and this includes one's own karmic opportunities and obligations. Therefore, veganism is not recommended although clearly if one has an allergy to milk products then veganism may be necessary. However, Steiner's research found that a vegetarian diet (including milk products) actually assists the development of that third and highest state of cosmic consciousness, which we called 'spiritual union' or **high-initiation** consciousness.

It is very important to realize that the dreamy 60's hippie mind-set, which appears to be induced in part at least, by an unwise

---

[141] From an intimate lecture to students given in Nov 1903 (archive notes).
[142] Lecture 9/Feb '05 (untransl.)
[143] Lecture of 1915, 27/March (untransl.)

vegetarianism, is neither the goal, nor the result of the kind of vegetarianism intended here. It is typical of people in the anthroposophical stream, that the will is functioning consciously and energetically devoted to helping society as well as seeking higher spiritual goals, not drifting off into dreamy bliss. To avoid the dreamy state, sufficient protein has to be in the diet, and that comes from eating the grains. If you want to work hard with sustained energy over decades, then vegetarianism, based on the grains, is the best possible diet.

Now the subject of vegetarianism has another aspect to it, namely that many people wish to be vegetarian, and would be already, but they simply can not find a satisfactory alternative to meat. The alternative is actually in using the basic grains in the form of a casserole or simply steamed, etc. However there is so very little worthwhile guidance available on the subject of how to prepare and enjoy the grains, I intend to produce such a book, complete with recipes for meals. A detailed nutrition guide obviously can not be included in this book.

Here I can only say in brief that it is recommended that you use the following as the basis of your protein needs: wheat, oats, barley, rice, millet, rye, and maize (referred to in the USA by the generic word for grain, 'corn'). Buckwheat, although not a grain as such, can be included in the list. Nuts and seeds and dairy produce should be used as well to supplement the grains. These will definitely give a vegetarian enough protein. The tables displaying essential daily nutrients which indicate that you must have meat are not as relevant as they appear. However, on the other hand, if you are not inwardly a vegetarian, then indeed you will need meat protein. However if you are inwardly capable of forming protein out of plant substance and its ether forces, then these plant foods will give you sufficient protein. It is an individual matter and until information is found giving clear guidelines on the use and preparation of grains, many people are required to have some meat.

However, it is also important to note that there are various 'pools' of etheric forces in various family groups whose bodies are resistant to etherealization, these bodies need meat protein. One should not try to survive without meat if the body is in danger of ill-health from this. I use the expression 'pools of ether forces' deliberately, because 'genes' are only the chemical material expression of these ether energies, and not to realize this is to stay in earth-bound thinking. And it is precisely such dead concepts that make it hard to experience real living wisdom, real **cosmic-spiritual** consciousness. Ideally, eggs are best avoided if you are capable of nourishing yourself as a vegetarian, but if you need something more dense, then eggs are a reasonably mild and neutral form of animal substance.

Regarding milk and its products, I will mention only two aspects briefly. Firstly, that it is not really animalistic, in so far as the cow's astral aura actually bypasses the area around its udder, according to Rudolf Steiner's research. Secondly, if you are allergic to milk you may be allergic only to the toxic agricultural chemicals used, and which readily tend to accumulate in the fatty substances of the milk. There is a further cause of milk intolerance, due to the unwise procedure used in the milk industry of homogenizing milk; that is, of spinning the milk with such speed as to disperse the molecules of cream, to prevent cream from accumulating on top of dairy products. This procedure causes the tiny particles of fatty substance in the milk to pass right through the wall of the stomach, and accumulate in areas of the body, becoming a serious burden to the lymph system, and so on.

The other recommendation is, that adults should not consume raw or fresh milk; milk is an excellent food, but adults, according to Rudolf Steiner need it in a soured form, such as cheese, yoghurt, sour cream, etc., because mucus forms only from having fresh milk as an adult. Fresh milk is only suitable for children. But even organic/bio-dynamic milk may have been homogenized, and therefore may cause a health problem.

The student is also advised to minimize the consumption of soy products, they are not good for the person developing higher consciousness. This is firstly because they are legumes, and secondly they actually have too much protein, therefore there is a tendency is to subtly harden the body. The higher the protein content, the less suitable it is as food for those seeking higher consciousness. Soy is so permeated by forces which harden the body, that its own protein can be successfully combined with many kinds of 'dead' mineral chemicals, such as those dozens of (often toxic) mineral substances which are used in paint-strippers, dyes, plastics and industrial resins.

In fact Henry Ford once experimentally had an entire automobile body-work made from Soya bean protein; this is compelling testimony to its hardening influence, once digested by the human being. Such hardening influences inhibit awareness of the insights and holistic images present in your ether-body. Nutritional theories, including alternative New Age theory can be often incorrect, such is the sheer complexity of the digestive process.

For example nutritional theories formulated without spiritual insight will not include the fundamental principle of nutrition – namely, what kind of elemental/ethereal forces have built up the foodstuff? What kind of ether energy will you then take up into your own body and ether-energies? In ancient Ayurvedic knowledge there is some trace of this truth, otherwise it is in the detailed and expert research by Rudolf

Steiner into nutrition that such vital principles can be found. On this basis then, it is recommended that, above all, you avoid mushrooms and peanuts; in the plant kingdom these are the most un-spiritual of all vegetable foods. The reason for such conclusions are too complex to be dealt with in full here, but relate to the presence of unpleasant subtle elemental forces in these plants.

If you find it hard to credit the extraordinary powers of research possible through clairvoyance of a high initiate, you have the company of some young doctors on the 1920's. What happened was, they went to a lecture cycle by Rudolf Steiner on medicine and health, not sure what he could offer, and sat down in the front row of the hall. As he walked into the room, towards the podium, casting a quick glance around the room, he pointed towards these two young doctors, saying that they had been eating (European) asparagus and therefore they are to remove themselves, and sit at the back of the room. In utter astonishment the men, who had indeed eaten this for lunch, stood up and moved to the back of the room.

Steiner was not someone to reveal his powerful clairvoyant abilities for the sake of impressing others, on the contrary he was very discreet about this matter. So why did he act so prominently then? Because he was about to teach medical people about healing and health, and in those circles no understanding of nutrition existed. The understanding that an holistic approach to nutrition essential for good health must include the vital matter of ethereal forces in foodstuffs was simply not in existence then. European asparagus is grown often in a wrong manner, in between tall furrows of soil which force it to rise ever higher. However, in doing this the proper amount of solar ether energy can not be assimilated, thus the plant has a pale colour and an excess of earth-ethers, this produces a slightly malignant result.

Namely that forces from unpleasant elemental entities (nature spirits) permeate the plant. He explained that he saw these ugly forces as he entered the room, hanging off the edges of the lips of the two men. (One can only surmise what a vast amount of multi-levelled perceptions were constantly assimilated by him whenever he gazed around him.)

In the animal kingdom when you feel the need for meat, it is, surprisingly, fish which should be avoided, rather than bovine flesh. Clairvoyant observation carried out by him of the impact on the human being of fish, revealed that a potent revenge urge arises in them as they are fished out of the ocean, and this astral thought-form often finds its target. If this seems odd, just reflect on the death of a cow in the abattoirs, it is in theory anyway, quick and perhaps not too painful.

But poor fish slowly suffocate to death out of the water. In addition, for every quantum of shrimp or fish caught, untold numbers of dolphins, and each year about 40,000 wandering albatrosses and other innocent creatures die a slow death. Of course this harm to other marine creatures ('collateral damage') does not apply where age-old ethical techniques are used for fishing. In short, vegetarianism releases the animals from much suffering, and the human race from much karma.

Remember that it is in our dreams that the higher sacred reality of life first announces itself to us. So the sleep time should be attuned to this reality, as discussed in the Chapter Nine. It is in this connection important to avoid eating beans and other legumes, or at least to minimize them. These foods, inferior spiritually to the grains, have an effect on your ether-energies similar to the effect of meat on your astral being. And since the ether-body is where the dream images are stored as we awaken, this causes a tainting of the dreams. We do of course possess the power of the ego to overcome obstacles, and so one can, where it is unavoidable, break such dietary guidelines. Furthermore beans can obviously be a good transitional food for those striving to give up meat.

Alcohol
As with the question of eating meat, the freedom of the individual is always respected in this path. The students in the Esoteric School were reminded by the initiate, that they have freely decided to apply for entry to this school, and they are always free to leave whenever they wish. But whilst a person was a member, they had some rules to observe; in particular as regards diet, the consumption of alcohol was forbidden. So too today, alcohol is not to be consumed by a person who seeks to undertake the processes elucidated here. Why? Consider firstly the fact that alcohol is an extremely unusual item amongst our foodstuffs.

It is actually a poison, it is something which can kill (of course there are more potent poisons which kill in smaller quantities, like mercury.) Yet alcohol is the only poison that we allow to be regarded as a food. Whenever alcohol is consumed, since it is a poison, the liver is directly summoned to destroy or neutralize it if possible. This is a remarkable fact, a parallel food item would be mild arsenic tea.

However, the chemical toxicity is only an external obvious matter. Far more seriously, alcohol is the only 'foodstuff' which upon entering the mouth, actually 'targets' the frontal lobe of the brain, it reaches there within seven seconds. This brings it to the vicinity of the pineal and pituitary glands, the glands which are linked to the forehead chakra, a fact which we will consider again shortly. Once it is in the frontal lobe of the brain alcohol proceeds to kill brain cells there, to kill off as many brain cells as it can.

This is very significant because, firstly, the ego has its 'anchor point' in the frontal lobe, this convex area developed over long ages, as the sense of ego-hood grew. It is the 'organ' that makes possible the sense of selfhood. Secondly, we have only a limited ability to re-generate new cells in the brain. Therefore, as is now known to medical science, a persistently moderate to heavy drinker will actually have a smaller brain than other people.

Furthermore, alcohol targets our bloodstream, or more precisely the ether stream that flows within the blood, and what does it do in the blood? It pushes away the oxygen molecules and takes their place; but it is these oxygen particles which, as we saw in an earlier chapter, are the vessel of the prana or ether energy which is vital to the healthy functioning of the body. Here we have several startling facts – known to Rudolf Steiner, and explained in their deeper significance by him years ago in connection with lectures on the Bible story of the marriage in Cana – which should concern every meditator.

The third eye or forehead chakra must, like all other chakras form an etheric counterpart; it is this etheric counterpart that is destroyed by the alcohol. Hence when this initiate was asked, what would be the implication for someone in the meditation classes of the Anthroposophical Society of drinking alcohol, Steiner replied that such a person would no longer be permitted to be in the classes.[144] Secondly, as we noted above, it is in the frontal lobe of the brain that individualized thinking is made possible; this is the hallmark of an individual ego. If the brain cells there become damaged then the ego has less capacity to produce its own mental processes, to be itself, to experience selfhood.

But, as I pointed out earlier, Steiner uses the term, 'the ego' in a complex dualistic manner, because of his unequalled perception of human psychology. That is, the ego has both a personal, somewhat illusory dynamic, but also within this are influences from the eternal ego to greater or lesser extent. So, damage done to this area not only inhibits the presence of the normal self, it also therefore reduces the toehold of the eternal ego within one's personality. The effect of alcohol is then, that one has a limited ability to form the finest expression of the individual self, namely, spiritual wisdom. Alcohol destroys the ego's foothold in the organism, reducing ego-hood, and on an everyday level, this induces the well known tendency to group consciousness and then,

---

[144] Reported Dr. Med. W. Simonis, in Mitteilungen aus der anthroposophischen Arbeit in Deutschland, Easter 1964, p. 38.

in larger quantities to animal behaviour and then unconsciousness. So the consolidation of the individual self, which is required for inner development, becomes impossible.

Now regarding the fact that alcohol replaces the oxygen particles, what does this sinister process mean? Well, our memories are carried in our ether energies; all sense-impressions of our experiences in life are stored in them, and we access them when we want to recall something. As is known, one effect of alcohol is a reduced memory, even loss of memory. This tells the esotericist who has some understanding of the advanced psychological research of Steiner, that this poison is damaging the ether-body and interfering with its role in the memory function. However, the problem is deeper than this, for an essential and vital part of spiritual development is the expanding or reaching back of our memory to the past life.

The subtle processes in the ether-body which meditation brings about eventually enable such recall to occur. This was explained in Chapter Seven. However if alcohol is consumed then such recall, which places a demand on the ether energies, becomes very difficult. Recall of the past life becomes virtually impossible. So why did alcohol become part of human life? No, it was not because it brought relief by closing down part one's inner life, one's self-awareness, so that the worries could be forgotten. It does this nowadays, true, but it is completely wrong to assume that this was the case millennia ago.

Rudolf Steiner taught that wine was introduced by the spiritual leaders of humanity not so very long ago, about 800 BC, and for a specific reason. Alcohol destroys the etheric counterpart of the forehead chakra, the famous 'third eye' of ancient art. Now this may seem very strange at first, but if the reader recalls that as mentioned earlier in the book, all humanity once had a natural clairvoyance, to a greater or lesser degree. Now the remark takes on real meaning. Any such clairvoyance involves an active 'third eye'. The closing down of this third eye about three millennia ago was important, because human kind had to lose their psychic abilities and become isolated in the material world, that is, their awareness of a living nexus of spiritual reality had to be removed.

Through this, people would gradually awaken to their own separate self. Alcohol, especially wine, was therefore introduced by the priests for that purpose, and it has exercised its effect on humanity, leading to this result. However, in esoteric orders, the initiated priests always refrained from it, for example, the Essenes and Nazarites of the old Hebrew culture abstained from wine. Wine therefore, indirectly, assisted earlier peoples to discover their ego-hood, their self-hood.

Illustrations that have survived from the secret rituals of initiation in the Dionysian cult in Italy clearly show this.

A neophyte is given wine and is shown, reflected off its surface, an ugly face, a painting of which is held up by a priest so as to be seen in the surface of the wine. This countenance indicates the unevolved, or not yet ennobled earthly ego. The influence of the wine was to lead the person to encounter more powerfully their imperfect earthly ego, in order, throughout several lifetimes, to ennoble it.

However, earthly ego-hood has been developed over the last two millennia, it now needs to consolidate and spiritualize itself; so the remarkable effect of alcohol is totally obsolete. Now a new clairvoyance is vitally needed, and this arises from the spiritualizing of the ego consciousness.

Therefore the students in the Esoteric School were required to stop consuming alcohol, and warned to beware of liqueur chocolates. Where sugar and alcohol are mixed, these were described as especially bad. Also homoeopathic wine is especially potent in the damaging of the ether-chakras.(1903) So check that any homoeopathic medicine you buy is made without the alcohol being carried along in the potentising process. Many people are now actively reducing or stopping their alcohol intake, as a sensitivity to these dynamics develop in modern humanity.

I decided in my mid teens to never drink alcohol, and hence I have been a life-long teetotaller. In flavourings, like vanilla essence, the alcohol is still there, it remains just as real even if it disguised. As a brief note form an earlier lecture reports, "Water is the drink for those who seek spiritual development." (1903)

Any herbal medicine you use should also be non-alcoholic; the Wala/Hauschka firm produces this fine medicine, as do other smaller alternative firms. But one or two firms associated with the anthroposophical movement may well use alcohol in their medicines as they do not regard these above matters as so important. Indeed, for the bulk of the consumers, who are not involved to the processes of specific inner development, the consumption of small quantities alcohol is not inconsistent with their life reality. Nevertheless, Rudolf Steiner showed pharmacists how to prepare and preserve herbal medicine without the use of alcohol; the above named firms use his process. The Weleda company does often use alcohol, but it can make alcohol-free medicines as a special order.

Psychedelic drugs

The effect of psychedelic drugs on the ether energies and soul is such that they **force** the petals of the chakras into activity instead of this being achieved by the presence of higher spirituality. Once stimulated into action, the chakras rotate backwards, anticlockwise, which is the same way they rotated in previous centuries with the old non-egoic clairvoyance.(1906) All this is harmful, in two substantial ways. Access to the higher worlds is forcibly attained, therefore one's consciousness is itself not in attunement with the higher realities underlying those realms.

Hence visions of higher worlds are grafted onto the still subtly materialistic consciousness which is not yet spiritualized. This is a dangerous union, for the mind then becomes vulnerable to certain entities, who distort the underlying significance of the already warped visions. The idea that underlies the use of such drugs is itself born within these same beings, who encourage the underlying concept that through a substance, the soul could become at one with higher worlds. This is itself an intensely materialistic idea. It is essentially that one can graft onto the normal thought qualities in the mind genuine and direct experiences of other realms.

The result is that the drug user has forcibly crossed over the threshold, ignoring the subconscious warnings of the guardian, and possibly has a malignant spirit as an assistant, who has opened the gateway. The materialistic concept underlying the action has to be overcome, before any further spiritual development is possible, otherwise one could become a 'materialistic esotericist'; such people are a reality. They do accept that higher worlds exist, but they nevertheless carry an attitude that is strongly self-centred and linked with earth-bound ambitions. This could be called a sinister materialistic esotericism. The end result can be an interest in a high-technology future for humanity. A future in which humans become electronic-bionic humanoids, with electronic circuitry and some form of genetic engineering integrated into their person.

Only that person can objectively assimilate an encounter with the spiritual reality of the higher worlds, who has learnt to think holistically, in a way attuned to the spirit. Lacking the development of such empowered thinking, such a person can be imbued with potent anti-life, anti-spiritualization ideas, such as the bionic humanoid. The fact that chemical substances do work to produce actual visions of scenes in the astral world – amongst delusions and distorted images of one's own astral forces – can be clearly explained. Namely that all experiences of the astral world are transmitted to the person by their ether-body. Our ether energies are the mediator, the transmitter of such images to physical awareness. What has this to do with drugs? Simply that all psychedelic chemicals, although they can be produced chemically in laboratories, actually derive from plants, namely from the most etherically concentrated part of the plant, its reproductive organs, the seeds and flowers. In the plant seed is a concentrated package of life force. A force so strong that it was used in ancient times, in Atlantis, as a power supply for their aerial craft.[145]

But we human beings have a plant-like aspect to our inner being, it is our ether-body, our ethereal life energies. A plant is really cellulose and ether energies; our ether-body has all the properties of a plant. Reproduction is only possible by it, growth and healing are likewise governed by it. When the substance that comes from the ether energies of certain plants is ingested it then has the ability to stimulate the person's ether-body.

The hallucinogenic substance causes the chakras in the ether-body to be activated, as if our own aura had been forming them over years of meditation. As they are made active in this way, however, they transmit in a distorted manner various images from the astral body. This is the inner meaning of the expression, 'flower power'. This process is a violent way to approach the "temple of God", and as such brings its negative results. In the potent drug, heroin, the ether-body flowers strongly into activity, just as does the poppy, and then proceeds to prematurely die, withering the physical body, as does heroin.

As is obvious in the above remarks, Rudolf Steiner was totally and utterly opposed to all use of psychedelic substances.[146] Marijuana is **not** excepted. Indeed some twenty years before this became suspected in the mainstream, which happened in mid 1995, anthroposophical medical literature advised that marijuana would cause harm to the user. For readers who are unaware of its danger, it has been established, amongst other problems, that a chemical in this plant which produces altered consciousness remains after ingestion for an entire month in the brain itself.[147] The main damage that marijuana causes appears to me to be to the ether-body, the result of which can be an immediate and incurable schizophrenia. Healthy development of higher consciousness

---

[145] See "Cosmic Memory - Atlantis & Lemuria" by R. Steiner

[146] It was disturbing to hear the slander in a BBC radio program years ago when a speaker declared that Hoffman, the developer of LSD, had taken up this idea from R Steiner. There is of course, absolutely no truth in it at all; the speaker cunningly connected his theme to some of Rudolf Steiner's medical advice to doctors. Namely he advice to develop mineral analogues to the active substances in medicinal herbs, as the herbs may no longer be so effective in healing people.

[147] 1995/96 publications from medical sources on the nature of this drug available from various community centres will now, hopefully, reverse the liberal attitude towards marijuana. The anthroposophical publication from 1975 is "Marijuana today" by G Russell, from the Myrin Institute, New York.

demands that the brain functions are not altered by chemicals. That is like trying to play a newly inspired musical work on a piano which has had its keyboard and strings re-shuffled by an accident.

Asceticism and sexuality

The guiding initiates of this path respect fully the freedom of the individual, and so no requirement is placed on the meditant to repress their desires. If however someone wishes to gently relinquish their interest and involvement in sexual activity then that person is given to understand that such an impulse, providing the soul-life is healthy, will assist them on their way to realisation of their divine potential. Initiation wisdom, in its original genuine sense, does not agree with occult ideas that imply that the higher-self and the divine worlds can be attained through sexual activity.

The initiate regards such occult ideas as deriving from lower spirits of Earth-egotism from the lower astral plane. The falseness of this concept is known to our higher-self, but its influence in our adult ego is often muffled. However, its influence is quite naturally present in childhood, resulting in a natural chasteness, returning us to the theme of chapter three, namely re-awakening the child spirituality as the path to the spiritual realms. The acolyte is advised that no matter how convinced and convincing such a 'sensuality occultist' may be, this doctrine of achieving nearness to the spirit through use of the ethereal and physical energies via the genital area is false.

Just as the view of the world from behind a brownish-red window that convincingly portrays the world in shades of that same colour is always false.[148] So, if a person becomes subject to the influence of the spirits of earth-bound egotism, sensual activity will indeed have an undeniable strong persuasive influence.' But the ambience created by such influences are clearly seen by the spiritualized ego as very harmful. When a reserve of ether energies are stored in the higher counterpart to the groin from a life-style aiming towards chasteness, then avenues for experiencing wholesome spiritual realities are bestowed. These higher counterparts to the lower generative glands are the pituitary and pineal glands, and these can only be fully developed as chasteness is attained.

However, and this is a most important point, the initiates of the path presented in this book would never require a person to suppress the sexual drive in an unhealthy manner. The tragic case of the theosophical clairvoyant Leadbeater, whose desires became malignant through conceitedly pretending he had no lower desires, illustrates this

---

[148] Those readers who have some ability to perceive the astral aura will know that a repugnant brownish-red colour occurs in the aura of people involved in such occult activity.

point. Respect for the freedom of the individual and understanding of the complexity of the issue makes such an attitude impossible.

Rudolf Steiner recommended to those who are serious in the quest for higher consciousness to have a moderate wholesome asceticism, and to focus on the transformation of the soul, then gradually the ether-body will become spiritualized as well. The soul does of its own accord lose interest in sexuality. This attitude of the initiate is not naive, it does not deny that there is a high spiritual force underpinning the sexual force, but rather that this is indirectly glimpsed, heavily veiled, as if from behind by lovers.

This is not to deny that there can be a loving non-lustful mood in sexuality, the point is that only when sexual desire is gone, and chasteness is achieved, can a particular higher stage of esoteric development be achieved; this high force can then be accessed and integrated directly into one's own spiritual being. "The procreative force is the fundament of higher forces, these higher forces develop in a person as the procreative power is transformed through abstinence."(1906)

It may be of interest to the reader to know some of the theoretical esoteric reasons why those rare persons who are high degree Grail initiates maintain abstinence. The higher force associated with the ether-body, mentioned above, is called the 'life-spirit' by Steiner. It is the spiritual (or 'Devachanic') essence of the ether-body. It is indirectly present in the process of procreation, and it is this power which is sensed by the couple at that time. The initiate in the stream of the Holy Grail Mysteries, is aware that deeper esoteric meditating needs to utilize the warmth-ether[149] (one of four ether energies in our life-force organism) in a beautiful way.

This ether starts to be the bearer of the higher insights one is experiencing, yet it is this ether which is central to ensuring that the body is fertile, and which is most drawn upon in reproductive activity. The life-force organism (or ether-body) can either 'go to seed' or start to blossom, a self-transforming process which can offer up the essence of our masculinity or femininity to the soul-body.

One of the tragic facts of those striving for esoteric-spiritual development is that all too often people lack the knowledge or the will to undertake really vigorous meditating. Such people are especially prone to wildly intensified desires, and can, despite a respectable

---

[149] This detail was mentioned by Steiner to Martina von Limburger, her notes were published in Vol. 29, No. 2 of the journal of the Anthrop. Soc. in Grt. Brit., "Anthroposophical Movement", London, 1952.

exterior, commit seriously improper sexual behaviour. This outcome does **not** occur when the person undertakes real meditation, because then the mysterious inner force behind sexuality, which the initiate knows to be the warmth-ether, is used in meditating.

It is called upon by the angels to bring about a flowering or blossoming of the life-force organism, rather than a literal 'going to seed'.[150] However, despite the above, a false asceticism is very damaging indeed, and so the earnest meditant has to find a balanced, reasonable life-style based on truthfulness and inner honesty. To take the "middle path' or 'golden mean' is the finest achievement in this regard.

When the higher-self begins to manifest in the soul, the ether-body develops a natural tendency to conserve its finest forces for the heart chakra. It is these forces which underlie the miraculous healing and occult powers of the very advanced adept. It is also this process which enables such a person to share in the sacred powers which intensify in the Earth's ether-body at the winter solstice, see my "Living a Spiritual Year". Nevertheless the main point here is that the meditant's freedom is paramount, and in the course of inner development the matter of the body's role in love, affection and desire becomes resolved by each meditating individual in their own way, and hence is not discussed in detail.

Conclusion
I have attempted to make available in this book, as a response to the search by many people for guidance in spiritual development in the deeper sense, as much as is advisable of the practical guidance given by the initiate, Rudolf Steiner. Through these pages, we have considered the three states of higher consciousness that can be developed, and learnt of exercises to develop the will and inner tranquillity necessary to make progress with meditation. The crucial importance of studying spiritual concepts and of developing the right mood of heart, have been considered. Explanations for the actual reasons why various mysterious phenomena occur have been given, as well as guidance through the initial experiences.

Then we looked at the solemn but really important fact that until the lower self has been encountered, the attainment of higher consciousness through meditation, i.e., crossing the threshold into a spiritual state of consciousness is not advisable, and in fact impossible

---

[150] Persons who acquire conceptually-based spiritual ideas, but who do not at the same time commit themselves to spirituality in their hearts, hence at least an earnest striving towards celibacy as an ideal, are prone to this difficulty, as the lower nature has its inherent energy potential stimulated by such study, although it need not manifest if the inner development is properly undertaken.

on any moral esoteric path. We also have discovered that the guardian of the threshold has an important role in all this, and that Rudolf Steiner's book *Knowledge of the Higher Worlds* is an essential book for the earnest meditant.

We then learnt of the auras of soul and of spirit, and how to prepare for going into sleep, and how to become more aware of our own guiding angel. Then a new perspective on the chakras was revealed, namely that only by actively spiritualizing the soul-life and really seeking for the freedom from the illusory drives of our current personality could one expect the chakras to develop.

This process is itself connected to the light from the cosmic Christ and if properly developed, leads to the Grail mysteries. In Chapter Eight we considered the new clairvoyance, and the way to expanding the present sense of self to encompass our past lives. Then practical advice about precisely what is done in meditating was given, followed by a chapter on actual meditation verses, for different purposes, but principally the Rose-Cross and the Foundation Stone meditations were introduced and explained. It was pointed out that meditating on these will allow the meditant to slowly and wholesomely experience the spiritualization of the soul, and increase the capacity to understand spiritual truths.

Finally, some pragmatic life-styles issues were addressed, such as diet. It is now up to the reader to begin the process, using the advice, experience and information collected and carefully contextualized in these pages. With this, the book is at an end. By the 36th century AD, when according to Rudolf Steiner's research, a Golden Age is due to prevail on the planet, a significant number of new initiates will be needed to help humanity, which at that time will be desperately rejecting a materialistic approach to life's problems based on a technology far beyond what we already have.

For now, may each reader find within its pages insightful and practical guidance of value for the joyous obligation of actively seeking spiritual development, with its resulting benefit for the community:
"But you {student on the way to the sacred} – know your self, and take hold of the pathway to the gods !" (Mani (4th cent AD)

Appendix 1

Brief note regarding initiation and the crucifixion of Christ

There are remarkable similarities between the old three-day rite, and the crucifixion and resurrection. Further, of this event it is recorded that the veil covering the Holy of Holies was rent into two. This was the cloth curtain that veiled the innermost sanctuary of the Temple from the eyes of the general community. Access to the divine was forbidden by the priesthood, in accordance with Old Testament requirements. This is entirely in accordance with the traditional priesthood's task to mediate between laity and deity. In the esoteric theology here, it is understood that this change in the human self was made possible by the union of the cosmic Christ, the leader of the sun beings to the soul of the Earth. By including this detail in the Gospels, however, the initiated Gospel writers conveyed to acolytes of the Christian esoteric schools, that the way to initiation has been opened up by Christ to everyone who so seeks. Hence also the dependence upon other persons, needed for the out-of-body-state is no longer necessary.

Appendix 2

The Colour Black

Black is not really a colour, but simply the darkness caused by absence of light; i.e. the reflection of light off the surfaces of the object. Hence the artistic gesture for black is the opposite of pushing/raying directly out from yourself, it is an inwards-going gesture. In contrast, white is not a colour but the reflection to our vision of the entire colour spectrum; its artistic gesture is an out-raying, out spreading one. Certainly in grief or in negative and depressive states the aura takes on a darker appearance, hence black is associated with sadness and brooding/negative attitudes. And as Rudolf Steiner mentions, when this depressive mood exists, it certainly causes the soul to wither for that time. However, a colour or other naturally occurring phenomenon can have two effects, hence there are two aspects to its symbolism, just as water can symbolize the emotions or the life-forces.

A specific group of people for millennia have worn black; a group with a direct connection to the spiritual realms, namely priests and priestesses. It was worn either all the time or when in meditation. It has long been the case historically that black is the colour chosen for use when one is involved in activity connected with the other worlds. So, black was not worn (only) by those who were depressed or of a malignant nature. The stark contrast between these two aspects of black is obvious and leads to confusion. The wearing of black by a child is indeed unhealthy and ill-advised. The same is true for young adults – it is a cause for concern to see youngsters today clad in black. This does not apply to a young woman's formal dress, or someone wearing one article of black, perhaps offset by green or white. I am referring to young people having virtually only black clothing. We feel that it is not good, but why? There is black as an expression of the soul-mood (or auric 'colour tone') of grief, depression and gloom. But yet, mysteriously black is chosen by those whose profession is to represent the glorious intensely radiant higher worlds. How can this paradox be understood?

Consider the living phenomena of human life! What colour do we wear for formal occasions, where interaction with others will be challenging, where the encounter will challenge you to be really centred, inwardly strong? Do we wear luminous pink, or some other pastel colour? No, we wear black. In business and political meetings, at high-key social gatherings, black is predominant. But there are times when one does not wish to focus inwardly and act out of an empowered centre with a strong sense of selfhood; namely when on holiday (or just at the weekend). On holiday, the urge is to forget the stresses, and to leave oneself a little behind so to speak. The need is felt to flow out of oneself, and merge with the environment. So we choose bright colours even if in pastel shades. Why?

To answer this, we need to consider what happens when you encounter a person in a coloured garment (as distinct from non colour, i.e., black). Suppose they are wearing bright red; then the next day, pale green. You become aware that the red was just fine for them, but the green is somehow quite off putting. If you know them fairly well, they could put on the entire colour spectrum and you could say straight away which is appropriate and which is really "clashing". Clashing with what? What is it that we sense is not in harmony? The garment's colour with the aura's main colours. We do have a faint semi-conscious awareness of what every person's auric colours are; and through their clothing we can actually sense this; for there is a clash (or harmony) with the aura. This is a remarkable fact ! It indicates that a coloured garment, but not black, allows a spectator to sense much more clearly one's aura. That is, the suitability of a coloured garment is not only related to the subtle colour tones in a person's physical presence, it also related to the sub-conscious perceiving of their soul qualities.

The colour conveys the astral auric quality into the physical environment, that is to the perceptions of people. It does this by loudly proclaiming whether the auric colour is or is not attuned to the garment's colour. But if they wear black, you have no idea what colour to suggest as harmonious (unless you are strongly psychic). When clad in black, it is as if a person's aura is "held back" from announcing itself to the environment, it does not ray out from the wearer so freely, for the environment to sense.

This gives the feeling of a protective-sheath effect around the person; and one also finds that the ego is more easily centred and empowered. It is this quality of not raying out and not intermingling which has a centring effect for the wearer, it enhances the sense of self. One feels more contained. It is precisely this not raying out, and the consequent enhancement of self which can be felt by others as 'bracing' or 'severe'. And unless the person is known to be involved with the higher worlds this colour has a slightly anti-social effect. (When one is almost entirely in black, not just with one garment). People could also by association project onto this the second factor; namely the association of black with the auric message of sadness or gloom. That second factor however, would normally be an illusion, which is dispelled upon meeting the priest or person.

Appendix 3

Countess Johanna von Keyserling

Countess Johanna von Keyserling was strongly clairvoyant, she had the ability to raise her consciousness to the higher worlds from within her body, and also could experience out of body journeys as well. To help her comprehend the nature of time, and transcend its effect, she was given an experience of scenes from ancient India through this technique (for it is possible to journey back in time in the astral plane). On another occasion, this advanced meditant was taken on an astral journey to assist spiritual beings to protect the life of her son, fighting near Calais during World War One. The experience was confirmed the next morning as correct and regarded as wholesome when Rudolf Steiner spoke to her about it. But as indicated above, in this case the esotericist was already powerfully clairvoyant, her consciousness was by nature highly spiritual, and such an experience is then not inappropriate.

She had already been able to encounter consciously the protector of the threshold, and become aware of its concern at the tragic lack of spirituality in the twentieth century. She had considered that perhaps this spiritual being had erred in regard to the timing of such expectations from humankind. Rudolf Steiner assured her however that there was no error in regard to its expectations for substantial spiritual development to be manifest already in the early decades of this century. In an unpublished manuscript from her archives given to the author she refers to this.

Appendix 4

Deeper esoteric notes about breathing and the Philosopher's Stone

This refined body will be a carbon-based body so to speak. Namely a diamond-carbon body not a coal one, the carbon will be raised up to its highest form, diamantine, although not in its present very hard state. The carbon becomes subject to the vivifying life-bestowing powers of the prana, and sets in motion a process which over lifetimes allows carbon to become a form of soft diamond, so to speak. The alchemists referred to this process as seeking the Philosopher's Stone.

When exhaling in the process of a certain esoteric breathing technique, one starts to release oxygen into the air, but in extremely tiny quantities. This does not mean that it is possible to suddenly develop magical powers and ignore your need for oxygen; although exactly that will occur in the far future. (The Indian fakirs already do exactly this and therefore can be immersed in water or an airless container for hours; but this is a result of occult techniques, rather than spirituality.) The point is that just as the constant dripping of water can make a hole in a stone, so too the meditant can gradually achieve an etherealized state which begins the process of transforming the body, releasing it at last from the 'original sin' condition of inner decay.

However such a perfected state of the body, physical yet not fleshy, requires that the passions become plant-like as regards selflessness and purity, too. This achievement can also be described as the ability to become plant-like because it causes the exhaled breath to contain some oxygen, although not enough to be registered by a mechanical instrument, just as plants exhale oxygen. However one can sense a finer quality in the exhaled air of an innocent child as compared with that of a degenerated person; this is not entirely astral, there is also an etheric aspect to this.

The physical body of people in the far future will become plant-like in the above sense, namely that we can form a body based on carbon, which is what plants have, and in addition, we can then use the released oxygen, exhaling any surplus. Hence what is exhaled out into the air will be no longer polluting but enlivening for the Earth. If oxygen was visible, perhaps as a gentle mauve colour, then trees and bushes would be vastly more valued than they are! Imagine being an entity whose exhalations are of such exquisite purity and life that it gives life to other beings. This is what the flora is, and this is what the future human being may become. It may all sound very unlikely, but then how likely is it that inky-black soft coal is made of only one substance, one molecule, and that a diamond is made of exactly the same substance, simply subject to different energies when it was created?

In this process of finding the Philosopher's Stone there is an overcoming of the death-process; for this to happen, the lower self must be in the process of dying out. "When all corrupting influences have been cast out of the soul, when it is spiritualized by divine ethical forces, then the meditant will be able to build up the glorious physically-existing but not fleshy, future body of diamond-like quality.." These notes from one of the esoteric lessons also refers to the matter of the lower-self, which we of necessity dealt with in detail earlier...

"from deep within, from the core of one's ego the esoteric meditant learns to work upon and transform his or her soul. This also involves knowing and recognizing evil, and then fighting against it in one's own soul." (ca. 1905)

This process then, gradually etherealizes the flesh body, for it enables the regenerative pranic energy within the air to become far more active in it. This in turn causes the very high faculty of **high- initiation** consciousness to develop (see Chapter One). For it is the relative density or 'lightness' of the body which determines how far these subtle higher states are able to manifest. This process of etherealizing the body does not lead to an unusual unique condition, rather it actually anticipates the future evolutionary dynamics of the body. For humanity is destined to eventually cease incarnating into flesh-animalistic bodies. We will live in an ethereal crystalline body; referred to in alchemical literature as "The Diamond-body". The term diamond is very accurate, for as we have discussed, carbon, of which a diamond is made, will become the main substance of our body. Not carbon in the form of earthly dark coal, rather in the nature of transparent, radiant diamonds. As this state approaches the body will become less heavy, less dense, and eventually, looking ahead into a future time-cycle, we will live in ethereal bodies and no longer in matter.

Naturally the future diamond body will be as real to us as our present 'fallen' one, because by then perception of the ethers will be fully attained. This truth has been known to Initiates for a long time; it is reported that the ancient Greek Mysteries taught that humankind will in the future live in bodies which cast no shadows, and require no food. On a more practical note, the person who seeks to develop in this specific way as presented here shall incarnate into an ever more refined and ethereal body, in succeeding earth-lives, and gradually it will become the 'diamond body'.

Science is aware that carbon becomes diamond rather than coal when it is subject to fire and pressure. Diamonds were formed in the primeval Earth amidst the immense heat and turbulent energies of that age, which derived originally from the sun. The advanced meditant subjects the carbon in the air to firstly the inner fire of her or his bloodstream, and secondly to the pranic forces, for as we have considered earlier the etheric forces permeate the blood. When these special conditions are operative on the carbon, they allow the plant-like diamantine body of the future to form. Our ego may be regarded as a sun in the microcosm, that is, in the little world of the human organism, where its place of manifestation is the bloodstream.

Our blood is therefore not only permeated by a warmth which is physical, there is also a spiritual warmth present in it. Once the dark fire or warmth of the lower self is conquered then the radiant fire of the inner sun can begin to transform the body, and release its inherent spiritual qualities. All such activity of the higher-self is connected with the being from whom the higher-self derives, the cosmic Christ. Just how did this being manifest to the great prophets? Remember the bush burning with a spiritual fire which Moses saw, from which he heard the words, "I am the I am" ? Then, too, on Mount Sinai again Deity was manifested in the fiery pillar of light.

Such references to the element of fire indicates how the cosmic Christ, now united to the planet, has a connection to the inner fire of the human being, namely our ego. For earlier esotericists knew that the higher thoughts and will are connected to the element of fire. Rudolf Steiner also indicated that this means that the deep task of using the fire-force of the blood to uplift the body helps redeem certain malignant subterranean fire-forces from which the lower self is empowered. This fact of the connection of fire with this being is indicated in the ancient esoteric 'Christian' documents, such as the Gospel of St. Thomas. One of the activities undertaken by the cosmic Christ is that of spiritualizing the body, which means the forming its future 'redeemed' body. It was for this reason that it was graphically emphasized in the accounts of the crucifixion that His bones were not to be broken, as prophesied centuries earlier.

An undamaged or perfect physical body would be involved, so that this as well as an archetypal, perfect soul-reality and life-force would enter the sphere of human existence. But here you must understand that 'physical' does not have to mean 'fleshy'; a physical organism can be very delicate, and tenuous, yet still exist in a spatial reality. This is actually a very important subject, which if not understood, could lead to very false ideas, as in exoteric Christian theology, about the flesh body being something that we shall always have to live in, even after the end of the Earth Age.

These three archetypal elements of human nature could then be present enabling humanity to resonate with them, to become 'like unto them' so to speak. In an esoteric lesson on this subject, which is inter-woven with the Rose-Cross theme, the following notes were later made... "and the purified soul forms for itself a body in each new incarnation which will increasingly approach the ideal future body, a body permeated by the fire of the divine love-forces of Christ and by the radiance of wisdom {of the higher-self, nurtured by the Holy Spirit}.... Through the sacrificial death of Christ {the sun god} and in devout acknowledgment of this pure, innocent death, the human being can bring the plant-like chaste life-force to manifestation within itself. The very life-blood of Christ purifies the human being. The student of the spiritual truths of life should learn to feel the connection of this sacrificial death of Christ with the plant-world that blossoms towards the sunlight". (ca.1912)

In considering this inspiring secret of our future, we are at the threshold of understanding one of the many deep themes explored in alchemy. As mentioned earlier, this process of forming the diamond body was known to the genuine esoteric alchemists; finding the "Philosopher's Stone" (or the Stone of the Sages) is the name given to this in alchemical tracts.

I cannot go into the details, as the subject is made complex through the fact that the same terms were applied to another aspect of alchemy. Namely, learning about 'archetypal' chemistry, that is the forming of metals, and matter in general, from out of the ethers. This remarkable knowledge allows one to metamorphose one substance into another, but materialistic souls become obsessed with the idea of making gold in this way. It is important that these matters are mentioned, for those souls with an interest in alchemy will find that the esoteric wisdom here provides a valuable key to their study. The breathing exercise presented earlier, is designed to assist serious meditators with this process of spiritualizing the body.

INDEX

10 petalled, 196
12 petalled, 194
16 petalled, 182
Alcohol
   dissoves third eye ether chakra, 298
Angel, 2, 29, 44, 48, 107, 111, 112, 121, 127, 131, 133, 141, 151, 152, 156, 157, 175, 176, 177, 178
Archangel Michael, 43, 176
ascend and dissolve, 136
astral projection, 105, 218, 219, 220, 221
atavistic, 104, 204, 205, 211, 212, 217, 250
Atlantean, 193, 208
Aum, 3, 275
aura, 19, 22, 25, 26, 27, 29, 30, 31, 32, 52, 55, 69, 74, 75, 78, 89, 93, 95, 98, 104, 107, 113, 122, 127, 128, 130, 132, 133, 135, 136, 140, 148, 175, 176, 178, 182, 185, 186, 187, 188, 190, 191, 192, 194, 197, 201, 202, 205, 209, 210, 211, 212, 215, 216, 218, 220, 245, 250, 251, 271, 275, 279, 281, 294, 301, 306, 307
avatars, 191, 224
Beatitudes, 3, 183, 184, 276, 277
breathing exercises, 234, 236, 237
Buddha, 4, 183, 184, 191, 193
Caduceus, 202, 256
caution, do not meditate, 241
chakra, 3, 30, 69, 88, 100, 107, 113, 177, 178, 179, 180, 182, 183, 184, 185, 186, 187, 191, 194, 195, 197, 201, 223, 276, 279, 296, 297, 298

seven planets, 197
chakras, 26, 32, 51, 66, 71, 82, 96, 98, 100, 104, 117, 141, 151, 154, 175, 176, 177, 183, 184, 185, 194, 197, 201, 202, 212, 213, 215, 218, 271, 275, 297, 299, 300, 301
Chastity, 182
chatting, 251
childhood, 106, 115, 206, 229, 230, 231, 302
Christ, 54, 55, 116, 130, 183, 191, 193, 233, 256, 262, 274, 276, 278, 279, 281
clairvoyance, 3, 12, 18, 25, 26, 28, 30, 31, 33, 34, 35, 37, 94, 98, 100, 104, 115, 184, 186, 187, 204, 205, 207, 208, 209, 210, 212, 213, 226, 236, 251, 295, 299, 300
consciousness
   body-free, 23, 105, 170
   divine illumination, 44
   dreamless, 152
   eternal higher-ego, 45
   eternal/continuity of, 153
   inner hearing, 37
   intuitive, 21, 105
   spiritual, 40
   the unity of all life, 45
   transcendental, 39
Contemplation, 1, 39, 45, 201
cosmic Christ, 3, 20, 52, 54, 55, 56, 58, 59, 88, 100, 129, 159, 181, 183, 191, 192, 193, 194, 195, 213, 222, 223, 246, 256, 257, 267, 274, 277, 280, 281, 288, 305, 311
cosmic-spiritual, 27, 33, 34, 35, 36, 37, 38, 39, 41, 44, 53, 78, 82, 99, 100, 117, 158, 167, 168, 175, 180, 182, 203, 211, 220, 227,

313

229, 232, 233, 235, 250, 254,
  259, 292, 293
Cosmos-Spirit, 52, 55, 59, 93,
  130, 160, 184, 191, 193, 194,
  252, 274, 276, 306, 311
criticism, 1, 68, 69, 183
depression, 52
Devachan, 34, 39
diamond, 275, 308, 309, 310, 312
divine feminine, 156, 280
dizziness, 110
Double, 126, 127, 129, 130, 131,
  133, 134, 142, 224, 248
doubt, 144, 211, 214
dreaming, 152
dreams, 75, 106, 148, 151, 152,
  153, 170, 178, 184, 296
ego-spiritualization, 278
Egypt, 99
Egyptian, 54, 55, 222
Eight-Fold Path, 184
enlightenment, 20, 117, 120, 181,
  191, 220, 235
esoteric, 1, 2, 3
'esoteric', 11
Esoteric School, 136, 169, 201,
  213, 217, 254, 296
eternal egohood, 177
eternal self/ego, 288, 290
ether heart, 188, 194, 195
ether-body, 24, 27, 29, 71, 99,
  100, 105, 110, 121, 134, 147,
  184, 187, 190, 201, 209, 210,
  231, 277, 287, 296, 304
ethereal vision, 3, 210, 215
etheric energy-centres, 201
etheric vision, 116, 122, 213, 214,
  215
faith, 28, 72
false images, 136, 247
fear, 141, 146, 147, 154, 281
God, 3, 46, 54, 98, 182, 191, 222,
  262, 264, 265, 266, 273, 274,
  276, 280, 301, 311

Guardian, 2, 117, 119, 122, 127,
  140, 141, 142, 152, 175, 176,
  300
Guiding Angel, 2, 3, 142, 151,
  155, 156, 157, 158
half suffocating, 148
hallucination, 28, 29
hallucinogenic drugs, 119
hate, 78, 145
Hierarchies, 36, 45, 180, 184, 290
higher self, 35, 45, 51, 55, 62, 65,
  88, 93, 95, 103, 107, 111, 120,
  121, 142, 148, 152, 154, 170,
  180, 183, 184, 197, 232, 264,
  275, 277, 278, 279, 280, 281,
  289, 290, 302, 304, 311
high-initiation, 43, 44, 45, 47, 48,
  49, 50, 53, 168, 211, 237, 259,
  292
Holy Grail, 193, 195
horror-films, 147
humility, 12, 82, 109, 136, 142,
  170, 251
illusion, 28, 113, 137, 177, 178,
  181, 247, 266, 308
indecent, 13, 114, 131
infant, 93, 231
initiate, 11, 30, 35, 44, 54, 55, 58,
  130, 142, 182, 184, 190, 191,
  197, 224, 253, 256, 272, 275,
  295, 297, 303
initiates, 52, 54, 78, 132, 172, 224,
  257, 270, 280, 302
initiation, 54, 98, 100, 101, 117,
  133, 160, 177, 182, 213, 214,
  222, 224, 233, 271, 280, 288,
  299
Jonah, 100
joy, 67, 77, 102, 103, 114, 120,
  230, 231, 240, 251, 264, 265
karma, 9, 48, 52, 69, 121, 131,
  137, 140, 141, 147, 156, 177,
  178, 179, 209, 232, 248, 296

Knights Templars, 88, 109, 193, 257
kundalini, 176, 202, 204, 256
Love, 11, 36, 41, 78, 107, 129, 192, 194, 226, 263, 264, 265, 289, 290, 311
Lower Self, 2, 117, 121, 122, 127, 129, 140, 309
Manichean, 193
mantram, 20, 201
Mars, 184
Masters, 2, 169, 171, 172, 182
meditation
　practical advice, 241
mediumism, 205
miracles, 71
Moon, 3, 19, 43, 54, 93, 177, 178, 215, 225
nature spirits, 187
nausea feeling, 148
Nazoraean, 55
nervousness, 62, 225
Osiris, 54, 222
pain, 41, 65, 66, 67, 107, 110, 113, 179, 217, 277
past life, 30, 104, 109, 122, 136, 137, 206, 210, 212, 226, 229, 232, 234, 289, 298
past lives, 78, 109, 137
peace, 10, 35, 38, 40, 64, 148, 178, 225, 229, 240, 244, 262, 264, 265, 273, 280
Philosopher's Stone, 275, 309, 312
pineal, 182, 186, 296, 302
pituitary, 178, 182, 296, 302
planetary rays, 198
pleasure, 65, 66, 67, 217, 231
Practical advice, 241
prana, 23, 189, 234, 236, 238, 297
prayer, 25, 51, 194, 262, 264, 275
Primeval Self, 275
Protection, 245

psychic-image, 24, 25, 27, 31, 32, 33, 35, 37, 43, 44, 53, 78, 98, 125, 182, 211, 213, 229, 232, 233, 236, 247
Pyramid, 55, 99
Recalling the past life. *See* **past life, past lives**
reproduction, 301
reverence, 2, 41, 88, 89, 91, 146, 147, 251, 255
Rose-Cross, 20, 256, 271, 273, 311
seeing faces everywhere, 210
sensuality, 94, 302
seventh degree, 55
sexual, 42, 99, 130, 292, 302
shadow side, 120, 121, 142, 143, 224
skhandas, 291
solar plexus, 206, 207
spirit-body, 36, 153
spiritual body, 223, 275
spiritual sun, 65, 262
spirituality, 1, 9, 10, 18, 33, 35, 41, 55, 78, 93, 95, 98, 101, 114, 120, 121, 122, 131, 139, 141, 142, 143, 149, 151, 156, 160, 177, 182, 190, 192, 193, 194, 195, 212, 216, 223, 225, 226, 228, 250, 252, 271, 278, 279, 281, 292, 300, 302, 308, 309
St. John of the Cross, 180
stars, 23, 60, 82, 87, 204, 224
subtle materialism, 83, 144
Sun-God, 54, 191, 222
The Masters, 171
thinking
　holistic-intuitive, 35, 169, 181, 280
third eye, 107, 177, 178, 182, 297
thought-form, 89, 245, 295
throat, 3, 134, 147, 182, 183, 185, 191, 195, 255

315

transcendental insight, 27, 33,
    34, 39, 44, 182
two-petalled, 107, 177
untruthfulness, 134
vegetarian, 108, 292, 293
visions, 2, 25, 26, 28, 29, 30, 37,
    41, 43, 98, 101, 102, 103, 104,
    108, 109, 115, 118, 135, 137,
    184, 185, 207, 211, 246, 300
winter solstice, 304
yoga, 51, 236
zephyrs, 106

Illustration credits

Copyright acknowledgements:

1: This illustration was published as the dust cover of *Das Wirken Rudolf Steiners, Band 3, Novalis Verlag; Schaffhausen, 1980. It is copyright by this publisher, who has kindly given permission for its use.*

2: The photograph was published in the Fortean Times, ed. B Rickard; London; 1981; issue No. 35, p. 32. The editor has kindly given permission for its use. The photo is, so far as the current editor is aware, copyright to FT.

3: The photo of the red window in the current building which was used for this illustration was published in "The Goetheanum Glass Windows", by Georg Hartmann, Verlag am Goetheanum, Dornach, 1993, who owns the copyright to it; it is used with kind permission of the publisher.

4: This drawing was made by Turgenieff who carved the windows in ca. 1918-1922. It is published in "Die Goetheanum-Fenster Bildband", Rudolf Steiner Verlag; Dornach, 1996, who owns the copyright to it; it is used with kind permission of the publisher.

5: A rough sketch of a rose-cross made by the author.

6,7,8,9,10: These paintings are copyright to Adrian Anderson; and were drawn especially for this book by Julie Harmsworth, an exhibiting artist in Melbourne.

11: This pastel drawing by Rudolf Steiner is copyright to the Rudolf Steiner Verlag, Dornach, Switzerland, and is used with kind permission of the publisher.

Diagrams 1, 2 and 3: these graphics are copyright to Threshold Publishing; and were made for this book by Joel Harmsworth.

1   From about 1910, this photo was taken by Dr. Felix Peipers after an esoteric lesson.

2 A coloured photocopy of a black-white photo. A roof-top in Murten, Switzerland, from 1981.

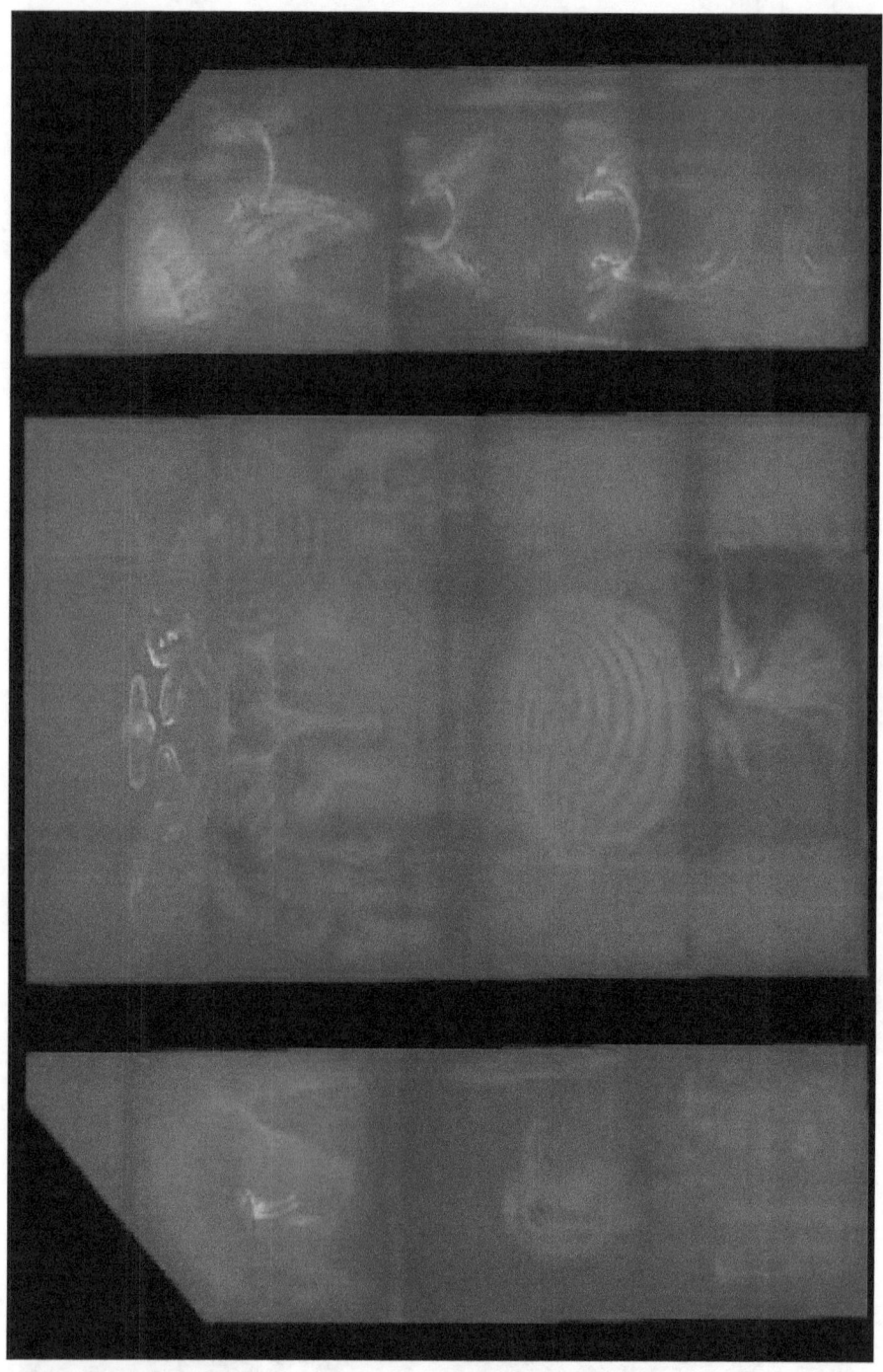

3 This image of the red window in the Goetheanum in Dornach, has been enhanced to show the details more clearly.

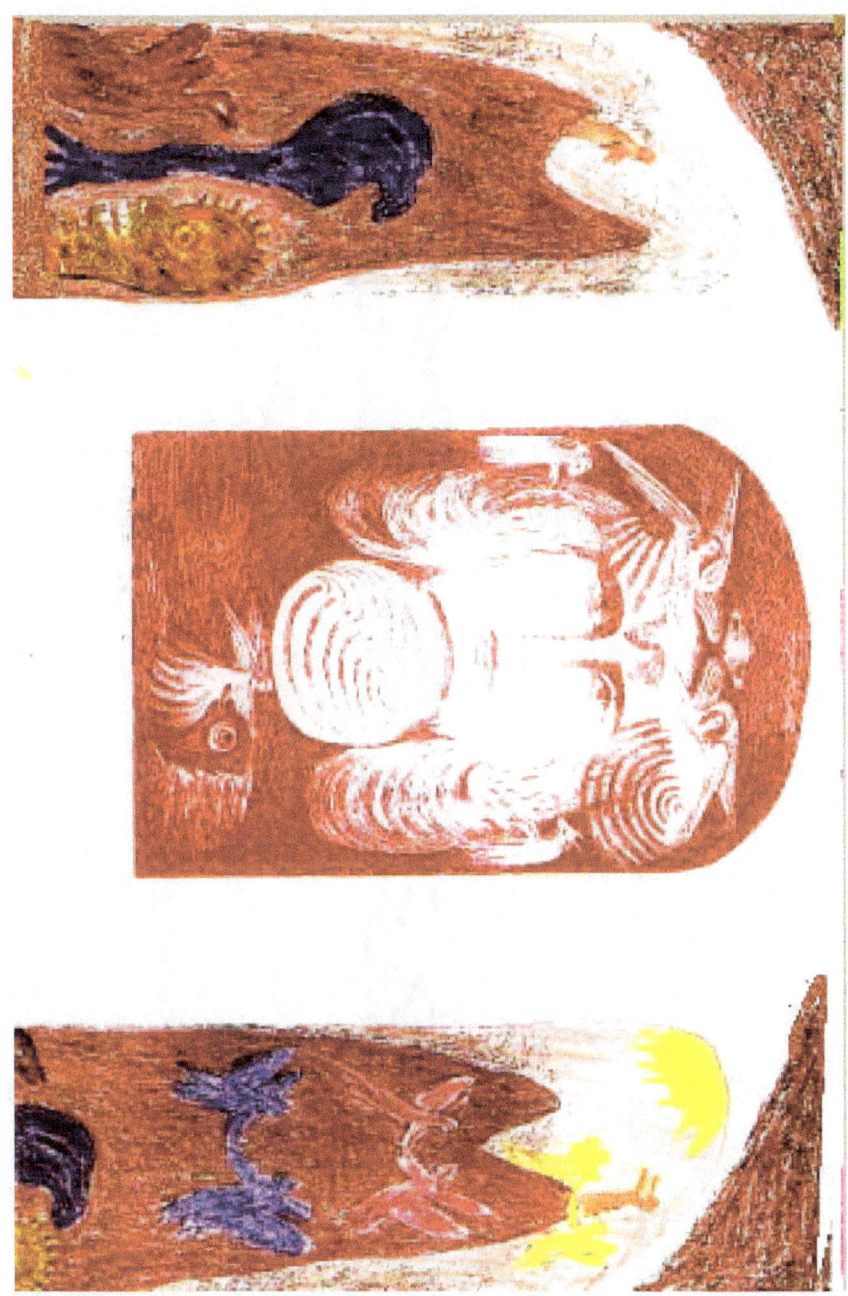

4 This coloured photocopy of the red window shows clearly the three beasts, which refer to the triune lower self, referred to in chapter 5. It shows clearly the triad of divine spiritual beings from whom spirituality flows into the aspirant. This makes possible the crossing of the threshold.

5　The Rose Cross

6 The colour-impressions in the not-evolved astral aura.

7 The colour-impressions of a finely spiritualized soul-aura. No attempt has been made to depict an actual aura, and hence no chakras are indicated.

8 The colour-impressions typical of the evolved **lesser** devachanic aura (or spirit-aura). This aura has similar qualities to those of the spiritualized soul-aura, for this aura – a part of our spirit – has imbued the soul aura with its qualities. This is what causes spirituality'.

9
The colour-impressions of the unevolved higher spirit-aura, or second devachanic aura; this is the Life-Spirit and the Atma or Spirit-human. It is much smaller than the normal astral aura.

9
The colour-impressions of the unevolved lesser spirit-aura, or first devachanic aura; this is the Spirit-Self. It is smaller than the normal astral aura.

10 The evolved higher spirit-aura, the Atma or Spirit-human. Such an exquisite aura or higher 'mental' body is found only with high initiates.

11 Rudolf Steiner's pastel drawing, "The human being in the Spirit". The Guiding Angel (green) is bestowing a radiant light for the spiritual sun; and also protecting the person from a Luciferic spirit (orange-red) who instills pride.

www.ingramcontent.com/pod-product-compliance
Lightning Source LLC
Chambersburg PA
CBHW060310240426
43661CB00059B/2714